RODEN
CUTLER, V.C.

THE BIOGRAPHY

Also by Colleen McCullough

Tim
The Thorn Birds
An Indecent Obsession
A Creed for the Third Millennium
The Ladies of Missalonghi
The First Man in Rome
The Grass Crown
Fortune's Favourites
Caesar's Women
Caesar
The Song of Troy

RODEN CUTLER, V.C.

THE BIOGRAPHY

COLLEEN McCULLOUGH

RANDOM HOUSE AUSTRALIA

Random House Australia Pty Ltd
20 Alfred Street, Milsons Point, NSW 2061
http://www.randomhouse.com.au

Sydney   New York   Toronto
London   Auckland   Johannesburg

First published 1998
This paperback edition published 1999

National Library of Australia
Cataloguing-in-Publication Data

McCullough, Colleen, 1937– .
   Roden Cutler, V.C.

   ISBN 0 091 84018 X.

   1. Cutler, Roden, Sir, 1916– . 2. Soldiers – Australia –
Biography. 3. Governors – New South Wales – Biography. 4.
Diplomats – Australia – Biography. I. Title.

352.23213/092

Designed by Yolande Gray
Typeset by Midland Typesetters Pty Ltd
Printed by Griffin Paperbacks, a division of PMP Communications

10 9 8 7 6 5 4 3 2 1

Contents

LIST OF MAPS

THE PRESENT

He sits in his special chair, impeccably clad, puffing away at a Havana cigar, his dark eyes twinkling impishly beneath thick black brows. One leg is stretched out stiffly, one long and beautiful hand lies at peace. Around him is an aura of immense dignity, of unruffled calm: this is a man, I think to myself, who has overcome every obstacle and met every challenge life has thrown in his path, a man who in his old age can look back without fear, dread or regret. It has been a life very well lived.

He is still a remarkably handsome man; I am irresistibly reminded of Clark Gable. Sexy, even in his eighties. He will hate that observation, but it is a valid one: the man has everything. 194 cm of height, a splendid physique, a film star face, high intelligence, an acute sense of humour, an air of approachable friendliness—and, underlying all of that, you take one look and know that he is an unshakable rock in any sea.

His name is Arthur Roden Cutler, winner of the Victoria Cross for valour, Knight of the Order of Australia, Knight Commander of the Order of St. Michael and St. George, Knight Commander of the Royal Victorian Order, Commander of the Order of the British Empire, Knight of the Order of St. John of Jerusalem, war hero, diplomat, governor, company director, family man.

That his story be told is necessary, and not only because it is a

3

part of Australian history; it is also necessary to dispel the myths of silver spoon and landed gentry, of those old bugbears wealth and privilege, so often trotted out to diminish personal achievement. The reality is actually very much to the contrary. Roden Cutler is a self-made man. What he is begins in his forebears, who emigrated from the British Isles at a time when the Great South Land was no milk-and-honey America; continues through the agonies of personal tragedy, adversity and economic depression; and ends in his own unconquerable courage.

What exactly is heroism? Most people are under the impression that heroic persons display fearless bravery in war, or put themselves at risk of their lives in some other activity. The usual assumption is that heroism is physical, but this concept is inadequate. Persons willing to risk life and limb in the line of duty or principle are persons whose valour encompasses all aspects of their existence. Heroes are formidable people in *every* respect. Simply, heroes refuse to be cowed, cannot be intimidated.

One of my tasks as Roden Cutler's biographer has been to examine in some detail the lives of other accoladed war heroes—a fascinating exercise in itself.

From Colonel Lew Millett (U.S. Congressional Medal of Honor) I learned that there are families having a history of war heroism going back hundreds of years; the Millett family of Massachusetts produced its first war hero during the first half of the seventeenth century, and there has been one in every generation since. From Julius Caesar I learned that heroism can be a deliberate, cerebral choice, for this particular war hero went after high military decoration in order to use it as a future political tool. The legend of Sir Galahad points up an interesting premise: that the soul of the hero is untainted, and that heroism will endure as long as the soul remains untainted. From long talks to the late Jack Hinton, V.C., I learned that some war heroes can be stubborn to the length of courting suicide, yet retain a deliciously wry humour about their plight; an observation reinforced by Jack's fellow New Zealander, the late Charles Upham, twice a V.C. winner. And I have yarned to those other Australian Victoria Cross laureates still alive during the genesis of this book—Keith Payne and Ted Kenna.

From all with whom I have conversed I learned that the one subject they are reluctant to discuss is battle. Getting the details of Roden Cutler's own war exploits out of him was as painful as picking buckshot out of a behind—one tiny bit at a time.

'It's all in the official citation,' he'd say.

'But what did you *feel*?'

'Too busy to remember.'

'What did you *think*?'

'About what I was doing.'

And so on. The secret, I discovered, was just to keep on picking away, one tiny bit at a time.

Of course it is no longer fashionable to adulate war heroes. These days they tend to be dismissed as dinosaurs, relics of an age perceived as gone. Yet if my research has taught me anything, it is that war heroism is an innate aspect of character. There is no real difference between heroism on the battlefield, while a ship is sinking, being burned for one's religious beliefs, in facing a crowd understanding that assassination is probable, or in the struggles of a lone woman without means to educate her promising children.

The Hollywood action movie is founded on heroism. If we laugh at how Arnold Schwarzenegger can gun down dozens of villains without sustaining a scratch himself, we are nonetheless looking at a celluloid caricature of the hero, and the more susceptible among us go home from the cinema to fantasise in Schwarzeneggerian mode: to dream of being bigger, better, braver. All the while seriously doubting our own individual potentials for heroism—and praying that we never have to find out the hard way.

Perhaps, in a nutshell, heroes are people who put the needs and plights of other people ahead of their own welfare: who do not think first and foremost of self. They want to live a very happy life very much, yet cannot do so at the expense of others. They are still with us, and always will be, no matter how strenuously society may strive to extol the mediocre or glamorise the anti-hero.

Heroes represent the finest in human nature. Their value to all of us is incalculable.

Time, then, to discover from whence came Roden Cutler, and see if we can discern why he is what he is: a great Australian.

GROWING UP

There have been Cutlers in New South Wales since 1833, when one Benjamin Richard Cutler, carpenter, arrived on the *Warrior* as a free settler. A Londoner, he brought with him his wife and a sixteen-year-old son, also named Benjamin. Shortly thereafter he set himself up in a joinery at Darling Harbour and did well enough to have fourteen benches in his shop. Adjacent to his premises was the wharf from which north coast red cedar was unloaded; Benjamin Richard Cutler made red cedar items his specialty. Soon he was able to bring his brother out from London, then shipped him to Wauchope to ensure the red cedar supply. No fool, Benjamin Richard Cutler! There are still many Cutlers around Telegraph Hill, near Wauchope, all descended from Benjamin Richard's brother.

Benjamin Richard's son, Benjamin, in his turn married and produced a third Benjamin, who was Roden Cutler's grandfather. *He* travelled over the Blue Mountains to manage the Western Stores & Edgley's general store at Bathurst, where he married Martha Abbott of Dungog. After he retired he bought a lush property at Raglan and renamed it 'Abbotsford' after his wife's family. Its homestead, convict-built out of sandstone blocks, was the oldest house west of the Blue Mountains. Later Roden's grandfather added a second property near Kelso to his little empire, and settled down to breed fine Hereford cattle. He had a large family of six sons and three daughters, but rather than subdivide his properties, he compensated those sons who did not inherit them with sufficient money to allow them to prosper in whatever occupations they chose.

Two of them bought a rich river flat property outside Blayney for three pounds an acre; one, Arthur, was Roden's father, and the other, George, was father of Sir Charles Cutler.[†] Five years of farming later, the brothers sold their land to the Fagans for six pounds an acre, and thought themselves made. George elected to move further west, to Orange, while Arthur preferred to invest his share in a produce store in Bathurst.

Produce stores were profitably essential: from them the farmer bought his feed and seed—bran, pollard, chaff, wheat and the like. Indeed, produce stores were a feature of nineteenth-century Sydney streetscapes as well, for Sydney ran on horses and everyone kept backyard chooks for eggs. They didn't die out in Sydney until well after the Second World War, as the baker, the milkman and the fruit-and-vegie man still drove horse-drawn carts, and everyone still kept backyard chooks.

Arthur was born at Raglan on 30 June 1875, and favoured the life of a bachelor for somewhat longer than most of his contemporaries. Family legends have it that the produce store—a huge shed rather than an orthodox shop—was more of a boxing arena than a bustling business; a keen follower of amateur boxing, Arthur set up a ring on the premises and held bouts there.

[†] Sir Charles Cutler became leader of the New South Wales Country Party and was a deputy premier of New South Wales.

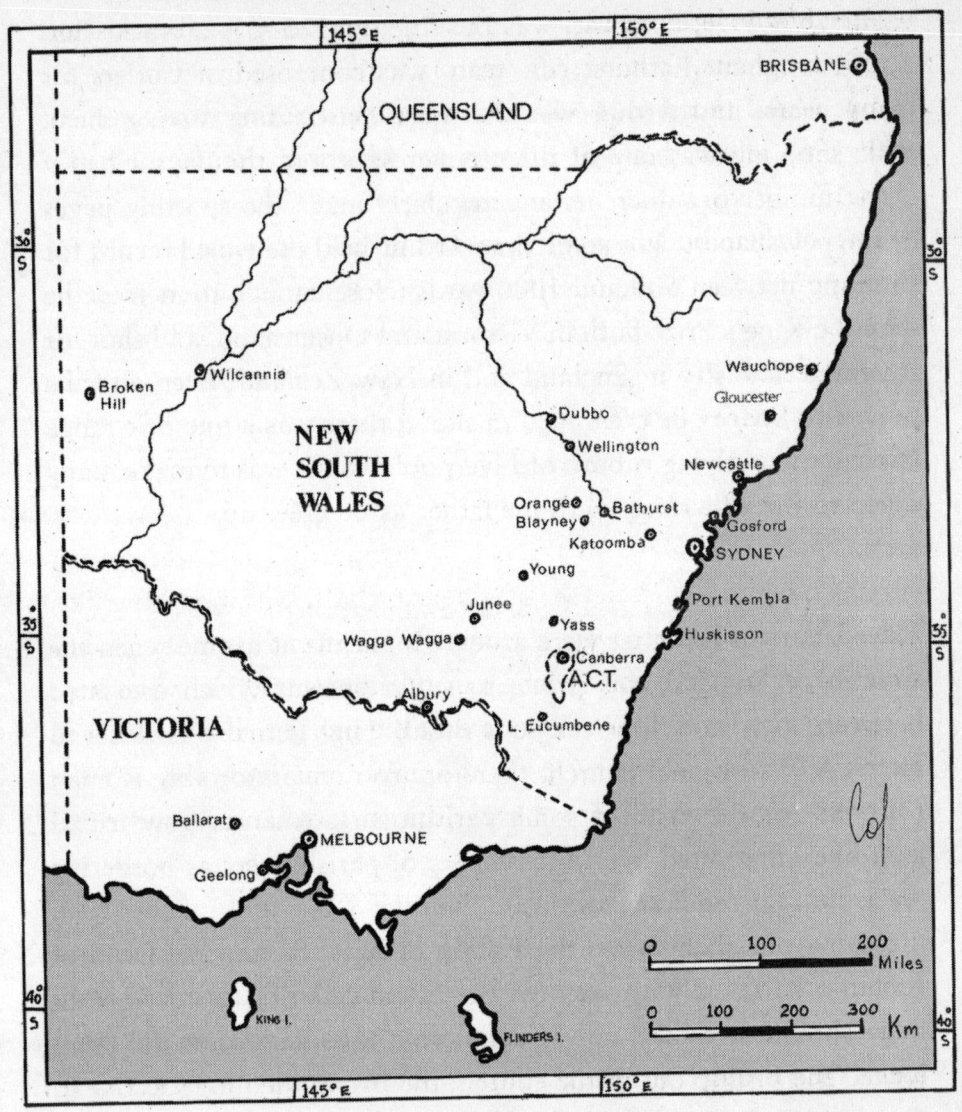

His chief love, however, was the rifle, and he was a crack shot. The triumphant Bathurst rifle team was composed of Cutlers for many years, and Arthur was the most outstanding among them. Rifle shooting was one of the premier sports of the day; it had a large number of adherents and regularly made the sporting pages of the newspapers. For some time Arthur held the world record for shooting between 500 and 1000 yards (close enough to metres); he won the King's Prize both in Victoria and Queensland, and shot for Australia at Bisley in England and in New Zealand. Even after he moved to Sydney he continued to shoot; there was a fine rifle range beyond the outlying suburb of Liverpool. Roden was to make many a trip to the rifle range with his father as he grew up.

The Cutlers of Bathurst were ardent Anglicans at a time when the Church of England was prone to suffer spasms which oscillated between 'high' and 'low' religious ritual. 'High' ritual was closer to Henry VIII's original church, therefore too uncomfortably Roman Catholic for the taste of some parishioners, whereas 'low' ritual could be interpreted by a different set of parishioners as bordering on Protestant fundamentalism.

During one such spasm the Bishop of Bathurst and the Dean of Bathurst had a falling out over the vexed question as to whether there should or should not be candles on the altar; when the Dean locked the Bishop out of the church, the Bishop fled for succour to the elder Cutlers at 'Abbotsford'. Some of their children, however, agreed with the Dean, with the result that—Arthur among them— they left the Anglican fold and went to the Presbyterian church instead. Difficult to believe in our day and age, perhaps, but in those days religion was a serious matter which involved a much larger percentage of the populace, in cities as well as in the country.

Church on a Sunday was the place wherein one said hello to God and to friends, exchanged news, had the opportunity to sing, and took the bad with the good if the sermon was a bit prolix or boring. Church was divinely sanctioned sociability.

Among the regular and devout congregation of the Bathurst Presbyterian church was a young woman named Ruby Pope. Born at Young on 23 October 1884, she was the daughter of Major Harold Hamilton Pope and Julia Roden, his wife.

On the Roden side the Australian experience went back to 1827, when Ruby's great-grandfather was posted to New South Wales in the British army. Subsequently the Rodens owned quite a lot of prime property in the Rocks, then one of Sydney's most thriving commercial and residential sectors. A small lane (misspelled as 'Rhoden') was named after one of them, though most of Rhoden Lane was sacrificed in the early 1930s when the Sydney Harbour Bridge was abuilding. A severe economic depression in the 1890s hit the Rodens hard, and their importance dwindled thereafter.

Major Pope came to New South Wales in the late 1850s, hard on the heels of the Crimean War. An engineer, he helped install the gun emplacements on Middle Head in Sydney Harbour, then did some of the work on converting the tiny Harbour isle of Pinchgut into gun-bristling Fort Denison, named after the then Governor, Sir William Denison. Russian fever was rife, and the British masters of the rapidly expanding colony of New South Wales were very perturbed at the thought that Russia might lust after lands in the Southern Hemisphere. Once the fortifications were finished Pope did other jobs for the British army for a while, then joined the Army reserve with a commission of major and became a prison warden. In this supervisory capacity he moved from one country gaol to another until he was appointed the Governor of Dubbo Gaol, wherein he always insisted that he be addressed as 'Major'.

Ruby Pope's childhood had therefore been a rather nomadic one; though Young was her birthplace, she spent time in Wilcannia and other towns owning gaols before the final move to Dubbo. Her photographs show that she was a very handsome woman of fine figure, yet she didn't marry early. Millinery—the creation of hats—was deemed a most respectable occupation for a young woman (no contact with *Men*!), so Ruby trained as a milliner. She was working in a Bathurst hat shop when she met the dashing, moustachioed Arthur Cutler.

They became engaged, but the wedding had to be delayed for a year when Ruby developed trouble in her left lower leg which required surgery. The operation was badly bungled, a not uncommon occurrence at the time; a post-operative thrombosis kept her in hospital for months. Though she eventually recovered, she walked with a limp for the rest of her life.

In the meantime Ruby's parents had moved to Manly, one of Sydney's remotest and most beautiful suburbs. Situated on the north side of the lower Harbour, it boasted several magnificent surfing beaches on the Pacific side of its promontory, the four-hundred-foot majesty of North Head, and several placid swimming beaches within the shelter of the Harbour. Manly was always the place in Sydney where country people preferred to go, whether it was to retire, like Major and Mrs. Pope, or on holiday. Somehow it never felt like part of a bustling metropolis, for it could only be reached after a forty-minute ferry ride from Circular Quay at the foot of downtown Sydney. How did it get its name? From Captain Arthur Phillip himself, commander of the First Fleet and the founding Governor of New South Wales. While exploring the fascinating reaches of what he called 'the finest harbour in the world', he came to the Harbour beaches of Manly and saw a group of Aborigines, Australia's indigenous people. He thought them fine-looking fellows, very 'manly'.

Major Pope bought a long, oldfashioned house on the corner of Darley Road and Victoria Parade, just opposite the Manly Public School. Ruby's favourite sister, the inimitable Aunt Dais, trained as a teacher and taught there. Like Arthur Cutler's, Ruby's family was also large: she had both sisters and brothers.

While Ruby was recuperating in hospital, Arthur had an offer of a job. Not any old job—this one was very special. The American Remington Arms Company was looking for an Australian sales representative. What attracted Remington's attention to Arthur was a combination of his prowess with a rifle and his easygoing, man's man charm. An ideal kind of person, Remington thought, to travel from north to south and east to west of the continent selling their finely wrought, world renowned firearms and ammunition. The Great War in Europe had made him restless; Arthur accepted the job with the Remington Arms Company and sold his produce store.

So when Ruby and Arthur finally married at Manly on 12 September 1915, it was already decided that temporarily they would live with her parents in Manly; Ruby would have company while he travelled, got used to the job.

Neither newlywed was in the first flush of youth. Arthur had turned forty, and Ruby wasn't far off thirty-two. They honeymooned in Queensland, where Arthur pursued his career as a rifle salesman with mingled happiness and frustration. For what Arthur really yearned to do was to join the Australian Imperial Forces, fight in the stalemated Great War. But the Army would not have him, not because of his age but because he suffered very badly from varicose veins—so much so, in fact, that he had already undergone surgery to have them stripped. No picnic at that time when surgery was still in its childhood. He had begged to be specially enlisted as a sniper, sure that his skill at long range shooting would more than compensate for those wretched varicose veins. To no avail. The Army was obdurate; it couldn't use his services.

Interesting, the fact that both Roden's parents had problems with their legs.

Ruby fell pregnant at once. While Arthur travelled the interminable distances of Australia on steamtrains or steamships, she lived in Manly with her parents and looked forward eagerly to Arthur's visits, which he made as often as he could. Her child was due about the end of the first week in June; she waited quietly and enjoyed good health.

A cataclysmic thunderstorm broke as night fell on 24 May 1916; buffeted by high winds and torrential rains, the house shook until a picture fell from the wall and carved a chunk out of Ruby's piano in the lounge room. But more urgent things were going on; Ruby was in labour.

And so it was that Arthur Roden Cutler entered the world in the teeth of a gale and in the midst of a war his absent father was not permitted to fight. He was long and dark, and no doubt to his ecstatic mother a wonder of perfection from the black hair of his head to his ten fingers and ten toes. Did she know what this son would become? No, of course not. But all mothers dream that their babies will be much to many, and Ruby Cutler would have been no different. Of all her babies, none would rest as close to her heart as her first-born did. He was to be her 'Laddie'.

A second pregnancy came fairly quickly after Roden's birth, and it was clearly impossible for the Cutlers to continue living with the Popes. So Arthur bought two adjoining blocks of land in Addison Road at Little Manly. They belonged to a bachelor solicitor named

Alfred Milford, who lived next door to them; *his* bachelor brother, John, lived next door to him in an amazing, fortresslike house. Rather different neighbours from the usual suburban motley, but destined to be good neighbours. On this generous allotment Arthur set about building a good but not ambitiously large house, though he was shrewd enough to ensure that it sat upon one block, while the other was given over to lawns and gardens.

The builder he hired says much about the kind of person Arthur Cutler was: remarkably fairminded and loyal to his friends. Through his rifle club he knew a builder with a German name, and also knew that the fellow was suffering much hardship from little work. People were fanatically anti-German. To him was given the task of building 'Kyeema' (the Aboriginal word for 'dawn', bearing in mind that in 1918 people did not know much about such matters), and he did well by Arthur. The solid brick house contained a lounge room, dining room, three bedrooms, bathroom, laundry, kitchen and a maid's bedroom off the kitchen. There was a generous verandah which was to come in handy later, when more people were squeezed into 'Kyeema' than Arthur had ever dreamed or dreaded.

But the Cutlers were still living with the Popes when Harold Hamilton Cutler was born in 1917. This time things were not right; little Harold Hamilton died three days after he was born. Not an uncommon fate, though a great sorrow to the parents and grandparents.

By the time the family moved into 'Kyeema' Ruby was expecting her third child. Homemaking was a thrill, from placing the piano— Ruby played competently—to arranging the furniture, which was substantial and comfortable. They had a telephone, a generous enough power supply to afford the luxury of an electric fire—*very* modern!—things for everyday use and things for best, and the services of a live-in maid.

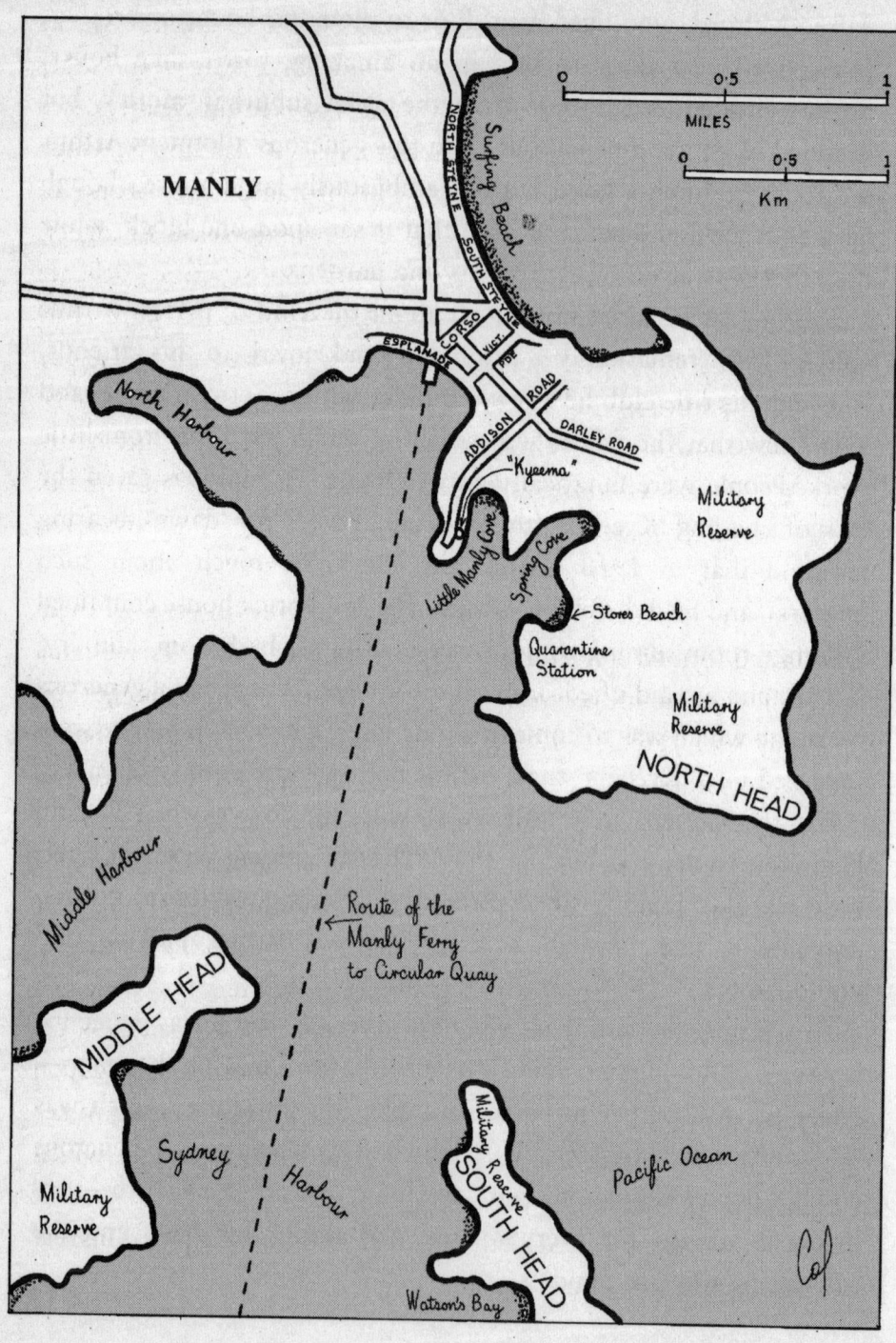

MANLY

Surfing Beach

North Harbour

Military Reserve

"Kyeema"

Stores Beach

Quarantine Station

Military Reserve

NORTH HEAD

Middle Harbour

MIDDLE HEAD

Military Reserve

Route of the Manly Ferry to Circular Quay

Sydney

Harbour

Military Reserve

SOUTH HEAD

Pacific Ocean

Watson's Bay

In those days the possession of live-in house help did not denote great wealth; rather, it was a sign that one was respectably circumstanced. There were no such things as vacuum cleaners, hot water systems, washing machines, refrigerators or fast foods, which meant that keeping house unaided was constant, heavy work; to care for children on top of it turned it into remorseless drudgery. Linens were boiled in a huge wood-fired copper, more delicate clothing was washed by hand in concrete tubs, excess water was removed from both by hand-turning a mangle, then all had to be hung, one item by one, on the clothesline. And that was just the washing. So Ruby Cutler didn't sit at her leisure or spend her hours playing with the children; she worked alongside her live-in maid, with whom she had to enjoy a pleasant relationship or suffer the consequences.

There was not a high turnover in Cutler maids; the two of them who lasted formed a startling contrast with each other. Violet came first. She was a jolly, unsophisticated country girl who got on famously with the Cutler boys, who thought her great fun, always ready to collaborate in a prank. One day she and Roden decided to shake up an unpopular neighbour by throwing stones on her roof. She lived on the opposite side of 'Kyeema' from the bachelor brothers, and had a habit of tossing the contents of her chamber pot all over Ruby's washing as it hung on the line. But crotchety old ladies who use chamber pots do not appreciate a hail of stones on the roof; she called the police while Violet and Roden took off for home. A young policeman arrived to make enquiries, whereupon Violet took a shine to him and he to her. His nocturnal visits to her room resulted in huge footprints in the garden bed, a sight which so alarmed Ruby that she too called the police.

'Oh, don't worry,' said the constable who turned up to inspect the garden bed, 'it's a policeman's boot.'

When the doctor was visiting 'Kyeema' one day he noticed a sore on the maid's mouth.

'I think, Mrs. Cutler,' he said tactfully to Ruby, 'that it's time Violet moved on.'

Violet had contracted what is now called a 'social disease'. So Violet moved on, and moved down until she became a prostitute who made the papers. Prostitutes did make the papers then.

Mary could not have been more different. Dour and abysmally plain, her Catholic orphanage upbringing had left her with a desperate desire to be a nun. For years she tried to join an order, but no one would have her; religious vocations were over-plentiful in those days. So she worked and lived in the Cutler household, went to Mass, and prayed nonstop to be a nun. Then one day the miracle actually happened! An unsuspected relative left her a legacy plump enough to enable her to be accepted, though she was too dull to be a teacher or a nurse. She went right on being a housemaid, but happy in her habit. Mary wasn't the hit with the Cutler boys Violet had been before her fall from grace, but Ruby certainly rested easier.

For by now there were boys in the plural. Geoffrey was born in February 1919, and Robert in December 1921. Then in October 1923 came the only Cutler girl, whom Ruby and Arthur christened Doone. Ruby loved the novel *Lorna Doone*.

'Kyeema' was a perfect place for a child to grow up during the 1920s. It stood atop a low, cave-ridden sandstone cliff on the western shore of Little Manly Cove, almost opposite Stores Beach and the old North Head quarantine station's austere semi-Georgian beauty. Serious crime was nonexistent, witness the alacrity of the Manly police to answer phone calls in person from crotchety old ladies bombarded with stones and perturbed mothers discovering huge footprints in the garden bed.

Caressed by unpolluted air, hide warmed by a brilliant sun, a boy could wander, adventure and explore with the same careless abandon as a soaring bird. Mothers did worry, but not at the prospect of a human predator, simply with that maternal anxiety which frets over where to draw the line between utter freedom and some prudent safety regulations.

Three years older than Geoff, Roden was more of a loner than the two younger boys. He taught himself to swim and ranged far and wide around North Head and the Manlys. School, where Aunt Dais was a teacher, interested him less than sun and sea and sky, but he was a bright boy and usually managed to do well.

Always inclined to be taller than his peers, Roden suffered spates of growth which sapped his strength and convinced Ruby that he was, as they put it then, 'delicate'. Much to his chagrin, his mother insisted that he wear grey flannel undershirts—flannel was considered a prophylaxis against chills and chest problems. Even when he joined the Boy Scouts at ten years of age, Ruby refused to let him doff his grey flannel undershirts, and ensured his compliance by becoming head of the Scout ladies' auxiliary; she was a person of great importance to a needy scoutmaster, so what she said went. Roden wore his grey flannel undershirts for years. Though they were not top of his clothing blacklist: that spot went to the knickerbockers Ruby thought looked just lovely. Ugh!

Family life was happy. Arthur had managed to construct a routine which mostly permitted him to return to 'Kyeema' on a Friday night steamtrain and remain at home until Sunday night, when he took himself off to the country platforms at Central railway station again to travel through the week, staying at modest hotels, making sure he was in a particular place on the local show day or picnic races, at which times the graziers and farmers were in town and business would be briskest. Trips to north Queensland, South Australia and Western Australia were aboard a ship; ships were faster and a great deal pleasanter than soot particles in the hair and an ineradicable smell of coal smoke.

Sundays were special. Religion wasn't something Arthur or Ruby shoved down their children's throats, but both parents were sincere Protestant Christians. If Arthur was home he and Ruby attended the evening service at the Manly Presbyterian church, but the children went to Sunday School irrespective of their father's whereabouts. Cars were still something of a rarity in Manly. One walked or one bicycled or one hired a pony carriage, which was an open landau drawn by two creamy ponies. People used to love creamy ponies. A pony carriage would arrive at 'Kyeema' to pick up the children, convey them to Sunday School and return to pick them up afterwards. When Arthur was home he and Ruby would be in the carriage, and the family would then go for a drive together before sitting down to a hot Sunday lunch. Sometimes of an evening after dinner the Bible would come out and a passage would be read and discussed, but not regularly enough for these active, restless children to find it a bore.

If Arthur had been on a long interstate trip he always brought presents home with him—meccano pieces, a train set, something significant: 'We kids thought it was Christmas.' Despite his enforced absences, Arthur was an understanding and a most generous father. He didn't believe in stringent discipline. Nor did Ruby. The Cutler children were not beaten. Simply, both parents expected a certain degree of good behaviour and mostly got it. When they didn't— and usually it was Ruby aggrieved, as she was always there—the culprit found himself on the receiving end of an unpleasant tongue-lashing.

Quite often on a Sunday morning when Arthur was home, his men friends from the rifle club would visit 'Kyeema'; the Scotch whisky bottle would come out, and a good time would be had by all. The men would toss a tin can or a small bottle out into the water and take turns to pot it with a .22 rifle. On one occasion some residents further down Addison Road decided to emulate this marksmanship, but kept missing the tin can, which floated on down towards 'Kyeema'. Arthur, who wasn't entertaining his cronies that day, got his .22 and tried to hit it without success. Then Ruby took the rifle and potted the tin can on her first try. (Church, the author adds, was in the evening.)

Not that Arthur spent all his precious time at home with a rifle. He was on good terms with both the bachelor Milford brothers, but it was John, the one who lived in a fortress, with whom he was better friends. John had a well-equipped metalworking machine shop, in which he amused himself by making scale models of railway locomotives. Roden still possesses the two miniature guns Arthur made in John Milford's machine shop, exquisitely turned out of brass: one was a field gun, the other a rail gun (that is, a gun mounted on railway tracks). Both could be fired, and Roden loved to fire them. His charge was black powder rammed home with a cotton wad, his projectiles ordinary lead buckshot. He pillaged the fuze from a Tom Thumb firecracker, stuck it into the fuze hole on the gun, then lit it; the gun went off with enough force to send the shot straight through a quarter-inch-thick piece of wood. Apart from almost killing brother Geoff when he appeared unexpectedly just after the fuze was ignited—Geoff leaped in the air like a gazelle, unharmed—this early artillery practice proceeded smoothly and was greatly enjoyed.

Good fortune didn't always smile. Ruby ailed from time to time, and on one occasion at least required hospitalisation. When Arthur departed in a pony carriage to bring her home, the children gathered on the front verandah to wait eagerly. Mum was better, they'd soon see her! The only Cutler girl, Doone, was eighteen months old, but she too was there, held sitting on the verandah rail by the maid. Who suddenly wandered off and left the child precariously perched. Doone fell to earth, but not cleanly. She struck her abdomen on a garden tap. When Ruby and Arthur appeared, it was Doone's turn to be rushed to hospital. The child suffered grave internal injuries which necessitated surgery, then developed peritonitis. She was sent home to die. But Ruby and Arthur were determined Doone wouldn't die. They hired a nurse named Biddy Morgan, who Roden remembers sitting hour after hour patiently swabbing the terrible open wound in the little girl's abdomen. Eventually Doone recovered. Nurse Biddy Morgan subsequently married Berkley Waugh, the local undertaker, and was progenitor of the Waugh family of cricketers—which delights Roden, one of the world's most ardent cricket fans.

Most of Roden's personal adventures took place in or on the water. He swam like a fish and fell in love with sailing. His first essay as a yachtsman was a ten-foot cadet dinghy which he and Arthur built out of wood and canvas; he sailed it all around the lower end of Sydney Harbour. Then he fashioned a canoe out of a sheet of galvanised iron by bending it lengthwise into a U shape, compressing its ends together and pitching them to make the canoe watertight. When he found it to be unstable he added an outrigger, and that did the trick. One day when a light southerly was blowing he paddled the canoe out to the notoriously choppy, mile-wide gap between the Harbour's Heads, put up a sail, turned around and came surfing in on the waves—right past the back of 'Kyeema' and under his mother's horrified eyes. Having beached the canoe unscathed, he arrived home to cop one of Ruby's most memorable tongue-lashings.

Bicycling and cricket absorbed him too, but though he liked Rugby Union, he never played football; Ruby abhorred it as rough and dangerous.

Whenever his mother felt that Roden had outgrown his strength he was packed off to visit the Cutler relations around Bathurst, where he learned to ride a horse well, though never to love the country style of living. Other visits were to Aunt Dais, now teaching school in Albury, a big town on the New South Wales side of the Murray River border with Victoria. Teachers were paid well enough for Aunt Dais, a spinster, to be able to afford to live on her own and have house guests.

Aunt Dais was an absolute trump, as time was to prove over and over again. A stumpy little figure clad in antique mode, she ran whatever or whoever came into her ken with a rod of gentle iron that could turn into solid steel if she thought someone helpless needed protecting.

Though it was not to happen until after General Douglas MacArthur arrived in Australia in March 1942 as Supreme Commander of the South-West Pacific Area, here is the place to say that the Americans promptly requisitioned an alarming number of buildings from one end of the continent to the other. One such was the kindergarten section of the Albury school wherein Aunt Dais was now the headmistress. No doubt the Americans felt they would need a depot in this vital rail junction town through which to funnel the massive amounts of men and matériel the Second World War was sucking into its maw. General MacArthur's headquarters were then in Melbourne, at the far southern end of the mainland; economics dictated that all Australian cities should benefit.

The moment that she heard she was about to lose her kindergarten school, Aunt Dais hustled herself to the Victorian platform (the rail gauge in Victoria was different from that in New South Wales) and caught the express train two hundred miles south to Melbourne. There she marched into American headquarters and demanded to see General Douglas MacArthur. Some terrified junior officer, fixed by that martial basilisk eye, stammered explanations that General MacArthur wasn't in Melbourne. Did that get rid of Aunt Dais? Oh, no. She stood her ground until she was ushered into the presence of the American general holding down MacArthur's Melbourne fort, then she gave him a tongue-lashing on a par with Ruby's to Roden after the canoe episode. How *dared* they deprive her little ones of their school? Never, never, never! They would have to step over her dead body first! Having said her piece, she sailed out and caught the next train back to Albury. The American high command did not lay a finger on Aunt Dais's kindergarten school. One wonders if they so much as dared to put a depot anywhere in Albury.

The house was beginning to fill up to overflowing.

When Major Pope died, Grandma Pope came to live at 'Kyeema' as a matter of course, which deprived the Cutlers of a good big bedroom. Roden and Geoff were relegated to the verandah, closed in against bad weather—a sleepout. The old lady was not always the easiest of permanent house guests, but neither Arthur nor Ruby ever complained.

Ruby's youngest sister, Aunt Moon (Muriel), lived in Tasmania and became yet another victim of the shabby medicine so prevalent at that time. A botched surgical procedure left her paralysed down one side and unable to look after her two children, Meg and Bob Milligan. Aunt Dais took Meg, but felt unqualified to house Bob.

Grandma Pope decided to take him—which meant that he came to live at 'Kyeema' as well, and joined Roden and Geoff (he was in their age group) on the verandah sleepout.

At Christmas time the Pope family tended to arrive en masse to stay for the festive season; Aunt Dais and Meg Milligan took the double bed in the sleepout, while Roden, Geoff and Bob dossed down on mattresses laid along the more open part of the verandah. Not that it mattered. Everyone had a wonderful time, everyone looked forward to the Christmas crush and Christmas dinner, a rather ludicrous cold climate midday feast of hot roasts and steaming pudding served with hot sauce. The temperature was usually into the nineties Fahrenheit, could reach the hundred. But there they sat, up to eight adults around the dining table and ten children around the emergency second table, eating away and politely wiping the perspiration from their faces.

Grace was always said, people had to be properly dressed for dinner, good manners were insisted upon.

There were pets. Roden's favourite was a white cat he was given as a kitten; its name was Tom. What Roden loved about Tom was the fact that the animal genuinely thought it was a dog. It would come when Roden whistled it, and always followed him down Addison Road until it reached its girlfriend's house, where it would wait until Roden returned, then follow him home again.

A dog named Montana, Monty for short, also occupied 'Kyeema', and after Tom, aged twelve, disappeared one day, another kitten arrived; it was black and its name was Jet, but Roden despised it because it didn't think it was a dog.

Early in 1930 the Great Depression cracked down. Suddenly people all over Australia were jobless, homeless, aimless. The degree of social devastation can hardly be imagined in our modern, cushioned welfare state. There was no dole. There were few laws to protect the workingman. When rent wasn't paid a family's possessions were sold by the evicting landlord. When mortgages couldn't be met foreclosure followed. In New South Wales a grim war went on between the federal Labor[†] Prime Minister, James Henry Scullin, and the New South Wales Labor Premier, John Thomas (Jack) Lang. Scullin's policy was the orthodox one of retrenchment and deflation; Lang thought that government spending ought to be accelerated and laws enacted to prevent eviction or foreclosure.

But for Arthur Cutler the increasingly violent wrangle between his State and his federal governments was a minor worry; the Remington Arms Company withdrew from its Australian market. Arthur was out of a job literally overnight without compensation.

He hadn't been a saving man. What he had, he spent on his family and his recreations, though his family came first. Not a gambler, his personal outlays were confined to Scotch whisky, his rifles and their ammunition. There had been more than enough.

That this state of affairs could change had not occurred to him any more than it occurred to hundreds of thousands of his contemporaries. Some people did manage to make money out of the Great Depression and some survived it relatively unscathed, but they were the tiny minority. For the vast majority the future loomed like an insurmountable wall, a grey amorphous barrier which sat there forbidding any ray of hope, any alleviation in frantic anxiety, any possibility of averting disaster.

A nation of settled people became a gigantic vacuum in which nomadic men roamed in thousands upon thousands in search of work, too dazed and too beaten to think properly. Their families

---

[†] The spelling 'Labor' was formally adopted in 1908.

tried to hang on, many in circumstances so reduced that shanty towns sprang up on public land and the queues at the soup kitchens went around the block.

At first Arthur tried to find work in Sydney, and if Roden were not in school he would go along to keep his father company. Arthur always wore his best three-piece suit, stiff cuffs and collar, carefully blocked hat. But the search was fruitless; jobs were just not to be had. Even so precariously situated, Arthur's nature didn't change.

'Got sixpence for a pie, guvnor?' a shabby man asked at Circular Quay before Arthur got on the ferry with Roden after yet one more empty day.

Arthur fished through his pockets and found a sixpenny coin, smiling wryly. 'Just as well that's all you asked me for,' he said, 'because I don't have any more to give.'

All he had kept was the ferry fare home.

The telephone had to go. So too did the electric fire, replaced by a coke-burning 'cosy' slow combustion stove in the lounge room—Sydney can be cold when the winter wind blows a gale and the sea spume coats the windows. The maid had to go. Ruby did it all herself, with the boys helping. At least they owned 'Kyeema' free and clear, and at least there was enough money left for Arthur to buy a battered old Studebaker car.

Like so many other men, he had decided that he would go on the road. Car was cheaper than train because he could live out of it, subsistence camp by the roadside and carry within it whatever he had managed to persuade some Sydney merchant to let him have for speculative sale: leather goods, tools, rifles and ammunition of course. To some extent it worked. He managed to sell just enough to cover his own expenses, feed and clothe his family in Manly.

The war between the Lang Labor State Government and the Federal Government became even more acrimonious after Scullin's

Labor Party lost the federal elections in December of 1931, and Lang found himself pitted against a conservative enemy in Canberra. He refused to pay the State's interest obligations, especially to London lenders, and began to talk about a general cancellation of debts. Scullin's Government had paid the interest owed by New South Wales, but the new Federal Government was not so inclined.

A right-wing organisation called the New Guard began to flourish in New South Wales, dedicated to bringing Jack Lang down in any way it could.

Two or three of Arthur's friends from the rifle club coaxed him into attending a New Guard meeting in Manly; their object was to enlist him among the New Guard's ranks. Ruby and Roden accompanied him to the meeting and its ringing oratory, then followed behind after he left while he talked to one of the friends.

'We need you, Arthur!' said the friend. 'We need men who are good shots because that's what it's going to come to. Civil war.'

'No,' said Arthur, 'no! You handle these things through the ballot box, not through violence.'

Roden, listening, was sick with disappointment; his mind had whirled off on imagined battles on Sydney's streets—what a terrific fight there'd be with Father, a world champion shot, in the midst of it! Now here was Father condemning the New Guard so strongly that he said later to Ruby and Roden, 'I'm just sorry I ever went to that meeting.'

It took some years for the lesson to sink in, but it did. Roden was to learn at first hand the difference between shooting people and shooting pennies tossed into the air.

Jack Lang went in May of 1932, after withdrawing all the State's money from the bank and barricading the Treasury. The Governor of New South Wales, Sir Philip Game, dismissed him from office for defying the law and he suffered a crushing defeat in the ensuing elections on 11 June. The federal policy had prevailed; States' rights were redefined; and Arthur had been vindicated. The ballot box had decided the issue, as it always must.

Someone else went in 1932: Grandma Pope. The sixteen-year-old Roden found her in extremis and raced up Addison Road to the nearest house owning a telephone, but nothing could be done.

Not that the numbers at 'Kyeema' diminished. Ruby kept on taking in the needy among her brothers and cousins, and Arthur never complained or criticised.

They ate. Bread was tuppence ha'penny a loaf, enormously expensive but also filling. Butter was a thing of the past; now the family ate bread-and-dripping—a layer of leftover fat from the frying or roasting pan coated the bread and was sprinkled with salt and pepper. (Sounds dreadful, but the author loved it as a child, and so did Roden.) Stews went a lot further than roasts, which were for special occasions: neck of mutton, beef shanks, some sort of curry. Sausages were cheap and produced plenty of fat for bread-and-dripping later.

For Roden and the younger children life went on, even if Father couldn't give them pocket money. Everyone they knew was in the same boat; everyone slipped stout cardboard inside their shoes until the hole in the leather was just too big not to be mended; everyone scrimped to find second-hand textbooks; everyone thought longingly of the matinées at the picture show.

Roden's first proper school was the Manly public school, where he started at the age of five and proceeded through the classes with a minimum of effort and reasonable marks. His best subjects were English and history, but he had little trouble with mathematics either. Aunt Dais was a teacher at Manly for the first few years. Though it had been a primary school only, Manly public school was elevated to Intermediate level in time for Roden to continue attending it until he sat for his Intermediate Certificate (which happened at about the age of fifteen).

In better times Arthur and Ruby had intended that their boys should go to the Sydney Grammar School, but the Great Depression made that aspiration absolutely impossible. Jobs were so hard to get that it seemed, provided they could manage to feed the boys, easier to keep them at school. Sooner or later the Great Depression would be over, and a good education is more precious than pearls. But it would have to be a State school education.

The four As and two Bs Roden earned when he sat for his Intermediate Certificate were sufficient for him to obtain an admission to Sydney Boys' High. This State funded school had—and still does have—an excellent academic and sporting record, and belonged to the G.P.S. (Greater Public Schools) system, which meant its pupils competed with those in the best private schools. It was an eternity away from Manly, for it sat (together with Sydney Girls' High) in a big triangle of land between Cleveland Street and Anzac Parade, on the inner fringe of the Eastern Suburbs. Roden took the ferry and then a tram to school, an hour each way: the fares amounted to fourpence per diem, and lunch was cut from home.

He wasn't a model pupil during the first year he spent at Sydney Boys' High in 1932. This was the year of Jack Lang's collapse, certainly, but more importantly for Roden, it was the year of the 'bodyline' series of test cricket matches between Australia and England, with English Harold Larwood chucking the hard red leather ball at a hundred miles an hour down the pitch and Australian Don Bradman, a mere fledgling, whacking sixes off him at peril of head and groin. And there was Roden attending a school only a hop, skip and jump away from the Sydney Cricket Ground! He was crazy about cricket, which even then he deemed the perfect sport—individual yet team oriented, consummately strategic. Naturally he played cricket himself, though never for the school.

So whenever there was a cricket match on at the Sydney Cricket Ground, Roden wagged school. Even when he was at school his head was full of cricket, and Don Bradman was his hero. The trouble was that school had always been so *easy*. He could coast through, no trouble. Then came the shock: at the end of 1932 he was informed that his marks hadn't been good enough to earn promotion. If he wanted to stay at school, he would have to repeat Fourth Year, as it was then called.

The shame of having to go home and confess his sentence to his mother! The mortification of watching most of his fellow Fourth Yearers become Fifth Yearers at the end of January 1933!

But Roden swallowed his pride and repeated Fourth Year, which meant that he was about a year older than most of his classmates. This time he buckled down to it and learned to study. He also gave up playing cricket and wagging school. Not that his behaviour was always exemplary. The boys had developed a habit of pitching orange peels through the open window of a staffroom on the top floor of Sydney High's two-storey pile. To find themselves shelled by orange peel did nothing to improve teacher temper, but Roden observed that their first reaction was always to close the window. So one day he organised his troops, made sure that they were amply provided with orange peel—and added a stink bomb to their arsenal. Then he scooted upstairs and shoved a wedge under the door to the teachers' common room. The moment the orange peel flew, the staff inside shut the window. Before they realised that they also had a stink bomb to deal with. Their instinctive reaction was not to open the window; they headed for the door. And couldn't get out. By the time they did Roden was sitting in the library, studying assiduously.

'We knew who thought it up,' said one of the teachers, Vic Hyde, to Roden years afterwards, 'but not only couldn't we prove it, we also considered it a rather admirable piece of strategy and generalship.'

To represent one's school in a sport on a champion level did not automatically earn one what was called a 'Blue'—a Blue was awarded only to the most outstanding. Roden gained Sydney High Blues in swimming, water polo and—perhaps inevitably—in rifle shooting. Though later events were to make it impossible for Roden to pursue this sport for the many years his father did, he had certainly inherited Arthur's skill.

It was generally expected that Roden would gain an 'honours' pass in English when he sat for his Leaving Certificate a year later than most, but he didn't. Those students aiming for a distinction level had to sit for two separate examinations in the same subject; the 'pass' paper was compulsory and graded as A or B, whereas the 'honours' paper was elective and graded as first or second class honours—or none. In subjects like English, a great deal depended upon the idiosyncrasies of the unknown person who graded an individual's paper. Since his English master had expected Roden to gain his honours pass, one can only conclude that Roden was unlucky; there is an element of luck in all external examinations. However, he did secure a second class honours in History, As in Maths I and English, and Bs in Maths II, Latin and Chemistry. This standard of pass was more than sufficient to matriculate—that is, qualify for entrance to university.

•

However, the first necessity was a job, in a time and place when and wherein jobs were almost impossible to get. The aim of most of the Sydney High boys in Roden's economic situation was to find employment in the New South Wales public service, which from Jack Lang's time had a policy of taking one hundred young men per year. But one's Leaving Certificate results were not admissible; one had to sit for a special examination set by the Public Service Board. Along with most of his classmates, Roden sat it at the end of 1934, the year he did his Leaving Certificate.

He wanted desperately to go to university, but in order to afford to go he needed a job; his tertiary education would have to be undertaken at night. The public service appointments were painfully slow, strung out over the entire year, and Roden's placement in that examination was not high enough—though he did qualify—to get a quick public service guernsey.

As a little boy he wanted to be a bus driver, but by the time he left school his ambition was to become a barrister in commercial law. This meant taking a double degree: Economics first, then Law. At least eight years of tertiary schooling, during which he would have to work to support himself.

No, he was not dux of his class, but he was highly placed, and voted a prefect by his schoolmates. Roden Cutler had qualities his masters understood and very much admired: he was a trier, a leader, a bit of an idol to the younger boys in the very best way. An influence for the good. He *must* fulfil his potential!

So it was that on the very last day of school, a Friday early in December 1934, the headmaster, Frank McMullen, appeared as Roden was cleaning out his locker.

'Cutler, do you want a job?' Frank McMullen asked.

'Yes, sir!'

'I've just had a telephone call from the Texas Company. They're looking for a bright young lad to work in their offices.'

The next morning, Saturday, Roden went for an interview, and started work on Monday morning at eight o'clock for the princely sum of one pound per week. The imposingly tall young man's title was 'office boy'.

The Texas Company Australasia (later known as Texaco) was located in one of Sydney's highest buildings—it rose a whole twelve storeys—on the corner of George and Margaret Streets, which wasn't very far from Circular Quay, where the ferries docked. The chief executives were all American, but there were a few Australians in middle management. Among them was a man named John Leplastrier, who soon noticed the cheerful and willing efficiency of the new office boy. One day in January 1935 Leplastrier summoned Roden.

'Cutler, are you interested in going to university?'

'Yes, sir,' said Roden.

'Good, because I think you must go. What would you like to do, Cutler?'

'Economics first, sir, then Law.'

An answer which pleased John Leplastrier, who was an Economics graduate himself.

'By the way, it turns out that you're being underpaid. The award says you should be getting twenty-four-and-a-penny.'

Good news! As twenty shillings made up the pound, the extra four shillings and one penny represented an increase of twenty per cent in Roden's pay packet. It made university feasible.

Roden enrolled in the Faculty of Economics as a night student, to commence at the beginning of March. He would be able to afford the minimal fees, buy his textbooks—second-hand, of course—pay his fares, and give Ruby generous board.

At this time the whole of New South Wales and the Australian

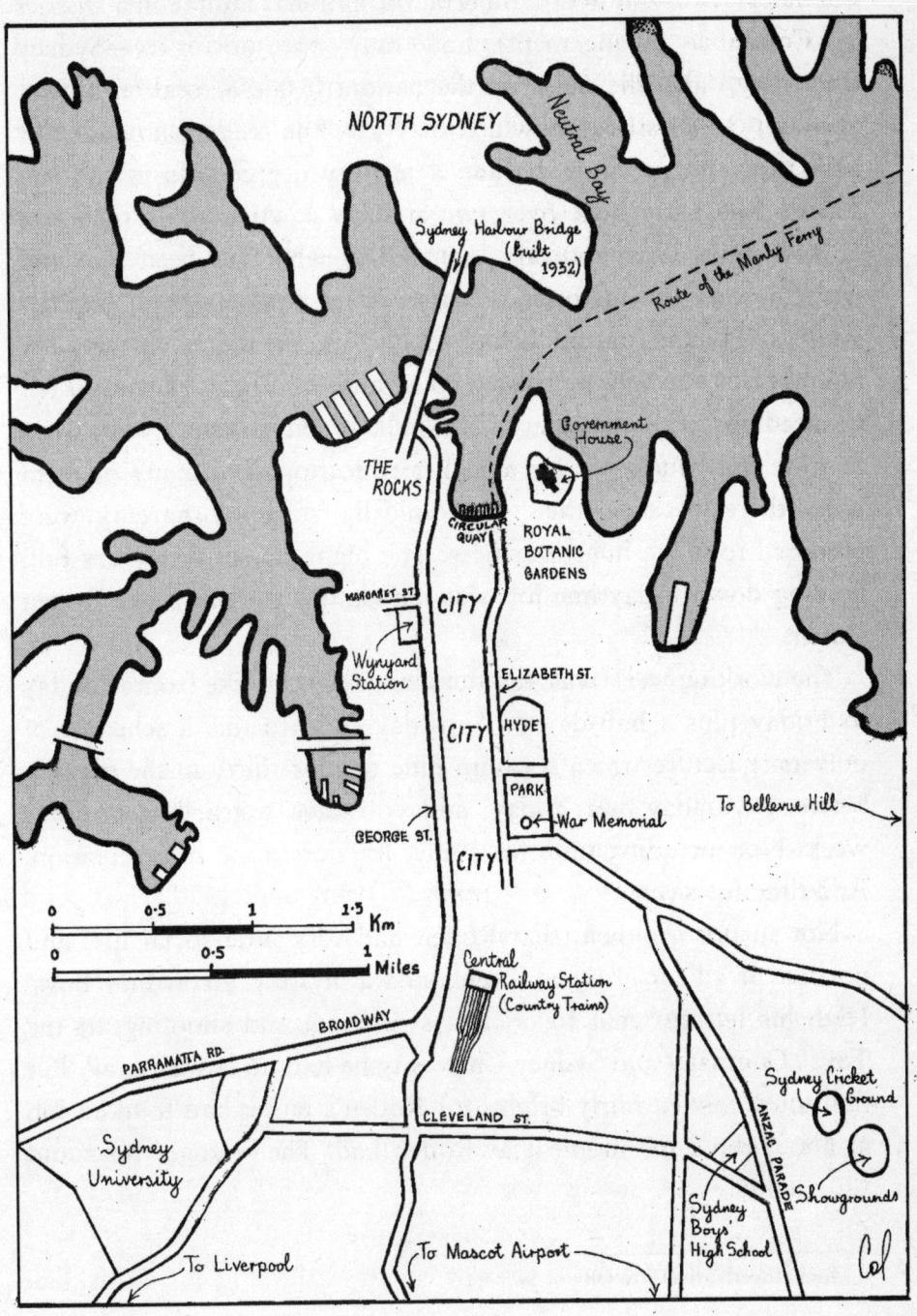

Capital Territory (it held Canberra, the national capital, in a District of Columbia arrangement) had only one university—Sydney University,[†] also the oldest in the nation. It had a total enrolment of about 3,600 students, which may give the reader some idea of how rare and precious a thing a tertiary degree was in the late 1930s. The State held over two million of Australia's then five million souls. Nor, contrary to much of what has been said and written, were the majority of these 3,600 students from wealthy families. Human nature being what it is, the scions of wealthy families not strongly motivated to acquire a tertiary education felt no need to go to university. The bulk of the students were there because they hungered for a higher education, and many of them were there because their economically strapped parents were prepared to make huge sacrifices. The night classes were very full; holding down a daytime job was mandatory for those like Roden Cutler.

The working week was 48 hours long: eight to five from Monday to Friday plus a half-day on Saturday. Add to this a schedule of university lectures from six until nine or nine-thirty in the evening between Monday and Friday, and you have a gruelling 65-hour week. Not including time for study, let alone time for recreation. And time for sleep.

Not surprising, then, that Roden had very little social life, and no time at all for girls, who remained a mystery. At Sydney Boys' High his leisure went to cricket, swimming and shooting; at the Texas Company and Sydney University he had no leisure at all. But the future looked fairly bright, for Roden's father had found a job at about the same moment as Roden had. The younger boys and

---

[†] More properly, the University of Sydney.

Doone would be able to follow in Roden's footsteps. *Surely* the Great Depression wouldn't last much longer!

Arthur went to work for Paul & Gray, a large firm of ships' chandlers, hardware and small arms merchants, as their travelling sales representative. His employment was on a commission basis, but he had the advantage of being very well known in almost every medium sized town from one end of Australia to the other, and the economy was beginning to make a very slow recovery.

At first he used the steamtrains or steamships, as he had in earlier times, but occasionally he'd climb into the rackety old Studebaker and set off in that, though he was never quite at ease when driving a car; Arthur was a horse and sulky man at heart. Paul & Gray were pleased with him, his sales and commission mounted steadily.

Roden too was prospering. From office boy he was promoted to petty cash clerk, armed with a lockable tin box in which reposed five pounds in assorted notes and coins. Imperial currency had twenty shillings to the pound and twelve pence to the shilling, but its nicknames were more usual than its formal names. The ten pound note was a 'brick' from its terracotta colouring; the five pound was a 'spin'; the pound was a 'quid'; the silver shilling was a 'bob' or a 'deener'; the silver sixpence was a 'zack'; the silver threepence was a 'trey bit'; and the penny was a 'brownie'. Out of his tin box Roden would disburse the minor sums which, on presentation of a docket, paid for office supplies of pencils, ink, paperclips and the like. He also had other clerical duties—and a raise in pay to thirty shillings a week.

At the beginning of March 1935 he started Economics at Sydney University as a night student. There was no difference between the day and the night course; both had to be completed in four years, both involved exactly the same number of lectures and assignments per week, and both kinds of student sat for the same examinations at the same time. Only his school uniform had allowed him to travel the trams and ferries on a child's fare, as he had virtually reached his final height while still at school. Now, however, he had to find the adult fare, which was threepence. It sounds such a tiny amount, but it bought a bit more than a loaf of bread. So Roden walked the two miles (about three kilometres) from the Texas Company to the university, then paid threepence to catch a tram back to the Quay after lectures were finished for the night.

In May 1935 Paul & Gray were so delighted with Arthur's sales figures that they gave him the use of a company car. It was a gleaming new Chevrolet coupé. Arthur collected it on the 20th of that month to drive to Newcastle, where he was due in the early afternoon. But the car wouldn't start, so he had to waste some hours in Sydney having it fixed.

He didn't get on the road until into the afternoon, a little upset at the fact that he would be very late into Newcastle, a hundred miles north. However, he couldn't push the car, which was brand new and had to be run in gently. At Gosford he stopped for a quick meal, then set off again at the regulation speed of thirty-five miles an hour. Driving the Chevrolet was more awkward than he had expected, for in 1935 cars were not standardised. This new vehicle's brake and accelerator pedals were the reverse of those in his old Studebaker.

Rounding a sharp bend not far from his meal stop he put his foot on the accelerator thinking it was the brake. The car left the road and careered wildly into a field, then came to rest in the midst of a clump of blackberries. But behind the thorny thicket was the only dangerous obstacle in the field, a huge and jagged tree stump. The accident had been witnessed; Arthur was rushed to a nearby private hospital, but died of his terrible injuries before he could be sent by ambulance to Sydney.

Roden had spent an ordinary kind of day at the Texas Company, where he had now been working for six months. He went to his evening lectures as usual, and returned to 'Kyeema' about half-past ten that night.

Uncle Roy was now in residence. Like many among Ruby's family—he was one of her brothers—he had turned to Ruby for shelter when he had no job and nowhere to go. Roden's dinner was sitting on its saucepan of simmering water on top of the stove, but Ruby wasn't present to give it to him. In itself that didn't perturb him. While he ate Uncle Roy sat with him, oddly silent.

Suddenly Roden heard someone weeping. He got up from the table and went into his mother's bedroom, where he found her lying on the big double bed in spasms of dreadful tears.

'What's wrong, Mum?'

The answer came amid those wracking sobs: 'My son hasn't got a father! The police have been and told me that your father was killed in a car accident and it wasn't his fault but that's what happened. He's dead!'

What could he say? What could he do? Reeling with shock, he got the full story from Uncle Roy, who had been under strict instructions that he was to say nothing about Arthur's death until Roden had eaten his dinner.

There was a simple funeral to arrange, and the Texas Company to obey; one didn't get sympathy leave in 1935, one got the day off (without pay) to attend the funeral.

Roden's job was now of paramount importance, for Arthur had left no savings. A tiny payment under workers' compensation law was the only other income the family now had. Oh, for the days when, in such a situation, all the young males could leave school and go to work! Not possible in jobless 1935.

The tragedy felled Ruby. She couldn't walk, couldn't move, couldn't look after herself. Everything had to be done for her. The children and Uncle Roy and kind neighbours clubbed together and did what they had to; she lay, unseeing, with her world in ruins. Things had been so hard for so long, and now this.

Roden ached for her and wept for her, but the Texas Company had to be obeyed and the burden of caring for the mother became something the family couldn't handle. So Aunt Dais came to the rescue. She was teaching school in Albury, where her sister (Aunt Victoria), married to the Albury inspector of police, also lived. Send Ruby to Albury, said Aunt Dais. Roden and Uncle Roy got her to Central railway station, where Roden had to carry her on board the train; her condition had made it necessary to buy her a sleeper ticket—prohibitively expensive—on this night express to Melbourne. Albury was four hundred miles south-west, a twelve-hour journey.

They had Ruby settled in the sleeper bunk when she suddenly seemed to understand what was happening. With a huge effort she lifted herself into a half-sitting position to kiss Roden and wish him well. It was the start of her recovery process.

While Ruby slowly improved in Albury, Roden looked after Geoff, Rob, Bob Milligan and Uncle Roy. Now almost twelve years old, Doone was sent to Albury in the wake of her mother, and was to stay there until after she sat for her Intermediate Certificate at fifteen. Poor Uncle Roy wasn't very domestically inclined, so it was Roden who kept house. When university began again he had to resume attending lectures, but part of his mind was always fretting over his family's plight. The high-spirited boy so fond of unmalicious pranks had gone ghosting away in the moment after he asked his mourning mother, 'What's wrong, Mum?' It had happened three days before his nineteenth birthday, five weeks before his father would have turned sixty.

Ruby came back, probably before she should have.

A new regimen began. The most important aspect of it was to save every penny possible; the tiny amount paid as workers' compensation couldn't begin to cover expenses. It was now Roden's job to head the family, do all the things Arthur used to do, from seeing to payment of land and water rates to dealing with income tax—not that there was much if any tax to pay, but on the surface of it Roden was a single man without dependants.

Ruby was up before the late winter dawn of a morning to see to breakfasts and get the children ready for school, after which came the housework. Roden left to catch the ferry armed with a double lunch, sandwiches and a thermos of cocoa to be divided between lunch and a pre-university snack. He walked from the ferry to the Texas Company, then at five-thirty he walked the two miles up George Street, Broadway and Parramatta Road to his night classes. He paid threepence to catch a tram back to the Quay after lectures were over, transferred to the ferry, and was home somewhere between ten and ten-thirty. His dinner was always sitting, covered with a plate, atop a saucepan of simmering water on the gas stove, and Ruby would be there to greet him.

'Everything all right, Laddie?' she would ask.

'Yes,' he would smile.

Then he sat down to eat while his mother sat opposite. They talked, though not over a 'cuppa' tea. Ruby loathed tea, refused to drink what was the usual liquid staple in an Australian home; this dated back to her childhood, when in some country town or other the Popes had lived near a Chinese laundry which stank of what Ruby thought was tea, but was more likely the boiling brew of dirty washing. Be that as it may, Ruby could never be persuaded to drink tea.

By eleven o'clock both of them were asleep.

Life at the Texas Company was not idyllic. The parent company sent one of its high executives to Australia to smarten the local operation up, and chose—of course—an axeman for the task. After several weeks of watching batches of six to ten employees walk into the Great Man's office and shuffle out jobless, the Texas Company got a new name among those remaining: Seek 'em, Suck 'em & Sack 'em. The sacking process was pure expediency—considerations like a man's having a young family to support did not enter into it. This activity disgusted Roden, who suffered at the manifest injustice of the statistical approach.

Roden's own experience with the Great Man concerned the petty cash. His tin box was seized and upended onto a desk, spilling its contents everywhere. Roden's books balanced, but a count of the money when compared to the dockets revealed that the petty cash box was threepence short. The Great Man began to roar, Roden saw his job disappearing. But even in this ghastly predicament he kept his head; it suddenly occurred to him that perhaps the tiny errant coin had fallen to the floor when the box was emptied. He bent, looked about, and found it. His job was safe, but he was growing a certain dislike of and contempt for American ways of business which was never to leave him, despite later and much happier experiences with things American. It had been the American Remington Arms Company which had dismissed his father without notice or compensation, and the American Texas Company which so detachedly stripped people of their employment when the Australian economy was just beginning to show signs of recovery. Roden's ethics and principles are unbending.

When he and two other young men were called in to see the Great Man, Roden went with a hardened attitude; he knew he needed this job desperately and he knew dismissal would brand him, but a touch of iron was entering his soul, and that iron would not let him diminish his pride by fawning or begging. The three stood there while the Great Man informed them that they had been chosen 'to learn the oil industry from the bottom up'—a euphemistic way, Roden thought, of getting field supervisors for much less than the Texas Company would have to pay older, more senior men.

It was Roden the Great Man asked for an answer first.

'I'm sorry, sir, I can't accept.'

'Why?' asked the Great Man, taken aback.

'I'm doing Economics at night at Sydney University, sir, and I wouldn't be able to get to my lectures on time from depots or the refinery.'

'You can't do two jobs at once!'

'I have been, sir, for almost a year.'

'But you *can't* do two jobs at once!'

'Sir,' said Roden steadily, chin up, 'if you have complaints about the standard of my work, you can sack me.'

He and the Great Man stared at each other; then the Great Man's eyes fell.

The second young man was a great deal better off financially than Roden, and chose to resign.

The third young man accepted.

When Roden left the Great Man's office he was sure that the end of the week would see his pay made up with a dismissal slip, but to his amazement he found himself promoted to invoice clerk at a salary of two pounds ten—fifty shillings—a week!

At which point, October of 1935, Roden's number came up in the New South Wales public service. The wait had been so long that he had almost forgotten, but now he learned that he could have his choice between two positions, one in the Trustee section of the Justice Department, or one at the Registrar-General's Department in births, deaths and marriages. Roden chose Justice.

To enter the public service meant a significant drop in salary: he would be paid thirty-five shillings per week instead of the fifty shillings he was now earning at the Texas Company. But public servants worked a 40-hour week, which meant a nine o'clock start in the mornings and no Saturdays. By this time he had better assessed the amount of studying he would have to do to pass Economics at a credible level, and understood that a 48-hour week made that almost impossible.

He and Ruby talked it over. Every spare penny he earned he gave to her, nor did he dream of asking her how she spent it. Not a ha'penny was wasted, and he had good reason to suspect that she herself went without regularly. Even so, she was adamant: he must transfer to the public service. It meant security of tenure and enough time to do Economics. Besides, who knew if the next Great Man the Texas Company sent out from America would prove more—or less—tractable than the present one? Better by far to be safe than sorry. The Cutler family would manage.

In the examinations at the end of 1935, his first year of Economics, he did well, but the fifteen shillings a week less at the public service was a handicap. Then a friend in the Trustee section at Justice suggested a partial solution: join the Sydney University Regiment, as he had!

So in March 1936 Roden joined the Sydney University Regiment. It belonged to the infantry reserve of the citizens' militia and was therefore not a part of the professional army, though in a state of emergency its soldiers were liable to be put to defence work on the home front. At the time it comprised about 300 men (no women!);

it did not assemble on a regular basis, nor while university was up. Instead, it held two camps of ten working days each within any one year, and public service rules said that he had to be paid his normal public service salary while in camp. As he was also entitled to three weeks' annual leave, belonging to the Sydney University Regiment meant he could have a proper holiday twice a year (for so he regarded the two camps) and use his public service leave to study for the three weeks prior to his annual examinations.

'I joined for entirely selfish reasons,' says Roden.

So he never was a natural military man. His ambitions lay in law and commerce, his academic qualifications were aimed at that, and life in an army camp was a holiday.

Though he had not had time to shoot for the university, Roden did shoot for the regiment. The unsuspecting instructor detailed to teach him how to use a rifle did so with praiseworthy kindness, but also, not unnaturally, with something of the air of an expert. Whereupon Roden threw himself down on the mound and bullseyed the target with every shot. Though his tally wasn't perfect; a stray shot from his neighbour landed in an outer ring of his target—a 'magpie'—and had to be counted as his bullet. Even including this stray shot, he was the regimental marksman. The instructor swallowed painfully and said no more.

The kind of life the regiment led in camp appealed to Roden immensely. Plenty of exercise, plenty of shooting, and the chance to ride a horse, keep it and his equipment spiffy. This he did well enough to carry off the equitation prize regularly. However, custom dictated that a man should not accept more than one prize. Roden always preferred to take the shooting prize (worth a pound) over the equitation prize (worth a mere seven shillings and sixpence). Those shooting prizes came in very handy financially, and once he presented Ruby with a crisp five-pound note—three weeks' wages.

He went in as a private and was content to be Driver Cutler in Transport, riding his horse postilion with a limber (a small, two-wheeled vehicle rather like a cupboard or chest, used to carry equipment and supplies) behind, and look after mount, tack and gear. Trucks were a luxury not accorded to a university regiment. Between the old iron huts and the ice-coated water, the winter camp at Liverpool was less comfortable than the summer one at Douglas Park or Menangle Park.

Though from 1936 onwards Roden's public service job let him earn a Blue in swimming and he played an occasional game of Rugby Union, it was the regiment which gave him his best opportunity to rub shoulders with students from other faculties. There were budding doctors, engineers, architects, classical scholars, veterinarians, physicists, economists and lawyers, all doing the same kind of thing in an environment having nothing to do with normal university life.

1936 was also the year when gathering war clouds in Europe began to rival the ravages of the Great Depression or political doings in the newspapers. The black American Jesse Owens offended Adolf Hitler at the Berlin Olympic Games by beating the Aryans even as Hitler's Germany rearmed and began to reach for territories it considered pilfered from it in the aftermath of the Great War. The Rhineland, Silesia ... Now leader of the New South Wales Labor Party in opposition, Jack Lang was advocating that Australia should withdraw from the League of Nations and never repeat its mistake of following its mother country, Britain, into war.

When Germany reunited with Austria (the Anschluss) in 1938, Roden was in his final year of Economics and doing very well in his slot at the Justice Department's Trustee division. He turned twenty-two and looked forward to graduating in the top percentile of his class. Somewhere along the way he had even managed to gain one Law credit by doing Roman Law; the examination required that half the paper be written in Latin. Roden passed. He also topped the university with a high distinction in Commercial and Industrial Law.

However, he could see that doing Law was going to be a big problem. Though a student could attend university full-time to do Law, most men in those days attained their law degrees through 'articles'; they were apprenticed as legal clerks in a law firm and attended university lectures as part of their (lowly paid) positions. So one could not do Law at night. Lectures were from eight to ten in the morning or from four to six in the evening, which meant they could not be divorced from the 40-hour working week.

He could do Law and continue to work in the public service, but that rigidly institutionalised body of bureaucrats insisted that any public service employee doing Law enter into a bond—to the tune of ten thousand pounds. It required that once the Law degree was attained, the employee must remain in the public service for ten years doing whatever kind of law his masters decided. To resign meant disgorging ten thousand pounds—an absolute fortune. Yes, he could seek a job as an articled legal clerk, but it had no guarantee of continued employment, and he *had* to keep a job. Ten thousand pounds were twenty years' salary. An outrage!

It should not be difficult to understand that in all this lay little time for balls, dances, parties and the other trappings of an existence in reasonably close proximity to girls, though he was tall, dark and handsome enough to attract plenty of feminine attention. But like many other young men of the period, Roden worked and sported himself to the point of daily exhaustion. He had no girlfriend. The only woman on his mind was his mother, who relied on him with ever-increasing trust.

Geoff went up to university to do Economics as well, and Rob entered his last year of high school. Doone, never scholastically inclined, did her Intermediate Certificate in Albury and then trained in secretarial work; nor was she ever in the pink of health. The old injury sapped her.

As he was not due to have his degree conferred on him until late May of 1939, Roden continued in the Sydney University Regiment.

War rumbles were continuous, and Jack Lang became such a small voice crying in the wilderness that he lost his position as leader of the New South Wales Labor Party. Robert Gordon Menzies (called 'Ming the Merciless' after the villain in the popular Flash Gordon movie serials, because he preferred to pronounce his name the Scottish way, Mingies) became conservative Prime Minister of the nation, and no more ardent supporter of Great Britain existed than Menzies. Everyone knew that if Great Britain went in, so too would Australia.

Suddenly the regiment, always infantry, acquired an artillery battery of one 18-pounder field gun. After three contented years as Driver Cutler in Transport, Roden took the army examinations, topped them, and became sergeant of the gun detachment. The solitary 18-pounder was an old Great War gun which the regiment fired only once. At first it was towed by six horses, but then the regiment obtained a farm tractor, and it was behind the farm tractor that the detachment hauled their gun to the Liverpool shooting range on that one glorious occasion when they were allowed to spend five pounds per projectile. The bill for the day was twenty-five pounds.

●

Ruby was present, of course, when Roden had his degree of Bachelor of Economics conferred upon him; no prouder mother sat watching. The long slog wasn't over, but the initial phase of it was, and Roden's salary had gone up.

Graduation was almost the last civilian thing he was to do, though he was still officially in the public service and therefore not eligible to enter the professional army; simply, citizens' militia units like the Sydney University Regiment kept being summoned for more and more exercises. The Government had the right to call on any citizens' militia or Army/Navy/Air Force reserve unit if it perceived a necessity to do so. Formal war was still in the future, but it was considered expedient to start putting those already in quasi-military activities into full martial mode. The public service, however, continued officially to employ Roden.

In August 1939 he received a phone call at the Trustee's office about eleven in the morning.

'Report for full-time duty, full marching kit, two o'clock at the university, Cutler. Don't know where you're going or how long it will be for.'

He raced home, changed clothes, collected his kit, explained to Ruby and reported at the university. A sergeant, he was put in charge of a guard of fifteen men and was directed to Moorebank ordnance depot, where they were to draw camping and kitchen gear and five rounds of live ammunition per man.

From there his detachment went to guard the Vacuum Oil Company on Duck Creek at Auburn (not very far from what is now the Year 2000 Olympic complex), as any oil facility was of vital strategic importance. Good practice.

The unit was instructed to look after itself and was given three shillings per day per man with which to buy everything from food to toilet paper. Unfortunately the management at Vacuum Oil did not appreciate the company's strategic importance and did not want a guard of fifteen young university graduates and undergraduates at the entrance gate, busy whitewashing stones to mark a boundary. So Vacuum Oil flatly refused to let them on the company premises. Nothing daunted, they set up camp just outside; Roden's second-in-command, a lance-bombardier, proved the best cook among them, so he found himself appointed cook and they lived very well on their three bob a day. When the *Sydney Morning Herald* asked if it could do a story and take some pictures of one of the Sydney University Regiment's guard detachments, Sergeant Cutler's operation outside Vacuum Oil was nominated. The resulting feature in the newspaper impressed Vacuum Oil sufficiently to relent and let the guard inside, even give them an office not much bigger than the latrine they dug.

It was while he was inside that guard room on 3 September that Roden heard Prime Minister Menzies announce that Australia was following Great Britain into war against Germany.

'Are you going to join up?' a tight-lipped Ruby asked Roden on his next leave.

'Yes, Mum.'

She nodded, didn't argue.

Times have changed; people at the turn of the millennium have a different attitude to war than people did in 1939, probably due in some measure to Vietnam—and to far franker media coverage of war's more gruesome side. Ruby didn't object because she, like Roden, considered that it was his patriotic duty to go to war.

In December 1939 the regiment was notified that it would serve for at least three months. Several members, including Roden, had clubbed together and bought an old Dodge tourer car for twenty-

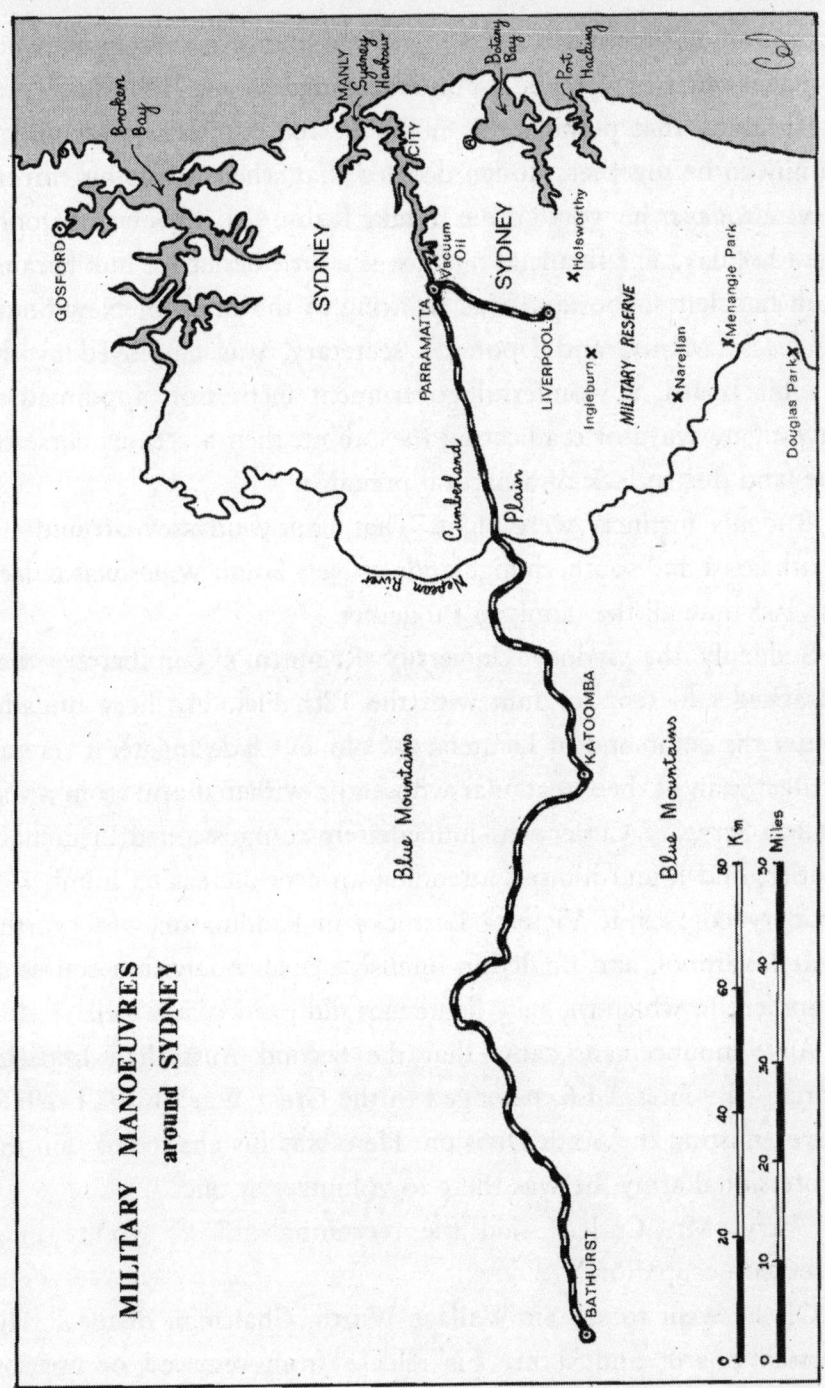

MILITARY MANOEUVRES around SYDNEY

four pounds. They named it *Diogenes*, though Roden forgets which Diogenes or why. Maybe a pun on 'Dodge'?

Thinking that perhaps this might be the last chance for all the family to be together, Roden decided that when it was his turn to have *Diogenes* he would use it to take Ruby, Geoff, Rob and Doone on a holiday. The financial pinch was a little easier for him because Rob had left school and was working in the Bank of New South Wales at Manly, and Doone, a secretary, was employed by the Rabbit Board, a wonderful government institution appointed to investigate ways of eradicating the rabbit, then a serious curse on the land due to lack of a natural predator.

Roden's instincts were right. That happy odyssey around the south coast and southern highlands of New South Wales was indeed the last time all the family got together.

Suddenly the Sydney University Regiment's gun battery was detached and sent to train with the 18th Field Artillery Brigade, under the command of Lieutenant-Colonel Clyde Ingate, a veteran artilleryman of the Great War who had a withered arm from a war injury. Sergeant Cutler was immediately commissioned Lieutenant Cutler, and found himself attending an ever-increasing number of artillery courses at Victoria Barracks in Paddington, Holsworthy near Liverpool, and finally an intensive Eastern Division course at Narellan, in which the new lieutenant did particularly well.

An announcement came that the Second Australian Imperial Forces (the First A.I.F. belonged to the Great War of 1914–1918) were enlisting the Sixth Division. Here was his chance to join the professional army; he was there to volunteer at once.

'Sorry, Mr. Cutler,' said the recruiting officer, 'you're in a reserved occupation.'

Off he went to see Sir Wallace Wurth, Chairman of the Public Service Board, and secure his release from reserved occupation status. Then, after the inevitable interminable wait while the bureaucratic wheels went round and round, it was back to the recruiting office, now enlisting the Seventh Division.

'Sorry, Mr. Cutler, can't give you a commission, but you can go in as a sergeant.'

This demotion was economically important; as a lieutenant, Roden's pay would be sufficient to ensure that Ruby could continue to live fairly comfortably even if Geoff and Rob joined up, though Roden hoped Geoff at least would stay at home to look after Ruby and Doone in a physical rather than a financial sense; he seems never to have wanted to burden his brothers with the money side.

Oh, well. He could certainly get into the Air Force as a sergeant, and he felt an attraction for the Air Force. 'Thanks,' he said to the recruiting officer, 'but if I have to start all over again, I'd rather do it in the Air Force.'

Once in possession of the application form to join the Royal Australian Air Force, Roden discovered that he needed a reference from the C.O. of the 18th Field Artillery Brigade, Clyde Ingate, before he could lodge the form.

Ingate frowned. 'Cutler, why on earth are you going into the Air Force?' he asked.

'I can't get into the Seventh Division as a commissioned officer, sir.'

'Tell you what,' said Ingate, handing back the R.A.A.F. application form, 'why don't you sit on this for a couple of weeks while I see if I can get you into the Seventh?'

Not long afterwards Roden got a telephone call from Ingate asking him to lunch at the Imperial Servicemen's Club.

'You've got the guernsey,' said Ingate when they met.

'But I have to go before the appointment committees!'

'Don't worry, you've passed all that. You'll be joining me in the

Royal Australian Artillery. Second Fifth Field Regiment. Next time you're up at university, how about sounding out any of the chaps you think would make good artillerymen?'

This was Clyde Ingate's way of collecting men. In the 2/5th Field Regiment there were at least twenty university graduates, a goodly number of undergraduates, some top up-and-coming young men from the business world, some doughty Sydney workingmen, and some countrymen who could shoot and live rough.

Roden did his bit the next time he was up at university; he secured a friend in Economics, Jack Robinson, and Dr. Adrian Johnson, his best friend, came into the 2/5th as its medico. Then when crippled Aunt Moon from Tasmania begged him to help his cousin Bob Milligan achieve his burning desire to enlist, Roden got Bob into the 2/5th Field Regiment as well.

Because Clyde Ingate preferred whenever possible to recruit men who already knew each other, right from the outset the 2/5th owned a peculiar and almost familial sense of identity that soon embraced all its members, bonded them as one rather than as cliques; many of the university graduates never became commissioned officers, whereas some of the workingmen did. For the time, it was quite amazingly classless.

And time was to prove that the 2/5th was a superlative field artillery regiment. Morale was always high and splendid teamwork its hallmark. Both stemmed originally from Clyde Ingate, the 2/5th's first commanding officer.

'Clyde was a wonderful psychologist,' says Roden. 'He knew how to pick men and how to mould them.'

Thus it was with some relief that Roden transferred from citizens' militia to the A.I.F. in April 1940, while the Phoney War in Europe was still dreaming on. Decisions about Law and his future were in temporary abeyance; there were more important things to do.

He was not yet twenty-four years old, though he had long been 'a man' in the sense that phrase was used in 1940. The boundary between love and duty is blurred, but when duty overrides all other considerations including self, one has become 'a man'.

WAR

At the beginning of May 1940 Roden was among the first members of the 2/5th to go into camp at Ingleburn, a part of the huge military reserve around Liverpool and Camden. Though even today there is still a big military reserve in the area, in 1940 the city of Sydney hadn't spread its tentacles further than Liverpool, the terminus of the suburban electric railway in the south-west. Beyond Liverpool all was farmland, eucalyptus forest and military reserve.

Everything was a bit of a disaster. Few of the new soldiers had been issued with uniforms, though most had bayoneted rifles, bolt-action .303 Lee-Enfields. Training hadn't begun; no one knew how to march, let alone organise himself in military mode. Mounting a guard was ludicrous. Having exhausted the number of men in uniform before he filled his ranks on his first duty as officer of the guard, Roden asked for men in civvies who could shoot. Several put up their hands, but admitted they didn't know how to drill with a rifle.

'We're rabbit-ohs, sir, haven't been taught to drill.' A rabbit-oh was a man who shot rabbits and sold them as food or fur.

'You'll do,' said Roden.

The 2/5th Field Regiment had a few Marman-Herrington trucks to haul its artillery, a step up from the university regiment's farm

61

tractor, but anything which tows a gun and limber is always called a 'tractor' in artilleryman's language. These vehicles, English-made by Ford, were two-wheel-drive with a shift which converted them to four-wheel-drive in rough terrain. Powered by a Ford V-8 gasoline engine, the Marman-Herrington towed the gun and limber (this held the gun's ammunition) and accommodated the gun detachment, their kit, gun stores (cleaning and repairing tools) and items like tents and camouflage nets.

Unfortunately the guns themselves were still the old 18-pounders. The 2/5th had been promised new 25-pounders,[†] the field gun of choice among all British forces during the Second World War. Most of the exercises, however tactical they might purport to be, were called 'TEWTs'—'Tactical Exercises Without Troops'—because employing soldiers meant shipping them by train. Far easier to manoeuvre without them, really. The other name for a TEWT was 'playing silly-buggers', but somehow all of it started to make sense and the men began to feel at home both in the Army and with each other. For the majority of them this communal life was a bit of a jolt; a well-off young businessman would, more often than not, find himself tentmates with a rabidly left-wing labourer. Most learned to put these civilian matters aside.

When the ranks were finally filled, regimental strength was a variable number around 630 to 640, with a tiny detachment of men of the L.A.D., the Light Aid Detachment, whose job was to keep all machinery in running condition, from tractors to motorcycles. The L.A.D. was a new phenomenon; until 1938 and the arrival of the first tractors, Australian artillery had been horse-drawn, and required the services of veterinarians rather than engineers, mechanics, fitters and turners.

[†] The bore of the gun was 3.45 inches (about 88 mm).

After three months at Ingleburn came camp at Bathurst—good news for Roden, who had plenty of relatives there. Officers of the 2/5th were now mounted upon Norton motorcycles.

'Terrible things,' says Roden.

Roden's Norton was an old and cantankerous one, but Clyde Ingate preferred to ride pillion with Roden than on a machine of his own or with anybody else.

On 1 September the move from Ingleburn to Bathurst began, but not by train; a motley collection of vehicles had been rustled up. Some of the trucks had to be rigged with life-lines to prevent runaways on the cruel haul up the escarpment of the Blue Mountains, while others, bulging with soldiers, had never been designed to transport human cargo. The drivers had no idea that a military convoy stuck together by proceeding at the pace of the slowest, with the result that the vehicles straggled over a long interval into the resort of Katoomba atop the climb.

Here some high official in the Department of the Army had decided that the 2/5th would parade before the brigadier in an effort to show the residents of Katoomba that Australia was serious about the war. The brigadier was a pompous sort of fellow who was not amused by the sight which greeted him as he stood stiffly to attention taking the salute on the steps of the Katoomba post office, which was halfway up a very steep hill—not an ideal locale for the 2/5th to strut its stuff.

These were the first troops en masse Katoomba had seen, so as they marched along various enthusiastic people kept gifting the soldiers with bottles of beer. A regimental ball held just before leaving Ingleburn only served to add to the chaos that the brigadier beheld from the post office steps. Most of the men were so happy or so hungover they forgot to salute; the brigadier was furious enough to want to insist that the whole parade be repeated, but

Clyde Ingate managed to smooth his ruffled feathers, and the journey to Bathurst continued.

In Bathurst things settled down and more equipment began to arrive, though Clyde Ingate still insisted that Roden transport him on trips when his destination might necessitate a social get-together. Ingate disliked the prospect of keeping an N.C.O. or gunner waiting for him to finish socialising, whereas Roden, an officer, could join him. And knew everyone in Bathurst.

The TEWT became a thing of the past. Marman-Herringtons were in more plentiful supply, other vehicles were arriving too, and the old hands from the Great War or the peacetime army were slowly getting used to the presence of the L.A.D. mechanics. People were becoming accustomed to each other, friendships forged.

Conscription had come in, but the 2/5th had no conscript soldiers; volunteers were not inclined to view conscripts with sympathy or approbation. The Menzies Government had instituted conscription.

On Sundays, Roden and his cousin Bob Milligan would climb through the fence and (with permission) walk up to 'Abbotsford', the Cutler homestead adjacent to the camp. There they would have a non-army-issue roast dinner; food in camp was 'not exactly gourmet'. The people of Bathurst were just as keen on the military as the people of Katoomba; there were always more invitations than men to fill them. Now that Clyde Ingate had a staff car, he would ask Roden to chauffeur him to social occasions.

By this time the war in Europe had entered its most serious phase. The Phoney War gave way to the real thing in May 1940 when von Manstein's panzer divisions punched through Belgium and reached the English Channel and Paris by early June. By July France had fallen and that part of France not physically occupied by the

Germans was governed from the town of Vichy (of mineral water fame) as a nominally sovereign state required not to hamper Hitler. Josef Stalin had made a pact with Hitler guaranteeing Germany's hold on western Poland in return for eastern Poland and a pledge that Germany would not invade the U.S.S.R.

But what really sent a thrill of fear through the nations of the vague institution Great Britain and Winston Churchill still called 'the Empire' was Italy's entry into the war on Germany's side in June 1940. The Empire nations east of the Suez Canal were suddenly faced with the potential removal of the fastest shipping route between Great Britain and their own shores; to send shipping around the southern tip of Africa added at least four weeks to a voyage. Italy straddled the Mediterranean and had a huge army in North Africa as well as another in Ethiopian East Africa. If those armies invaded Egypt and took that thready umbilical cord linking the Mediterranean with the Red Sea, things would look very grim for India (Pakistan and Bangladesh were administered as part of India at the time), Burma, Malaya, Indo-China, Hong Kong, Singapore, the Dutch East Indies, the islands of the Pacific, Australia and New Zealand. All of those places traded far more with Europe than with North America.

At about the same moment as Mussolini brought Italy into the war, Australian Prime Minister Menzies appointed the managing director of the Broken Hill Proprietary Company (B.H.P.), one Essington Lewis, as Director-General of Munitions Supplies, and the administrative head of this steel and mining giant buckled down to work immediately. (John Curtin was to keep him in the job when Labor came to power, and add aircraft supply to it.) Lewis had ordered gargantuan amounts of machine and manufacturing plant from Great Britain, and he needed them delivered yesterday. For everyone's sake, the Suez Canal had to be held.

It was decided that Australia would send its Sixth Division to Egypt, and follow that up with the Seventh Division as soon as possible. Growing alarm about Japan's intentions meant that the Eighth Division, still enlisting, would be sent to Malaya.

So when the 2/5th motor cavalcade headed for Bathurst, its human cargo knew more or less that they were going to the Middle East to help defend Egypt and Suez.

The Battle of Britain was raging in the air over the fields of Kent and Surrey, the bombing of London and the Midlands had begun, and in Canberra, Australia's national capital, a different kind of war was going on.

The earliest years of the Second World War were peculiarly difficult for Australia, which wanted to be in it yet didn't want to be in it. Political turmoil was a symptom of this dichotomy, rather than a cause of it. On 21 September 1940, a federal election was held. The results in the lower house (House of Representatives) showed very clearly how divided the nation was: Menzies' Government (a coalition between his own United Australia Party and Arthur Fadden's Country Party) gained 36 seats; John Curtin's Labor Party gained 36 seats; and the balance of power was held by two independents, A.W. Coles and Alex Wilson, who usually voted with Menzies.

The upper house (Senate) had been returned with a clear Menzies majority, which the press saw as an indication that public opinion still slightly favoured Menzies and Fadden. Labor leader John Curtin decided that now was not the time to make a bid for power, and turned down Menzies' first offer to participate in a 'national government' of all parties, saying that he much preferred to see Australia continue to have a Loyal Opposition. Curtin was also aware that he hadn't yet gained the upper hand in his struggle to reconcile the warring elements within Labor's ranks. In New South Wales (a state Curtin hated to visit) there were effectively three Labor Parties, nor did he have the unswerving allegiance of men like Dr. Herbert Vere ('Doc') Evatt, or the left-wing leader Eddie Ward, who wanted to conciliate the communists, or John Albert Beasley, who led a non-communist faction. Curtin did, however, propose an Advisory War Council, half-and-half with the Government. Menzies accepted; the gesture was better than nothing.

A lot of names, but the strange course of Roden Cutler's life makes a description of political doings at this time very necessary, for his fate was to become entwined with the outcome of what was going on in Canberra in 1940 and 1941.

The Communist Party was a force to be reckoned with in the labour movement of that era. Its members were highly influential in some of the more sensitive trade unions, especially in the coalmining and stevedoring industries. With a federal budget due to come down in November, anything was possible. John Curtin's best friend and most consistent adviser, Joseph Benedict (Ben) Chifley, had made himself an impressive authority on banking and finance, but like Curtin he did not think it politic to wrest government from Menzies. Whereas Doc Evatt, Eddie Ward and others wanted Labor in government at any price. Curtin and Chifley won the internecine Caucus battle and Menzies survived the budget debate. It was the second Australian budget to reach one hundred million pounds; the first was the budget of 1939.

Part of it was to be expended on the 2/5th's promised 25-pounder guns, but when after six weeks in residence at Bathurst the regiment packed up and left that October of 1940, the guns were nowhere to be seen. The old 18-pounders went with them for embarkation. They were on their way, they were going overseas.

Everyone was very brave, and Ruby bravest of all as she said goodbye to Roden consumed with private fears she had never experienced through the worst of his daredevil exploits as a boy. Where he was going, he would not always be in charge of his fate.

The *Queen Mary* was anchored in Neutral Bay; along with the rest of the 7,000 troops of part of the Seventh Division, the 638 members of the regiment boarded with the 13 mechanics of the Light Aid Detachment. The *Aquitania* took several thousand more soldiers, and together the two great ships moved slowly down the Harbour on a perfect, sunny, southern spring day.

The wrench of parting was over, the band had played the 'Maori Farewell' (to this day Roden hates that plaintive lament—it has memories too many and too bitter to bear), the streamers and bunting had trailed away, sad and sodden, into the depths, and ahead were 6,000 miles of rough and open ocean. In Port Phillip Bay they hove to and let the *Mauretania*, bearing more men of the Seventh, join them; from there on the three mighty liners were escorted by the Australian cruiser H.M.A.S. *Perth*.

They rolled and pitched the notorious waters of the Great Australian Bight, rounded the southernmost tip of Western Australia and lay off Fremantle while the three ships were provisioned once more. No shore leave, alas. After that it was the vast reaches of the Indian Ocean, past the Cocos Islands (still owned by the Clunies-Ross family), apparently headed for Ceylon. Then in that wonderful, idiotic way only bureaucrats, be they civil or military, can conceive, course was changed to a new and top-secret destination. Destination top-secret, when suddenly there were lectures on the role of the British Raj in India and lessons were offered in Hindustani? Oh, we're going to India! No, no, no! Antarctica, perhaps.

For some days there was little to be seen save porpoises, flying fish and an occasional whale. When the *Perth* handed convoy escort over to another cruiser, everyone girded himself for another rendition of the 'Maori Farewell', but as the trim naval vessel ceremonially sailed down the length of the three troop transports, its band played 'Roll Out the Barrel' instead. To see the *Perth* go hull down over the south-eastern horizon was to relinquish the last link with home.

For the enlisted men life on the fabulous *Queen Mary* was no fun. People got lost—sometimes on purpose—the mess queues stretched from one deck to another, far too many men were packed far too closely together to permit healthy exercise, and propinquity in the throes of seasickness was very hard to cope with. Ocean liners were not air-conditioned back then; the *Queen Mary* was suffocatingly hot, especially for the hapless souls crammed into airless cabins below the waterline.

For the officers life was more bearable, though not quite up to first-class passenger standards. They were more spaciously housed, and the meals in the officers' dining room contained six or seven courses of excellent food. But the best part about the voyage on the *Queen Mary* as far as the officers were concerned was the fact that they had feminine company. The ship was also carrying contingents of army nurses, who had officers' privileges. A bright, pretty lass named Mollie Nalder sat at Roden's table; the two of them became good friends later, under very different circumstances. But on board the ship there wasn't much chance for friendships to develop into romances, for the girls were chaperoned and guarded by some really fierce professional army nurse dragons.

In Bombay (yes, of course the destination was India!) the ships were too deep-draughted to berth; the *Queen Mary*, the *Aquitania* and the *Mauretania* stood in the roads about three miles out while the troops were unloaded into ferries and brought ashore. The smell of India was a foetid stench that stole into every passageway and cabin—where were those alluring odours of spices and exotic perfumes? Certainly not in Bombay, where the heat and the humidity competed to reach the century mark on the old Fahrenheit scale. To these Australians, culture shock took the form of smell shock.

The convoy had left Sydney on 20 October; landfall in Bombay occurred on 2 November. A very fast voyage of thirteen days, which most aboard deemed a mercy.

In Empire countries of the time there were always jokes going around about the British Raj, for BBC radio comedy shows were hugely popular everywhere, and there always seemed to be a fraightfulleh-fraightfulleh pukkah Indian Army colonel character who reminisced about a place called 'Poonah'. The Seventh Division was sent to Poona and laughed about the fact all the way there on the train, a bit of a rattletrap, but heaven after the confines of the *Queen Mary*. Most of the soldiers now had rupees, and threw the coins blithely to the beggars along the line without realising that a whole rupee to an Indian beggar in 1940 was an absolute fortune.

The delights of Poona didn't last long. Then it was back to Bombay, where the 2/5th (together with the 2/6th) was transferred to an old East India Company troopship, the *Lancashire*, which had been specifically built to transport Indian soldiers. This was coming down to earth with a rush; the *Lancashire* was an abominable experience for everyone, including the officers. The cockroaches, so the theory went, had been selectively bred for size and ferociousness, the food caused perpetual sickness, the medical facilities were minimal, and the *Queen Mary* suddenly seemed a cool and airy vessel even below the waterline. To make matters worse, the

Lancashire remained at anchor in the roads for what seemed an eternity. From now on no ship sailed unless part of a big and heavily escorted convoy, and the convoy took some days to assemble.

It had taken thirteen days to sail 6,000 miles of ocean, but the much shorter voyage from Bombay to Suez also took thirteen days.

When landfall came at the Red Sea end of the Suez Canal, Roden was instructed to leave the *Lancashire* and take charge of the 2/5th's equipment, which had to be offloaded in Suez to allow the ship free passage of the canal itself. Lieutenant White of the 2/6th Field Artillery Regiment was detailed to go along to help, and they thought it wonderful that they wouldn't have to suffer the *Lancashire* up the canal to El Kantara (spelling will conform to the English-language concept of the place names during the Second World War), where lay the Egyptian terminus of the railway to Palestine. Their pleasure lasted no longer than it took to set eyes on the squalor of their billet in Suez, and they both came down with extremely sore throats; Roden's sore throat, in fact, was to persist for so long that it was feared he had contracted diphtheria.

But after four days in Suez the equipment got under way to El Kantara, where the two men rejoined the regiment, which was heading for training camp in Palestine. The railway carriages were box cars of similar construction to the flat cars on which rode the equipment, but on this first of what were to be several journeys on the Palestine-Egypt railway the 2/5th was fascinated. Hardly any of them had ventured further from Australia than New Zealand, so the sight of donkeys, camels, tiny fields walled in stone, biblically clad peasants and mud-brick villages was novel enough to provoke endless comment; they had expected desert, not orange groves and agriculture. Though of dust there was plenty.

By the time the train passed through Gaza darkness had fallen;

nothing could be seen because the 'blackout' was complete. Dust-caked and weary, the 2/5th stumbled off the train a few miles beyond Gaza at a place called Deir Suneid (pronounced Deer Suneed), unable to see through the impenetrable, lightless night. But they had been 'fostered', as it was termed; a similar regiment already in residence had made camp for them, just as, in their turn later on, they too would 'foster' new arrivals.

It was the end of November 1940. The regiment had been on the sea or on the railway for six weeks.

Dawn was to reveal that theirs was simply one in literally twenty miles of army camps interspersed between tumbledown Arab villages and orange groves. The road which bisected the area went from Gaza to Jerusalem, but no biblical landscape lit up that vast, saucer-shaped depression; the makeshift, pitiless, cheerless military mockery of a city around Deir Suneid, Barbara, Khassa, Julis and Qastina was destined to be home in the Middle East. To quote from the history of the 2/5th, *Guns and Gunners*: 'It was from these places that the units set out to campaign, and it was to these places that they invariably returned.'

What the 2/5th did expect was to find themselves in the midst of an equipment paradise; that everything they desperately needed, from the promised 25-pounders to more Marman-Herringtons and other vehicles and gear, would be waiting for them at Deir Suneid. But nothing was waiting. In this lay the desert.

It took time for the regiment to understand how hopeless the equipment situation was everywhere. When the British Expeditionary Forces were evacuated from Dunkirk in June 1940, they left all their equipment behind to be gobbled up by the Germans. No field guns, no anti-aircraft guns, no tanks, no trucks, nothing much bigger than a rifle got back to England, and England could not replace the losses overnight. Australia had no plant to manufacture weapons or machines of war; even automobiles were imported. Yes, things were going onto a war footing, but factories are not thrown up in a day.

British jitters over the situation in the Mediterranean caused most of the equipment destined for Egypt and Palestine to be shipped down the length of the Atlantic shore of Africa, around the Cape of Good Hope, then up the Indian shore of Africa to Suez. All that saved the British Seventh Armoured Division's hide when the Italians did decide to invade Egypt was Churchill's decision to brave the Italian menace in the Mediterranean by sending a convoy holding three armoured regiments (as it turned out, safely) directly to Alexandria. The sheer size of Mussolini's armies in North Africa had intimidated the British high command, but, as General O'Connor was to prove, the British mouse walloped the Italian elephant at every engagement.

So, rather dismally, the 2/5th settled down in camp at Deir Suneid to drill, drill, and drill again. All it had were the old 18-pounders, and not enough of them to make up full batteries. What could be done to cheer the men up, Clyde Ingate did; leaves were plentiful for all ranks, which enabled sightseeing trips to Tel Aviv, Jerusalem, Galilee and, for a few, Cairo.

Roden went to Cairo with a regimental friend from university days, Jack Nagle, later a Supreme Court judge in New South Wales. He also went to Galilee, eager to tread the same earth Jesus Christ had; that is a sense of history. What he still remembers most vividly was the eerie sound of a cock crowing thrice, for it brought back Jesus' words to Peter in the garden at Gethsemane.

The regiment's religious experiences in camp were not so inspiring, for the padre of the moment was a doleful character who preached a burdensome sermon. After the first Sunday morning parade, none of the officers went to the next. Clyde Ingate was not amused.

'I have to go, and if I have to go, so bloody well will the rest of you!' he snapped.

Among the padre's gems was this statement: 'I take church parades on Sundays, and when you're dead I bury you.'

Not exactly what troops expecting to go into battle sooner or later wanted to hear. He was full of warnings about buying drinks from the locals, as he was convinced they were urine. But he did manage to obtain a piano for the regiment; in those days before music by professionals was so easily acquired, a great many men played a piano well enough to accompany sing-alongs.

The interminable drills were varied by courses on technical subjects for the officers, commissioned and non-commissioned. One N.C.O., sent to Cairo to attend a seminar on field security, reported back to Ingate that the course was so secret none of the participants ever discovered what it was about.

Two Great Men inspected the regiment. The first, just before Christmas, was General Thomas Blamey, who was to become John Curtin's friend, ally and military adviser after Labor went into government in Canberra. The second, early in January, was Percy Spender, Minister for the Army. Roden remembers Blamey's visit because one of the regimental drummers accidentally fell into a slit trench in mid-roll (the whole area was perilously mined with them), and the minister's visit because he thought Spender's stirring oration to the troops was quite inappropriate—more like Julius Caesar before a battle than the few words of thanks a modern commander gives *after* the battle.

Aside from a splendid Christmas dinner during which the officers waited on the men, the winter in Palestine was drearily monotonous.

The weather was bitterly cold and very rainy, and the slit trenches which proliferated everywhere began to resemble the fields of Flanders during the Great War. Gunnery practice in dry periods was blighted by the little whirlwinds Australians call willy-willies, as they accurately mimicked bursting shells amid the real bursting shells.

One disease no one suffered from was scurvy, for the orange crop this winter of 1940–1941 could not be exported to its usual European markets; it was bought instead by the army city, and many a unit, sick to death of drilling, went into the groves and helped the locals pick. Orange juice ran like water, and tasted a great deal better.

News from the war front was happy; the British were doing unexpectedly well against the Italians, who were driven steadily out of Cyrenaica.[†] After the capture of Bardia and the battle of Beda Fomm, the British Foreign Secretary, Anthony Eden, was able to paraphrase Winston Churchill's famous remark about the air Battle of Britain: 'Never has so much been surrendered by so many to so few.'

But the astonishing British success against the Italians was to have unforeseen consequences; Adolf Hitler, gearing his massive (and relatively idle) armies for the planned invasion of the U.S.S.R., summoned General Erwin Rommel to headquarters on 6 February and ordered him to bail the Italians out in North Africa. His force was to be minimal, but Hitler's choice of a commander was one of his better decisions. Rommel was to prove a formidable enemy, shrewd enough in his early days to compensate for his lack of armour by disguising Volkswagen cars as tanks to hoodwink the British observation officers.

---

† Modern eastern Libya.

That same February of 1941 also saw one of Churchill's biggest blunders; he was still obsessed, as he had been during the Great War (Gallipoli), with the concept of 'the soft under-belly of Europe'—the Balkan states. Now he visualised the area united against Germany by being stiffened with an influx of British troops and armour. Greece under General Metaxas had courteously refused, stating that a British presence in Greece would only provoke a German invasion. Then at the end of January General Metaxas died; his successor was more biddable. Churchill got the green light, and orders went out to his Commander-in-Chief, General Wavell, in Egypt that he was to cease pursuit of the Italians and hold back much of his strength for diversion to Greece.

The battle-hardened Australian Sixth Division was pulled out of North Africa to go to Greece and was replaced by the poorly equipped and only partially trained Australian Ninth Division. The Fourth Indian Division (a magnificent fighting force) was shipped to the Sudan to curtail a tentative strike by the Italians in Eritrea, and the badly depleted British Seventh Armoured Division was replaced by a part only of the inexperienced Second Armoured Division. Everyone with a combat record was taken out of North Africa.

The 2/5th Field Regiment (a part of the Australian Seventh Division) now expected that it would go to Greece, but under a new commander. On 19 February it said goodbye to Clyde Ingate, invalided back to Australia; his heart was playing up. Shortly afterwards the new commander arrived, Lieutenant-Colonel John O'Brien, who was at the time the youngest C.O. in the A.I.F. A good man, he stepped up training even as he tried to convince these weary, disillusioned men that the promised equipment *would* come.

But marching orders came first. Roden was returning from that memorable trip into Galilee when he got word in Tel Aviv to get

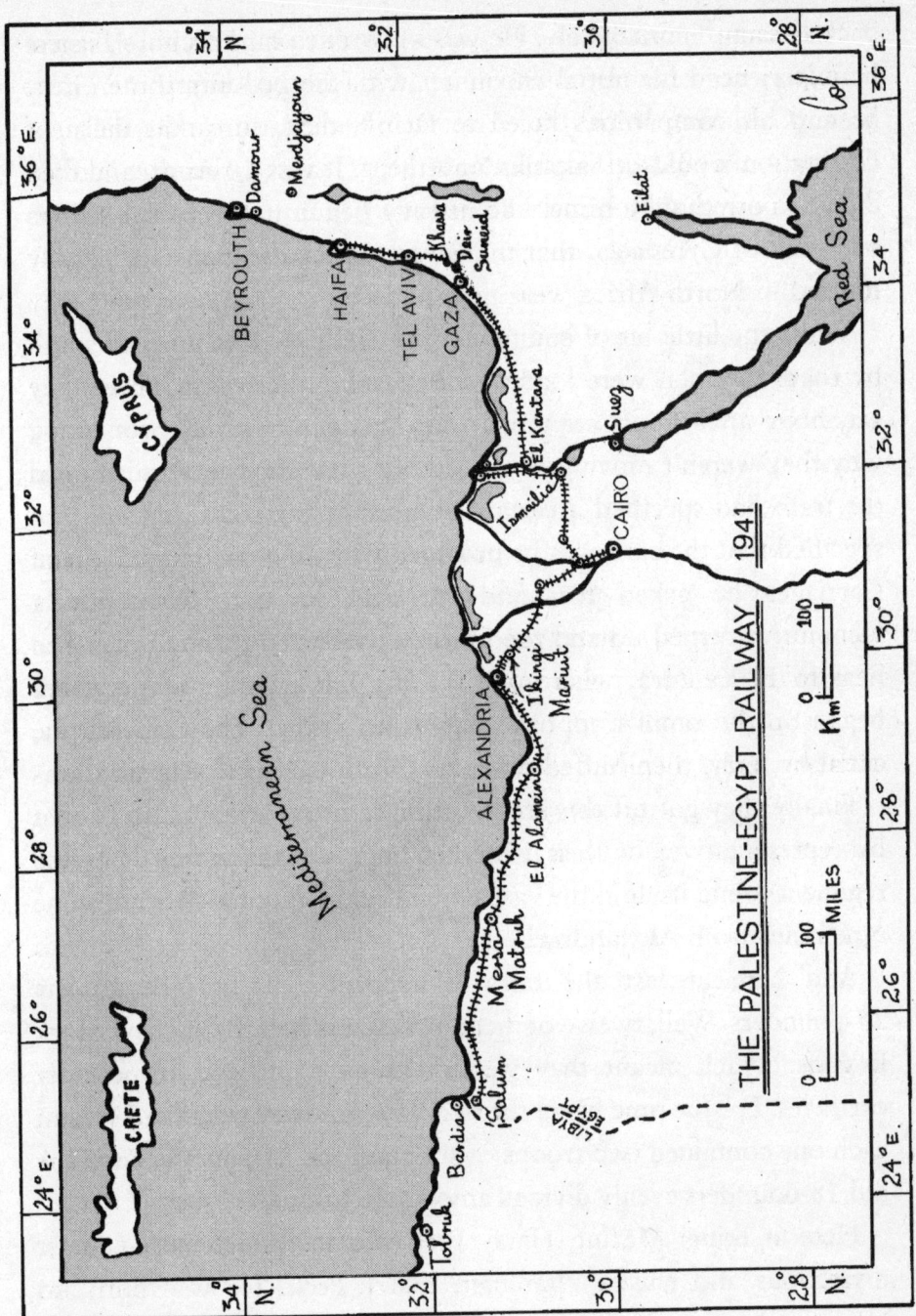

THE PALESTINE-EGYPT RAILWAY 1941

back to camp immediately. He wasn't sorry to quit his hotel, where he experienced his initial encounter with the bed bug. Bitten raw, he and his companions raced to Deir Suneid, sure that the next destination would be Salonika or Athens. It was 10 April, and they didn't know that Rommel had already begun to sweep the British back out of Cyrenaica, that thanks to Greece the gains against the Italians in North Africa were now lost.

While the little bit of equipment the 2/5th possessed rolled south by road, the men were loaded onto a train after dark. There they sat, hour after hour, crammed onto wooden benches, wondering why they weren't moving. It turned out that whoever requisitioned the train had specified a certain number of carriages, but had not specified that the carriages be provided with an engine to pull them. Carriages he asked for, and carriages he got. Eventually a locomotive turned up and the journey proceeded through dust and heat to El Kantara, where one railway line ended and the other began on the canal's opposite bank—no bridge. They crossed the canal by ferry, then huffed down to Cairo and up to Alexandria.

Finally they got off this second train in utter darkness, to be met by representatives of their fostering unit; a night march later the regiment found itself in the vast staging camp at Ikingi Mariut, some nine miles from Alexandria.

And here at last the miracle happened. The 2/5th got its 25-pounders. Well, twelve of them, which was half. Brand new Mark II guns, which meant they weren't mounted on old 18-pounder carriages. For the time being the two batteries were organised so that each one contained two troops of six guns, the 25-pounders and the old 18-pounders evenly divided among the troops.

Here at Ikingi Mariut, Harry Peck was in his element. A most mysterious and elusive character, Harry Peck. He was born, so regimental legend has it, during a hut inspection by an unnamed officer in the first few days of the 2/5th at Ingleburn. One of the camp stretchers was a mess, which deeply offended the officer and his retinue of attendants.

'Who owns this kit?' the officer demanded.

Among the debris on the bed was a bottle of something every Australian knows well: Peck's fish paste, a rather luridly pink, aromatic spread made from anchovies and intended to be smeared on bread or toast. Australians love it, won't be parted from it. Even in camp at Ingleburn, some soldier newly severed from his civilian luxuries had thought sufficiently ahead to bring along a bottle of Peck's fish paste.

'Harry Peck, sir!' said one of the hut's inhabitants.

The legend goes on to say that Gunner Harry Peck was then formally charged under the Army Act with 'conduct to the prejudice of good order and military discipline'. But an intensive search of the regiment's rolls failed to find an army number for Gunner Harry Peck, who thus made the first of many escapes.

A tradition grew up that Harry Peck was never involved in anything for personal gain or profit—which is not to say that his activities were always legitimate.

Simply, if you needed a tin of camouflage paint, Harry Peck would obtain it. He signed for petrol when the needy one was on proper regimental business, though perhaps not quite the kind of business another unit would approve of. Harry Peck made sure the 2/5th got its fair share of equipment at a time when the bun-rush as ships docked and unloaded at Suez might have seen the 2/5th's share go to someone else. He signed for goods at every ordnance depot anywhere in the 2/5th's vicinity anywhere in the Middle East, then later back in Australia, and later still in New Guinea and at Balikpapan, Borneo. His rank varied between Gunner and Lieutenant-Colonel, and he died at Merdjayoun, Ibeles Saki, and a dozen other places. In Syria he was sometimes known as Henri Pecque of the 31st Anchovy Division of *l'Armée Australienne*. In Palestine there existed a Jewish-Australian soldier named Heinrich Pfeck. Lieutenant Harry Peck was heard delivering a five-minute talk over Radio Jerusalem about Mohammedanism in Australia, and after he was heroically wounded an army program played him a song.

Gunner/Bombardier/Sergeant/Lieutenant/Captain/Major/Lieutenant-Colonel Harry Peck did brilliant work during the eight days the regiment spent at Ikingi Mariut. He found anything up to and including trucks on the wharves in Suez, then got them into the regiment's hands within hours, though Suez was a good 300 miles away.

During those eight days at Ikingi Mariut the 2/5th worked in shifts around the twenty-four-hour clock to get the feel of their guns and tractors. At night the detachments wheeled their guns inside huts and kept on practising; and the new equipment kept on flooding in, more and more and more.

Ikingi Mariut was a sea of sand. While the wind was blowing men got lost walking from one tent to another; sand even got into tightly lidded tins of cigarettes. Roden left his gun training manual on a camp table beside his camp bed while he went to get something to eat at the mess hut; when he returned the thick book had disappeared. But it was there, buried under an inch of newly deposited sand. To make matters worse, the vertical breech blocks of the guns jammed from sand the moment they were opened.

The last thirty vehicles arrived just in time for the L.A.D. to check them and the regiment paint them with desert camouflage. On

20 April the 2/5th moved out along the thin strip of tar, shimmering with heat, that connected Tripolitania[†] with Egypt. Finally the men felt confident they could deal with war, and knew too that they would not be going to Greece. They were to face Rommel and the Afrika Korps.

The British thrust into Greece was rapidly turning into a disaster. The Germans had come down from Bulgaria the moment the first British troops moved into Salonika, but not by the expected route down the Struma River. In a series of outflanking manoeuvres they split the Greeks from the Yugoslavs and the British from the Greeks, then drove into Thessaly well west of the Olympus massif pushing the Greeks and British before them like so much earth. The British high command had no choice; the order went out to evacuate everyone possible to Crete. It was Dunkirk all over again. Behind them the British left their artillery, their tanks and a great many captured soldiers, Australians and New Zealanders among them.

In North Africa all the advantages of winter 1940–1941 were now being lost. Save for a lonely outpost at Tobruk, Wavell's forces were out of Cyrenaica and back in Egypt, reforming at the great fortress of Mersa Matruh. Where the 2/5th was going.

In other times a delightful, balmy resort town sat on the jewelled lakelike bay of Mersa Matruh. Its ancient name was Paraetonium, and there the rich, famous and royal disported themselves over the course of the millennia: Alexander the Great en route to Ammonium, Cleopatra, Roman emperors and many more, culminating in the visit of the Prince of Wales and his American friend Mrs. Wallis Warfield Simpson in the 1930s.

Even the 1941 wilderness of barbed wire, minefields, concrete

---

[†] Modern western Libya.

pillboxes and twisted wreckage could not completely strip Mersa Matruh of its air of magic.

'It was not an unpleasant front,' says Roden.

During the few weeks the 2/5th was to spend there, they saw no real action save for bombing raids by the Italian air force. These raids were cunningly timed to catch the soldiers in Mersa Matruh with their pants down, as they usually happened in the morning while the queues to use the latrines were at their longest. The bombs would start exploding and men would erupt from the latrines with their shorts around their ankles while those still waiting their turn ran in all directions. Shrapnel tended to hit exposed behinds. Air raids at other times could be expected if the few Egyptians remaining in the area suddenly bolted for their ramshackle conveyances and hightailed it into the desert; either their hearing was more acute, or they could smell planes.

The real fighting in April and May was going on around Tobruk, where the Australian Ninth Division was holed up together with an infantry brigade from the Seventh and some fifty tanks of the Royal Tank Regiments. A state of siege developed in which Rommel could not dislodge the Australians, but Wavell could not relieve them; their only supply line was from the sea, imperilled by Italian submarines, mines and bombers.

It is important to remember that the British War Cabinet had no idea that Hitler was planning to invade the U.S.S.R. Churchill, who had a strong sense of history, was so convinced that the Germans were not foolish enough to repeat Napoleon's mistake that he seriously thought the German offensives of 1941 would be directed towards an invasion of Great Britain and towards the oil supplies of the Middle East, through Syria now that there were large German forces in Greece and Thrace, and through Egypt. The War Cabinet's opinion was shared by the British generals. For this reason the

Mediterranean gauntlet was run occasionally, using very fast cargo ships to carry tanks, anti-aircraft guns, field guns, howitzers, mortars, landmines and all the other trappings of modern warfare. These convoys mostly made it safely to Alexandria. No one had any idea that Hitler and his chief of staff, General Halder, were so determined to minimise German involvement in the Mediterranean that they sent General von Paulus 'to head off this soldier gone stark mad', as Halder described Rommel in his diary. Everything possible had to be conserved for the coming Russian offensive, delayed a month due to enormous flooding of the Bug and other undisciplined rivers on that eternal Russian plain.

In Mersa Matruh the 2/5th continued its gun practice under the supervision of an Australian brigadier, Frank Berryman (who went on to become a knight and a lieutenant-general). Though later he was to esteem Roden highly, Berryman early on took a very dim view of this cheeky lieutenant, who seemed, as Berryman saw it, to take great delight in showing him up. Despite his lowly rank, Roden was developing a tendency to speak his mind and act as his own commonsense dictated, no matter what the military tactical manuals said, or how custom and tradition said a junior officer should behave when carpeted by the boss.

There were some difficult escarpments around Mersa Matruh, and some gunnery exercises involved hauling the guns up to the top of one of these ridges. During one such exercise Roden worked very hard to get his troops down a precipitous incline; the troop responded superbly well, and the precious guns, limbers and tractors arrived at the bottom unharmed. There they chanced to pass Brigadier Berryman at close quarters.

'Good on you, Cutler, you're the only one who made it,' said the battery commander, Major Bill Courtney.

But at the conference the following day Berryman claimed that the troop were smoking and skylarking around—and that no officer was present. Instead of taking his medicine in silence, Roden contradicted Berryman, insisting that no one was smoking or skylarking, and that he, the troop commander, had been there the whole time. Berryman was most annoyed.

The second occasion was more embarrassing for the brigadier. In this particular exercise Berryman was cast in the role of the enemy, detailed to take the ground atop a very steep escarpment. There was a sort of a road which was confidently deemed to be the only feasible way up. Roden asked himself what he would do if he were the enemy, and decided that he'd attempt the ascent on a goat track in order to come round behind the defenders. So while the other gun officers trained their pieces on the road, Roden put a 25-pounder just out of sight of the goat track to cover it. When Berryman got to the top, he found himself looking straight down the muzzle of a 25-pounder. He was very upset; Roden got another roasting in conference.

Every junior officer had to take his turn as officer of the night watch, during which he sat looking in the direction of the enemy. Very boring, when the enemy was at Tobruk and the Italian air force didn't fly after dark. Candles and kerosene lamps were not to be had, but in a war zone under strict blackout conditions, the men became hungry to enjoy some kind of light their commanders would not object to.

Cigarettes were the anodyne of soldiers of both the World Wars; lightweight and easy to stow in all sorts of crannies, they were issued freely. They came in tins of fifty, but no one threw the tin away when the fifty were gone. Handy things, tins. The soldiers used to make a tiny lamp out of an empty cigarette tin by half-filling it with petrol, punching a hole in the lid and threading a piece of string through it. A dangerous device, but no one worried.

To keep wide awake, alert and intelligently on the lookout, the watch kept their cigarette tin lamp well down out of sight and entertained themselves by wreaking vengeance on the hated bed bugs, which were endemic at Mersa Matruh—as were other vermin. The trick was to spear a bed bug on a pencil and then sizzle it in the flame. The front was deathly quiet at night, not so much as a flare on the horizon from artillery.

The days were now soaring past the century mark—one day the mercury stood at 126°F (52°C). In temperatures like that movement was almost impossible, nor could the guns be relied upon, but of course the heat was having much the same effect on Rommel, still slugging away at Tobruk.

The water ration was a gallon a day per man, but in actual fact no man ever got more than two pints for his personal use. In such matters officers had no privileges of rank. Out of the two pints (a little over a litre) a man had to wash, shave and keep himself hydrated, though one big mug of tea was supplied with a meal. Every spare drop of water had to go into the radiators of the vehicles (and there Rommel had the advantage, as many of his vehicles were air-cooled).

Naturally there were plenty of army stuff-ups. No one had thought to provide the men with salt tablets, so sodium depletion was omnipresent. But there are ways around most things, and the water/salt problem was no different. The sea wasn't far away and the rocks held pools of crystallising salt, or were caked with a layer of salt. After a swim (the only kind of bath Mersa Matruh had to offer) the soldiers would return to camp bearing a treasure trove of precious salt. It was risky to bathe, of course. The Italian air force would swoop in, but the laughable little 'gun boat' in the harbour had the loudest siren in the Middle East, and the fellaheen who operated it seemed to know the planes were coming long before anyone else did.

There were still not enough 25-pounders for the regiment's batteries. The 18-pounders were so old that they couldn't hope to maintain air pressure when fired for more than two or three hours. The 2/5th did, however, inherit two naval 6-pounders made in 1890; the rifling inside the barrels had been worn absolutely smooth, so no gunner could predict within two thousand yards whereabouts the projectiles the guns fired would land. Fascinated, the L.A.D. thought the best thing was to aim them out to sea as part of the harbour defences.

The L.A.D. mechanics were very busy, for the area around Mersa Matruh was a wasteland of abandoned tanks and vehicles, British and Italian. Out they'd go to fossick among the debris, whooping whenever they found some delectable item they could strip from a piece of shattered equipment and tuck it into their stores against a rainy day. Keeping the regiment mobile was a nightmare, particularly in the matter of springs. The L.A.D. became geniuses at reshaping spring leaves and remaking springs.

It turned out too that the factory calibrations for the new 25-pounders bore no relationship to the distance the guns actually shot. 25-pounders could be used as true guns on a low trajectory over a longer distance, or as howitzers on a high trajectory over a shorter distance; the maximum effective range was 13,400 yards (12,250 metres).

Each gun consisted of two parts, the basic structure (wheels, trail, axle and firing platform) and the superstructure (barrel and breech, sighting system, recoil system and saddle, the latter including the traversing and elevating mechanisms). The total traverse (that is, the arc the barrel could be moved from extreme left to extreme right) was 8°, whereas elevation (that is, the vertical angle of the barrel) was to a maximum of 45°; theoretically the gun could be used as an anti-aircraft weapon, but in practice that was unfeasible. Under the trail which linked the gun to the limber was a circular metal firing platform which was detached and then dropped on the ground in the spot where the gun was to be positioned, after which the gun was wheeled onto it. This enabled the whole structure to be rotated through 360° by the gun sergeant if it became necessary to swing the gun more than 4° to the left or right of the midline. To fire accurately the gun had first to be sighted, which had nothing to do with pointing the barrel at the target. Sighting meant getting the gun structure itself perfectly level. The gun layer directed this procedure by consulting a two-bubble spirit level device incorporated in the gun's sighting system.

The gun detachment consisted of six men—the gun sergeant, a bombardier second-in-command, the loading number, the layer, and two ammunition numbers. The sergeant took his instructions from the command post and controlled the gun and its detachment. The accepted rate of fire was five rounds per minute, but a seasoned detachment could fire faster than one round per twelve seconds for a considerable period of time if asked to do so.

Artillerymen like to hear the ammunition referred to as 'projectiles' rather than 'shells', though 'shell' is also used. The 25-pounder fired separated loading ammunition (that is, the fuzed projectile was loaded first, then a brass cartridge case containing the charge in cloth bags was placed in the breech behind it). The explosive in the projectile was fuzed either to detonate twenty metres (yards) above the ground or on touchdown, but it was the charge in the cartridge case that pushed the projectile out of the barrel and on its way to the target at enormous speed. By bagging the charge the range of the gun could be altered; red bag always, white bag added to red for additional range, and blue bag added to red-plus-white for maximum range. Under normal circumstances all three bags were used, and that was how the cartridge cases were supplied, holding all three bags.

Each man in the detachment had a specific job and worked as one with his fellows. The gun sergeant (Number One) spoke to numbers rather than names because events did not always guarantee that the same names would be working the gun. The bombardier second-in-command (Number Six) was responsible for care and supply of ammunition, and knew the Number One's job in case he had to take over. He stood closest to the limber and knew which kind of fuze and how many charge bags were needed on a particular fire mission; he checked the projectile fuzes and the bags in the cartridge case, removing blue or blue-plus-white bags if so instructed. Afterwards he had to burn any unused charge bags and ensure—if feasible—that the spent cartridge cases were returned to base (they would eventually be melted down and recast). One of the two ammunition numbers (Number Five) stood between the Number Six and the other ammunition number (Number Four) who stood at the gun, and passed the ammunition. First he passed the fuzed projectile, which the Number Four put inside the breech. The moment his hands were out of the way the loader (Number Two) shoved the projectile into the commencement of the barrel with a hand-held rammer. Once his hands were out of the way the Number Four placed the brass cartridge case into the breech, which freed up the extractors holding the breech block open. The loader then operated a lever to close the breech, and the gun was ready for firing. Firing was the layer's job; he was Number Three. All of this happened in twelve seconds or less.

Very little was automated and nothing was computerised because computation beyond a slide rule, mathematical tables and a human brain did not exist. Which was probably a good thing. Conditions in the field—be they related to sun, sand, salt spume, snow, rain or the vicissitudes of transportation—surely militated against any kind of extremely delicate working part. A gun or howitzer was simply required to pierce armour or explode and scatter shrapnel.

Accurate calibration figures were vital. A battery or troop command post set its guns up according to these figures so that by the time the observation officer phoned or radioed his co-ordinates in to register the guns, the guns were already more or less aligned. This alignment with the target's vicinity was called 'ranging'.

'Registering' was the fine tuning. Because the targets were mostly some miles away and the guns were concealed in some fairly safe place, targets were usually invisible to the gunners and the command post at the guns (firing on tanks was the exception to this). It was the duty of the observation officer at his observation post to register the guns. This post was in a position from which the observation officer could see the target. He was armed with two vital objects: a contour-detailed survey map and a communication device, either a radio or a field telephone. His responsibility was to bring the guns to bear exactly on the target, and in order to do this he had to know his guns and ammunition intimately. He worked out the location of the target, its height and the direction from himself to the target, then he contacted the command post at the guns and gave them the information. They consulted their firing tables, diagrams and a gunnery slide rule to calculate the bearing, range and angle of sight from the guns to the target; where science transmogrified into sleight of hand was in the more elusive factors these calculations involved—weather, wind velocity, temperature of the propellant (charge), rotation/spin both of the globe and the projectile as it zoomed to the target—factors which made an infantryman regard an artilleryman with awe. When a troop or battery was firing at the same target, all the guns were given a common bearing and a common range. The gun layer would apply the range to the cone-shaped calibrated range indicator and elevate his gun accordingly.

Under ordinary circumstances the observation officer's occupation was not more dangerous than anyone else's in combat, but when the guns were going into action to cover an infantry advance a forward observation officer was employed, and things could get hairy for him.

The forward observation officer accompanied the infantry but could find himself ahead of the general advance. Naturally the last thing a commander wanted to do was fire on his own men; gunfire preceded the infantry to soften up the enemy. This sometimes meant that the forward observation officer was a lot closer to the target than prudence recommended. It was his job to direct the fire onto a line between himself and the target, after which one round was fired. After this he had to correct for both line and range, and another round was fired. From then on range was normally the factor needing further adjustment, so he went on giving directions which 'bracketed' the target by falling behind it and in front of it, narrowing the range until the target and the round were spot-on. Sounds easy, and in good terrain it can be; but in craggy country in close proximity to the enemy it can be difficult, especially in 1941, when craggy country meant the radio didn't work and the communication device was a field telephone with all its sometimes miles of vulnerable cable too easily spotted by the enemy.

The procedure might go something like this:

After the first round: 'Right 2°, drop 100.' Correcting line and range.

After the second adjusting round: 'Add 100.' Range only.

After the third adjusting round: 'Drop 50, six rounds fire for effect.' Range felt to be correct, target zeroed.

Each gun in the battery or troop would then fire six rounds at the target and, with any luck, the F.O.O. could get out.

At Mersa Matruh the 2/5th discovered that the factory boffin calibration figures were nothing like the field performance of the guns. This meant that the guns had to be recalibrated by the regiment's ballistics experts, and that meant test-firing the guns what seemed like endlessly. As things turned out, it was to be almost another year before calibration and field performances were finally married.

A bit of the old Palestine gloom was descending again. The Italian bomber raids became a part of the daily routine, the heat kept getting worse as summer neared, the water situation was no better, frying bed bugs palled, and the L.A.D. had exhausted the resources of the equipment wasteland. What would happen now that Crete was becoming a disaster too? Where was the next action going to be? And *when*?

Syria was held by the Vichy French[†] with a very professional army of some 65,000 French Foreign Legionnaires, Moroccans, Algerians

---

[†] That part of France not physically occupied by the Germans was governed from the town of Vichy as a nominally sovereign state. French colonial possessions tended to adhere to the government in Vichy, not to the stateless Free French led by Charles de Gaulle. The Vichy French in the French colonies were *not* at Hitler's beck and call; if left alone, they tended to sit pat and do nothing to aid either side. The British hope was always that a Vichy French colony would declare for the Free French, but many French in the colonies, while not at all enamoured of Germany, felt that their allegiance was to the soil of France— that is, to the French Government in Vichy. This was particularly true in 1940 and 1941; actual collaboration with the Germans by Vichy came in 1942, with the return of Pierre Laval.

and other French colonials; it included the Lebanon. Fears were that it would ally itself with the Germans, which is why the Syrian campaign was mounted. Perhaps because it was one of the shortest in the annals of the Second World War and because, contrary to London's fears, the Germans never did aim for the Middle East oilfields, the five-week-long Syrian campaign of early summer 1941 merits but a small paragraph in a single-volume analysis of the Second World War—and not much more in a multi-volume one. A contributing factor may well be that no one wants to remember that in one theatre of war the British fought the French to a standstill. At this time Churchill was very close to Charles de Gaulle, leader of the Free French, and the whole French tangle of divided loyalties was considered extremely politically delicate.

Determined to conserve his strength for North Africa, General Wavell hadn't wanted to fight Exporter (the code name) in Syria. When Churchill and the War Cabinet insisted, Wavell then opposed the use of any Free French in Exporter, explaining that he was sure the presence of Free French would only serve to stiffen Vichy French determination to resist. London was equally sure Wavell was wrong; Churchill was searching for an excuse to fire him, therefore not inclined to listen to anything Wavell said.

What chiefly perturbed London was the assistance Vichy Syria was giving to German planes en route to Iraq to fan the flames of a rebellion there. Reports had also come in that an advance party of German military had already arrived in Syria to pave the way for a strike against the Arab oilfields. Moreover, London had received a flurry of intelligence to the effect that Vichy Syria would transfer its allegiance to Free France if the British arrived there in force. Wavell protested that all London's intelligence was being manufactured by the de Gaullists, but de Gaulle was right there to whisper in Churchill's other ear. The result was that Wavell fell into

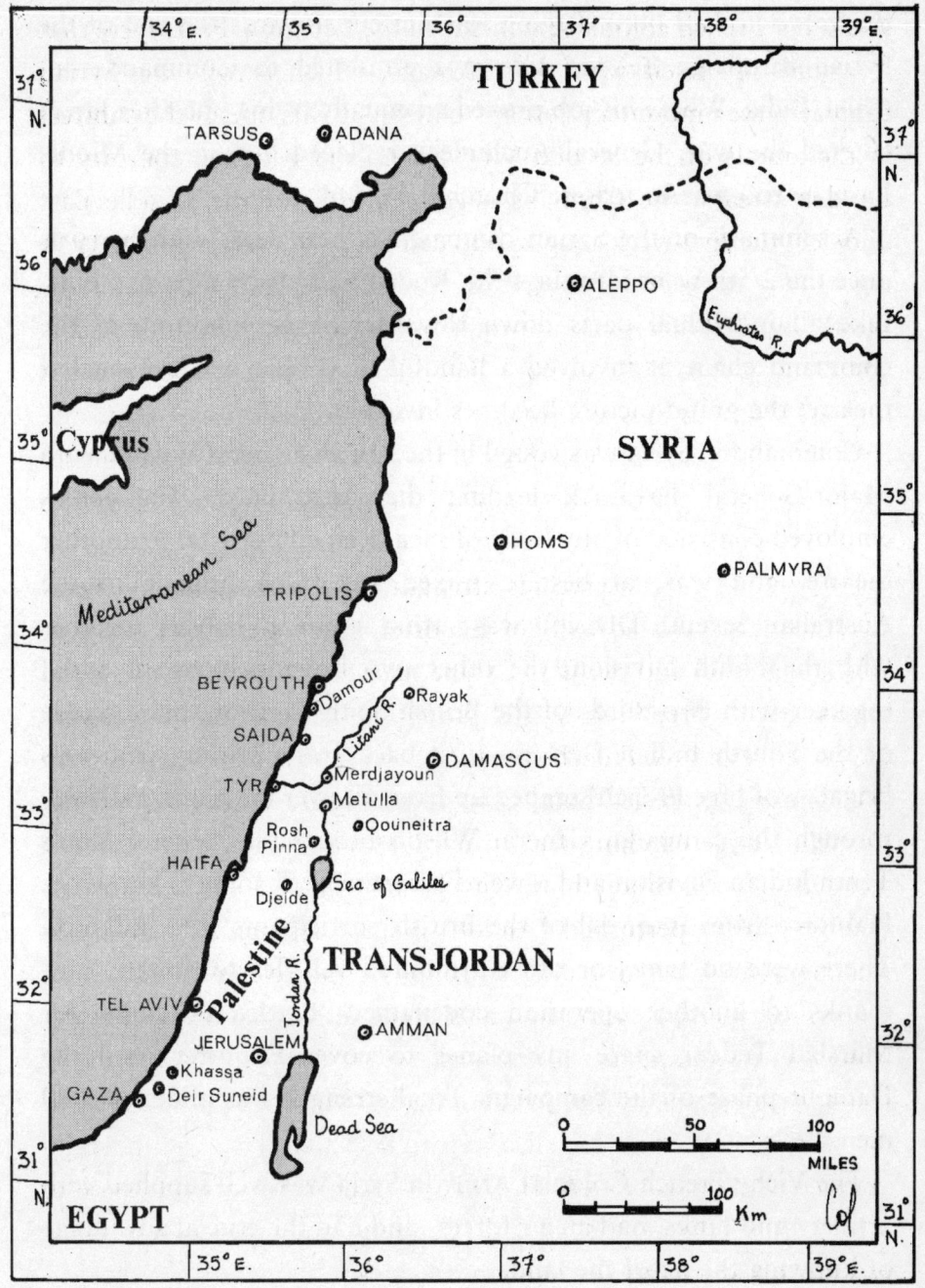

TURKEY

TARSUS ●ADANA

Cyprus

SYRIA

●ALEPPO

Euphrates R.

Mediterranean Sea

●HOMS

●PALMYRA

TRIPOLIS

BEYROUTH
●Damour
●Rayak

SAIDA

Litani R.

●DAMASCUS

TYR
●Merdjayoun
●Metulla

Rosh
Pinna
●Qouneitra

HAIFA

Sea of Galilee

●Djeide

Palestine

Jordan R.

TRANSJORDAN

TEL AVIV

●AMMAN

JERUSALEM

●Khassa
GAZA●
●Deir Suneid

Dead Sea

0   50   100
MILES

0   100
Km

EGYPT

the grave he had been digging for himself; towards the end of the Syrian campaign he was sideways promoted to Commander-in-Chief, India. Where his job proved an equally trying one after Japan entered the war. General Auchinleck replaced him in the Middle East; he too was to irritate Churchill.

A summary of the Syrian campaign is best dealt with here, as once the 2/5th went into the field, Roden had his own part to play. Like all individual parts down towards the very bottom of the command chain, it involved a handful of people in a far smaller theatre; the grand picture becomes invisible.

Command in Syria was vested in the British General Wilson, with Major-General Lavarack leading the Australians. The forces employed consisted of any body of men deemed not vital to another theatre, and was, at best, a mixed bag. One brigade of the Australian Seventh Division was sitting it out in Tobruk together with the Ninth Division; the other two brigades went to Syria, together with two-thirds of the British Sixth Division, one brigade of the Fourth Indian Division (just back from Eritrea), and two brigades of Free French scraped up from all over the place. Halfway through the campaign General Wilson brought in General Slim's Tenth Indian Division and a weird assortment of soldiers known as Habforce from Iraq. All of the British participants were infantry. There were no tanks or other armoured vehicles to donate, nor, thanks to another operation codenamed 'Battleaxe', could Air Marshal Tedder spare any planes to cover Exporter until the Damour phase of the campaign. Total strength was about 40,000 men.

The Vichy French Colonial Army in Syria was well supplied with artillery and tanks, had an air force—and had the crucial advantage of knowing the lie of the land.

The battle for Syria was indeed a battle, for the action never ceased. It lasted from 8 June 1941 until 10 July, though hostilities were not to cease until the small hours of the 11th; the Vichy French commanders did not all agree with the supreme commander, General Dentz, when he asked for an armistice. In the event General Dentz did not sign the armistice until 14 July, which was Bastille Day.

The 2/5th stayed on in Syria until midway through January 1942 as part of an army of occupation, as the French colonial soldiers left in Syria were without the professionally trained French. The regiment left when the threat of a German thrust from Turkey dwindled due to Stalingrad and other reverses in the U.S.S.R.

The fighting in Syria was hard and almost guerilla style; no great sweeping tank engagements, no droning Vs of planes to darken the sky. Both sides fought cleanly, as that term is used in war, but with absolute determination. Crevasses, crumbling escarpments, gulches, steep mountains and dense, jungly banana groves created problems that the North African warriors never suffered. At times the terrain was so impossible for vehicles that mules and horses were employed instead. It could take all day to get a tractor and a gun over a mile or two of a boulder-strewn dry watercourse or a track halfway down the side of a cliff; the miracle is that such tasks were usually accomplished without losing tractor or gun.

In the initial phase of the campaign three separate drives were made, all originating in Palestine. The first route was along the coast through Tyre and Saida (Sidon) to Damour and Beyrouth (Beirut); the second was parallel but inland along the valley of the Litani River from Metulla, through Merdjayoun, and on up to Rayak; the third headed straight for Damascus. The Australian Seventh's two brigades took the coast and the Litani route, with the British Sixth and Indian Fourth Divisions aiming for Damascus. Some of the British Sixth were also involved in the Litani drive.

When bitter fighting and better knowledge of the extreme difficulty of the terrain gave General Wilson pause towards the end of June, he summoned Habforce from Iraq (where things had quietened down) and sent it to take Palmyra, after which it was to push on to Homs. Then he obtained permission to use General Slim's Tenth Indian Division (based in Basra) to drive up both banks of the Euphrates River, destination the big loop of the Baghdad–Aleppo railway between Tel Kochak and Aleppo.

Nowhere was it easy. Slim's Tenth Indian couldn't manoeuvre properly because of drastic lack of transport, and the Vichy outpost in Palmyra held Habforce off until 3 July. Once Damascus was taken, the British and Indian troops couldn't negotiate the superbly defended wilderness between Damascus and the coast.

The big breakthrough came from the Australian Seventh at the beginning of July, when it overcame General Dentz's main defence position along the Damour River on the approaches to Beyrouth. After five days of desperate fighting, Dentz saw the hopelessness of further resistance, and asked for an armistice. Had it not been for the Frenchness of the enemy in Syria and the embarrassment which followed when 90 per cent of the 38,000 European Frenchmen involved elected to be repatriated to Vichy France rather than join de Gaulle, the success of the Syrian campaign might have been more trumpeted. For the fact remains that Syria was a much needed boost for British morale, already becoming slightly war weary.

Now back to the 2/5th in Mersa Matruh. On 25 May 1941 the regiment handed over much of its cherished equipment to the 2/8th Field Regiment, newly arrived in Mersa Matruh. Orders were to travel light, only personal kit and regimental property to be taken. Which didn't stop the L.A.D. managing to convey much of its precious loot, nor the gun layers from smuggling the new anti-tank telescopes out in their kits (when shooting at tanks, the guns were positioned to shoot at them directly).

The train which had brought the 2/8th to Mersa Matruh took the 2/5th back to Palestine, though at one stage of the journey it looked as if they might wind up being detained in Egypt. The Egyptian Government was wavering in its pro-British neutrality; Rommel was beginning to make the Germans and Italians look like a better bet. Which fact didn't help when an unknown member of the regiment (*not* Harry Peck!) chucked an Italian hand grenade towards a throng of Egyptians on the line at Hammam. Italian grenades were so useless that one of the ways the 2/5th used to pass the time at Mersa Matruh was in tossing these grenades from one man to another. To chuck one in the direction of a crowd was a stupid and thoughtless thing to do; quite why remains a mystery, but probably concerned a certain Australian intolerance of the eastern habits of pushing, pestering and begging. Alien, temper-trying. Certainly it wasn't done with the intention of killing or maiming, more to watch the delight at spying largesse turn into terror when the nature of the largesse was discovered. But the grenade exploded, the first to do so in the regiment's experience. Some of the Egyptians were badly injured; Roden thinks one died.

The outrage of the Egyptian Government threatened to put a stop to future artillery activity by the 2/5th, but a day of high diplomatic intervention calmed the situation and the regiment continued on its way, very chastened.

They went into camp at Khassa, where the fostering 2/1st Field Regiment was heartbroken at losing a lot of its gear, for of course it too had fossicked and scavenged over the months it had been in the Middle East.

By now the 2/5th had sixteen 25-pounders, which it broke into four troops of four guns each and thankfully abandoned the last of the old 18-pounders. Just as well. The four-gun troop (a troop normally had six guns) turned out to be a blessing in Syria, where the mountains and ravines made this smaller sized troop more flexible and more effective, besides freeing up more men to relieve the existing gun detachments.

The stay in Khassa was very short. On 30 May the regiment moved up to Jdeide, ten miles to the west of Nazareth. Here was country surely not unlike that Jesus Christ had looked across, fertile timeless fields dewed with forested hills. The inhabitants of Jdeide were Jewish and lavishly hospitable, even to offering bunches of flowers. It was a land of milk and honey.

Training intensified. Peculiar shivers ran down the spines of men like Roden who were acquainted with the Bible, for most of the exercises took place on the plain of Armageddon. An omen, or merely a coincidence? Those who knew their Bible wondered.

And when on 8 June the attack finally began, the order was that the Australians were to wear their felt slouch hats rather than their steel Tommy helmets. So confident were the Powers-That-Be that the Vichy French wouldn't fight.

They went in over the Jordan River north of Rosh Pinna and made their way to Qouneitra and the Banias Road bridge over the Wadi Hasbani. The units around them were partly Australian and partly British territorials, Scots Greys among them. Roden says that the Free French weren't much use, but that the Australians did like General Legentilhomme, the Free French commander. Of all the many nationalities of soldier who fought on the British side and the Vichy French side, no hatred existed save between the Free French and the Vichy French; General Wavell had been right.

Roden accompanied the 9th Battery to Qouneitra (the guns were split into two batteries of two troops each, 9th and 10th), where warfare proceeded as it was supposed to; after some talk aimed at persuading the Vichy French to give in gracefully, the Vichy French informed the British that they preferred to fight—that hostilities would commence at noon. Which they did, with some rivalry between the 9th Battery of the 2/5th and a battery of the Royal Horse Artillery, but honour was satisfied when the 9th Battery got its first shot away ahead of the Royal Horse Artillery. The Vichy French fired back for a short while, then asked for a truce. This being granted, the members of the outpost disappeared in the direction of the coast while the 9th Battery rejoined the 10th near Wadi Hasbani.

At Khirbe the regiment fired its first full scale barrage, slowly beginning to understand the problems this Syrian campaign was going to present to discourage good gunnery. For one thing, there was no meteorological data whatsoever until Damour, still over three weeks in the future; for another, a radio (also called a wireless) hardly ever worked in the rugged and mountainous terrain. No one had really planned on carrying many miles of telephone cable, which was to remain in desperately short supply throughout the campaign. Most of the barrages fired in Syria to accompany infantry advances had to stay on the opening line until the infantry could see whereabouts the shells were bursting; the soldiers had perforce to be held well back from the opening line, then would close up and stop until the barrage lifted—that is, moved forward enough for the troops to gain ground in its wake.

At Khirbe the fire from forty 25-pounders preceded the infantry, rolling slowly across the little town and on towards the next one, Qleaa, lifting another hundred yards only every four minutes because the ground was so rough and hilly that the foot soldiers were hard put to struggle across it.

Another difficulty soon manifested itself. Whenever possible gun positions are protected by having forces in front of them to make sure the enemy cannot capture them, but in Syria it became commonplace to site them where there was no protection. Luckily the hazardous nature of the countryside made direct attempts to take the gun emplacements virtually impossible.

At Khirbe, Captain Adrian Johnson—unruffled, unfailingly pleasant, tenderly reassuring—began to shine. The regiment's medical officer, he had been Roden's best friend for a long time. He set up a forward dressing station and treated anyone in need, from Australian through British, Free French and Vichy French to local people caught in the crossfire and injured by shrapnel. All were grist to his mill, nor did working under combat conditions dismay him. Baptisms of fire under fire make or break, but nothing broke Adrian Johnson, who didn't just sit and wait for casualties to come in. He went looking for them as well. Day after day as the battle went on he stayed as close to the forward lines as he possibly could. A 'fighting doc'.

Khirbe fell, then Qleaa; the way was clear to the main fortress in the region, Merdjayoun. At times the big, clumsy ammunition transports had trouble negotiating the so-called roads and demand often exceeded supply. Observation to register the guns would, nine times out of every ten, have to be done by field telephone; the additional burden of having to transport great coils of cable only made matters worse. But when Merdjayoun fell the regiment was overjoyed to find more than thirty miles of telephone cable stored in the barracks. Booty was suddenly very important, though before these first few days of action no one had actually thought—save with distaste—about booty. The 2/5th now understood that there was booty and booty. Real booty was anything of value to an artilleryman, from telephone cable to a giant thermometer nicked off a pharmacy's outside hoarding. That thermometer did sterling

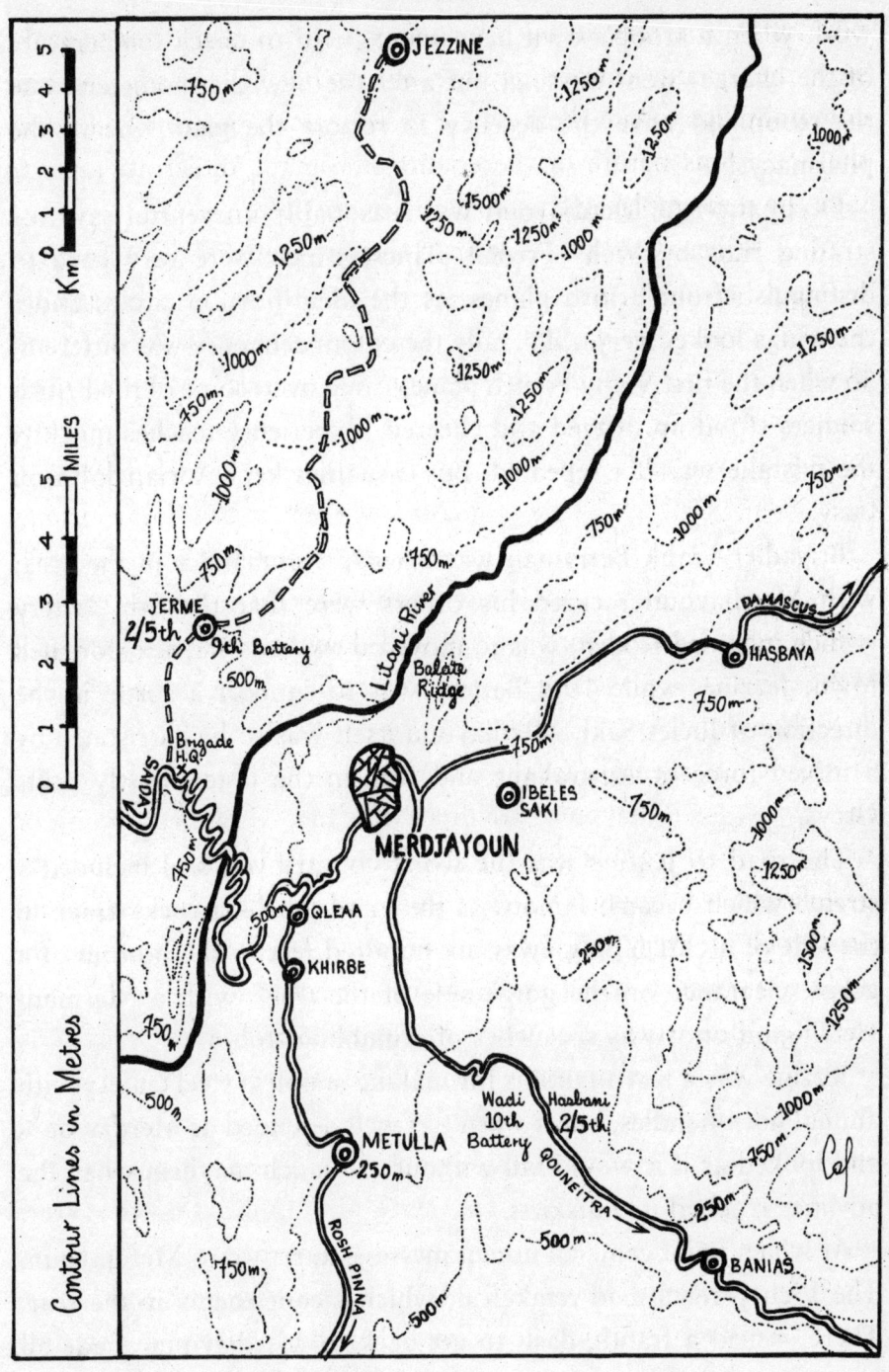

work when a troop's own instrument (used to check temperature of the charge) went missing, but after the new thermometer came the troop did have the decency to restore the giant one to the pharmacy.

Occupation of Merdjayoun was reasonably uneventful save for strafing runs by Vichy French planes, which were very hard to distinguish from British planes, as the identification circles under the wings looked very alike; only the colour sequence was different. So when the first Vichy French planes came over, some of the British soldiers stood up, waved and cheered. Experience teaches quickly; the mistake was not repeated. But casualties kept Adrian Johnson busy.

Brigadier Frank Berryman was brigade commander in the area; with Merdjayoun secured his orders were that the 9th Battery (which included Roden) was to move on towards the next fortified town, Jezzine, while 10th Battery was to support a sortie in the direction of Ibeles Saki. Merdjayoun itself was to be garrisoned by a mixed force of Australians and British, the latter mostly Scots Greys.

The road to Jezzine was the worst country yet, and included a stretch which became famous as the 'mad mile'—a rocky track in the side of a cliff falling away six hundred feet to the bottom of a gorge; clearance on the gorge side of the track with a Marman-Herrington on it was six inches of crumbling stones.

Jezzine was a town famous for making stainless steel cutlery with animal horn handles, but it wasn't as well defended as Merdjayoun, and looked as if it would fall without too much mayhem when the advance reached its outskirts.

At which point came an urgent message to return to Merdjayoun. The Vichy French had retaken it, which meant enemy in the rear. There ensued a frantic dash to get back to Merdjayoun, made all the more perilous because most of it was done in darkness and without lights during the night of 15–16 June, a week after battle had begun. People were going without food or a bath; the cook truck with SIR HENRY PECK & FAMILY painted on its side did its best, but somehow whenever the cooks got a savoury mess of stew together, enemy action intensified and the stew had to be tossed away. Bathing was something one did in a chilly river pool when and if there was a lull in the fighting.

Roden chiefly remembers returning on the mad mile, an uphill tussle around one bend after another. At most of the bends the Marman-Herrington tractor just couldn't get the gun around the curve in its wake; the gun had to be unhitched, the tractor and limber driven around the corner, then the gun manhandled back and forth until it too was around the bend and could be hitched up again. With the 9th Battery was a British anti-aircraft battery which lost one gun over the edge of the road into the gorge, but when, as light came, a Vichy French plane began strafing the road, the anti-aircraft battery brought it down.

At one point the labouring 9th Battery had to get a vehicle past a gun; afterwards the driver couldn't get it back again. Having had some experience as a line wagon officer in the dim days of his Australian training, Roden took over and drove the truck back, an exploit which enhanced his standing among the drivers tremendously; lieutenants are usually thought of as people who can't change the washer on a tap. In one place they encountered some British going forward to Jezzine. When Roden told them that orders were to fall back towards Merdjayoun, they wouldn't believe him; it took a lot of talking to convince them.

On 16 June, a week after hostilities had commenced, the 9th Battery parked its guns in an olive grove outside the village of Jerme; 10th Battery was on the far side of Merdjayoun at Wadi Hasbani.

Frank Berryman had been ordered to command the retaking of Merdjayoun, where the Vichy French were now in strength. Their guns were mainly 75 mm anti-tank weapons, but very adequate for the kind of defensive firing they were called upon to make. They quickly got the range of the regiment's advance headquarters in a culvert beside the Saida road, a position also occupied by some of Berryman's staff. Lucky Vichy French! They didn't really have to register anywhere; it had all been done during the years the French had exercised all over Syria. So getting in and out of the culvert called for some fancy footwork. Here all the British telephone cables gathered together like roads converging on Rome, the switchboard. Radios were utterly useless, situation normal.

9th Battery established observation posts to register the Merdjayoun fortress-barracks atop a hill as well as some gun emplacements to the west. 10th Battery had finally been linked up to the culvert by telephone, and was doing its bit by shelling installations on the eastern side of town. A troop belonging to the 2/6th Field Regiment was brought back from Jezzine in great haste to be added to the 2/5th; it got the code name 'Duku E', and its six 25-pounders were to remain with the 2/5th for some time to come. With the 9th and 10th Batteries separated by over twenty miles of rough track, the addition of Duku E to 9th Battery made a lot of difference. It also brought regimental strength to twenty-two guns.

The infantry unit designated to make the attack on Merdjayoun was the Australian 2/25th Battalion, and here for the first time in the campaign the forward observation officer came into his own. None of the safer observation posts could register the guns, so Captain C.A. 'Joe' Clark went forward with the Australians of the 2/25th. The mission was a headache from the start, for Clark and his tiny party of signallers had to carry an enormous quantity of telephone cable and string it as they went. If possible this was done from the back of a truck, but all too often in Syria it had to be done on foot, as with Clark. The route made a goat track look like a super highway; at one stage they had to scramble a thousand feet down the wall of the Litani River gorge, then cross the deep and powerful stream in pitch darkness.

Because his party was so hampered by the telephone cable, Clark himself went on alone at a faster clip. To compound his party's woes, they ran out of cable as they stumbled along, and had to wait for more. In the meantime they had lost all contact with Clark, and were learning that keeping the cable already laid on the ground in one piece was a worse nightmare than laying it; the mules commandeered to bring supplies forward to the infantry, the boots of those accompanying the mules, and shellfire all wreaked havoc on that meandering string of wire, which necessitated that someone should keep going back to check that it was still intact, if possible tuck it out of the way of feet and hooves.

Clark reached the 2/25th infantry at dawn, in time to see the covering barrage from the regiment's guns commence. But the advance was soon halted; very heavy fire from the defenders made it impossible to go forward. The troops were, besides, exhausted after scrambling over and around the obstacles in their path. As the day wore on the heat in the wadi, more a gorge, increased to a point which rendered any aggressive action unfeasible. The troops had had to wade chest-high through the Litani River, a torrent capable of sweeping men and mules away, and this was the first time the men of the 2/25th Battalion had gone into action. The omens were not propitious.

On the far side of Merdjayoun the 2/2nd Pioneers were looking after things. This battalion of Australians was basically a support unit whose usual work was sapping: that is, using a spade and shovel to dig trenches, holes, dugouts, tunnels and gun emplacements, but—sometimes supplementing their meagre arms issue with machine guns and other weapons scrounged from God knows where—they could also fight. Though their attack was a feint designed to conceal the real attack by the 2/25th Battalion, the Pioneers thought it would be a very good joke if they could reach the Merdjayoun barracks first. Blithely ignoring the regulation that said an infantry force stayed 150 yards behind the gun barrage, they moved up until they were within 15 yards of it. 10th Battery was covering the Pioneers, and established its observation post in a church belfry at Qleaa which survived intense fire from the enemy and a stick of bombs from a plane.

Regimental headquarters in the culvert were too far from the action on the north side of Merdjayoun, so 9th Battery's fire was directed from 9th Battery's command post. At noon, when things fell quiet, the presence of tanks inside the fortress-barracks was reported in; Berryman ordered 80 rounds of gunfire. The barracks had already been registered during the original taking of Merdjayoun, so the target was a sitting duck. More than eleven hundred rounds fell in concentrated fire upon the great building and hit the magazine, which went up with a huge roar and a vast column of smoke. 10th Battery saw the smoke and started pouring in fire from its side too.

During this lull at the apex of the day's heat 10th Battery was moved closer to Merdjayoun, an enormous saving in telephone cable and signallers to string it out, as the front between Jerme and Qleaa was across open ground perpetually bombarded by Vichy French gun batteries and bombed and strafed from the air.

By 18 June no one had heard from Forward Observation Officer Joe Clark, though, unknown to headquarters, a party sent with more telephone cable to find him had actually done so. The trouble was that the field telephone had not emitted a single ring from him.

'Cuttles,' said C.O. John O'Brien (who had taken to calling Roden that), 'you'd better go out and locate Joe Clark.'

Understanding the Australian army maxim that if you asked for volunteers you got killed in the rush, whereas if you ordered men to go you got killed in the retreat, Roden asked for volunteers and got more than the two signallers he needed. They set off with a day's rations, confident that they would be back within twenty-four hours. Naturally they lugged more telephone cable.

As he and the two signallers neared the front line it was easier to see why Merdjayoun, successfully taken once, had fallen to the Vichy French again. The enemy in this area was all French Foreign Legion, very tough and seasoned troops, and the Scots Greys who had been detailed to garrison Merdjayoun were not the famous professional regulars but poorly trained and inexperienced territorials. They hadn't had the panache to hold their ground; the moment the Vichy French attacked, they fled.

Roden also encountered some of the Australian soldiers now trying to retake Merdjayoun, and found them terrified, more anxious to retreat than advance.

In the meantime C.O. John O'Brien was talking to Brigadier Frank Berryman, who was worried that no one had heard from Clark. O'Brien said he'd sent someone to find him.

'Who?' asked Berryman.

'Cutler.'

'What, *him*?' asked Berryman incredulously. 'He's wet!'

Wet Cutler had commandeered the services of a reluctant soldier from the 2/25th Battalion and was finally led to where Clark had set up his observation post.

It was decided that the telephone wire to Clark's observation post was so vital a second line should be paid out, which necessitated more wire, more signallers and more rations from the command post. The route was still so arduous that it took all day of 18 June to accomplish the mission, which lost a donkey over a cliff, was pinned down by fierce enemy fire, and needed the services of a guide towards the end.

At this stage no one in command was sure whether a second advance was going to work; Berryman and O'Brien set out in the tracks of Clark and Cutler to investigate the situation for themselves. They evolved a battle plan, but the route was so fraught with dangers and over such rough terrain that by the time they arrived back at the regimental command post they had been away far longer than they had expected. It was too late to do anything before dark.

Clark and Cutler, up forward, were very busy. Two of the key points in the new battle plan were located on the crest high above their observation post, and overhung the forward positions of the 2/25th Battalion. One was a copse of pines, the other a steep, red-hued escarpment, and both were heavily occupied by Vichy French guns in a perfect place to blow the infantry advance to pieces. The general area, called Balate Ridge, lay to the north of the town; once registered, the guns plastered it, but the copse area remained relatively untouched.

Clark and Roden decided to find a better observation post from which to register the copse area; the party had one rifle and one revolver between the several who ventured out. They encountered rifle and machine-gun fire and one of the gunners was wounded. After a little backtracking they found a safer route and managed at last to register the target.

The salvo subsequently directed at the copse area was one of the most effective single series ever fired by the regiment. The projectile fuzes were set to explode at treetop level; the hail of shrapnel, wood splinters and burning branches devastated the Vichy French emplacement. Men ran in all directions and the garrison commander and two of his three officers were killed, with over half the rest of the garrison killed or injured.

The attack on Merdjayoun on 19 June was to be of the pincer variety, with the 2/25th Battalion coming down from the copse area and the red escarpment, while the 2/2nd Pioneers were to come in from the south and link up with the 2/25th on the western slope of the barracks hill. One company of the 2/25th was left to guard the Balate Ridge and protect the left flank; there was reason to think the Vichy French had more gun emplacements behind Balate.

Because the attacking troops were moving up from the rear and the regiment's gun batteries were on the opposite side of the target, fire was progressively shortened in range instead of lengthening; unusual techniques were becoming the rule rather than the exception in Syria.

Roden's bed on the night of the 18th consisted of rocks, as it was again on the night of the 19th; by the end of his participation in the Syrian campaign, he was so used to sleeping on rocks that he couldn't sleep in a real bed.

At dawn on the 19th, Clark and Cutler parted, Clark going forward as far as his wire would take him, Roden joining the lead attacking troops. In the midst of the carnage yesterday's salvo had made of the copse area, Clark set up another observation post and registered the suspected Vichy French battery just visible over the top of Balate Ridge. Once the regiment's 25-pounders had the target, firing from it ceased, though Clark decided that the guns hadn't been destroyed. But he had done what he could, and the enemy guns were registered. He moved onward in Roden's direction, noting that on top of Castle Hill, a hump just to the west of the town, was a concentration of very troublesome machine guns.

Once Clark joined Roden near Castle Hill the two of them decided that the 2/25th Battalion had found its steel and would move forward again when ordered. But first it was necessary to silence the machine guns. Clark, Roden, two gunners (Geoff Grayson and Bruce Buckingham), two 2/25th riflemen and a 2/25th Bren gunner, Private V.G. Pratt, set off to register Castle Hill, taking telephone cable to pay out as they went. Under heavy machine-gun fire they made their dash towards a derelict mud hut used as a stable. When bullets cut the wire Roden went back and mended it while the fire continued all around him. By some miracle he wasn't hit; nor was the wire again. The hut, they thought, would make a good observation post.

The Pioneers came up on the right, but were decimated by the machine-gun fire. It became vital to register the target and silence those machine guns, but Vichy French artillery fire hit the telephone line and broke it again. This time Grayson went out to mend it; then it was hit and severed a third time. Two more gunners coming to locate them mended this third break, but after they discovered that the telephone in the hut was still dead, the two gunners elected to return to the 2/5th command post checking the wire all the way.

Two medium R.35 enemy tanks appeared, grinding uphill and accompanied by some fifteen *poilus* (French foot soldiers). Pratt the Bren gunner grabbed one of two .5 calibre anti-tank rifles the group had with it; Roden, a fine shot, grabbed the other. But it soon became obvious that the so-called anti-tank rifle (named the Boyes) was incapable of piercing a tank's hull or turret. The *poilus* began firing; Pratt abandoned his Boyes rifle and returned the fire with his Bren gun—a lightweight, hand-carried machine gun. Bullets came screaming into the hut, killing one of the 2/25th riflemen and wounding the other.

It occurred to Roden that if a .5 calibre anti-tank weapon couldn't pierce a tank's armour, maybe it could damage the tracks, which were driven on a kind of cog system around a series of wheels inside the track belt. Both tanks were positioned to shelter the *poilus*, as was a stone wall. Roden switched the sights of the Boyes rifle to fire at the track mechanisms.

The 2-pounder turret guns swung to bear on the hut. The first shell hit the roof and brought down an avalanche of bricks, one of which struck Buckingham in the belly, badly bruising him.

'I'm dead!' he gasped, joking to reassure the rest.

They grinned.

The second round exploded inside the hut. Pratt the Bren gunner was killed instantly and Clark was literally eviscerated by a piece of shrapnel. Grayson was hit in the groin, a wound which bled copiously but did not enter his pelvis or prevent his walking. The only one now without an injury, Roden just kept on firing round after round at the tank tracks.

Then suddenly both tanks wheeled and left, their crews apparently worried that the fire on the tracks would damage them. The *poilus* edged away under their cover.

The interior of the hut was a shambles. Only Roden had survived unscathed, though Buckingham and Grayson were able to walk and the second rifleman could walk with assistance. Grayson was kneeling by Clark, a horror of blood and spilled guts; the two stuffed them into the ruined belly and managed to bind Clark up enough to move him. The 2/25th, by now a mere two hundred yards behind them, were coming up: time to make a run for it.

Roden swung Clark across his shoulders and they dashed for the 2/25th lines, where medical orderlies found a stretcher for Clark and took charge of their own wounded. Clark was still alive as a rescue party from the 2/5th command post carried him away.

Though still bleeding and in great pain, Grayson (who later became a deputy town clerk of the City of Sydney) walked beside him all the way, encouraging him to hang on until Adrian Johnson could fix him up. But just before the group got to the Litani River, Captain Joe Clark died.

Once he had seen Clark, Grayson and the rest safely away, Roden suddenly realised that he had left his Rolex watch behind in the hut. It had been his mother's parting gift to him just before the *Queen Mary* sailed, and so great was this man's presence of mind that even in the midst of the shattered ruins of men and hut, he remembered to take the Rolex off before poor Clark's blood and intestines smothered it. He couldn't leave it there, he simply couldn't! Back he ran under fire, retrieved the watch, put it carefully into his pocket and returned to the staggered men in the 2/25th forward post. No bullet touched him. He knew, you see, for how long Ruby must have gone without, pinched and scraped, to buy that watch.

Clark's death made Roden the only observation officer in the forward part of the advance, and Berryman urgently needed to know what was the situation, whether or not the attack on Merdjayoun should continue. The field telephone was working again, so Roden had a conversation with Berryman. In his opinion, he told the brigade commander, the Vichy French were dithering and unsure how much was being deployed against them. The infantry wanted to hold where they were, having met an assault in the Merdjayoun cemetery which had cost many men, but Roden thought that the infantry should press for another advance and get into the town itself, where cover was better. The Vichy French gunners behind the Balate Ridge would then have to cease firing for fear of hitting their own men. In the end Berryman decided that he would order the 2/25th to hold its present position pending further intelligence from Roden as to conditions inside Merdjayoun.

So it was off to the outskirts of the town, accompanied by five volunteers from the 2/25th Battalion. They managed to penetrate the narrow streets without being detected, and learned that patrols of the 2/25th and the Pioneers had already made contact at Castle Hill on the west. The pincers were closing. Roden got on the field telephone to Berryman and said that an attack on the town should be made immediately. The time was about 3 p.m., and his instructions from Berryman were to register the road in and out of town at a bottleneck which the Vichy French would have to use when quitting the area.

Leaving four of his five volunteers in a house, Roden and one companion, a 2/25th Battalion lance-corporal named Williams,[†] sneaked into the cemetery lumbered with the usual gear of the forward observation officer: a field telephone and a big, heavy coil of cable which they paid out behind them in a way they hoped would hide it from sight. There were a number of tanks growling around through the dirty, dusty lanes, accompanied by transports holding *poilus*, but when shells suddenly started lobbing exactly on top of them, they panicked. *How* did the British know where to direct their fire?

He had ample time to register the bottleneck very carefully against the moment when the Vichy French started to withdraw. Then, as dusk was falling and he and Lance-Corporal Williams were thinking of pulling out, two R.35 enemy tanks appeared. They were lying in a street drain and looking down on a flat turning bay about fifty yards below them; one tank remained in the flat circle, where it was joined by a truck, while the other tank ground up the slope towards them. A detachment of *poilus* jumped out of the truck,

---

[†] Despite exhaustive enquiries, the author has not been able to find out which of the twenty soldiers surnamed Williams in the 2/25th was the man who accompanied Roden.

laughing and chattering, and proceeded to erect machine guns. The second tank stopped before it got as far as the drain, and there was just time to wind the field telephone handle.

'Is that you, Ro? Thank God!' said the voice of Lieutenant John Firth.

'For heaven's sake, don't ring me!'

Hardly daring to breathe, they lay there while the tank clanged and pinged as it cooled off and its crew drifted towards the *poilus*, exchanging idle banter. As long as he and Williams didn't move they were fairly well concealed, but Roden knew that the enemy was massing for an attack on the left, which placed the two of them in a very awkward position. They would have to wait until much later and then sneak through the cheerful, confident enemy lines.

As the night thickened and the Vichy French began to doze, Roden and Williams took off their boots, strung them around their necks, picked up the field telephone and as much of the cable as they thought they could carry noiselessly, and crept off.

The Australian advance was coming into town from the right and hooking around on the left, and what worried Roden more than being shot at by the Vichy French was being shot at by the Australians. When he thought they must be very close to the Australian lines he stood up and called out their names loudly.

'Halt! Who goes there?' came a familiar voice.

'Is that you, Cam?'

'Is that you, Ro? I was just going to shoot you!'

By some amazing fluke, in a unit of a thousand men he had stumbled upon Lieutenant Cameron Robertson, a friend since Economics days at university. They had met again only days before.

Just behind the Australian lines a party from his own regiment picked Roden up; the closeknit 2/5th had a habit of prowling when some of the friends had gone missing, and those not rostered for gun duty would always be there to haul the forward observation officers back into the fold. After a parting word of thanks to Lance-Corporal Williams, Roden and the group from the 2/5th commenced the journey back to the regimental command post.

It was a long way away—six miles of the same ghastly trek down the thousand feet of steep gorge to the Litani and up the other side. Roden was so tired that he literally went to sleep as he walked, alarming the rest of the party so much that they decided he must be wounded after all.

And when finally, dead on his feet, he trudged into the regimental command post, he couldn't sleep—no rocks to lie upon. The date was 21 June, two weeks into the battle for Syria.

But the battle for Merdjayoun wasn't over yet, though the regiment's chief duty became counterfire. A few of the Vichy French guns were very big, up to 155 mm, and the two sides blazed away at each other while ever there was ammunition to do so.

The usual harebrained things happened, like Roden's friend Jack Nagle's foray forward of the lines with a three-ton truck and some gunner friends to pick up badly needed ammunition. They loaded the truck quietly under the Vichy French noses, then drove away tranquilly. To discover when they returned, safe and sound, that the load had weighed nine tons.

Medico Adrian Johnson had been everywhere, mainly helping the battered 2/25th Battalion's medical officer, who was swamped. A dab hand at commandeering Arabs, Adrian Johnson used them as stretcher bearers with such cheerful and friendly courtesy that these usually unwilling people trotted back and forth with their stretchers under heavy fire without turning a hair. At one stage Johnson had no sleep for over forty-eight hours. He could never rest if anyone he knew personally was missing or reported to have been injured, would con a gunner or a signaller into accompanying him on a search mission to locate the victim.

Merdjayoun was an unusual campaign because it fell upon the forward observation officers to keep Brigadier Berryman and command headquarters informed as to what was going on and how the troops were faring. This is not normally the duty of an artilleryman, but in wild countryside wherein mountains had a habit of plunging a thousand feet down to a roaring river, the customary intelligence systems didn't function. Radio was out of the question, nor were there any observation planes; the Vichy French owned the skies.

Many years later Lieutenant-General Sir Frank Berryman told Sir John Carrick that he wished he had had more young officers of the quality of those who assessed the position and kept him informed at Merdjayoun. 'In my experience, the best junior officer from either World War I or World War II was Cutler.' A sentiment about which Cutler himself knew nothing during the Syrian campaign.

Towards the end of the battle for Merdjayoun Roden was despatched with one 25-pounder to cover an attack by the Sixth Division Cavalry Regiment, owner of a few lightweight armoured vehicles. Two tanks came out every morning just inside the Vichy French forward line and fired on them; they just couldn't get rid of the things. Roden remembers that their commander, Major (later Colonel) Denzil Macarthur-Onslow, had a 'Yoicks, tally-ho!' fox hunt approach to combat.

Roden's orders were to fire with open sights on these tanks—a very risky business involving sitting the gun on a hillside a scant two miles from the target with the Marman-Herrington's engine running in case a quick getaway became necessary. Not only were enemy planes a danger, but so was an anti-tank gun emplacement the Vichy French had at the junction of the Hasbaya and Banias roads; it was just as able to shoot at his exposed 25-pounder as he was to shoot at it, which he couldn't do until he got the tanks.

Firing with open sights left no time for instruments. It happened on a 'guess-by-God' basis: the gun commander stuck his arm straight out in line with his eyes, fist clenched, and used the distance between his knuckles as line-of-sight, while range was a matter of instinct and experience. It involved a whirlwind of decisions by the gun commander. In this case, Roden had come armed with the best gun and gun detachment, and they did him proud. They got their shots in very fast and smoothly as soon as Roden made effective corrections. The two tanks were knocked out and the Sixth Divisional Cavalry Regiment was able to tally-ho its way into an attack. Roden then destroyed the anti-tank gun.

When he got back to the command post he discovered that the King's Own Royal Rifles had made the telephone lines hot complaining that the gun's fire had landed on it. Off went Roden to see the irate C.O. of this British unit and explain that the missiles landing on his riflemen were Vichy French mortar shells. But the C.O. insisted that Roden's gun was the culprit.

'Only an infantryman doesn't know the difference between a 25-pounder and a mortar shell,' says Roden in disgust.

By 28 June, Merdjayoun was firmly in the hands of the Australians and the ridges to its north and east, Balate especially, were hammered into subjection.

10th Battery lost one of its 25-pounders when a projectile exploded inside its barrel and bulged it; the gun was permanently out of action. Its replacement had to come from Duku E of the 2/6th, as it had six guns to everyone else's four. There is strong fellowship between artillerymen, and Duku E had been fighting with the 2/5th since the beginning of the battle to recapture Merdjayoun, but some things stick in the gullet, like losing a gun. Number five of Duku E's troop was known to be unreliable, so 10th Battery knew that number five gun was going to be palmed off on it. But 10th Battery was determined that it wasn't going to accept number five gun. The duel of wits was tortuous, but when 10th Battery drove its new gun away, it wasn't towing number five.

The L.A.D. had toiled nonstop throughout the action, mostly hauling overturned trucks or vehicles which had fallen down a mountainside to a place where they could be put back into commission. They also repaired the guns and even manufactured new parts for them. Some of the genuine advances in gun design were first invented by L.A.D. or gun personnel in the field.

At the beginning of July the regiment was moved with great secrecy to the coast below Damour. With it came the 2/2nd Pioneer Battalion from Merdjayoun. The coastal drive had been fought by the 21st Australian Infantry Brigade, to which the 17th Australian Infantry Brigade, back from Greece, had been added. The 17th was severely under strength, hence these reinforcements from the interior. As well as the extra artillery provided by the 2/5th, a battery of Royal Artillery 6-inch howitzers appeared, together with some other small supporting units. Gunfire was also poured in from British naval cruisers off the coast, and there were actually British planes in the sky. General Wilson had decided that here at Damour, where the Vichy French General Dentz had concentrated his main defences, was the make-or-break of the whole Syrian campaign.

Roden travelled with the 2/5th, his feelings as mixed as everyone else's. To move from one theatre of war to another is a refreshing change, but also the unknown factor. So far this hadn't been an idle campaign; the action had been continuous since entering Syria, and the move to Damour did not promise a cessation in hostilities. A lot is written about morale, esprit de corps and the exhilarating effect of victory, but when a body of soldiers is obliged to go week after week without a proper bath or a good meal or clean clothes, even a Harry Peck can get a little blue. To some extent, high morale is dour determination combined with the confidence that comes after blooding. Camaraderie is perhaps more important than morale, unless one chooses to view them as opposite sides of the same coin.

The lie of the land south of Damour was just as difficult as it had been along the Litani, for the Wadi Damour, a very wide river bed here at the coast, had the kind of steep escarpment which rendered forward observation virtually impossible. Nor did radios work; the regiment still had the incubus of the field telephone about its neck. The cheering news was that there were actually reports on wind velocity, barometric pressure and air humidity. And at last there were decent maps. The artillerymen who fought at Merdjayoun used maps on a scale of a quarter-inch to the mile; the entire sector measured 3 × 3 inches (75 × 75 mm). These sweat-soaked and tattered squares pulled out of shirts were all they had to go on, though anyone with talent was put to drawing panoramas. Now they even had a survey unit!

The 2/5th, including Duku E, was accommodated around Jiye, well south of Wadi Damour and, though on relatively high ground, beneath a mountain which the Vichy French artillery used for ranging. The regiment's wagon line was stretched all the way back to Saida, fifteen miles south, and meals for the troops closest to

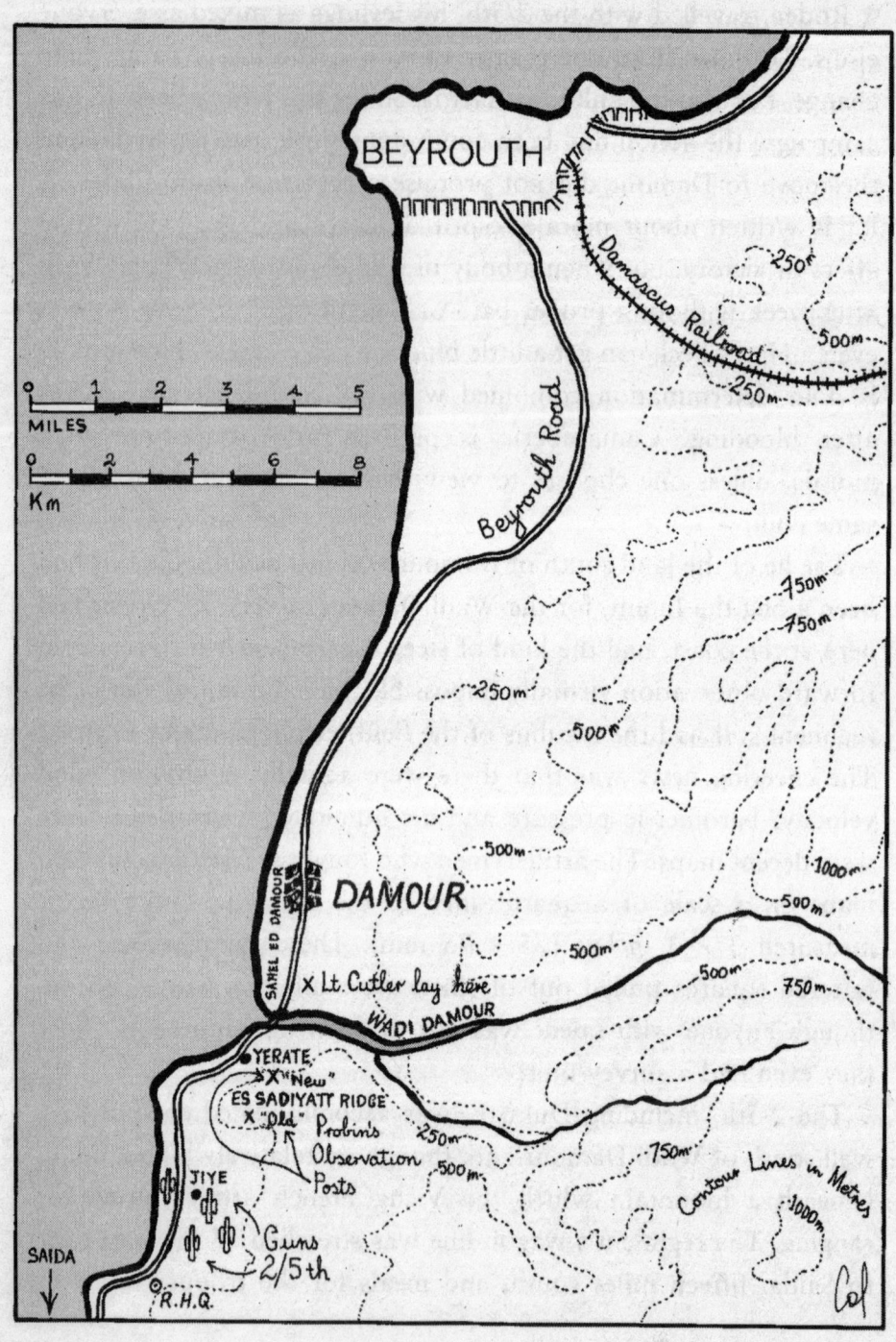

BEYROUTH

Damascus Railroad

Beyrouth Road

250m

500m

250m

750m

750m

250m

500m

500m

1000m

500m

DAMOUR

SAHEL ED DAMOUR

X Lt. Cutler lay here

WADI DAMOUR

500m

500m

750m

YERATE

X "New"

ES SADIYATT RIDGE

X "Old"   Probin's
            Observation
            Posts

250m

500m

750m

1000m

JIYE

Guns
2/5th

Contour Lines in Metres

SAIDA

R.H.Q.

MILES
0 1 2 3 4 5

Km
0 2 4 6 8

Cd

Wadi Damour had a long journey. One troop of guns had to be set up in the midst of a banana grove, where it was certainly invisible from the air or the heights east of Damour, but the growth was so dense that it proved impossible to site the guns absolutely parallel with each other, an essential for gunnery.

The general battle plan required that the infantry, having crossed the bottom of the wadi, should mass for attack on the north bank, facing a flattish area of banana grove jungle from the Beyrouth road westwards through the Sahel ed Damour to the sea. Once the troops were in position at the startline, a lifting barrage would precede them as they moved north; the assault was confined to the area of the Beyrouth road because east of it the land rose precipitously to the thousand-metre contour line, and to the west of it the banana groves were literal jungle. Damour itself straddled the Beyrouth road a little over a mile beyond the Wadi Damour bridge, which the Vichy French had already blown up (the Australians replaced it with a temporary structure, but as far as the general battle plan was concerned, there was nothing to transport that needed a bridge). Not a large town, Damour was nonetheless distinguished by having a number of sizeable buildings on its outskirts, suggesting that there were industries in the area.

The trouble was that the ground at the southern escarpment of the wadi reared much higher than the northern one where the infantry startline was; it then flattened out in the Yerate area before suddenly and steeply rising to the Es Sadiyatt Ridge, behind which were the British gun emplacements. This meant that though the guns had superb views of Damour itself, the wadi and the first thousand yards beyond its north bank were completely invisible. The Vichy French still held the south bank of the wadi and Yerate in strength; observation posts closer to the wadi would have to be put in enemy territory, though the 2/5th was busy firing into the Yerate sector.

The two brigade commanders, accompanied by their artillery officers (C.O. John O'Brien of the 2/5th and Captain Harry Probin of Duku E), made a personal reconnaissance on 3 July, battling their way over trackless terrain at less than a mile an hour. As a result, Probin went forward and established an observation post on the Es Sadiyatt Ridge, where he hoped that the north bank and the thousand yards beyond it would suddenly come into view. He was disappointed. Though the observation post to become known as 'Probin's' was dangerously unprotected, it still failed to register those crucial thousand yards. The only way to monitor progress of the infantry across them was to send a forward observation officer into battle among the advance units.

During the night of 4 July the ammunition was trucked in (500 rounds per gun); next morning all the guns were to register on a building to the east of the Beyrouth road known as the 'blockhouse'. Unfortunately no two observation officers could agree on the identity of the 'blockhouse', so a new target had to be selected. It looked like a brewery—horrors! No artilleryman wanted to carry the stigma of having bombarded a brewery. Then news came that the structure was a silk mill, which was all right. Observation Officer Hodge registered the factory so accurately that one of his rounds punched a hole in its chimney.

The fire-plan for the assault on Damour called for the full gamut of programmed shooting:

- Concentrations of fire were to be put down on the enemy defences south of Damour town, while harassing fire was to be directed simultaneously up and down the length of the Beyrouth road.
- A preliminary barrage was systematically to search every inch

of the north bank and the wadi itself.

- A protective standing barrage was to be directed at the north bank of the wadi just before the infantry moved to its startline.
- This box barrage was to persist as the startline was reached.
- Once the start was made, the main barrage was to roll forward 100 yards ahead of the infantry through the Vichy French defences.
- Duku E was to direct a curtain barrage to the east of the Beyrouth road to prevent troops from straying too far east.
- The southern section of the Sahel ed Damour was to be subjected to an enfilade[†] barrage after the main barrage was finished.
- The naval vessels offshore were to direct their fire at coastal installations.

This immense fire-plan was all the two brigade commanders and their artillerymen could do to protect the foot soldiers, for there was no armour to roll ahead of the infantry thrust. Save that there were no horses, it was almost nineteenth-century war. And the first phase of it entirely depended upon the forward observation officer's ability to keep in touch with the artillery.

In the early afternoon of 5 July, the 2/5th C.O. summoned Roden to regimental headquarters and informed him that zero hour for the big push on Damour was to be shortly after midnight on 6 July—less than twelve hours away. Roden was to be the forward observation officer attached to the spearhead force, 2/16th Battalion, composed of men from Western Australia. He was to take Lieutenant Trevor Macmeikan with him as his junior support

---

[†] An enfilade barrage is fire brought to bear into/onto the enemy's flank.

officer, and liaise through the 2/5th's second-in-command, Major Bruce Watchorn.

'It'll be a bit of a holiday for you, Cuttles,' John O'Brien said. 'You'll have a box seat at the show—nothing to worry about, we and the Navy will be sending everything we have at them. I know you're overdue for leave, but you're the only one I've got left for the job. The rest are dead.'

A little later Roden and O'Brien met with Watchorn, who told Roden that the forward observation officer's telephone line would be taken cross-country towards the Wadi Damour from Probin's observation post on the Es Sadiyatt Ridge. Rendezvous with the 2/16th unit was to be at Probin's observation post.

'Which unit of the Second Sixteenth is it?' Roden asked.

'I'll let you know later,' said Watchorn.

After he parted from O'Brien and Watchorn, Roden went to find a friend from Economics at Sydney University, Jack Robinson, who was a sergeant in signals with the 2/5th, and asked him to organise getting the telephone line up to Probin's, together with enough cable to carry forward with him after Roden met up with the unit from the 2/16th Battalion.

And that's that, thought Roden. But what neither he nor Jack Robinson knew was that at 5 p.m. on this day, Forward Observation Officer Probin moved his post a whole mile closer to Wadi Damour. The field telephone went to the old post. Not Probin's fault—the message about his relocation wasn't passed on.

Hearing nothing further from Watchorn, Roden enquired if there were any further instructions yet: Watchorn said no.

Why then didn't he feel good about it? What was wrong, what? Something *was* wrong! And suddenly he knew what. This was it. This was the mission from which he wasn't going to come back.

Family matters tremendously to Roden; he went to find his cousin

Bob Milligan, who was off duty in anticipation of the coming night's work, as indeed were most of the 2/5th's men.

'Let's go for a swim, Bob.'

The two of them scrambled down to one of those beautiful beaches with aquamarine water which make the coast of ancient Philistia so bewitching. They stripped off, dived in, swam about. While they dried themselves in the long gold rays of the sun Roden told Bob Milligan that he was going up as F.O.O. that night to the attack and that he had a presentiment he wouldn't return. A long-time member of the 2/5th, Bob Milligan had seen enough and been through enough not to want to argue and to keep the emotions he was feeling under some degree of control. Roden asked him to collect his things and keep any among them that he could use.

They parted, Bob desperately worried. Further instructions had come through from Major Watchorn: Roden was to go along the track skirting the Es Sadiyatt Ridge in the direction of the Wadi Damour bridge until he came upon a disabled Vichy French anti-tank gun just opposite another track leading upwards. A guide would be there to conduct him to the rendezvous.

Just after darkness fell Watchorn told Roden that it was time to go. Roden and his junior support, Trevor Macmeikan, each armed only with an officer's revolver, set off along the track. A long trudge later and sure enough, there was the anti-tank gun—but no guide. They waited for a while—still no guide.

'Maybe,' said Roden, 'there's another gun somewhere else.'

They started walking again, getting steadily closer to the wadi and further away from Probin's observation post, hundreds of feet higher and a thousand yards behind them. Or what they thought was Probin's.

Suddenly just to the side of the track, a looming shape in the night, stood a disabled Vichy French anti-tank gun. Beside it was a soldier from the company of the 2/16th Battalion to which Roden had been attached.

No one had realised that there were two anti-tank guns at two different intersections on the track nor, back in the 2/5th command post, had anyone yet understood that Probin had moved his observation post a mile closer to the Wadi Damour.

With sinking heart Roden understood that the place to which he was led was not the place where his field telephone and spare cable were located. The company commander was one Major A.E. Caro, and he wasn't very pleased when Roden told him that he had neither telephone nor wire. All he was carrying in person was his radio.

'I'll have to go back and find Probin's O.P., then I'll catch up with you,' said Roden.

'You've got a radio,' said Major Caro.

'Yes, but it will be useless, sir. Believe me, radios just don't work in this sort of country. I have to go back and find my telephone,' said Roden.

The men of the company were tense and edgy; this was the big night and no one wanted to hear about artillery blunders. Major Caro insisted that he be accompanied by a forward observation officer because he didn't want to see his men blown to pieces by fire from their own side.

'The radio *will* work, it's not all that hilly,' said the Major, growing more irritated.

'Sir, it won't,' said Roden. 'I have to have a telephone.'

A junior company officer sneered. 'You're yellow!'

There was silence for a moment, then Roden shrugged. 'All right, I'll come with you, but I'm warning you, the radio won't be operational,' he said.

By now it was nearly midnight and Major Caro wanted to move

out. The trek to the wadi over this rocky landscape would be a long and arduous one, and he wanted to be at the wadi the moment fire lifted further than the north bank and the startline.

So it was Trevor Macmeikan who had to leave the company and wander about in the darkness looking for Probin's. He knew as well as Roden did that the radio would be useless, and he was frantic. Then, well after midnight and in the midst of the huge barrage, Macmeikan encountered Gunner Ron Reid of 10th Battery.

Reid had experienced his own chapter of disasters. When he and his party, carrying cable, finally reached what they believed to be Probin's to find no one and nothing there, he contacted 10th Battery and learned that Probin had moved onwards about a mile. Perhaps because of the noise, which must have been deafening at 10th Battery's command post, whoever Reid was talking to misunderstood the situation and ordered Reid to return to base. Reid protested and tried to explain that he had to carry on, but the voice was adamant: return to base. On the way down from old Probin's he and his companions became separated, and he was on his own when he chanced upon Macmeikan.

A lot of time elapsed before a party from 9th Battery, the lost souls from 10th Battery, Macmeikan and Reid finally met up with Major Watchorn on the track junction to Es Sadiyatt Ridge.

It was easy now to sort out the confusion, but everyone knew that it was much too late to help Roden Cutler. Still, they tried. They strung cable up hill and down dale, but by dawn the Wadi Damour was still ahead of them, they had run out of wire, and the infantry assault had begun.

The 2/16th Battalion company reached the last stretch before the Wadi Damour to find that the Vichy French dug in on this near side were provided with watchdogs; they began to bay and yammer, and the mortar shells began to rain. A huge projectile fell to earth not twenty feet from where Roden stood, but it failed to explode.

Ah, thought Roden, that's something in my favour!

The heavens erupted into fire; the barrages began and were to continue unabated for the next six hours. Six hours of brilliant, flaming sky, of invisible missiles screeching, whining, whistling overhead, the massive Navy shells roaring and thundering like a fleet of express trains. Up in the hills to the south the men of the 2/5th and other units laboured, stripped to the waist, feeding their guns until relieved, when they would fall to sleep right beside the gun wheels, oblivious to the racket just above their dreamless heads.

The moment the fire lifted out of the wadi the soldiers scrambled down to the Damour River, a knee-deep and sluggish stream at this time of year. They waded through it, raced to the north bank and went to earth under a ledge at its bottom, there to wait until dawn.

Of course he had been right; the radio didn't work. Roden crouched with the rest and waited for the command to move forward, aware that all he had was an officer's revolver. No one had a spare weapon to donate to him, one of the finest shots in the army. And it was terrifying. The waiting always is.

The sky was alight with gunfire but the first streaks of genuine dawn hadn't yet appeared when the company stood up to loosen its muscles and took off at a run up the north bank of the wadi. Ahead was barbed wire; Roden hung back until it was cut and the men were away again, still running, then he followed with revolver drawn. But the pace was too precipitate. No one saw the machine-gun nest save Roden. Its inhabitants were stirring, as they too had grown used to sleeping through barrages; it was the sound of boots aroused them. Everybody in the company was ahead of him, everybody was going to be mown down. Waving his revolver,

Roden leaped feet first into the nest among the three legionnaires it contained. Confronted by six feet five of steel-helmeted Australian, the Vichy French put their hands in the air and were shepherded outside.

These were French Foreign Legion, the most professional of troops, yet presence of mind on a battlefield is rare, even among professionals. No one tried to overpower Roden, who had spied a second nest. He called out to its occupants to surrender in his atrocious French, whereupon three more men emerged, hands in air.

By now the rear men in the Australian company had noticed what was going on; the six prisoners were disarmed and pushed off to one side. A third and bigger nest opened fire, its crew wide awake. Roden grabbed at a Bren gunner's arm.

'You've got your gun, so give me your Mills bomb,' he said. 'Cover me while I try to get close enough to toss it in.'

As Roden wriggled, prone, towards the nest, the Bren gunner noticed someone moving the machine gun around, and fired a short burst. One bullet went straight through the legionnaire's cheek. That gave Roden time to throw the Mills bomb into the nest, which was a big one built on a zigzag principle; the blast which followed injured no one. The five legionnaires inside had had enough, however, and came out with arms up, a senior N.C.O. in the lead. Even in the midst of so much action, a corner of Roden's mind was busy being amazed at how the pie slices of cheek in the wounded man's face flipped and flapped as he breathed.

There were now eleven prisoners no one knew what to do with. Labouring over his French, Roden told them to walk back to the wadi and give themselves up to the Australians there. They clearly thought that the battle was lost.

Every man going into action carries two things: a water bottle and a field dressing. As the eleven prisoners shuffled off Roden gave his water bottle to the wounded one, for their water was still inside the nest.

But there were more machine-gun nests ahead, too many of them too well dug in and positioned to take front on. This was the kind of situation where drawing down artillery fire became a vital necessity. The laggards of the 2/16th company took refuge inside a small, circular animal pen surrounded by a high stone wall. They had no idea what was going on, whether the assault had succeeded or failed, but it seemed to them that failure was more likely than success. That they were isolated among the enemy. One of them went off to find out what was happening; when he didn't return, another man followed.

There were twelve of them left inside the sheepfold, sure they were surrounded on three sides.

'Look,' said Roden, 'I'm just lumber you have to carry, so I'll take a tack through the bananas and see if I can find my officer and the telephone. Once I call down fire you'll be able to get out.'

The edge of the nearest banana grove was scant yards away; Roden sped to it and ran along its edge. The morning was wearing on, the time about 11 a.m.

He didn't see this machine-gun nest, just inside. Nor did he feel the bullet which smashed his right leg apart below the knee. Blood was spraying everywhere! He saw before he felt a thing, spreadeagled on the ground, the enormous gaping wound on full display because he was, like all the Australian troops in Syria, wearing shorts, his socks slipped down around his ankles.

Two men bearing hand-held machine guns came out of the nest and headed towards him—to finish him off, Roden was sure. But then, close enough to observe their victim's condition, they said a few words to each other and returned to the almost invisible nest. No point in wasting a bullet, the *cochon* was nearly dead.

The first thing to do was to stop the bleeding. His field dressing was no use, couldn't hope to plug or cover the hole in his leg, its bones sheared and splintered, flesh mangled. A tourniquet. A tourniquet—*what*? His lanyard! He detached the thick piece of cord connecting the butt of his revolver with his shoulder and wrapped it about his thigh just above the knee, then twisted it until the blood stopped spurting. After that he managed to squirm out of his shirt, tore it into strips, used some of it as a pad and the rest as a bandage.

There was no shade where he lay and the sun seemed to stay at its zenith forever and ever; the heat was intense, his shirt no longer shielding his skin. Thirst raged, but he had given his water bottle away. And the pain! Oh, God Jesus, the *pain*!

Every so often he loosened the tourniquet, understanding that the shattered leg had to have its share of oxygen lest it died. But *he* couldn't die!

The sky whirled, consciousness began to slip away, yet he knew the moment it did he would lose control of the tourniquet; he would bleed to death unknowing. Whatever he did—however he did it— he *had* to stay conscious.

Despair came as the unbelievable, unbearable pain grew even worse; his head turned, his eyes contemplated the revolver. One shot to the temple and it would all be over, this terrible, remorseless, ghastly pain ... Then he thought of his mother. What would she do if he died? How would she manage if she was cut off from the allotment automatically deducted from his army pay because he was dead? What would happen to Geoff, to Rob, to Doone if he died? His father had died, and think how dreadful that had been. If he died, who was there to look after them?

Darkness fell, the damp chill of night invaded his almost bloodless body. The pain ground on, the gunsmoke reeking the air was gradually dwindling before the eternal mystery of the stars. How long had it been? How long would it go on? He couldn't die, he *couldn't* die!

The machine-gun nest was utterly silent; perhaps the men in it had stolen away, though Roden never knew that answer. But suddenly the eleven soldiers from the sheepfold were gathered around him in the night.

They had heard the machine-gun fire, heard Roden cry out in a great voice, 'My God, they've got me!'

Someone had actually brought his army greatcoat into battle with him; the men buttoned it and slipped a rifle through each arm, then lifted Roden onto this makeshift stretcher. He could not help the groans and cries as they bore him up, began to carry him. After a short walk they put him down, terrified that some enemy post would open up on them; they were still under the impression that the attack had failed, that there was no help this side of the wadi. They had drunk all their water so had none to give him, though they promised in whispers that they would come back for him as soon as they could. Roden thinks they were absolutely sure he was going to die.

About his own height away from where the soldiers left him was a little irrigation channel, and he could hear the water gurgling and chuckling as it flowed along. Tongue swollen, he tried for hours to reach that elusive sound, bury his head in it, but no matter how he tried, he couldn't get there.

Dawn came. The bananas rustled and sighed, but he was even further from their shade. The water splashed along its channel, he could hear the faroff sounds of artillery, some cruiser firing a round—BOOM! The leg when he looked at it was grossly swollen, the flesh beginning to blacken. And the pain just went on and on and on. Even so, he regularly loosened the tourniquet, noticing that the blood didn't spurt much any more. So tired, so very tired ...

Thirsty, so thirsty! The blazing summer sun beat down, beat down ... Ants. They swarmed to dine on his leg.

No one was going to come, he understood that now. Noon went, the sun began its westerly slide. He had been there for more than twenty-four hours.

At the 2/5th command post Roden's absence went unnoticed all day on 6 June. Everyone was exhausted after firing a six-hour barrage, and lack of reports from a forward observation officer had meant that the first thousand yards of the attack had had to take place without gunfire lifting before it. The best the artillery had been able to do was concentrate upon what they could see beyond that. During the afternoon of the 6th the brigade commander asked for another enfilade through the Sahel ed Damour; a lot of soldiers were stuck at the southern end of it not very far from where Roden lay, though other infantry groups had penetrated further forward than command headquarters realised.

At 10 o'clock on the night of the 6th a message came to the 2/5th that Roden Cutler had been hit; the assumption was that this had just happened, rather than happened twelve hours earlier. C.O. John O'Brien went out to see if he could locate Roden in the banana groves, but found nothing.

By dawn on the 7th, the hunt was on with a vengeance. Dr. Adrian Johnson, so good a friend of Roden's that Ruby thought of him almost as another son, went down beyond Yerate to the edge of the wadi, then led his party down into the wadi and began to search up and down its length. Not long afterwards he found a dozen wounded Australian soldiers and got to work amid the bursting shells and shrapnel; a surveyor helping him was wounded in the chest. One more to treat.

No sooner had Adrian Johnson finished with them than Sergeant Jack Robinson appeared in the wadi; he had spent the night in the Sahel ed Damour because someone told him Roden was there. They armed themselves with as much emergency medical equipment as they could carry together with a stretcher, then set off up the north bank and into the mess of barbed wire and war detritus between the wadi bank and the commencement of the banana jungle. There they found four French Foreign Legionnaires, one an N.C.O., all disarmed but not under guard. Between sign language and halting French, Johnson and Robinson learned that the legionnaires had encountered the retreating soldiers from the sheepfold and noticed that the enormously tall officer was no longer with them. The soldiers simply passed on and left them to their own devices; now they communicated to Johnson and Robinson that they thought the enormously tall officer was either dead or wounded.

Hearts hammering, the two gunners walked with the four legionnaires to their own machine-gun nests, then on to the sheepfold, and so down to the edge of the banana grove nearby. And there they found Roden, still alive twenty-six hours after he had been wounded.

The legionnaires thought kindly of Roden; he had helped the wounded one (long since vanished with the rest). While Adrian Johnson applied a Thomas splint to the ghastly-looking leg, Jack Robinson gave Roden water and the four prisoners stood watching. When the 2/5th medico gave them the signal, they got Roden onto the stretcher (little wonder the earlier attempt to carry Roden on an army greatcoat had provoked such agony—until the Thomas splint was applied, all that held the leg together was muscle).

The N.C.O. was very concerned. '*Doucement, doucement!*' he kept crying while they lifted Roden. 'Gently, gently!'

There is an old, blurred, black-and-white photograph of Roden being carried down the road on the flat section towards Yerate by four combat-clad legionnaires, his friends from the 2/5th flanking them and Vichy French shells bursting athwart the road behind them.

Near Yerate was a mud-brick hut used as an animal shelter; the floor was smothered in dung. There the legionnaires handed the stretcher over to three men who had brought a utility truck forward at Adrian Johnson's orders earlier in the day. It was hidden from the Vichy French gunners behind the hut.

The shells were getting closer. Johnson had just injected another shot of morphine when one exploded just outside the doorless entrance. The blast threw Johnson on top of the ruined leg and Robinson and the others flat amid the dung, but when no second explosion came hard on the heels of the first, the 2/5th emergency party decided it was time to get out. They loaded Roden into the tray of the utility truck and took off at top speed down the road with the Vichy French trying to land a round on them. Bits of shrapnel peppered the utility, but the engine kept going and no one was hurt, even though those in the open back were completely unprotected.

The advance dressing station was a long trip to the rear of the gun emplacements, but regimental headquarters were on the way. Out of danger now, the driver of the truck slowed to a more normal speed. At headquarters he pulled up and the men piled out, yelling that Cutler was found, but he was in a very bad way. While this was going on, Roden, conscious, understood whereabouts he was. His thirst was so insatiable that he had drunk every drop of water Johnson and Robinson had with them; these familiar buildings meant only one thing to him—*beer*. A bottle of this nectar cost a shilling, and each man in the regiment was entitled to two bottles per week. Nothing else would do than two bottles of beer. Adrian

Johnson shouted out for the beer, someone brought it, then the truck got going again.

The first bottle of beer went down without touching the sides, but between the morphine and the sudden surge of alcohol in an empty stomach inside a body almost empty of blood, Roden passed out with the second bottle of beer clutched to his chest. Which was not in very good shape either; at some point while he lay in the open near the bananas his own side had bombarded the area, thinking all the troops were well forward of it. A piece of shrapnel had thudded against his chest on the left side, bruised the flesh and cracked some ribs.

The rest of the journey south towards Saida and the advance dressing station swam in and out; each time he regained his senses he cuddled the beer and felt nothing beyond the agony of being moved along a road pocked with shell craters.

When they reached the advance dressing station he was in a conscious phase; the last thing he remembers before the general anaesthetic took effect was Adrian Johnson ripping his shorts off.

Doesn't hurt a bit, he thought.

The moment he woke he knew that they had taken his leg. It was a crude procedure, what is called a 'guillotine amputation'. Though the wound was well below the right knee, gangrene had set in and was spreading rapidly, so the surgeons simply cut the leg off above the knee without allowing for skin and muscle flaps to cover the stump, which had to drain and receive plenty of air.

His chest hurt, but not because it cushioned a bottle of beer— someone had taken his beer! When an orderly came along Roden's thirst was so great that he was very peevish.

'Where's my bottle of beer?' he demanded.

The orderly blinked. 'I'll find out, sir,' he said, checked the dressings and did all the other minor investigations orderlies were required to do, then vanished. Some time later he returned to do another round of checks.

'Where's my bottle of beer?' Roden asked.

'Sorry, sir,' said the orderly courteously, 'I've been round every pub in Sidon, but there's not a bottle of beer in town.'

It wasn't until weeks afterwards that Roden learned who had pilfered his second bottle of beer; Adrian Johnson and another friend, Volney Bulteau, had drunk it while they waited to see if Roden was going to survive the operation.

His thirst raged without let, he drank gallons and gallons of water. Of blood transfusions he had none, for of blood there was none. All the blood was spilled into the rubble, the dust and the banana groves. To drink copious amounts of water was the only avenue his body had to build up blood volume. He couldn't eat, wouldn't eat. Water! More water, *please*! Always more water.

The advance dressing station possessed no beds; its many patients were accommodated on stretchers laid flat on the floor. Roden's neighbour was a colonel, Selwyn Porter, whose wound enabled him to get around, even if in some pain. Because the battle was at its height the traffic in casualties consumed most orderly time, so it was Selwyn Porter who fetched and carried for Roden.

At the end of three days the medical consensus was that he would probably survive an ambulance journey to the much bigger British casualty clearing station in Haifa. Along with others he was loaded into the vehicle and driven the fifty-odd miles from Saida to Haifa. Another road ruined by shells. Roden yelled in pain, but he was not alone; the interior reverberated with moans and screams from every occupant.

The battle for Damour was still going on, so the British station in Haifa was equally chaotic. Stretchers of wounded lay everywhere, and a man simply had to wait his turn.

It was the custom if going into battle to remove all trace of rank; Roden's revolver and lanyard, hallmarks of an officer, had long gone. Not that he cared. He lay quietly on his stretcher and watched the hive of industry all around him through a haze of pain. Someone came to fumble at his meat discs, two small metal dog tags strung on a sink-plug sort of chain around every serviceman's neck. Army medical procedure was, once a man looked as if he might live, to leave one meat disc on the chain and detach the other, borne away to identify its wearer.

Suddenly a voice cried, its tone aghast: 'Oh! Oh! This is an *officer!*'

Very important to the British, that distinction.

There was a mad stampede to pick up his stretcher, bear it to a small room somewhere in the middle of this local nabob's mansion doing duty as a hospital and put him into bed, change his clothes and give him water to drink—but not enough water.

'By then I'd had it,' says Roden.

The enquiries from the 2/5th and divisional headquarters must have started coming in; someone more senior came along and said to her retinue, 'This officer has to go into the big bedroom with the water view.'

Roden begged and pleaded to stay where he was, that he just wanted to rest, that there was no need, that he wouldn't appreciate a big bedroom with a water view, but the cluster around the bed refused to listen. It was off up the stairs to a room which admittedly did have a glorious view of Haifa harbour, but the trip almost killed him.

Still his thirst didn't diminish. Now he discovered the difference between British and Australian nursing training; the British nurses thought it appalling to drink so much water, and tried to ration it. Had it not been for an Australian night nurse, Sister Gordon, who brought him jug after jug of water during her shift, Roden might not have lived to go further than the big bedroom with the glorious view of Haifa harbour. He couldn't eat. Nor could he stomach the small bottle of warm, syrupy black stout to which all officers were entitled with a meal.

The battle for Damour got itself over; Vichy French General Dentz asked for the armistice he delayed signing until Bastille Day. He was proud of the fact that here at least France had fought well, given an enemy a run for his money. The war would not end with the British and the Germans able to say that France had crumbled everywhere without a fight. The identity of the enemy mattered little; the important thing was that Frenchmen had fought hard and gallantly to an honourable finish.

Syria had fallen to the British and there only remained the mopping up, to which duty the 2/5th was assigned along with other units; not every French officer had agreed with General Dentz, so there were still flareups.

About six days after he first set eyes on the glorious view of Haifa harbour, Roden was informed that his condition had improved enough to allow of his being transported to an Australian general hospital. He was offered his choice of two such: the Seventh A.G.H. at Rehovoth or the First A.G.H. at Gaza. He knew some people at Rehovoth, but many more at Gaza, where the remnants of the Fifth A.G.H. from Greece had been combined with the First.

'Thank you, I'd rather go to Gaza,' he said.

It never occurred to Roden—in fact, it seems still not to have occurred to him—that he was being talked about in very high military circles. A mere lieutenant (he had been about to be made a captain, but promotion ceases upon an incapacitating wound), he had been given the best room in the Haifa casualty clearing station, then he was offered his choice of hospitals.

The journey to Gaza, about a hundred miles to the south, was done on a train. A hospital train. The patients were put on stretchers and slotted into racks along each side of the carriage like meat pies on trays in a delivery van. The train arrived in the middle of the small hours to the usual blackout regulations. The nurses and doctors came down to the train and personally dealt with transfer of the men to the hospital.

Brigadier Frank Berryman got in touch with Kingsley Norris, head of the Australian medical support services in the Middle East, and asked him to make sure that Roden Cutler got the best of everything; Berryman's opinion of 'wet' Cutler had changed poles, as Sir John Carrick was to confirm later. Every eminent man in Australian medicine serving in the Middle East would see Lieutenant Roden Cutler, from the neurosurgeon Rex Angel Money to the chest physician Edgar King. Even those on the staff of the First A.G.H. read like a list out of a *Who's Who* of New South Wales medicine after the war: Lorimer (Professor Sir Lorimer) Dods, Sir William Morrow, and many more. Including Adrian Johnson, who was to marry the sister of their 2/5th friend Jack Nagle, and become a distinguished Sydney dermatologist.

It must be borne in mind that the quality of medicine for the time was excellent, but that medicine in 1941 was only remotely like medicine at the dawn of the new millennium.

He had visitors while at Gaza, one just after he had arrived there: his cousin Bob Milligan.

Though the action at Damour was over, Roden knew battle orders still prevailed, so he stared at Bob in amazement.

'For heaven's sake, Bob, who was mad enough to give you leave at a time like this?' he asked.

'I didn't bother to get leave,' said Bob simply.

He had gone A.W.L. A signaller, he had found it easy to pinch a motorbike, which he fuelled by signing for petrol at British depots, gone to Haifa and then followed Roden's trail down to Gaza.

Roden was winded. 'Bob, they can shoot you for deserting under fire! Go back—*now*!'

'You're more important to me, Ro. I couldn't bear it a minute longer, everyone saying you couldn't possibly pull through—I had to see you for myself,' said Bob.

It took a great deal of persuasion to convince Bob Milligan that Roden was sure he was going to live, that everything was all right—if he'd survived thus far, he'd certainly survive Gaza!

They talked about Ruby and the rest of the family; Roden was adamant that his mother not be told what had happened, though Bob thought it inevitable that she would find out.

Eventually Bob climbed back on his motorbike and returned to Damour, signing for more petrol at British depots. If anyone had noticed his absence, no one had reported it.

Adrian Johnson came whenever he could, another who told Roden that Ruby was sure to find out about his condition and his leg. Oh, he didn't want that! Not yet. Not for a long time to come.

Thinking Roden was dying, C.O. John O'Brien sent him an 'in requiem' letter that said men like Roden Cutler and Joe Clark had given the regiment 'a soul above butter and guns'.

At first Roden was put into a cubicle on his own, lapping up water to his heart's content. One of the first to pop in and see him was Mollie Nalder, his table companion in the officers' dining room on the *Queen Mary*. An eternity ago for both of them. She and some of the other nurses when on leave would spend a part of the tiny amount of money in their paybooks on eau de Cologne for Roden's back rubs; the hospital methylated spirits was very raw stuff. They loved him, which means that he was a courteous, co-operative, uncomplaining patient. Nurses have their own ways of assessing patients, and a man's looks, no matter how tall, dark or handsome he might be, do not earn him eau de Cologne in an army general hospital during a war.

At first Roden did well after he was transferred to Gaza, started to eat, grew less thirsty. His weight had gone down from 200 pounds (90 kilograms) to 133 pounds (60 kilograms); he 'looked like a bag of bones'.

Then he began to have shortness of breath and his temperature went up. The shrapnel blow to his chest, not of itself so serious, had been festering through those long days of terrible pain and too much immobility. He had developed empyema, a collection of pus between the lung and the pleura (the envelope wrapped around the lung) in what was called the pleural cavity.

Antibiotics scarcely existed save for a few early forms of sulphonamide which were known to be toxic in the high dosages required for grave infections. Nothing for it: the pleural cavity would have to be drained surgically. His condition went down so rapidly that Bill Morrow decided they couldn't move him to an operating theatre. The accumulating pus would have to be drained right there in the cubicle. So they rolled him over onto his stomach, drilled a hole through a rib and pushed the tube through it until it pierced the pleura. Atmospheric pressure inside the pleura is less than that of air, therefore the moment a connection is made between the outside air and the pleural cavity, the lung collapses like a pricked balloon. It can no longer do its job of putting oxygen in and taking carbon dioxide out of the bloodstream. Luckily this was the left lung, the smaller of the two.

Lorimer Dods concluded that Roden was in shock and would have to have a transfusion of blood. This precious fluid had just arrived from Jerusalem, where it had been donated by the civilian Jewish population, no lovers of the Vichy French. Having given his opinion, Dods went off elsewhere on his busy rounds.

The doctor instructed to give the transfusion to Roden was Dr. Noel Bonnin, who had been in the Middle East long enough to understand that there were many perils for blood on the trip from Jerusalem to Gaza. Two other soldiers had already been given some of this shipment of blood; both of them died.

The transfusion apparatus was readied, but news of the two deaths gave Bonnin pause; he demanded to see the blood, and pronounced it unsafe. There was some argument about the matter, but Bonnin held firm. After finding a volunteer with the same blood type as Roden, he took new blood and gave it to Roden, sure that it was fresh.

Afterwards Dr. Noel Bonnin had words to say to a very senior man from Headquarters, with the result that he was 'loaned' to the British Eighth Army—in a *transfusion* unit attached to the 1st Scottish Mobile Hospital. Whoever did the posting had a rather nasty sense of humour. Roden didn't find out about Dr. Bonnin's fate until 1987. There can be no doubt he saved Roden's life.

Best that Roden should have company and be under someone's eye constantly; the First A.G.H. didn't have sufficient staff to maintain a nurse permanently by Roden's bed, so off he went to the ward. Propped upright, hooked up to various tubes and pulleys, the faithful 'sucker' sitting on the floor pumping away, he looked like a Heath Robinson cartoon. The other men in the ward referred to the big glass jar of frothy-topped muck perched on the sucker's platform as 'Cutler's brewery'.

His condition began to improve again; he was allowed to lie at a more comfortable angle and the drain was removed. Cutler's brewery was no longer in production.

He began to get out of bed to have a proper bath—what utter bliss that was! And then one day a nursing sister announced that he was to go for a ride in a wheelchair about the hospital's grounds. Roden felt as if there might be a faint ray of light at the end of this tortuous tunnel. Oh, the sun! No, not the most fetching of hospital surrounds, between the dust and the dirt, but better by far than lying in bed.

Ten minutes into the perambulation, the orderly behind him at the chair handles and the nursing sister beside him chatting cheerfully away, he started to gasp.

This time the right lung was in trouble, and there was absolutely nothing could be done. The left lung had not yet reinflated, so he was going it alone on a member which now threatened to desert him too. Everybody knew this was the end; by the middle of the night Roden's bed was encircled by every doctor and nurse available. It is never easy to lose a patient, but the more the patient has been through and the braver his battle to live against all odds, the more intolerable death is. After *so much*! It just wasn't fair, it wasn't fair!

Propped bolt upright again, he gasped, choked, hacked weakly, wondering if he had the strength to knock on the Pearly Gates. Something inside his chest seemed to break, he felt suddenly so much worse, as if he were drowning, and started to cough with all his might. Cough. Cough. Cough. Cough. Until the dam burst. He coughed up what seemed like pints of blood and pus, the doctors and nurses encouraging him, flying off with one bowl, presenting him with another.

And that really was the first faint light at the end of the tunnel. He began to get better, properly better. Or as properly better as a man with one leg can get.

He has never said what went through his mind during that long convalescence in Gaza, with the worst of it over and the long haul levelling out. When he learned that his mother knew what had happened he had a nurse friend take a picture of him in a wheelchair, positive that he looked chipper, unworried. It was sent off to Manly.

His army career was certainly over, though it had never been a true career, nor had he become enamoured of army life.

'Can't I stay in the Middle East?' he pleaded when two doctors came to assess him for the Department of the Army. 'Surely I could do a useful job in Cairo?'

The answer was no. He was going to be shipped home.

But he did make one very illuminating statement to Mollie Nalder, who spent a lot of time with him at Gaza. They had been reminiscing over the fuss which had ensued after she took Roden down to the beach with some other patients. The day had been so perfect; the water twinkled and sparkled, a translucent blue-shot green and calm as the Mediterranean can be, since it has no tides to torment it. She caught the look on Roden's face, came to a decision.

'Come on, Ro, let's get you into the water,' she said.

The sheer heaven of that swim! For the first time since the leg had come off he felt as if his body belonged to him.

The fuss blew up because the group had been seen taking Roden into the water; Mollie Nalder was reported. Her crime was not frolicking with a bunch of male patients on a beach in a strange land. Her crime was that she had taken a handicapped patient into the water and let him swim out. He might have—he might have *drowned*! The punishment for a crime as capital as this was to be sent back to Australia in disgrace, and for a while it looked as if Mollie would indeed be sent home in disgrace. Cashiered, permanently besmirched. But then it blew over. Who knows why? Who knows who said what to whom?

Anyway, now they could laugh about it. And about other things. The conversation turned serious; Roden spoke of his mother, wondered how she felt about the leg. Communication with one's family was very difficult. No telephone calls, just letters which took forever to arrive or looked like windowed skyscrapers, so many words had been neatly cut out of the text. A Red Cross friend, Betty Larke, had been to see him and tell him that someone, presumably his mother, was bombarding them with enquiries about his condition.

How would he manage when he did get home? It was nearly November, he had been in hospitals since 7 July, and he had no idea what was going to happen to him after he got back to Australia.

'Though,' he said finally, 'I expect what I'll wind up doing is selling matches on the concourse at Wynyard station.'

Very illuminating, that statement to Mollie Nalder.

For most of the hours and days and weeks and months he lay in a bed or travelled in a wheelchair or got around on crutches he must have thought about little beyond the mess his future promised to be. What use was he now, a cripple? The Army didn't want him. Why would anyone in civilian life? Sooner or later the war would be over and the soldiers, the sailors, the airmen would return, most of them in one piece, and all eager to carve up the civilian roast among them. How could he possibly help his mother in this parlous state? What *would* become of him?

At the beginning of November, Roden got his marching orders back to Australia. But before he went Brigadier Frank Berryman sent his car and driver to Gaza to pick Roden up; he was to have the opportunity to say farewell to the regiment. Oh, what a pleasure! There was Adrian in the back seat! Though Adrian had visited whenever he could, it was terrific to have the chance to sit at their ease (the roads were in much better repair than they had been on that ambulance ride to Haifa) and talk, catch up.

Adrian himself had not been well; he was, in fact, to be invalided back to Australia shortly after Roden, having suffered a series of illnesses. Apparently it did not occur to Roden that this was pretty special treatment for a lieutenant, chauffeured in the brigadier's car, though of course he *did* know it was; he put it down to kindness, was intensely grateful, thought no more about it. Perhaps the chief emotion it aroused in him was pure satisfaction that Berryman had about-faced on the subject of wetness. This was Berryman's way of apologising, simple as that.

In Beyrouth, where divisional command headquarters were located, they stopped to have dinner at the mess with Berryman himself. He was very much the affable host, introduced Roden and Adrian to all sorts of top brass; what Roden remembers most vividly is that the dining table had a glass top, under which a mass of flowers was arranged. Quite stunning. Not so surprising in the Lebanon, a country of urbane and sophisticated French-educated people.

After dinner the car went on to Tripoli, where the 2/5th had its headquarters. That was a grand reunion, though some of the old faces were gone. Major Bruce Watchorn had been transferred to a staff position. And there was a new battery, the 55th, so the regiment had expanded.

He was regaled with lots of stories about the concluding days of the battle around Damour—which Roden had not been there to witness, of course. Like the one about the commander of the 212th Battery of the Royal Artillery, pressed into service as part of a barrage on a point north of Damour called 'the road block'. The eight 6-inch howitzers of 212th Battery were nestled at the bottom of a gully just beyond Damour; howitzers can do that sort of thing because of the high, soaring trajectory which makes a howitzer a non-gun. C.O. O'Brien visited the 212th Battery in person to make sure the battery's commander got the fire-plan—after all, he *was* an Englishman. O'Brien discovered him sprawled in an easy chair on a vined terrace, shaded by an awning. At his side was the telephone. Having perused the fire-plan, he picked the receiver up and in a pear-shaped accent relayed the orders to his command post, very visible a mere fifty yards away, then hung up. He could have walked across! thought O'Brien.

'Oh, fraightfulleh sorreh, didn't offer you a cup of tea! Do have one!' said the battery commander.

Well, there were still thirty minutes until zero hour, so O'Brien accepted. The tea was poured by a turbaned Indian servant; while this ritual was going on the 212th Battery commander pensively contemplated his neat row of massive howitzers, then proceeded to chat to O'Brien on every subject under the sun save Damour and the coming barrage—cricket, the weather, a decent cup of tea, the memsahib.

Zero hour came. The howitzers sat all in a parallel row as quiet as mice. The battery commander picked up the telephone.

'Have you cracked orf yet?' he asked his command post.

'No, sir,' came the answer, equally pear-shaped.

'Well, crack orf, old man, crack orf!'

Five minutes later the howitzers cracked orf, right on target if not on time. Deafening.

The regiment was pioneering a new foot-firing mechanism designed by Gunners Hogan and Douglas, Roden was told; with it, a layer should be able to make every round a hit. Later on, well after Roden had departed for good, Gunner Bob Valler of 55th Battery got six hits in quick succession on six different and fast-moving targets while demonstrating the new gear.

A wonderful visit, too quickly over. Adrian Johnson was with him on the way back as well. They detoured up into the high mountains to a ski resort—there was snow everywhere in early November—and stayed overnight at a hotel called, appropriately, Mon Repos. The bathtub was a beauty, hugely wide and long, and hot water gushed forth like a geyser. The most considerate of nurses, Adrian got Roden in and out of the bathtub: a born dermatologist. Dermatologists don't like to see people hurt.

Next day it was back to Gaza and farewell to Adrian, who returned to duty in Tripoli. Brigadier Frank Berryman had done Roden proud.

Within a week Roden was informed that he would be going home on a Dutch hospital ship, the *Oranje*. With the 49 pounds of kit he used to carry on his back in pre-leg days and his tin officer's trunk, he was loaded into an ambulance and conveyed to El Kantara on the Suez Canal, where the Sixth A.G.H. was situated. More fuss! What *was* going on? Between bouts of fending off twittering nurses and probing doctors, he rested and fumed and wondered why so much exasperating fuss. When he wondered aloud, a nursing sister told him he was going to be awarded a decoration. So the Military Cross really was going to come through. But why so much fuss? Unwarranted.

They asked him whether he preferred to embark on the ship as walking or carried wounded; since he was quite knacky on his crutches now, Roden elected to be walking wounded. Whereupon they put him on a stretcher anyway. Why ask? thought Roden, fuming.

Thus he arrived in Suez and alongside the *Oranje* on a stretcher, an orderly hovering nearby. The next moment his stretcher was deposited on a platform, the orderly hopped on too, and both of them were lifted high into the air. It seemed like hundreds of feet to Roden, who had been given enough medication to be drowsy in that spinning, disembodied fashion medication induces. But once the platform was plopped on the deck he reached for his crutches and announced that he was going to walk.

'Oh, no, you won't!' said a New Zealand nursing sister.

Off down the faintly humming passageways on his stretcher, growing steadily more disorientated. They passed a door which said BAD HEER.

'Well, this is a hospital ship, so I suppose that's the ear, nose and throat department,' said Roden to himself.

Next moment they passed a door which said BAD DAME.

'Wacko, what service!' said Roden to himself.

Male and female bathroom in Dutch.

He slept very well for a very long time, knew nothing about the flurry of leaving port.

The *Oranje* was a big, speedy vessel built as a one-class ocean liner; she had been converted to a hospital ship with intelligence and professionalism. Though her passengers were New Zealanders and Australians, her medical crew was Dutch, as was dour and reserved Captain Potger. She had been painted white from stem to stern and bore gigantic red crosses on her sides, her funnels, her stern, any place the eyes peering through a submarine's periscope might see. One of the most stringent rules of war was that no vessel or vehicle painted with huge red crosses could be fired upon, so Captain Potger hustled the *Oranje* out of Suez harbour and into the Red Sea the moment he was informed that all his passengers were aboard. His ship was not escorted, nor was she part of a convoy. Hospital ships could sail the high seas safely. However, knowing that fact did not prevent his pushing the *Oranje* along as hard as he dared; the water broke in glassy curls on her bow and hissed along her hull.

Because the patients were Australians or New Zealanders, the Dutch medical staff had been supplemented by two New Zealand women, Sister Porteous the nurse and a physiotherapist whose name Roden cannot remember. A team of three Australians, two doctors and a nursing sister, made up the liaison staff: Colonel Galbraith, Major Major and Sister MacFarlane. Roden had a particularly soft spot for Sister MacFarlane, a delightful woman. Later on in the war the same three—Galbraith, Major and MacFarlane—went down with the hospital ship *Centaur*, torpedoed and sunk with the loss of almost all hands by a Japanese submarine. No rule is sacrosanct forever. Captain Potger was also to be the victim of a torpedo, on a different ship—not a hospital ship—in the North Sea, by a German submarine. He survived.

There were no ports of call for the *Oranje* as she steamed steadily eastward, stopping occasionally to bunker, then away again. It was a pleasant voyage, so different from the one that brought them to the Middle East and combat. Plenty of space, lots of tender loving care and attention, edible food, the stunning cleanliness for which the Dutch are justifiably famous.

After zigzagging through the islands, straits and channels of the Dutch East Indies, the *Oranje* docked at last in Sabang, a tiny, almost-island attached to the west coast of what was then called the Celebes, now called Sulawesi. The wife of the Dutch Consul-General in Sydney at that time was working aboard the ship as a volunteer nurses' aide; her name was Michelle Elink-Schuurman.

And there it was again! The Dutch colonel-administrator of Sabang arrived and rushed straight up to Roden, who was on his crutches beside Michelle Elink-Schuurman. The colonel-administrator was diminutive in size, but he went right up on his toes and tried very hard to kiss Roden on each cheek, a salutation which greatly embarrassed Roden. *Why* did this sort of thing keep on happening? *Why* did half the world—even in a lost corner like Sabang!—make such a fuss about what was, after all, only a Military Cross? Yes, a Military Cross was very nice if they insisted he deserved one—though he didn't think he did, and had said so—but a lot of chaps were awarded Military Crosses. Grr!

From Sabang the *Oranje* entered the Indian Ocean again to sail down the coast of Western Australia, that arid, cheerless littoral the Dutch navigators of the seventeenth century thought worthless, despite Dirk Hartog's pewter plate hammered in 1616 to a post by the shore at Cape Inscription. If only they had known of the riches beneath this brazen red landscape!

It had become the daily custom to go up to the lounge just before noon to hear the BBC news. Perth was drawing near when Roden, carrying the book he was reading, joined the group clustered around the wireless. He listened to the major news—Japan was expected to declare war any day—but the tailend stuff he deemed boring, so he moved into a corner, sat down and opened the book *With Malice Towards Some*.

A shadow darkened the pages. Roden looked up, brows raised.

'Are your Christian names Arthur Roden?' an acquaintance asked, expression peculiar.

'Yes.'

'Well, mate, you've got the Victoria Cross.'

'Ha, ha!' said Roden with heavy irony.

'You have, you really have! It was on the news!'

'A mistake,' said Roden, closing his book because all the people in the lounge were beginning to crowd around him.

A hospital ship is a dry ship. The only way a patient can obtain alcoholic beverages is to produce a doctor's prescription. Among the throng congratulating Roden was the Dutch physician responsible for his care. Suddenly Roden found a little piece of paper in his hand: it said, R_X *Champagne ad libitum.* A carte blanche for as much champagne as he could drink for as long as he wanted to drink it!

A bottle of good French champagne cost twelve shillings and sixpence, which made a big dent in an army paybook, especially because no one was permitted to have more than five pounds at infrequent intervals unless special permission was given.

He didn't believe it, he just didn't believe it. There was bound to be a mistake somewhere. But everybody else believed it, and that meant he'd have to do the right thing and send the French champagne around that night in the officers' dining room. So he took himself off to see the paymaster and explained his problem. After much hemming and hawing, the paymaster agreed to let him draw ten pounds. That bought sixteen bottles—enough. There were riotous toasts, clinking glasses, beaming congratulations.

But he didn't believe it. There was bound to be a mistake somewhere. *The Victoria Cross?* Not King nor Country could honour a man more than by awarding him a rather dowdy-looking bronze Maltese cross dangling from a plain, dull red ribbon. All it said was FOR VALOUR. A mere handful of men won it. To the best of his knowledge, only three had been given out to Australians since the beginning of the war—three among eighty thousand men. They won it for dazzling feats of arms—they were front line troops! Not artillerymen. He had not done one thing more than anyone else had done—wasn't that what he had said after Merdjayoun when the C.O. told him that Brigadier Berryman was recommending him for the Military Cross?

'I'd rather you didn't,' Roden had said then.

'Why on earth not, Cuttles?'

'Because the last thing I want is to walk around sporting a medal. It'd be dreadfully embarrassing! It'd set me apart from the other chaps, and I'd hate that.'

'The other chaps think you deserve it too, Cuttles.'

'No. I've done nothing anyone else hasn't done.'

Though he had written to his mother to give her the news that he was being promoted to captain and was being recommended for a Military Cross, he had not felt entirely comfortable about it within himself.

But a *Victoria* Cross? No, there had to be a mistake. It was a dream, it wasn't really happening, they had the name wrong, or there was an Arthur Something Cutler in the British Army. Oh, this was awful! The *Oranje* would dock in Perth and the whole ship's company would learn that Arthur Roden Cutler's Victoria Cross was just a figment of some wireless announcer's imagination.

It was Friday, 28 November 1941.

THE CITATION

'For most conspicuous and sustained gallantry during the Syrian Campaign and for outstanding bravery during the bitter fighting at Merdjayoun when this artillery officer became a byword amongst forward troops with whom he worked.

'At Merdjayoun on 19th June, 1941, our infantry attack was checked after suffering heavy casualties from an enemy counter-attack with tanks. Enemy machine gun fire swept the ground, but Lieutenant Cutler with another artillery officer and a small party pushed on ahead of the infantry and established an outpost in a house. The telephone line was cut and he went out and mended this line under machine gun fire and returned to the house, from which enemy posts and batteries were successfully engaged. The enemy then attacked this outpost with infantry and tanks, killing the Bren gunner and mortally wounding other officers. Lieutenant Cutler and another manned the anti-tank rifle and Bren gun and fought back, driving the enemy infantry away. The tanks continued the attack, but under constant fire from the anti-tank rifle and Bren gun eventually withdrew. Lieutenant Cutler then personally supervised the evacuation of the wounded members of his party. Undaunted he pressed for a further advance. He had been ordered to establish an outpost from which he could register the only road by which the enemy transport could enter the town. With a small party of volunteers he pressed on until finally with one other he succeeded in establishing an outpost right in the town, which was occupied by the Foreign Legion, despite enemy machine gun fire which prevented our infantry from advancing. At this time Lieutenant Cutler knew the enemy were massing on his left for a counter-attack and that he was in danger of being cut off. Nevertheless he carried out his task of registering the battery on the road and engaging enemy posts. The enemy counter-attacked with infantry and tanks and he was cut off. He was forced to go to ground, but after dark succeeded in making his way through enemy lines. His work in registering the only road by which enemy transport could enter the town was of vital importance and a big factor in the enemy's subsequent retreat.

'On the night of 23rd–24th June he was in charge of a 25-pounder sent forward into our forward defended localities to silence an enemy anti-tank gun and post, which had held up our attack. This he did and next morning the recapture of Merdjayoun was completed. Later at Damour on 6th July, when our forward infantry were pinned to the ground by heavy hostile machine gun fire, Lieutenant Cutler, regardless of all danger, went to bring a line to his outpost when he was seriously wounded. Twenty-six hours elapsed before it was possible to rescue this officer, whose wounds by this time had become septic necessitating the amputation of his leg. Throughout the Campaign the officer's courage was unparalleled and his work was a big factor in the recapture of Merdjayoun.'

So reads the official citation published in the *London Gazette* on 28 November 1941.

The *Official War History* has the following to say:

'The artillery observers' line had been cut by shell-fire and the artillery team—Captain Clark, Lieutenant Cutler and Gunners Grayson and Buckingham (of the 2/5th Field Regiment)—and a few infantrymen who were with it were attacked by two of the tanks, which were followed by about fifteen French infantrymen. Cutler and Lance-Corporal Pratt (2/25th Battalion) each opened fire on the tracks of the tanks with anti-tank rifles and saw their bullets hitting, but with no effect except to cause the tanks to lurch and seek shelter. Thereupon Cutler and Pratt exchanged their anti-tank rifles for a rifle and Bren gun and fired on the enemy infantry, who took cover behind a stone wall and replied. The tanks advanced again and opened fire with their turret guns. The second shot killed Pratt, fatally wounded Clark, and wounded Grayson. Cutler took up an anti-tank rifle and hit the tanks' turrets, but without effect. Then he fired and hit their tracks, whereupon tanks and infantry withdrew to shelter.'

Here is Gunner Geoff Grayson's recollection:

'Had it not been for Cutler I'm quite sure that tank would have annihilated the lot of us . . . My last recollection is of him shooting, because he continued to engage the tank . . . He was firing at the tracks and he managed to stop the tank, which slewed around and couldn't fire at us any more. He was cool, he was calm, his orders were quite clear and concise. There was not one element of panic and that did a lot to inspire those serving under him.'

There follows the official citation awarding Gunner Geoff Grayson the Military Medal:

'Gnr Grayson acted as signaller to Capt. C.A. Clark during the operations against Merdjayoun on 19th June, 1941. He manned the telephone under continuous enemy fire until the Observation Post was attacked by two tanks and enemy infantry. He, together with three other occupants of the Observation Post, was successful in driving back this attack. During the course of this fighting, Gnr

Grayson was wounded, but in spite of this wound he immediately went to the aid of Capt. Clark, who had been fatally wounded by a 2-pounder shell. Grayson then walked about six miles over very rough country alongside the stretcher-bearers carrying Clark, but he collapsed when within half a mile of a Regimental Aid Post. Throughout the whole of the action, he showed himself a cool and courageous soldier and was a splendid example to others.'

The next item is the abridged text of the covering letter sent by Brigadier Frank Berryman to 'Aust. Div. Exporter'[†]:

'I forward herewith a report by Lieut. A.R. Cutler, describing in plain language the activities of Capt. C.A. Clark and Lt. Cutler. His report reveals a story of persistent thrustfulness and gallantry ... Unfortunately Capt. Clark died of wounds received during the encounter with the enemy tanks, but I should be glad if his gallant conduct could be suitable [sic] recorded if not posthumously rewarded. I have instructed C.O. 2/5 Aust. Fd. Regt. to recommend Lt. Cutler for the Military Cross.'

Lieut. A.R. Cutler's report is very long and exhaustive, varying in some minor details from the two accounts I possess of Roden describing events onto audio tape, but basically it is the account I have given in the description of action at Merdjayoun. I quote only the paragraph dealing with the evacuation of the mud-brick observation post:

'While two watched the flank the rest attended to the wounded. Our infantry had by this time advanced to cover our flank, and all made a dash to safety, two of us waiting and carrying Capt. Clark.

[†] Australian Division 'Exporter' (the code name for the campaign).

Apart from a few stray rifle shots, we were not molested and I began to realise:

'(1) That they must have been unsure of themselves.

'(2) That they apparently were ignorant—as we were to some extent—of the disposition of our forces and of our strength and

'(3) That the Boyes rifle must have troubled them to some extent.'

At no time does the report cover Roden in glory; rather, it is very businesslike and informative, and just a little disapproving of infantry unpreparedness for battle conditions (by that I do not mean the report criticises the troops; rather, it criticises the men who are supposed to train them for combat)—Captain Clark and Roden patiently sat in the thick of it and gave the soldiers, shaken by their first experience of enemy fire, a reassuring little talk about shrapnel.

Which, among other things the report details, gives one a truly heartwarming idea of what a wonderful man Captain C.A. 'Joe' Clark must have been. The bravest of the brave. Yet he was never decorated. He was 'Mentioned in Despatches', despite this long report's apportioning more credit to Clark than to Cutler. In a letter Roden wrote to his mother, he calls Captain Clark 'Alan', not 'Joe', the name given to him in the 2/5th's history.

All of the above is quoted for one reason only: it points up the fact that even a day or two after the battle, no one quite gets the story right. The data I have studied differ in some minor respects. My gift is basically to find the words to bring the story to life, but facts must be adhered to. The trouble is that the actual facts are often smeared with a tidge of camouflage. I do sincerely believe that Roden on tape, so many years afterwards, tells the true story. The first set of tapes was recorded in 1991, the second in 1997, and they duplicate each other. What I say in this brief chapter are my own thoughts, not Roden's. He vouchsafes no judgements whatsoever. But his mind is crystal clear, and no one forgets the kind of experiences he went through in Syria in 1941.

Returning to the Victoria Cross citation, what fascinates me is the paucity of information about events at Damour, which are tacked on almost as an afterthought, stripped of any detail. The answer Roden gives is that he was never officially interviewed about his share in the Damour campaign because of the gravity of his physical condition. Yet what had been a recommendation for a Military Cross on 29 June turned into a recommendation for a Victoria Cross after Damour.

My own opinion is that there were some monumental blunders made at Damour, and that the camouflage took the form of omission.

And that Lieutenant Arthur Roden Cutler, V.C., paid for those mistakes with the loss of his leg.

He remains the only artilleryman to win the Victoria Cross in the history of Australia to date. And, until Leonard Cheshire won his V.C., Roden Cutler's V.C. held the Empire record for the length of the period of action for which it was awarded—some nineteen days from 19 June to 7 July.

ON THE HOME FRONT

'Lieut. A.R. Cutler
2/5th Fd Regt R.A.A.
A.I.F. Abroad
29th June 41

'**M**um darling,
        'I got your 34th letter last night, and you really can't imagine the joy and pleasure I get from letters from home. You doubtless realise that my opportunities for writing now are extremely limited, and yet now, more than ever, I long for home news. Your letters have been arriving fairly regularly, but the others must be suffering from cramp.

'... While we are on the subject, Mum darling, please let me know how finance is with you, because I'm going to increase your allotment. You see George† is now a capt.

'That's the good drill, eh Mum dear? Capt. Cutler M.C. Sounds a bit on the nose doesn't it? Don't address me as Capt. yet, because it has to be gazetted, and I'll put Capt. on my letters, when it is

---

† 'George' was the name Egyptians used when addressing Australian officers. Though the uniforms were similar, they had no trouble distinguishing a British from an Australian officer. British officers wore black boots, Australian officers wore brown boots. To be called 'George' tickled Roden, who referred to himself thus in his letters to his mother.

done, and DON'T UNDER ANY CIRCUMSTANCES PUT M.C. after my name, because I'd feel a twirp. Anyrate the M.C. has not yet been awarded, but as the Force Commander himself recommended me, I suppose I'll get it. You know, dear, it never rains but what it pours, and both promotion and decoration have come at once, but are not connected.

'Unfortunately Col Morris, the Troop Commander, Peter Braithwaite and a signaller were killed on Fri. 13th, and as Col was a capt. it left a vacancy. I was lucky in getting the recommendation to fill the vacancy. And then on the 19th June I was lucky enough to be recommended for decoration. As far as I know it is one of the first recommendations in the Division, certainly the 1st in 7th Div. Arty. The boys in the regt are funny. Not one of them begrudges me all I've got, all of them practically knew of it before I did (one gunner congratulated me 5 days before I knew myself on my captcy) . . . I'm going back to Batt. H.Q. and this will keep me away from any danger—glad? Gee I had some fun though on the 19th Jun., and wouldn't have missed it for the world, except that I would give all to bring back to life those killed not only here, but in this war on the whole. My experiences will be with me all my life, and I'll never forget some very vivid flashes.

'Again the 19th was one of the saddest days possible because Alan Clark, whom I respected and liked, and with whom I've spent some very pleasant leaves, unfortunately was wounded, and died on the way back. I did all I could for him, but it was hopeless.

'I'm getting off the track, Mum dearest. On Bty H.Q. I'll be safe as a house, and the show here is very nearly over—in fact we are being relieved within a day or two, and then they'll just "mop up".

'This letter must be a bit boring because it's been George! George! George!, but still I'm as pleased as punch at the promotion and I know you will be too. I feel that it is all due to you and it is for you that I want to get on. You can tell your cobbers a lot of ballyhoo now, Mum. Crikey it would be crook to be in the offing and have to listen to it all, though.

'Old Bob came over to see me last night, as proud as a puff pigeon, but demanding (demanding! mark you) that I take him with me whenever I move. Incidentally he solemnly ticked me off, told me I wasn't to do it again, and then heaved a sigh as much as to say "Well! I've done my duty." ... We are both looking forward to our first leave and wondering where we'll spend it.

'... Poor old Mum, you must have been nearly run off your feet when you had the whole household down sick. Take it easy, dear, and I'll send you some money to have a quiet fortnight's holiday ... I'll be home very soon, and I want to see you looking fighting fit. Your health means all to me.

'Well, there is not much news this side of the ocean, Mum dear. Nothing exciting ever happens here.

'I'll send you the story of my escapades some day—nothing much to it.

'Well God bless you, Mum. Please give Doone enclosed stamps and give my love to all, and remember me to friends.

'All my love for yourself
'Laddie'

She kept everything. A tiny doily he had drawn a bird on and embroidered when he was Laddie. He seems never to have doubted his masculinity or cared whether some small thing he could do or make for Ruby was 'cissy'. It was all carefully hoarded, and she would go on hoarding everything until the end of her life.

The worry hadn't gone away from the moment she waved the *Queen Mary* goodbye; women of Ruby's generation had gone through the Great War, had waved the soldiers off to the War to End War, never dreaming that one day their sons would follow in Father's marching footsteps to fight yet another war. And the Great War had slaughtered so many! So many. Country dweller though she had been, well did Ruby remember the slaughter, for she had been a woman in her late twenties in 1914.

Everything was so mysterious! Roden's letters never held cut-out windows because he was too intelligent to put a foot wrong where the censors were concerned, but that in itself made the letters vague. She never knew quite where he was. And though he thought the letters gave nothing of his activities away, they are reminiscent of the small child who says, 'I'm not going to tell you what I've got you for Christmas, Daddy, but you can throw away your old wallet.' The one quoted, written at the end of June between the fall of Merdjayoun and the journey to Damour, does its best to lull maternal anxiety, yet the grief of losing comrades in arms cannot *not* be told to this most beloved of all ears. '*Gee I had some fun though on the 19th Jun., and wouldn't have missed it for the world, except that I would give all to bring back to life those killed not only here, but in this war on the whole.*' Much is made of the promotion and of the Military Cross. As things turned out, he was to get neither.

There is nothing to say when Ruby got that letter, whether it was before or after she got the news of what had happened to this most precious son at Damour. Such letters were often months in transit; he had had thirty-four letters from her between his departure on 20 October 1940 and 29 June 1941. That works out to about one per week, but Ruby would have written more often than once a week. After all, the others had cramp, as Roden himself puts it wryly.

She must have hovered near the front gate waiting for the postie to appear in Addison Road every morning and every afternoon; the mail came twice a day—you could set your clock by it—preceded by the cheery shriek of the postie's whistle. But when you have a son you *know* is in the thick of action you don't wait for a whistle right at your letterbox, you're hovering in the vicinity. Not that you fear the postie. He means good news. What sets your knees to knocking and your heart to thumping is the sound of the doorbell— will there be a telegram boy outside holding a small thin envelope as he asks your name? That is how the really bad news comes, by telegram.

That is how Ruby got the news that Roden had lost his leg as a result of battle, and that his condition was 'grave'—the word used in 1941 rather than the modern 'critical'. 'Grave'. A word loaded with significance. The telegram ended with the name Percy Spender. Minister for the Army and also, ironically, the Manly member in the Federal Parliament.

She was found wandering, confused and incoherent, along Manly Beach.

After that came constant bombardment of the Department of the Army, the Red Cross, any institution the family in Sydney could think of to get news of Roden. *Was he still alive?*

Doone was living at home now; she had obtained a job with the Manly Steamship Company (which ran the Manly ferries) as secretary to its managing director. Geoff was in the Royal Australian Air Force, training to get his pilot's wings, though Roden had wanted him to stay out of the services, look after Ruby and Doone. Having begged, pleaded and cajoled Roden into signing the papers permitting him to join the A.I.F. (necessary when the rest of the eligible males were already in the services—policy was that every mother was entitled to keep one son), Rob had left the Bank of New South Wales and was in the Army at Geraldton in Western Australia.

News did come through, but slowly. Yes, your son has lost a leg, but no, your son is not going to die. Oh, people *die* of disease and infections in the Middle East! Your son is not dying, Mrs. Cutler. Yes, Mrs. Cutler. No, Mrs. Cutler.

At some time she got the photograph of himself Roden had sent from Gaza thinking he looked so well. Ruby stared at it and rocked with grief.

When the news broke that he had won the Victoria Cross, a dozen reporters were knocking at Ruby's door. One article in the *Sun* (a Sydney afternoon paper) contained a photograph of her holding a photograph of Roden, smiling and smart in his officer's cap. It concentrated on a story Ruby had told the reporter about Roden, aged fifteen, swimming with friends at Bondi Beach; the shark bell rang, people scrambled out of the water, and there was the dreaded dorsal fin cruising between a friend and the sand. Roden swam out and guided his friend in safely, later describing to his mother how eerie it was to look down and see the fourteen-foot monster just below him. Roden deprecates the story, which is why it was not mentioned earlier: 'Grossly exaggerated!'

Perth saw confirmation of the Victoria Cross. When the *Oranje* docked, the reporters were waiting to see Arthur Roden Cutler, who spent the few brief hours the ship was in port discovering what fame was like; he didn't think it was all that it was cracked up to be. A mercy to be out of there and on the high seas again.

Especially because he had worked out how to keep on drinking champagne. He was not alone in his taste for it; everyone was happy to quaff the odd glass or two of French champagne.

'Listen,' he said to his friends at the dining table, 'my paybook is out of bounds, the paymaster won't let me have more money. But the rest of you can draw your five quids. I have the prescription. You provide the funds and I'll buy the bubbly.'

From then on, his table had a bottle of champagne with dinner every night.

The *Oranje* was just emerging from the awesome waters of the Great Australian Bight, Adelaide around the corner, when the news came through that the Japanese had bombed Pearl Harbor. A shocking disaster, but it had one good side, and one good side only: the United States of America was in the Second World War. Everyone knew that meant the tide was bound to turn sooner or later in the right direction. It wasn't just 'the British' any more— that is, the Empire—it was now 'the Allies'.

More reporters in Adelaide, but Pearl Harbor deflected a lot of attention away from winners of Victoria Crosses, no grief for Roden. And by the time that the *Oranje* tied up in Port Melbourne, the focus was firmly on Japanese intentions in Asia and the Pacific. Oh, good. Sydney would be no different.

In Melbourne the ship stayed long enough for Roden to go ashore, which he did under the clucking thumb of Michelle Elink-Schuurman. They dined at the Australia Hotel—heaven! Melbourne was absolute heaven. Good food, hordes of proper-looking people walking everywhere, not a burnous or a fez in sight, and the smell was *clean*. A faint tang of smoke from a fire somewhere up in the Dandenongs—summer was here—the indefinable scent of eucalyptus—newly mown grass—good old meat pies. There really is no place like home.

But he was tired. Any kind of activity took it out of him these days, and the stump was still draining, naked.

•

One couldn't just sail straight on into Sydney Harbour; a submarine boom had been erected between Watson's Bay and Middle Head, which meant ships caught on the wrong side of it after it was closed had to wait until the following day to proceed. The *Oranje* just made the boom in time, but had to moor at a buoy for the night. The pilot came out to meet the ship, in its stern a piper skirling in kilts and full regalia—for Roden. It was a small sample of what was to come.

Next morning the patients disembarked and were taken to the Sydney Showgrounds (just next to the Sydney Cricket Ground and a hop, skip and jump from Roden's old school, Sydney Boys' High) for their medical check-up. And there waiting were Ruby, Doone, Geoff and Rob.

His mother wept as if her heart were broken, which in a way drew everyone's attention from *him*, and that was good. When his turn came the doctors examined him, informed him that he would have to have a spell in hospital for further assessments—but not, said their chief with a smile, until the New Year. He could spend the rest of December at home with his family. Christmas at 'Kyeema' in Addison Road, Manly.

All he wanted to do was get there.

'Let's take the ferry,' he said eagerly.

The family looked awkward.

'No, we have to catch the one o'clock ferry,' said Ruby, more composed now. 'They're expecting you on that.'

So they were driven into town and had lunch at the Carlton Hotel, then driven to Circular Quay. Its dowdiness looked just beautiful to Roden—the squalor of the Rocks to the west of the cove, the grim grey sheds, the shabby Customs House, the tram depot on Bennelong Point to the east, the tired row of ferry wharves groaning softly, water slip-slapping around their weedy piers. Oh, this was home! How many times had he loped his long legs on this familiar ground, leaped onto the ferry with six feet of water in between—well, now it would have to be on crutches.

There were crowds of people everywhere, and they were cheering him. The one o'clock ferry was decked from funnels to waterline with bunting, streamers, placards saying WELCOME HOME. He felt—he didn't know what he felt, save enormously moved. One trouser leg pinned up, he boarded the ferry while everyone cheered, waved, beamed. The Harbour swam beyond a wall of tears.

All the way to Manly the ferry cock-a-doodle-dooed its siren— these sleek monsters did the trip in exactly thirty minutes. 'Seven miles from Sydney and a thousand miles from care' was the Manly motto. Oh, more people on the Manly wharf! More people than he had realised Manly owned.

The Mayor of Manly, Alderman Bob Miller, mayoral chain about his shoulders, formally welcomed Manly's pride to Manly's shore. Then it was into the back of an open car for the drive down the Manly Corso on one side and up the other, schoolchildren lining the route and cheering, Roden thinks, because they had been given a half-day off school. On the steps of the Manly town hall Roden had to give a speech—not an activity he was accustomed to in those days.

There was another Victoria Cross winner present; the Manly member of the State parliament, Bill Curry, had won a V.C. during the Great War, and during the reception inside the town hall which followed the speeches outside, Bill Curry solemnly warned Roden about accepting drinks in bars because everyone in the bar would want to buy him one and that was the road to drunken perdition. Roden said politely that he didn't think that would be a problem for him.

'Kyeema' at last. Only when he had arrived there and was settled in an easy chair did Roden realise how exhausting the day had been. His tiredness smothered him. But there were many little gifts to open, including a tiny bedside lamp from an elderly retired teacher of his primary school days. She had no money, but she wanted to show him how proud she was. Though the shade was plastic and the bulb soon burned it brown, Roden treasured it. Bed. It had to be bed, while he could still get there. A long, long day. Oh, how good it was to be home!

Where Ruby came into her element at last. She fussed and fetched and carried, kept him in bed for as long as he could stand it, settled him in a comfortable chair under a tree on the lawn during the hottest part of the day. The family finally had the space to see for themselves how desperately ill Roden still was. Other people were not so perceptive, so the stream of visitors seemed neverending; Ruby firmly limited visiting hours to the time Roden spent in the shade of the tree. Reporters came regularly. So, much to Roden's surprise, did artists, from newspaper cartoonists to serious portraitists; he found himself charcoaled, pencilled, pastelled, watercoloured and oiled. He was famous. The only consoling fact was that his fame would pass. There would be more Victoria Crosses, so much was sure.

The months between January and September 1942 were spent in and out of the Prince of Wales Hospital at Randwick, a stately Georgian pile in buttery sandstone on the far side of Sydney from Manly; it was the servicemen's hospital then.

At first the doctors thought the stump would heal well enough to permit of his wearing an artificial leg, but in March they decided that was not going to happen. He would have to have another amputation sufficiently further up the thigh to allow plenty of healthy muscle and skin to form a 'flap'—a properly sealed stump capable of supporting Roden's weight, on the increase at last.

Not that people left him alone for long. With Japan in the war things were more serious on the home front. The far northern parts of Australia were suddenly vulnerable, and in February 1942 the town of Darwin was heavily bombed, with the loss of 243 lives. A tiny drop of life in other places, perhaps, but to Australians? Terrifying. Hong Kong was gone, Singapore was gone, Burma was under threat, so were the Dutch East Indies, which Japan had to have because they produced oil. The only internal resources Japan had in sufficient quantity were citizens and technical skill; it lacked oil, iron, coal, the full gamut of raw materials. Well, the Dutch East Indies had the oil, but Australia had the rest.

Air raid shelters became the rage, and naturally a V.C. winner must know all about air raid shelters. So it was off to 'Kyeema' or the Prince of Wales Hospital to consult the expert, who was simply too sick to care. With a look of mild surprise, Roden answered those who were appalled to discover he hadn't turned 'Kyeema'—so vulnerable, right inside North Head!—into a fortress like John Milford's two doors down.

'The cliff between our house and Little Manly Cove is riddled with caves. Why should I excavate an air raid shelter?'

Not the right answer. As the months wore on the queries and consultations never ceased. What did he think about this, what did he think about that? All he thought about was pain.

In Canberra, the national capital, a great deal had occurred while Roden was away. The Prime Minister, Robert Gordon Menzies, had also gone away. He left Australia in January 1941 and was absent for four months. It was not a jaunt, but it looked like one to many Australians on the home front. Menzies could not have done a more imprudent thing, though it might be debated that what he accomplished in England and the United States could not have been done at long distance. The official reason for his trip was that he was the Australian Government's representative to the British War Cabinet on matters of policy regarding the war.

Always an Anglophile, Menzies' experiences in England reinforced this tendency, and, after he saw how fearlessly King George VI and his wife went among the civilian victims in the burning, crumbling East End, Menzies also developed a passionate affection for and admiration of the British royal family. They lived on the same austere rations as their people, they stinted nothing by way of effort or compassion.

Distance from the home front led to indiscretions: Menzies was quoted in the Australian newspapers as saying in London that he had high hopes for peace in the Pacific and thought Australia could remain friends with Japan. This was before economic sanctions were applied to Japan by Great Britain and the United States of America, but many Australians were terrified of the Asian masses living on their Pacific doorstep—and convinced that Japan was after both *lebensraum* and resources in Australia.

Though Menzies does appear to have realised that Winston Churchill was a colonialist to his bootlaces—the people of the Empire were there, first and foremost, to serve Great Britain—he also admired Churchill enormously; he was present in London to see the British Prime Minister at the height of his reputation and glory. The two men became sufficiently close friends for Menzies to be a rather exclusive guest of Churchill's at 'Chequers', the country residence of all British prime ministers. In letters he described, for instance, his being the third member of a 'Chequers' triumvirate:

the other two were Churchill and Charles de Gaulle. It pleased Menzies that he could participate fully in the hours-long conversation, as he spoke fluent French. Despite his feeling that he was on an equal footing with these two titans, the correspondence betrays a certain naiveté; the colonial boy was party to the doings of the leaders of the free world.

Little wonder, perhaps, that upon his return to his native shores Menzies was acutely unhappy. Australia just wasn't where it was at; where it was at was London, and he hungered to be in London. So his demeanour was chilly, arrogant, patronising. He thanked nobody for running the country in his absence, least of all Arthur Fadden, who had been Acting Prime Minister. Fadden was leader of the Country Party faction of the conservative coalition, and in 1941 rural influence in Canberra was far greater than it is nowadays (witness the change of name from Country to National Party). Nowhere near as urbane, witty or eloquent as Menzies, Fadden knew it. The press could hate Menzies yet never find a way to poke fun at him, whereas the press had a field day with Artie Fadden.

Nonetheless, Fadden had survived the four months he governed Australia with a slender majority in the Senate and a tied House of Representatives; he had kept the two independents, Coles and Wilson, who held the balance of power, on the Government's side. Now here was the real Prime Minister back on the home front, with never a word of thanks. Nor did Menzies thank the Advisory War Council set up late in 1940 at John Curtin's instigation, though it had actually done a good job. This Advisory War Council had become a forum wherein both sides of the political fence could meet in relative harmony and exchange information as well as views. Because of the Government's precarious hold on power, the Labor members of the Advisory War Council had come to wield a peculiar influence; Curtin was a brilliant strategist as well as a brilliant tactician, though sometimes he had more trouble opening the eyes of his colleagues to these facts than he did his conservative opponents.

One sceptical colleague was Dr. Herbert Vere Evatt, who joined the Advisory War Council later in 1941. Evatt had been a formidable but contentious force since he had entered the political arena in the 1940 elections. Neither Menzies nor Curtin was fond of him, Menzies because the Doc had been a judge in the High Court of Australia (the supreme Bench) and should therefore have eschewed politics, Curtin because he didn't approve of the Doc's brand of socialism or his erratic, sometimes bizarre behaviour. Possibly, too, Curtin disliked the Doc's stunning academic background, just as he disliked career soldiers—he himself was not educated in the formal sense.

As June ran into July 1941, while Roden was contending with the Syrian campaign, Menzies grew more frigid and overbearing. Doc Evatt and John Beasley kept putting pressure on Curtin to seize government, but Curtin maintained that he would rather wait until Menzies shot himself in the foot, as he would. He wanted Labor to have a clear mandate without needing to go to the polls. Menzies asked again to form a multiparty 'national government'; Curtin refused again. Resentment of Menzies within his own ranks was fanning from a smoulder to a blaze. The nation was beset by strikes in the most crucial war-effort industries, and there was Menzies not applying all his energies to solving the situation. Both sides of the Advisory War Council were most unhappy. So too was the Director-General of Munitions, Essington Lewis.

And so indeed was Menzies, who yearned to be back in London. When he proposed to his Cabinet that he return to that hub of events wherein the press adored him and the British War Cabinet listened to his opinions with respect, his Cabinet said yes, of course.

But the Advisory War Council said a firm no; it was not appropriate that the Prime Minister of a nation on the brink of war with Japan should go gadding off to the opposite end of the globe on a more or less permanent mission. The holder of this mission was to be the Australian representative to the British War Cabinet; it had taken Menzies time to wangle this concession out of Churchill, but he had succeeded. Now the Advisory War Council said no. If he wanted to be Prime Minister, then he must stay in Australia.

Much has been written about the reasons why Robert Gordon Menzies resigned as Prime Minister of Australia on 29 August 1941, but to this observer at this distance removed in time, the real reason seems glaring. It is unlikely that Menzies' character and personality would have permitted him to admit that *he* couldn't govern, nor does his resignation speech say as much.

'A frank discussion with my colleagues in Cabinet has shown that, while they have personal goodwill towards me, many of them feel that I am unpopular with large sections of the press and the people and that this unpopularity handicaps the effectiveness of the Government . . .'

The speech says neither that the Government couldn't govern, nor that he had been 'spilled' by his colleagues, only that his unpopularity perturbed them. His mood was chirpy, certainly not devastated. Why should it have been devastated? He was going to do what he burned to do: go to London as the Australian representative to the British War Cabinet. It never occurred to him that he wouldn't get the job; it was his idea in the first place, and he was the only one who had the necessary intimacy with London. He could do better work in London than in Canberra.

But it doesn't pay to appear ungrateful or unappreciative. Appointed Prime Minister of Australia on Menzies' resignation, Arthur Fadden promptly gave the guernsey as Australian representative to the British War Cabinet to his old friend, Sir Earle Page. *That* was devastating. Menzies had to be content with the portfolio of Minister for Defence Co-ordination. He had overreached himself and virtually ensured the collapse of the United Australia Party. Moreover, it was to take him years to regain his political credibility.

The Fadden Government lasted forty days, rocked by scandal about a 'secret fund' to counter communist propaganda. Beasley and Evatt renewed agitation to seize power, but Curtin wanted Fadden to present his budget to the Parliament, which he did on 29 September.

On the first day of October, Curtin attacked at last. The Opposition did not object to the *amount* of taxation; what it objected to was the distribution of taxes. Let the tax burden fall on those who could bear it. Labor formally rejected the Fadden budget.

After Ben Chifley paved the way, Curtin talked to A.W. Coles, one of the two independents. On Friday, 3 October, Coles rose in the House and announced that he would vote with Labor against the Government. Whereupon Alex Wilson, the other independent, defected too. Fadden's Government was defeated, 36–33.

John Curtin was sworn in as Prime Minister on 7 October. Francis Forde was Deputy Prime Minister and Minister for the Army. Ben Chifley was Treasurer. Dr. Evatt was Attorney-General and Minister for External Affairs. Norman Makin was Minister for the Navy and Munitions. John Beasley was Minister for Supply and Development. Eddie Ward was Minister for Labour and National Service.

So when Roden returned to Sydney on 13 December 1941, his country was governed by a different party without there having been an election. A general election was not to be held until August 1943. Curtin's strategy and tactics had worked.

Things weren't exactly looking up on the war front, and it was definitely moving closer to the home front. Curtin commenced his duel of wills and wits with Churchill on the subject of the Australian troops in North Africa, particularly those marooned inside Tobruk. Curtin wanted Australian troops home; Churchill wanted them in the Middle East. Nor was Australia informed of the decision reached by Churchill and President Franklin Delano Roosevelt: Hitler first, Japan later. Not exactly Curtin's list of priorities.

Roden's list of priorities was more personal, though his experiences in the Middle East had endowed him with a wish to serve Australia's servicemen. His military incapacitation had put paid to that promotion to captain, and he knew that as soon as the medical authorities decided everything possible had been done for his leg, he would be discharged from the A.I.F. The 'tin leg' was fitted as soon as the reamputated stump had healed to the doctors' satisfaction, though he was on crutches when he was invested with his Victoria Cross on 11 June 1942. The Governor-General of Australia, Lord Gowrie, pinned it on him; curiously, Lord Gowrie had won the Victoria Cross himself during the Great War. Clyde Ingate was there to see it happen. So were Roden's family, Ruby wreathed in smiles.

He had learned all about this dowdy little medal on its plain, dull red ribbon, learned that it had been the idea of Queen Victoria herself after a visit to a hospital near the port of Southampton. There she had spoken to one Corporal Byrne, whose injuries were ghastly, but who had held his ground despite them. There should be, she resolved, a unique decoration which could be awarded to any and all ranks across the full range of armed services; a decoration carrying so much honour that its recipient would be accorded his proper due by the entire British world.

The Imperial Order-in-Council authorising the Victoria Cross was issued at Buckingham Palace on 29 January 1856, and the first ceremony at which it was awarded to the men who had fought in the Crimea was held at Hyde Park on 26 June in the next year. Clad in a modified uniform of a British field marshal and mounted sidesaddle, the Queen herself bestowed her medal on sixty-two recipients; a crowd of over 100,000 watched.

All the Victoria Crosses have been made by the same firm of London jewellers, Hancocks & Company, out of the breech cascabel[†] of a Russian cannon captured at Sebastopol. Contrary to a story that the last Victoria Cross made from this chunk of bronze was awarded in 1942, the author is assured that there is still enough of the original metal left to make almost another hundred.

In the centre of the bronze medal itself is the British lion atop the Imperial Crown; below these is the motto, FOR VALOUR. The medal is attached by a V-shaped arm to a bronze bar adorned with laurel leaves, crimped over the end of a dull red ribbon one-and-a-half inches (38 mm) wide. On the back of the Maltese cross itself is the date on which the deed of valour occurred, enclosed in a circle; on the back of the bar the name of the recipient is engraved. In order to foil forgers, every Victoria Cross bears a secret mark. It must be worn on the left breast, and it takes precedence over any and all other orders and honours given by Great Britain or Australia.

The statistics of the Victoria Cross awarded to Australians are interesting:

Boer War, 1899–1902:	6
World War I, 1914–1918:	64

[†] Breech cascabel: the cascabel was the knob or pommel protruding from the rump of a cannon; the breech plus the cascabel constituted the entire rump end of a cannon.

North Russia, 1919:   2
World War II, 1939–1945:   20
Vietnam, 1965–1972:   4

These figures might lead one to think that as time has gone on personal deeds of valour on the battlefield have grown rarer, given that the number of men enlisted in the First World War is less than numbers for the Second. But the author believes that the last two of these five conflicts saw conditions on the battlefield alter. Opportunities for service above and beyond the call of duty were not nearly as numerous. The trenches of the Gallipoli Peninsula and of Flanders during the Great War of 1914–1918 marked the apex of hand-to-hand fighting, the source of most V.C.s.

All the above notwithstanding, as Roden saw it early in 1942, a Victoria Cross and threepence would get you a pot of tea; he had no intention of frequenting pubs to be bought all the drinks he could guzzle.

Geoff and Rob were both serving, while Doone suffered under the custom of the times, which was to pay women far less than men were paid. Rob had used his leave in Sydney when Roden had come home to transfer from the A.I.F. to the R.A.A.F., and got his pilot's wings in bombers. Then to his dismay he was posted to the same wartime backwater he had endured while in the Army—Geraldton in Western Australia. Later he was a sergeant pilot on the Mitchell bomber, and was based in Canberra. Geoff had become a test and ferry pilot, after which he became part of Toma Squadron and covered the ground action in Borneo.

How was he going to support Ruby? It always came back to that. He was the eldest, it was his responsibility.

During his convalescence in hospital after the second amputation he was skimming the Positions Vacant section of the *Sydney Morning Herald* when he saw an advertisement by the New South Wales branch of the R.S.L.; it wanted a new State secretary.

The Returned Sailors', Soldiers' and Airmen's Imperial League of Australia (known to everyone as the R.S.L.) was, in 1942, an organisation of Great War veterans. It had originally been founded (minus airmen, of course) in 1916 with the aim of preserving the memory and records of all those who served and suffered for the nation, to provide for their sick and dependants, and establish branches in all States with clubs in all possible cities and towns. It obtained the bulk of its funds from 'Poppy Day', on which volunteers sold a little artificial scarlet poppy all over the nation; the poppy was chosen in remembrance of the fields of scarlet poppies in Flanders. Anzac Day, 25 April, was the day on which any ex-seviceman, as well as current servicemen, could join in the march through the nation's streets to the Cenotaph war memorial, there to lay wreaths and remember the dead. Anzac was the acronym for the Australian and New Zealand Army Corps which fought at Gallipoli in 1915.

One of the first things Roden had done when he returned home was to join the R.S.L.; he was, in fact, the first veteran of the Second World War to do so. His motive for joining was simply that he felt he should put something back into the system. One would think that this gesture would have been welcomed, but he was viewed askance. The R.S.L. belonged to the veterans of the Great War, that was how its members felt.

So when Roden applied for the job of New South Wales branch secretary and got it against some forty other applicants, a great many members were hugely affronted. What did this young twirp know about war, fighting, the status of a veteran? The fact that this young twirp had won a Victoria Cross was dismissed. A job that paid 750 pounds per year belonged to someone who had *earned* it! How dared the State executive give it to a kid!

This happened shortly after Anzac Day 1942, and so great was the general dissatisfaction within the R.S.L. that news of it filtered through to Sir Wallace Wurth, Chairman of the State Public Service Board. He called to see Roden and asked him to come back to the public service, admitting that it had never been done to offer to re-employ a man who had resigned, but determined that Roden should be an exception. Roden weighed the 750 pounds the job with the R.S.L. paid against the 250 pounds a public service job would pay, and declined with sincere thanks.

The offices of the New South Wales branch of the R.S.L. were located inside the rather austere but quite beautiful War Memorial built in Sydney's Hyde Park behind a long pool. The author, curiously enough, remembers to this day being taken as a child to the public chamber of the War Memorial and looking down into a well which contained but one object, a bronze statue of a man stretched in agony over a sword. It made a profound impression on a little girl whose relatives had been soldiers, but who knew nothing about the suffering inherent in war.

It didn't take long for Roden, still on crutches, to realise that he was physically unable to make the journey from Manly to the office every day, Monday to Friday. So he moved into the Hyde Park Hotel on Elizabeth Street fairly opposite; it was run in those days by Len Plastoe, whom Roden remembers with affection. The walk was now a mere block-and-a-half, and that he could cope with. He had turned twenty-six that May of 1942.

Most of the internal strife within the R.S.L. arose out of the fact that the Great War had ended a mere twenty-three years earlier, so the members of the R.S.L. were still men in their prime, forties and fifties. Not incapable of being State secretary by any means. Nor did they like the habits and attitudes of the intervening years being disturbed by an ever-increasing flood of youngsters returning to the home front due to battle wounds or other illnesses. The modern R.S.L. club did not exist; these later and far more opulent premises came into being only after the State of New South Wales legalised gambling, and were built on gambling profits. No reflection on the R.S.L.; every kind of patron body did it. But to get an idea of what an R.S.L. club might have looked like just after the Second World War, visit the Norfolk Island R.S.L. Gambling is not illegal in Norfolk Island, but the community will *not* tolerate its overt presence.

Even putting the disapproval aside, the job of secretary was arduous. It need not have been, perhaps, but Roden believed in earning those 750 pounds. Monday to Friday he worked at the War Memorial offices, then on Friday night he boarded a steamtrain and travelled to a club somewhere in New South Wales to talk to the members, discover what their thoughts and feelings were, and give the inevitable speech. He was getting quite good at giving speeches, had learned that he owned the gift of speaking extemporaneously; he would talk to the members, find the kernel he needed, then get up and speak off the cuff around that kernel. By the time he started his Monday to Friday round of duties again, he was exhausted. That seemed to have become a permanent condition.

At which moment the Federal Government in Canberra entered his life in the person of Dr. Herbert Vere Evatt. The Doc invited him to take on an unpaid job as one of the members of a new body, the Aliens' Classification and Advisory Committee. It involved visiting internment camps and writing a report plus criticisms and recommendations. Roden accepted.

The chairman of the committee was the Victorian Labor politician Arthur Calwell, who happened to dislike the Doc with some passion, which made life interesting. Roden's fellow members of the committee were Bill Dovey, K.C.,[†] a highly respected, well-known Sydney barrister who was 'a pretty good cross-examiner but a bit brutal on the witness' (he was later a judge, and was the father of Margaret Whitlam, one of Australia's best known and best loved people); the Victorian Jack Barry, K.C. (also a judge later on); and Sir Walter Cooper, a retired senator from Queensland. Roden was the servicemen's representative.

The committee visited a number of these internment camps, areas designed to detain (behind barbed wire) German or Japanese nationals resident in Australia but not holding British citizenship (there was no such person as an Australian citizen until 1949). Before the Second World War a great many of these almost invariably German citizens had never thought about becoming British subjects.

Conditions in the camps were dreadful. In one such prison outside Adelaide the committee was horrified to see small children being marched off to school under armed guard; in the same camp Roden encountered a man he knew, a German married to an Australian who was, Roden thinks, the sister of the nurse who saved Doone's life, Biddy Morgan. Australia was his *home*! His wife was an Australian, he was a member in good standing of the wool trade—he had just never bothered to change his citizenship.

This camp outside Adelaide was one of the biggest, for a good proportion of South Australia's rural population was German; they

---

[†] King's Counsel. After the accession of Queen Elizabeth II to the throne, it became Q.C., Queen's Counsel. K.C. or Q.C. was a legal accolade confined to barristers—that is, lawyers entitled to practise at the Bar. The present term is S.C., Senior Counsel.

were among the first to establish the wine industry in the Barossa Valley and other places.

Arthur Calwell demanded to see the aliens' files. Dr. Evatt refused. As the attorney-general, he did not see why the committee needed to examine the files. Calwell said that the committee would resign, as it couldn't do its job properly. The Doc's dislike of Calwell was just as strong as Calwell's dislike of him, so he assumed that Calwell was 'having a go', as Australians say. He phoned each of the committee members in turn hoping to find support. Dovey, Barry and Cooper all backed Calwell. It came to Roden's turn.

'*You* wouldn't resign, would you, lieutenant?' he asked; he always addressed Roden as 'lieutenant'.

'Yes, Dr. Evatt, I certainly would unless we can see those files,' said Roden.

The files arrived. They were scrappy and inadequate, and all too often they revealed that many of the internment orders were based on emotions, not facts. 'Oh, heavens, they interned everybody on the flimsiest of evidence!'

So the report when it was issued was damning. Conditions in the internment camps improved a great deal, but to this day Roden is ashamed of how those people were treated.

Aside from infrequent trips to internment camps, the Aliens' Classification and Advisory Committee duties were not onerous; what was wearing Roden down was the R.S.L. job. His chief concern lay in the unwillingness of the old veterans to accept the new veterans. As the months went on he devoted more and more of his time and energy to smoothing down ageing but not yet elderly feathers, persuading people to pull in tandem rather than push and pull. The job was satisfying enough, but the travel made it increasingly difficult to bear.

The artificial leg was a matter of trial and error. In Gaza somebody had written to him and said he trusted that the amputation was below the knee; a man hardly noticed an amputation below the knee, but one above the knee meant an unmanageable limb ever after. This Job's comforter was right. The amputation was high, the result a struggle with or without crutches.

Finally the doctors issued him with an ultimatum: either he gave up the job with the R.S.L., or he sentenced himself to a life in and out of hospital. He feared to give up the job very much. If he did, then people would assume he could not—or would not—work. He would have no further offers.

Dr. Evatt came to his rescue; he seems to have been pleased with Roden's aliens work, unpaid though it had been.

'I'm looking for a deputy director of security in New South Wales,' said the Doc. 'Decent pay.'

'I doubt I have the temperament for spying,' said Roden.

'No spying, lieutenant, just paperwork,' said the Doc.

'I'll do it for six months, Dr. Evatt, see how I go.'

So Roden went to work for the National Security Service, which was the forerunner of ASIO, the Australian equivalent of the C.I.A. Dr. Evatt was correct; the work involved nothing but endless pieces of paper, few of which were riveting.

One aspect of the work, however, did prove fascinating, and that concerned informants. These people were not paid to inform, they simply wrote letters to the Government and eventually their missives were sent to the clerical staff of the Security Service. One such letter enclosed a newspaper photograph of—*himself*! He remembered the occasion the moment he set eyes on it, for of course Ruby had clipped it out to show him, highly delighted that they had made the society pages. They had gone to lunch at Prince's, one of the 'in' restaurants of Sydney at the time, and there he was, standing with Ruby and Michelle Elink-Schuurman, wife of the Dutch Consul-General in Sydney. *What*, asked the informant, was a V.C. winner doing in the company of a woman whose husband was undoubtedly a German spy? The letter was consigned to the circular filing cabinet immediately.

At the end of the six months Roden had said he would serve in the Security Service, no alternative employment was in sight. Oh, he didn't want to stay in security! Here it was, nearing the end of 1943, and all he had to show for it was a car.

The idea of the car had started when the New South Wales public service took up a collection to buy Roden a vehicle which a man with one leg could drive comfortably. In those days before the automatic transmission was incorporated into automobile design, that meant a very expensive car. It had to be provided with a 'hand throttle'—that is, a hand-operated accelerator—and the same foot could operate both clutch and brake because the transmission was geared through the brake—depress the brake a certain distance, and the gears disengaged. Cars were in very short supply anyway (and petrol was strictly rationed), but the kind of car Roden needed was almost nonexistent. Then, provided that Roden could obtain such a vehicle, there was the cost factor. The public service collection had been generous, but it was not nearly enough.

Six Ford Mercury cars of the right kind were imported into the country; Roden applied for one of them, but had little hope that his request would be viewed favourably. He made it through his local member of parliament, Percy Spender, who had long gone from his portfolio as Minister for the Army (that was in October of 1941). But he was still on the Advisory War Council, which was thriving, so he had clout. And at the beginning of August of 1943 there was to be a general election for the Federal Parliament due to the Brisbane Line controversy, of which more anon.

A great many people had approached Roden to stand for the House of Representatives at this election, and of course the most logical seat for him to contest was Manly, his own home territory. Percy Spender's seat. He was offered other seats as well, and from both sides of the political fence: a Labor offer here, a United Australia Party offer there. To all of them he said NO.

'I have never been political, Mark,' he was to say years later to his youngest son. 'The denigration of character and all the rest of it—quite frankly, politics was a game I had neither comfort nor confidence in.'

But Percy Spender didn't know that. Roden got his Ford Mercury car, which made a huge difference to the ease of his life.

Who produced the rest of the money for it? Aunt Dais.

For John Curtin the years since he had assumed the prime ministership were not easy either. 1942 had seen both joy and terror. Much joy upon the high seas, between the naval battles of the Coral Sea in May and Midway in June. He had won most of his encounters with Winston Churchill; only the Ninth Australian Division remained in North Africa, and it was to come home a year after the Sixth and the Seventh. The others were either in Japanese prison camps (the fate of many in the Eighth Division) or up to their necks in the Pacific war. Terror was Kokoda, the New Guinea campaign between July and November 1942. After their defeats at sea, the Japanese high command decided to launch a land attack on Port Moresby, capital of Papua New Guinea and gateway to north-eastern Australia. The attack was spearheaded from Rabaul, at the northern tip of the big island of New Britain, was to land on the north coast of New Guinea in the Buna-Gona-Salamaua area and cross the towering Owen Stanley Ranges by a pass that didn't exist called the Kokoda Trail. The hideous struggle along the Kokoda Trail ended with the Japanese driven back to the Bismarck Sea; they were never to get so close again.

Curtin's policy from the beginning had been to co-operate with the Americans; he held no faith in Great Britain's ability to protect any Pacific nations, had been sceptical of Singapore before Singapore fell. His hopes were pinned on the United States of America, and he felt that this country was far more Australia's natural ally than Great Britain. His greatest military friend, however, was General Thomas Blamey, whom he elevated to the status of Commander-in-Chief of Australian Military Forces. Blamey did not quite fall into the category of a Duntroon-trained career army officer: them Curtin despised, calling them 'scoutmasters'.

At the end of 1942 the Minister for Labour and National Service, Eddie Ward, accused the Menzies-Fadden Government of endorsing a military plan which drew a defence line across the continent of Australia at the latitude of Brisbane. It came to be called 'the Brisbane Line' and the political furore was to rage for a year. The trouble was that Ward's accusations also called into account Curtin's own Government, as the report upon which Ward based his case had been issued by General Iven Mackay (a Menzies appointee) in its original form on 14 December 1941, to Francis Forde, Labor's Minister for the Army. A revised memorandum by Mackay was presented to Cabinet in February 1942 and Cabinet rejected it, saying that all the people of Australia must be protected. Then General Douglas MacArthur got into the act by confirming on radio that the Brisbane Line did exist. The trouble was that Labor had been in office for six months by the time MacArthur arrived in Australia, so his statement impugned Labor too. The tenor of MacArthur's speech was typically grandiose: *he* would save Australia because it couldn't save itself. Pressed to produce further evidence, Ward alleged that the relevant paper had gone missing from the official files; Curtin denied this, demanded and got an apology from Ward. Then Arthur Calwell in Caucus accused Curtin of intending to defect and form a 'national government'. Fadden moved a vote of no-confidence in the House and was narrowly defeated; as an election was due, it would be held now.

Thus the election on 1 August 1943 was fought on the Brisbane Line. Labor won control of both houses of parliament, but the whole business took a terrible toll on Curtin's health. When Caucus insisted that Ward be given a ministry (he had been suspended from Labour and National Service pending the results of an enquiry into the missing document), Curtin retaliated by making Ward Minister for External Territories—still, over half a century later, the Outer Mongolia of all portfolios.

The tide was turning in the Pacific as well as in Europe; there were 820,000 Australians in the armed services, including 40,000 women, which wasn't bad for a nation that had not yet quite reached the seven million population mark.

It was growing ever clearer, however, that for both New Zealand and Australia the ties to Europe in the form of Great Britain were gradually unravelling; to use Geoffrey Blainey's phrase, the tyranny of distance ruled all other considerations. There were further disappointments for both countries. At the Cairo conference between Churchill, Chiang Kai-shek and Roosevelt, the shape of the postwar world was defined without thinking of consulting the two orphans down there in the Antipodes.

●

Towards the end of 1943, the Prime Minister contacted Roden and offered him another job. The Government, Curtin explained, was reorganising the Repatriation Department, that branch of the federal bureaucracy which looked after veterans' affairs. It was going to be expanded, and the present board of three commissioners wouldn't be able to handle everything—the steady flow of men back to the home front through injury or illness was increasing, just as the number of men under arms was increasing. There were hospitals to build, pensions to structure—so much! To help get things moving, two assistant commissioners were to be added to the top civil service echelons, said Curtin. And he would very much like Roden to be one of the two. The salary would be one thousand pounds per annum. The only hitch was that the job would be in Melbourne.

A thousand pounds a year! *A fortune!* This time Roden did not hesitate: he said yes, please.

His two Labor fairy godfathers were a startling contrast in almost every respect. John Curtin was self-educated, words did not come easily; he looked the complete intellectual, from his round, wire-rimmed spectacles to the detached expression he so often wore. Herbert Vere Evatt of the splendid academic background looked like everybody's favourite uncle; he was zany, bouncy, cuddly. Neither man was particularly tall.

As Roden was packing up his things and clearing his desk at the Sydney offices of the Security Service, the door flew suddenly and noisily open and a woman appeared in its aperture.

'Yes, madam?' asked Roden politely.

'I'm Jessie Street, and I'm taking your job here. Just wanted to see what you look like,' said this extraordinary person, then departed as abruptly as she had arrived.

She was an extraordinary person. On the one hand she was the wife of a judge of the Supreme Court of New South Wales; on the other hand she was politically somewhere to the left of Karl Marx and a militant feminist not far from the time when they had been called suffragettes. Her split-level life was to grow worse after her husband was knighted in 1956 and she had to suffer the indignity of being addressed as 'Lady Street'. When Sir Kenneth became Chief Justice and Lieutenant-Governor of New South Wales it really was complicated; upon receiving an invitation to an official function, Sir Kenneth would say that he had to consult his wife, then he would inform the person issuing the invitation that thank you, neither of them would attend, or thank you, he would attend but Lady Street would not.

The move to Melbourne was a sadness because it meant Ruby and Doone wouldn't see him as often as they had; he loved to take his mother to spiffy restaurants or—especially now he had his car— on picnics to some quiet spot around Sydney. But his duties, as he understood them, would necessitate his travelling to Sydney occasionally, so Melbourne wasn't a complete exile.

He had met a girl in Sydney during 1943, one of those odd encounters which, had it happened in any other way, might never have drawn her to his attention.

Of course he was highly visible to women, between the height and the face and the war hero status, but their ploys to attract him tended to discomfort him, especially if they were, as people said then, 'forward'. Many an eyelash was fluttered, many a heavy hint dropped into the conversation, but Roden, without realising it, only added to his desirability by being elusive. Happy to go out with a party including women, the only woman he was seen with alone was his mother.

Adrian Johnson was back in Australia, so too were other army friends, and parties—even on wartime ration books—were fairly frequent.

One such party was held at the Ditfords' house. Bill 'the Bull' Courtney, Roden's old battery commander in Syria, had come home, and Nell Ditford, who was his sister, invited Courtney's friends over to celebrate. She also asked some of her own crowd; among them were two sisters, Joan and Helen Morris. Joan was in the Navy; Helen had just completed her training and was a private in the women's army.

After one of the women in the lounge room unbuttoned a mortified Roden's shirt and then wrote her telephone number on his undershirt in lipstick, he retreated in terror to the kitchen, where—it was a typical Australian party, women in the lounge room, men in the kitchen—he had a far more enjoyable time talking to his male cronies. Nell Ditford entered, frowning.

'Ro, will you do me a favour?' she asked.

'Of course.'

'There's a very nice girl in the lounge room who refuses to take off her hat. She's just finished recruitment training up at Ryde, and they've dinned it into her head that if and when she meets a V.C. winner, she has to salute him. Well, she knows that you're here, and she can't salute you without her hat on, so she won't take the wretched thing off,' said Nell Ditford.

Back to the lounge room, where the young servicewoman, very neat in her uniform, stood among the rest. No need to ask which one; a number of the girls were in uniform, but only one was wearing a hat.

The moment Roden walked up to her she snapped to attention and gave him a smart salute.

'Now you can take off your hat,' said Roden, smiling.

He thought her charming, was immediately attracted to her. Very composed, very polite, very well behaved. No need to fear that *she* would give him her telephone number unrequested, even on a piece of paper, let alone in lipstick on his undershirt! She wasn't short, but she wasn't overly tall; her figure was very feminine, small in the waist, generous above and below, and she had, he noticed appreciatively, excellent legs. Her face was not beautiful, but he thought it pretty, and her smile was enchanting; widely set hazel eyes, clear skin, softly curled brown hair a little tumbled from the hat.

When he went to take his leave of Bill and Nell Ditford, he found the Morris sisters departing too, and offered them a ride home in his gleaming Ford Mercury car. They demurred, as they lived in Fairfax Road, Bellevue Hill, only a few blocks from where the Ditfords lived in the more exclusive of Sydney's eastern suburbs. Roden insisted, the two girls accepted, and he drove them those few blocks.

Two weeks later he asked both of them—he was cagey, was Roden—to dinner at the Hermitage, a French restaurant in Angel Place, downtown Sydney. A good time was had by all, but he did not tender them another invitation. Helen looked older than she was; she was actually only nineteen.

He didn't precisely forget Helen Morris, but there were many reasons why he didn't pursue the acquaintance. Chief among them at that time was his leg—how could any woman cope with that ugly, offputting stump? Nor was he sure that he would ever be able to support a wife and family as well as Ruby, whom he just could not let go short of a thing. The job as an assistant repatriation commissioner was still in the future.

●

So he went off to Melbourne still heartfree, there to assume his repatriation duties.

He found Melbourne a beautiful city, quiet and rather English to someone from flamboyant, razzamatazz Sydney; even in his middle twenties a person of some dignity, albeit genially approachable, Melbourne suited Roden's temperament. Because his own manners were impeccable, he liked to mix with people who shared this quality, and Melbourne abounded with them.

He found lodgings in a building in South Yarra called St. Caroline's; a glorified boarding house, it provided food and also would do washing. Yet it didn't make a huge dent in that thousand pounds a year salary. The Great Depression and his father's death had left a permanent mark on Roden, who liked to know that there was something put by for the future.

The Chairman of the Repatriation Commission was Norman Miles, but he had been seconded to the job of Coal Commissioner of Australia, so Jack Webster acted as chairman during Roden's tenure. The two other full commissioners were Bill 'Buncha' Keays and Cyril Smith. Roden's fellow deputy commissioner was Bert Wilkinson, who had been in the Repatriation Department since the Great War and knew all the ropes.

The commissioners worked Monday to Friday and Saturday mornings turn about. Most of the duties of the two deputies had to do with claims made by veterans to the Repatriation Department—pension applications, medical expenses, family hardship and the like. The appropriate section of the department assessed these claims and either approved them or disallowed them. When a veteran appealed against a negative internal decision, the claim was referred on to Roden and Bert Wilkinson. They did not act like judges in a courtroom. Neither the aggrieved claimant nor any witnesses were seen in person; it was all done by studying the files on each case. Some cases required travel to Sydney.

Internal assessment tended to be fairly ruthless, so there were a lot of appeals to scrutinise, and both deputies were of the same mind: a claimant always had to be given the benefit of the doubt. Unless the facts clearly indicated that the claim was not allowable under the letter of the law and regulations, Wilkinson and Cutler would reverse the internal decision. That was sometimes very difficult, as in a special war benefits claim by a soldier whose testimonials all confirmed his actions. The trouble was that Roden had been in the same action and knew that the soldier's claim was false. However, he couldn't permit his personal knowledge of the situation to colour what was a process of due law and regulations. The appeal was upheld. The case of the Don R (despatch rider) who had an accident after a night on the town and was claiming compensation for his injury was a very curly one: was it his fault because he was drunk, or the Army's fault for letting him climb on a motorcycle in that condition? The appeal was upheld.

He had flown down to Melbourne, but as soon as he was settled he booked a room for Ruby at the Australia Hotel, flew to Sydney and drove his Ford Mercury back to Melbourne with Ruby in the passenger's seat. It had taken a little time to save up enough petrol coupons for a V-8 engine purring along the scenic coastal road, but experience had shown that he needed the car. They stopped overnight at this place or that—so beautiful!

For Ruby the trip and her subsequent stay in Melbourne were blissful until she fell and broke her leg. At nearly sixty years of age her recovery was slow, her time in hospital a grind eased only by Roden's nightly visits. When she was discharged he put her in the

Majestic at St. Kilda, where he too now lived; St. Caroline's had decided to convert to apartments, whereas he needed his laundry and cooking done for him.

And of course there was only one way to get her home to Manly: by air. Even getting on a plane was next to impossible, but Roden, a veteran of this kind of thing, slipped the counter clerk some cash and got two tickets.

His mother was absolutely silent, gripped his hands in terror. So as soon as the aircraft levelled out he bought two brandies with dry ginger ale. Then he bought two more. Ruby relaxed her hold, knuckles pink again. Luckily the flight was a smooth one—a long, propeller-driven drone. She looked out the window, marvelled.

'This flying business,' she said then. 'Is this all there is to it?'

'Yes, Mum.'

'This is the way to go! There's nothing to it!'

He had been in Melbourne for a year and the job was going very well; 1944 was an improvement on the past few years in every way, and though he did not become involved with any woman (he did see Joan Morris occasionally, as she was obliged to visit Melbourne), he was coming to realise that these soft, fascinating creatures didn't mind if a fellow was maimed or incapacitated in some other way. His repatriation work had helped him reach this conclusion; every day he perused papers which revealed some woman's devotion to a man like himself, and among his own friends and acquaintances he saw further evidence. Women were so loyal, so compassionate, so caring. Perhaps it was not beyond possibility that he too might find one of these paragons for himself?

As he left the office one Saturday noon in company with Bill Keays, Bill showed him a shortcut to Flinders Street railway station.

It involved walking down a narrow lane with a dogleg kink in it. Among the buildings it contained was a facility offering food and accommodation to servicewomen. As he and Keays neared it, four women emerged; budding officers, obviously, from their white epaulettes. And there was *Helen* Morris! Her eyes slid his way, widened; she hurried to pass by him without saying hello. But he put his hand out and stopped her, whereupon she gave him that enchanting smile. Shyness had prompted her to cut him—she didn't want to appear a showoff to her friends.

'What are you doing here?' he asked.

'I'm just finishing the officers' course at Bacchus Marsh.'

'Good for you!'

And a little more of the same, pleasant chat the onlookers could not deem significant. So Joan had told her of his job? Mmmm. Where was Helen going next? She didn't know. Oh, pity ... They parted and Roden caught his train, accompanied by the memory of her smile. Oh, pity ... She was shortly to be a lieutenant, she clearly enjoyed the life she was leading. Oh, pity ...

Her circumstances were comfortable, even during the Great Depression. Her father was the accounting director of Snow's, a department store, and a great personal friend of Sir Sydney Snow's. There were three girls and one boy in the Morris family, which was descended from early settlers around Ballarat (later to be one of the State of Victoria's goldmining boomtowns).

David, the only boy, was the oldest child; then came Joan, Helen in the middle, and Marion-called-Mim at the bottom. The great family sorrow had come in 1936, when David, a student in his final years at Scots College, succumbed to lobar pneumonia and died. No one was to blame; in those days before antibiotics, pneumonia was one of the commonest killers, and it had no respect for age. As many young died of it as old.

The tragedy devastated the whole Morris family, though it affected Joan and her mother, Clare, most severely. Closest to David in age, Joan was never really to reach her potential, nor did she ever marry. Clare Morris withdrew into herself.

Helen had been educated at a private girls' school; she was bright, but she had no academic leanings. Mr. Morris decided to 'finish' her, so she was sent to Hopewood House, run by the Misses Kaye. A finishing school was an institution which concentrated upon the social graces—manners, deportment, good conversation, letter writing, a working knowledge of music, art, literature and history, what to do with all the cutlery at one's place around the dinner table, and so forth. As things turned out, the Morrises could not have chosen a more suitable education for Helen. Her own family background (Mrs. Morris used cake forks, a rare thing) and Hopewood House equipped her for the years to come.

Having been 'finished', Helen took a secretarial course and became private secretary to the managing director of the Trustees Executive Agency in Sydney. This lasted only as long as it took her to grow old enough to enlist in the Army. Her boss was quite desolate at losing her, but she was adamant.

Her reverence for the Victoria Cross was typical of her character. A man who had won it was more than just a hero: he was a great man. Some might swoon and sigh over Robert Taylor or Leslie Howard, but Helen was not the swooning and sighing kind. She had her priorities right. Meeting Arthur Roden Cutler, V.C., was an honour she had perhaps hoped might come her way, but it was not in her nature to resort to tricks or ploys; the business with the hat and the salute was sincere.

She must have carried the memory of him, even hoped a little when he invited her and Joan to the Hermitage restaurant, but as far as she knew it might as easily be her sister he had liked. And then—no more. Oh, well ... She worked hard, she enjoyed her military life, she took the opportunity to train as an officer. And then—there he was again! In the lane outside the assistance station where she had had a meal. He was with someone, a senior-looking fellow—important. He wouldn't remember her. All the girls pestered him, so she wouldn't. Best pretend not to see him, slip past him quickly.

How amazing! He detained her, actually chatted as if pleased to see her. As she didn't know where she was going, how could she tell him? But he had looked at her warmly, affectionately.

Her lieutenancy came through and she was posted to Bandiana, a transport depot near Albury, where, unknown to her, Aunt Dais lived. The job was enormously interesting—she was in charge of convoys of vehicles to Melbourne and had to learn to drive all sorts of trucks, even articulated ones. The major in command was a bit on the stodgy side, but she did good work and he had few complaints.

Of course she knew Roden was living in Melbourne and she knew where he worked, but she just couldn't summon up the courage to give him a casual phone call when she arrived in the city on convoy duty. What would he think of her? If she did phone him, it would have to be for a very good reason—something that would sound all right. Why did she have a feeling that now it was up to her to make the next move? She was in love, but he wasn't. Yet he *did* really like her, it had been there in his eyes.

The Majestic in St. Kilda was a far cry from Helen's abode whenever she was in town. Mr. Morris was an almost over-protective father and Melbourne was a strange city. So he insisted that she stay at Menzies', a most exclusive hotel—and cheerfully paid the bill. The hotel, by the way, had nothing to do with Robert Gordon Menzies, the ex-prime minister.

In the foyer of Menzies', with its imperturbable staff gliding around in waistcoats of vivid scarlet-and-white Menzies tartan, she recognised a famous singer of the time, a woman from Lancashire. As it was permissible to smile at her, Helen did so.

'You're in the Army,' said the singer, smiling back. 'Are you here to go to my concert?'

'I wish I was,' said Helen, 'but I have no ticket.'

Whereupon she found herself gifted with *two* tickets.

She telephoned Roden, explained about the tickets, and asked if he would like to go to the concert with her. Roden said yes.

They dined at Menzies' first, went to the concert and enjoyed it, then afterwards they dropped in to drink coffee at Elizabeth Collins. What a wonderful evening!

And that was the start of it. Whenever Helen was in town they saw each other. If Joan was in town as well, Roden took both of them out—together.

As a wartime economy measure, the Federal Government put a ceiling on how much a hotel or a restaurant was allowed to charge for a meal: three shillings for breakfast, four shillings for lunch, and five shillings for dinner. The trick was to go to an oyster bar and spend five shillings on oysters, then go to Menzies' or another restaurant and spend five more shillings on a main meal. That way, one had a feast. Highly illicit, of course, but everyone did it. Lieutenant in the Army or not, Roden wouldn't permit Helen (or Joan, or any other woman) to pay for her food.

The courtship proceeded at a snail's pace, on Helen's side because she didn't want to push Roden into anything, and on Roden's side because he didn't want to push Helen into anything.

Roden went up to Albury for a weekend and introduced Helen to Aunt Dais, who liked her and continued to see her, give her home-cooked meals, listen to her speak of a hoped-for captaincy.

At 'Kyeema' the family knew little about Roden's social life, though they knew he occasionally saw the two Morris sisters. For whatever reason, they assumed he saw more of Joan than of Helen. No one, including Ruby, sniffed a romance in the air.

In 1945 Roden had to go to Sydney; knowing that Helen too was going to Sydney on leave, he rang her and asked her if she would like a lift from Albury to Sydney. The only snag, he was careful to explain, was that he couldn't manage the drive in one day. They would have to overnight in Junee or Yass. Oh, yes, please! cried Helen. Best confirm it with your father first, said Roden, who had read Mr. Morris aright.

'I don't think so, dear,' said Mr. Morris gently.

So all Roden picked up in Albury was Helen's suitcase—at least she wouldn't have to lug that on and off the steamtrain. He promised to deliver it to Fairfax Road, Bellevue Hill, then left. Helen caught the train, a much slower trip because the trains were always full and one had to book a seat, usually not on the same day as one asked.

When Roden arrived at the Morris house he found a young girl sitting behind the wheel of a large English car in the driveway, trying vainly to turn it around.

'Having trouble?' he asked, getting out of the Mercury.

She looked at him in terror. 'You're at the wrong house!'

'Doesn't Helen Morris live here?'

'Yes, but you can't come in!'

Clearly the Morris girls were extremely sheltered. For answer, Roden got into the Wolseley and managed to get it nose out; Marion-called-Mim took off, panicked, to pick up her father from the Edgecliff tram stop. So there he was, in the driveway. Obviously unwelcome. What to do now?

A woman opened the front door. 'Come in and have a drink,' said Clare Morris, who knew why the strange young man was there.

Oh, did he need a drink! A large Scotch whisky.

'Sherry?'

Well, that was better than nothing, he supposed, but at least the sherry Mrs. Morris poured him was a gigantic one.

Then Mr. Morris came home, and things settled down. After discovering that David Eric Morris was very warm and pleasant, Roden deposited Helen's bag and went home to 'Kyeema'.

One of the major problems with this courtship concerned the other people who always seemed to delight in playing gooseberry. Simply because no one understood something serious was going on. You're going out? Oh, jolly good! I'll (we'll) come with you! In Melbourne it had been Joan; the twosome was often a threesome until Joan was posted to the Royal Australian Navy depot at Fremantle, Western Australia. In Sydney there were threesomes, foursomes, fivesomes and howevermanysomes—Joan if she were in town, Ruby always, Doone, Geoff occasionally, or Rob, or friends from the 2/5th Field Regiment, or a naval medico Doone was seeing for a time. It never rained but it poured people.

Neither Roden nor Helen was the kind to flout convention, especially with Mr. Morris as the father figure. If convention irked them, it did so subconsciously. Helen was used to being sheltered and guarded, while Roden was a gentleman with all the shibboleths that word conveys.

•

John Curtin died on 5 July 1945 after a long battle with what seems to have been congestive cardiac failure. Though the Canberra world and his family (he came from Western Australia) had known of his condition since he had fallen ill the previous November, it came as a shock to the nation, which loved him dearly because he had put Australia's needs ahead of Great Britain's.

Much of his energy towards the end was devoted to peacetime strategies; the war itself had become a painful and perpetual confrontation with General MacArthur, who kept insisting that Australian forces participate fully in the drive on Japan—and that they should take a hefty share of occupation duty after the war was over. The Prime Minister wanted Australia out before it was overwhelmed by debt.

Curtin had become—not mystical, precisely, but certainly philosophical; he wanted the world to order its doings more sanely, more softly, more subtly. War was an abominable business—the lives lost! The money the nation owed!

Though he was well aware that the persons who strutted the international diplomatic stage loathed Dr. Evatt, it was Evatt he sent to San Francisco (shepherded by Francis Forde) for the talks which were to result in the formation of the United Nations Organization. Interestingly enough, the Doc was to be one of the most influential forces in the framing of the U.N. Charter, and was President of the U.N. General Assembly during its 1948–1949 session. Though he disliked the Doc himself, Curtin simply thought him the best man for the job.

Francis Forde was Deputy Prime Minister, so on Curtin's death he assumed Curtin's office—for one week. Caucus preferred Ben Chifley, the Treasurer. He was to remain Prime Minister until Labor was defeated in the 1949 elections—at the hands of a rejuvenated Menzies leading his own offspring, the Liberal Party.

•

The war was well and truly over by the time that Roden took his courage in both hands (even winners of the Victoria Cross sometimes quail before their mothers) and told Ruby that he was thinking of getting married.

Aunt Dais had known for a long time, but Aunt Dais kept her counsel. 'Is this the one, Ro?' she asked him after he got into the habit of appearing in Albury occasionally to spend the weekend, when Helen would appear to keep him company.

'Yes, Aunt Dais, this is the one.'

Whereas Ruby knew so little. He chose to tell his mother when others were present.

'I'm thinking of getting married,' he announced.

Geoff looked stunned. 'You're joking!'

But she must have sensed something, for Ruby said, tight-lipped, 'I don't think he is. It's Joan Morris, isn't it?'

'No, it's Helen Morris.'

She wasn't pleased. Not because it was Helen rather than Joan; she knew neither girl very well. No, it was because she understood that her family was going to be forever changed, that this most beloved of her sons had needs she could not fulfil, that his blood family was not enough, that he wanted to create his own family. A kind of step away from her as unexpected as it was unwelcome. And he had been her mainstay since Arthur died—ten long years of worry, hardship, grief and loneliness. Yet thanks to Roden they had not been unbearable years. Thanks to Geoff, Rob, Doone too. But if Roden went, the others would go. Had to go. Oh, what would become of her?

She was to go through exactly the same emotional turmoil when Geoff found a girl, so much so that his first romance came to nothing. He became engaged in London. Rob was a little easier, and at least Doone brought a man *into* the family.

•

One of the last to know about the whole business was Helen.

They had had a tiff more than a quarrel when Roden passed through Albury; his telegram never arrived, so he found her on duty—and very annoyed with him.

'I can't get out of looking after these girls!' she said, paused for a significantly long time, then asked, 'What are *you* going to do?'

'I'm going up to Sydney to get engaged,' he said.

'Oh.' A very long and very significant pause. 'Let me know when you do. I'd like to be the first to congratulate you,' she said stiffly.

And so they parted.

1946 was drawing near; Helen came home on leave, and Roden at 'Kyeema' was suffering through his mother's patent disapproval of his impending change in marital status.

When Helen got to Sydney, Roden phoned her.

'I thought you weren't going to get in touch with me?'

'How about coming on a picnic with me to Palm Beach?' he asked, as if nothing was the matter.

'Right-oh!' she said offhandedly, and hung up.

When Roden arrived to collect her, Marion-called-Mim asked if she could hitch a ride; she was going to see friends. So off went the threesome. At 'Kyeema' the expedition became a mini-convoy as the party swelled to include Ruby, Geoff, Doone and her Navy boyfriend, Dr. John Fraser.

Mim hopped out to visit her friends; at the end of the day everyone else returned to 'Kyeema' and had dinner. No one had made any reference to the existence or non-existence of an impending marriage. Things were obviously not quite set between Roden and Helen, who behaved as if they were remote acquaintances. Maybe ...

A typical Sydney summer: the heat broke in a 'southerly buster'—a sudden dramatic drop in temperature, wind from the south, lightning, thunder and torrential rain.

Feeling quite as worn as he had in Gaza, Roden rose and offered to drive Dr. John Fraser and Helen home.

The threesome set off while the rain bucketed down. But for once the luck was running with Roden; John Fraser was based at Garden Island naval station, so he was dropped first. That left Roden alone with Helen. They drove in silence to Fairfax Road, where Roden turned the Mercury's engine off.

'About marriage—I have a lot of faults, you know,' said Roden, 'so I'd better tell you about them before you say anything.'

For the rest of her life Helen was to tease him about how he couched his marriage proposal. 'I didn't want to hear about your faults! I knew your good points.'

The Morrises accepted their son-in-law to be with unaffected pleasure, though Roden never did get around to asking Mr. Morris for his daughter's hand.

'We're so glad you're going to marry Helen!' Mr. Morris said when he came in all formality to ask. Approval at last.

They announced their engagement in Melbourne on 15 February 1946, but they didn't plan to marry in a hurry—people were more patient then, and assured economic prosperity was very important to Roden. When they did marry they would get a little flat somewhere in Melbourne and settle down; Roden would become Repatriation Commissioner one day, Helen was sure.

But Dr. Herbert Vere Evatt had other ideas. At one time he had enquired of Roden as to whether he would go as commercial attaché to Paris, just beginning to come alive again after the long

Nazi occupation. Roden had declined, explaining that he had been away, thank you, and didn't fancy another trip abroad.

A newly engaged man, he was going about his repatriation business one day when the phone rang.

'What's the weather like in Melbourne, lieutenant?' asked a familiar voice.

'Warm and fine, Dr. Evatt.'

'Ready to go away yet?'

'Where?' asked Roden cautiously.

'Oh, you'll like it!' chortled the Doc, and hung up.

Well, he could be a little strange sometimes. Shrugging, Roden continued with his work.

On his way out the door into the street the switchboard operator beamed at him. 'Congratulations!' she said.

'About what?' She'd done the engagement bit already.

'About going to New Zealand as high commissioner.'

'But I'm not!'

'Yes, you are! It's been over the wireless. You're going to New Zealand and Sir Keith Officer is going to The Hague.'

Even after he saw the announcement in the evening newspaper he didn't believe it.

The acting chairman, Jack Webster, summoned him the next morning. 'Why didn't you tell me?'

'I didn't know,' said Roden. 'In fact, I still don't know.'

Webster thought for a moment. 'Then I suggest we sit on it for a week or two,' he said.

A week or two went by, and still no word from Dr. Evatt or the Department of External Affairs. Webster summoned Roden again.

'Nothing?'

'Nothing.'

'You're off to Sydney to do appeals, so why don't you call into

Canberra on the way back and ask the minister in person if you still haven't heard,' said Webster.

Of course he had told Helen about it, though excited people around Bandiana had already let her know—her engagement was common property by now. They discussed it over the telephone, but at the end of it their chief emotion was bewilderment.

Nothing while he was in Sydney. Roden contacted the Doc's office at Parliament House in Canberra and made a five o'clock appointment to see the Minister for External Affairs.

When he arrived he learned that the minister was still in the House, so he sat and waited. And waited, and waited. About eight in the evening the Doc burst through the outer door.

'Oh, hello, lieutenant!' he said to Roden breezily. 'So glad you took the job!' He disappeared into his inner sanctum and did not emerge again.

'That's all I managed to see of him,' said Roden to Jack Webster on the phone.

'Then I suggest you see Charlie Frost before you leave Canberra and find out what he knows,' said Webster.

Charles Frost was the Minister for Repatriation, therefore Roden's ultimate boss. The interview was unexpectedly ticklish.

'That was the job *I* wanted!' said Frost.

Oh, dear. Frost was intimating that when—and if—Ben Chifley won the election due this year, Charles Frost would not be in Chifley's Cabinet—mightn't even get Labor preselection in his seat. The traditional goodbye kiss as thanks for Cabinet service was a senior overseas diplomatic or commercial post.

'I think we can safely assume that I'm going to be High Commissioner in New Zealand,' said Roden to Jack Webster when he returned to Melbourne. 'One of these days I imagine External

Affairs will get around to notifying me officially. In the meantime, you'd better give me my marching orders.'

There was no formal training in diplomacy in 1946. The top jobs usually went to ex-Cabinet ministers, as mentioned above, while the more junior ones were filled from the Department of External Affairs' own professional public servant ranks. But a proper cadet-ship in diplomacy was still on the drawing board; the new High Commissioner to New Zealand hadn't a clue what the job entailed or how to go about it. He'd graduated in Economics, been an office boy, a petty cash clerk, a very junior public servant in the Trustee's office, a lieutenant in artillery, an ex-servicemen's executive, a paper-shuffler in espionage, an assessor of aliens, and a deputy commissioner in charge of hearing ex-servicemen's appeals. Exactly the right training for a career in diplomacy!

Dr. Evatt had handed him a plum without his ever asking for it—without his ever dreaming of it. His salary would be *two* thousand pounds a year—astronomical!—and he would live in an official residence, be granted an allowance to cover legitimate expenses, have an office staff and a staff to run the residence. He was to be one of His Majesty the King's senior diplomats in a very delicate job at the ripe old age of twenty-nine.

He didn't have the time to waste in pinching himself—he had to do some boning up, and mighty fast. First, see as many people as he possibly could in External Affairs, read whatever they or his own intelligence suggested, then try to find an ex-diplomat to consult about things like protocol—what exactly *was* protocol? I mean, one sort of knew, but that wasn't anything like good enough for a high commissioner.

Secondly, he had to find out whether he was going to arrive in

Wellington (the capital of New Zealand) as a bachelor high commissioner or as a recently married high commissioner.

'You have three choices,' he said to Helen. 'One, you can wait until I get home on leave to marry me—about eighteen months, it seems. Two, you can join me at your convenience in New Zealand and we'll marry there. Or three, you can marry me before I go and come with me.'

She didn't hesitate. 'I'll marry you before *we* go.'

He got her out of the Army in two days.

Thus it was that Arthur Roden Cutler married Helen Gray Annetta Morris at St. Mark's Anglican church at Darling Point—one of the more socially distinguished places to marry. Frank Berryman and his wife attended.

Helen was a devout and practising Anglican, whereas Roden had mostly gone to the Presbyterian church to please Ruby; after their marriage he returned to the Anglican fold his father quit after the altercation between the Bishop and the Dean of Bathurst.

The date was 28 May 1946. Roden had just turned thirty and Helen (who was born on the 5th of May) twenty-three. They honeymooned blissfully in a cottage at Avoca, within easy reach of Sydney.

DIPLOMACY

The relationship between Australia and New Zealand has never been an easy one. Though geographically the two countries are in fairly close proximity for this part of the globe, their histories and cultural development have been different. Both are island nations: Australia is the world's largest island to which another large island, Tasmania, is tacked on; New Zealand consists of two large islands and a number of extremely small ones. Though both possess indigenous populaces, their ethnicity is very different. The Australian Aborigines crossed from the Indian subcontinent approximately 40,000 years ago and found a place more conducive to a hunter-gatherer, semi-nomadic way of life, albeit that tribalisation split the land up territorially. They were a peaceful people by nature, and though they resisted European inroads, they were never numerically strong enough in any one area to retard European encroachment. The New Zealand Maori were a maritime people who successfully navigated many thousands of miles of the Pacific Ocean in canoes to arrive in Aotearoa (their name for New Zealand: it means 'land of the long white cloud') about 700 years ago from other Polynesian islands far to the north. Fierce and warlike, they resisted European settlers in a series of bitter conflicts that resulted in a solemn agreement in 1841, the Treaty of Waitangi, which remains the only form of constitution New Zealand possesses aside from its laws.

The European settlement of Australia was the direct result of the American War of Independence. Until 1776, victims of Great Britain's extremely harsh criminal laws were acquired by speculators who shipped them to America and sold them as indentured servants. After 1776, they had to go somewhere else—but where? A colony in west Africa was abandoned due to fever and intolerable tropical conditions; those sentenced to 'transportation' kept piling up in English gaols and aboard prison hulks until *something* had to be done with them. So in 1788 the First Fleet arrived in the area later to be called Sydney, bearing about 760 convicts (together with their keepers) who were to serve out their sentences in this dry, inhospitable place. Over the succeeding sixty years many thousands of convicts were to be transported to New South Wales and the other eastern seaboard colonies of New Holland.

New Zealand does not have a convict history; its first European settlers were 'free', though a number of them were, of course, convict escapees from across the Tasman Sea. Climatic conditions and the more beneficent effects of being a relatively small place surrounded by vast oceans gave New Zealand a more English look and feel than anywhere in Australia; once the forest giants were felled the countryside was vividly green, gracious, succulent. Insects were not present in voracious and annoying millions; there were no deadly snakes; the mountains were coated with snow in winter; so much to remind the settlers of the place European New Zealanders called 'home' until very recently indeed.

The influx of settlers to New Zealand was basically English or Scottish; of Irish there were far fewer, of Welsh not many; and the 'class' of New Zealand's European settlers was somewhat higher than those, even free settlers, who went to New South Wales, Victoria, Tasmania, South Australia, Queensland and Western Australia—all separate British colonies, whereas New Zealand was New Zealand, one British colony.

By 1901 and the confederation of its separate colonies into the new Commonwealth of Australia, the differences between this new Australian nation and New Zealand were fully formed. In 1907 the Dominion of New Zealand came into being, another new nation more or less independent of the mother country, Great Britain (it did retain some control over both places). Prior to 1901 there had been plans to amalgamate Australia and New Zealand as the nation of Australasia, but the New Zealanders (originally incorporated in the early drafts of the Australian Constitution) rejected this, decided to go it alone. A wise decision, based in practicality.

Regrettable though the situation may be from every viewpoint between expedience and philosophy, the fact remains that Australians and New Zealanders are poles apart and tend to rub each other up the wrong way, though these days the feeling is more prevalent in New Zealand than in Australia simply because Australians do not think about New Zealand as much as New Zealanders think about Australia. Most emotions depend for their strength upon how an object or an entity impinges on existence, and in relative terms Australia hogs the news, is more prominent on the international stage, has more to say for itself. Which irritates New Zealanders, very naturally. They think of themselves as equally important, whereas Australians think they don't matter much.

The author has considerable experience in these matters, being of equal amounts of New Zealander and Australian, and coming from a family which has crossed the Tasman Sea more than once.

Attitudes in New Zealand in 1946 were pretty much the same as they are at the turn of the millennium, and may be briefly summed up as that New Zealanders deem Australians crass, vulgar, untutored oafs, and Australia as a combination of vast smoggy cities and arid wastes. When Australians think of New Zealand the usual phrase is 'dead from the neck up', and when they think of New Zealanders they apostrophise them as 'worse whingers than the Poms'. They pun on 'land of the long white cloud' as 'land of the long white whinge'.

The Wellington cosmos of 1946 incorporated all of the above New Zealand attitudes, but with some exacerbations. New Zealand's politicians had perforce to deal with their Australian counterparts, particularly during the Second World War, when both nations suffered from identical Lilliputian sensations as the Big Three or the Big Four divided up the postwar globe about as wisely as they had after the Great War. But the New Zealand politicians always felt like junior partners. As for Wellington's diplomatic circle, it downright despised Australians.

Finally, an explanation of the High Commissioner. Within the British Commonwealth of Nations, the ambassador of one B.C.N. country to another B.C.N. country does not call himself (take the feminine as read) 'ambassador'. He is the High Commissioner. In 1946 he did not rank as high as a full ambassador, but after 1948, when the status of British Subject was removed from the citizens of British Commonwealth nations, he ranked as equal with an ambassador.

Mr. Roden Cutler, V.C., and Mrs. Cutler elected to fly to their new post on a Sunderland flying boat, one of the more comfortable planes of the pre-jet era. It was mid-June—winter in the Southern Hemisphere—so Roden and Helen set out from Manly in darkness to make the trip to Rose Bay flying base on the other side of the

Harbour. Ruby, desolate but hugely proud, said goodbye to them in Manly, but Mr. and Mrs. Morris were supposed to meet the voyagers at the pier in Rose Bay, not far from Fairfax Road, Bellevue Hill. Roden and Helen waited as long as they dared, but her parents never came. Their alarm clock had failed to ring. Not a happy start, especially for Helen.

The 1,300-mile flight took seven-and-a-half hours, in bad weather the whole way. One of the conditions governing a flight on the Sunderland consisted of signing a consent form prior to embarkation in case passengers' baggage had to be thrown out of the plane to keep it flying rather than sailing. That did not happen on this flight, but Roden did wonder while the Sunderland dropped, soared, pitched, wallowed. Helen said little, though she was terrified; it was her first-ever plane ride.

There was no direct way to get from Sydney to Wellington; one had to fly to Auckland, at the northern end of the North Island of New Zealand. They arrived in New Zealand's biggest city as the early winter dusk was setting in, very glad to set foot on terra firma.

In the hotel dining room they had their first taste of New Zealand decorum as well as food; on the wall was a particularly fine painting of a female nude, which an English male guest got up to inspect closely. The New Zealand diners thought his conduct disgraceful; they didn't think highly of a nude on the wall in the first place, but to put one's nose nearly against it—horrors! The meal was good and they had their first sample of the tree tomato (tamarillo) and the Chinese gooseberry (Kiwi fruit). A kind guest showed them how to eat these delicacies.

After that came a steamtrain journey, mostly in the dark, down the length of the North Island to the national capital, Wellington, some three hundred miles south of Auckland.

'How green New Zealand is!' said Roden to Mr. Taylor, the New

Zealand Department of External Affairs protocol officer who met them at the station.

'*Green?* We're in the middle of a terrible drought,' said Mr. Taylor blankly.

'Oh, I am sorry. For how long?'

'Six weeks.'

Eastern Australia had been in severe drought since 1937—nine years. Lesson number one in relativity.

'We've booked you indefinitely into the new Waterloo Hotel just across the road,' Mr. Taylor said, shepherding them out.

'What's the matter with the residence?' asked Roden.

His companion looked uncomfortable. 'Well, I believe that it's not—er—very habitable at the moment.'

Inspection the next day proved that this had been a gross understatement. The residence of the Australian High Commissioner was a shambles.

Roden already knew that the previous Australian High Commissioner in Wellington had gone home under a cloud, but it took some time to find and weave all the threads of the story together.

The Government of the Australian island State of Tasmania was a Labor one headed by Robert Cosgrove. Not long after Ben Chifley became Prime Minister, Premier Cosgrove got on the telephone to Canberra with a very usual Tasmanian complaint: no one in Canberra ever remembered that Tasmanians and their so beautiful State existed. New South Wales was 'the premier State'; Victoria was 'the garden State'; Queensland was 'the sunshine State'; Tasmania could well have called itself 'the orphan State'. Once a place is separated by a wide body of water from another place which basically controls its destiny, the ties binding the two places together become tenuous, and the less powerful of the two places becomes deeply resentful of 'Big Brother'. The reader may perceive that the situation of Tasmania anent the Australian mainland was similar to the situation of New Zealand anent the whole nation of Australia.

No doubt Ben Chifley closed his long-suffering eyes as the complaint went on—why is it, Prime Minister, that when it comes time to apportion out the jobs for the boys, Tasmania never gets a job for one of its boys? Da de da de da . . .

'All right, then,' said Chifley when he could get a word in, 'nominate someone and I'll see he gets a good job.'

Premier Cosgrove nominated his ex-Minister for Lands, who had contrived to become somewhat of an embarrassment to the Tasmanian Government due to some of his ministerial activities. Though in size Tasmania is not small, in 1945 its population was sufficiently sparse to render it difficult to turn a high profile into a low profile. Better if the ex-minister was sent elsewhere.

Chifley appointed him High Commissioner to New Zealand, and off he went happily, accompanied by his wife and his ladyfriend, who was on the high commission's books as 'librarian'.

They were not precisely a sophisticated trio. In private life the new High Commissioner had been a rabbit-oh; driven a horse-and-dray around settled areas selling rabbits for eating and also peddling long poles with a forked branch at the narrower end. These poles were clothes props. When the clothesline sagged due to the weight of the wet washing, one inserted the forked end under the line, heaved and shoved like mad, and propped the clothesline up with the pole.

The trio's impact on the stiff, snobby, punctiliously correct Wellington Establishment was startling, to say the least. Not to mention fulfilling every last preconception New Zealanders had about Australians. Their grammar wasn't always perfect and they didn't dress very well; one of them was a poor, drab, silent little woman whom life had treated even worse than her husband had, while the other two laughed too loudly, drank too much and loved a rip-roaring party.

Mrs. High Commissioner was a perfect target. As soon as the Wellington Establishment sniffed out her vulnerability, it tormented her unmercifully. Mocked her, put her cutlery the wrong way around at dinner and kept on prodding until she shrank completely inside her shell. Finally she packed her bags and went home to Tasmania.

That left the High Commissioner in untrammelled possession of the residence; the librarian moved in, though they did try to keep up appearances. She would leave the residence to walk one block, he would drive the car out of the residence and pick her up at the end of the block. The parties began, and they were legendary. People danced on tables, fell into the fishpond, smashed glasses and china, kept the neighbourhood awake. As they had diplomatic immunity, the Wellington police could do nothing.

It came to a head in the queue to a cinema. Like the British they loved so much, New Zealanders respected the queue to the point of turning it into a fetish. Whenever one saw a long line of people, one tacked oneself onto the end of it; 'jumping the queue' was tantamount to a capital crime. The High Commissioner and his librarian arrived at the cinema and pushed into the front of the queue. When some of the members of the line could manage to speak through the foam around their mouths, the couple were told to get to the back of the queue.

'I am the Australian High Commissioner, so I don't have to get on the end of the queue.'

A brawl developed, punches were thrown, the police arrived, and the High Commissioner was hastily recalled to Australia.

•

Now, the Wellington Establishment discovered, the new High Commissioner was a beanpole of a kid with a wife who looked as if she was still in school. Yes, he had won a Victoria Cross and lost a leg in the doing, and a Victoria Cross winner was someone to be respected and honoured. *But* ... No Australian had ever won two of them, whereas Charles Upham, a New Zealander, had. Statistics were quickly calculated and national honour vindicated; per head of population, New Zealand had more Victoria Crosses than Australia did.

The bulk of the Cutlers' luggage was coming by sea, as the thought of having to witness one's suitcases tossed out the door of a Sunderland floundering along just above the wave crests had meant that nothing precious travelled with them. Roden had managed to pack what he considered the most valuable of his boning up books, so they spent their spare time with their noses glued to the pages and were rather glad they were staying in a nice, warm hotel. The residence was not very warm.

Some money had to be spent on making the residence livable again; from day one Helen took her duties very seriously and made sure that she had the repairs done and bought new furniture as cheaply as possible. The short commons of recent wartime rendered this more difficult, but as she had excellent taste the results were as pleasing as irreproachable.

Roden had to present his letter from the Prime Minister, a formality yet a very important one.

And the first calls had to be paid. Protocol dictated that the new diplomat should call upon all his opposite numbers plus all the New Zealand Cabinet ministers plus whoever was appropriate in the New Zealand bureaucracy. The new diplomat's wife also had to pay calls—upon the diplomats' wives. He left his card, whereas she left three cards: one of her own for the wife plus two of Roden's, one for the husband and one for his wife.

They seemed to exude an offensive odour; if a member of the Wellington Establishment noticed them on the street, the member would cross quickly to the other side of the road. Few returned their calls, so they gathered few cards and the visitors' book bore an almost blank page.

At the time Wellington contained only one diplomatic minister, the American ambassador; three high commissioners, from Great Britain (from now on to be referred to as the United Kingdom), Canada and Australia; and a number of consuls, chief of whom was M. Armand Nihotte, the Belgian Consul-General. It forever irked Nihotte that he was outranked by the American, the Englishman, the Canadian and the Australian, for he had been in Wellington the longest and felt that this earned him seniority; he was always badgering the New Zealand External Affairs people to be awarded seniority, and grew very angry each time he was firmly refused. As he was the only minister, Mr. American Ambassador (Avra M. Warren) was the senior among all the diplomats.

The New Zealand Government was a Labour one, headed by the Prime Minister, Peter Fraser. That at least meant some degree of community feeling between New Zealand and Australia, a socialist[†] government too. Unfortunately both External Affairs departments were minute.

This was particularly so in Canberra. Though in 1901 a

[†] The author is aware that over the past two decades Labor has been endeavouring to distance itself from the old tag of 'socialist', which of recent times has become more or less synonymous in some people's minds with 'communist'. In 1946 and for some decades after, however, 'socialist' was perfectly acceptable, and did not deny a democratic ethos. Similarly, the word 'conservative' is occasionally used to describe the U.A.P.-C.P. or Liberal-C.P. coalition.

Department of External Affairs had been created, it lapsed until very few ministers existed—one in London and occasionally one in Washington D.C. Most overseas appointments belonged to the Department of Trade, and were trade commissioner slots. Once he became Minister for External Affairs, Dr. Evatt set about remedying this, especially in the bureaucracy, which contained almost no senior people when he assumed the portfolio. It grew rapidly, but one of the reasons why it took so long for Roden to be informed that he was to be High Commissioner to New Zealand was simply that External Affairs had too few bureaucrats to cope with the Doc's gyrations. To increase the bureaucracy was a cornerstone of socialist policy, and the Doc did his best—but it took time to find good men. That he had a genius for finding good men can be seen from the way he tested Roden Cutler: once someone caught his eye, he proceeded to give him a series of trial runs, and watched closely.

Roden thinks that it was his Victoria Cross first drew him to the attention of men like Evatt and Curtin, but, as he says with truth, the V.C. may have helped initially, yet it was the quality of his work which saw him continuously promoted. He never disappointed anyone who took a chance on him.

Nor was he to do so in New Zealand. The Australian High Commission (a separate entity from the residence) was in close proximity to the New Zealand parliamentary buildings. He had an Official Secretary, Bernard Kuskie, of whom Roden became very fond; his health wasn't good, and he died in 1951, still in harness. His Third Secretary was Alexander Borthwick, who was to leave in 1947, but whom Roden was to meet again in Ceylon. There was a small office staff to do the typing, the filing and answer the telephone. His quarters also housed the office of the Australian Trade Commissioner, who came under the authority of the High

Commissioner, but had no political duties—his job was trade and commerce.

The identity of the Trade Commissioner came as a shock—he was none other than the brigadier who took the 2/5th Field Regiment's salute on the post office steps at Katoomba in 1940! The author asked how a brigadier had obtained this position—was he qualified? Roden smiled and said the brigadier's credentials for the Trade Commissioner slot were about on a par with his own for High Commissioner.

'I think he'd once worked in the mail order section at Anthony Hordern's department store.'

Diplomacy, Roden learned, was largely a matter of plain old commonsense. His chief duty was to liaise between the Canberra government and the Wellington government. This was not always easy, thanks to the Doc, who had a habit of forgetting that he had a high commissioner in Wellington. His opposite number in the New Zealand Cabinet was Prime Minister Peter Fraser, who held the portfolio of External Affairs as well; the Doc would phone Fraser directly, then neglect to tell Roden what was going on. But once Roden found his feet—that took him two months—he began painstakingly to build a really solid relationship with New Zealand, its government and its people. The New Zealand External Affairs people were unfailingly helpful. One of the best aspects of New Zealand's government and bureaucracy, he discovered, was that they disliked the pettifogging arguments men like the Belgian Consul-General considered true diplomacy.

In less than a year he stood on firm enough ground with Prime Minister Fraser and other members of his Cabinet to enjoy their full confidence; a situation which continued after Fraser's Labour went out of power and the conservative Sidney Holland came into power.

Some ministers would visit the Australian High Commission

rather than summon Roden to them, an indication that they had grown fond enough of him to want to spare him the walk. This reflects well on the kind of office Roden ran: a minister could feel quite secure there. He was often asked to attend Cabinet meetings when a visiting dignitary was sitting in on them.

His job necessitated that he travel throughout both Islands, speaking to bodies of all kinds, always emphasising the need for his country and theirs to draw closer together. In conferring with a minister or a senior public servant, it was his task to explain how Australia felt about an issue; his duty to Canberra was to explain how New Zealand felt about the same issue. But to Roden by far the most important aspect of his job was to enhance Australia's image and standing in Wellington.

On the more domestic side things soon settled down too. Calls were now repaid, the visitors' book boasted so many signatures that the pages had to be turned regularly.

There were some attitudes towards Australians among Wellington's high society that obviously stemmed from the fact that most affluent or prominent New Zealanders at this time affected pear-shaped English accents and often sent their children to school in England—Harrow, Roedean, Rugby. They knew perfectly well that these customs were not practised in Australian society to nearly the same degree. Yet both Roden and Helen spoke well; their accents were definitely Australian, but not what would now be called 'Ocker'—very broad, nasal and slangy. What used to be called 'educated'. They could cope with politesse familiarly.

'But you're not *Australians*!' a Wellingtonian would say.

'Yes, we are.'

'Well, you weren't educated there, then!'

'Yes, we were—why do you ask?'

An embarrassed pause would ensue until the Wellingtonian could find another subject to talk about.

They found themselves the object of much curiosity, between their evident ease with the social graces and their youth.

The Mayor of Wellington took Roden aside at a function to ask, 'You haven't been knighted—what did you do wrong?'

'I don't think I've done anything wrong, sir, it's just that I'm a bit young to have earned a knighthood.'

'But you're High Commissioner! High commissioners are always knights! At least the British ones are.'

One society matron enquired as to whether Roden knew 'our High Commissioner'?

'Do you mean the New Zealand High Commissioner in Canberra?'

She looked scandalised. 'No, no! Sir Patrick Duff!'

Sir Patrick Duff was the British High Commissioner to New Zealand; he mattered a great deal more than any New Zealand one.

They were so loyal to 'home', sent the United Kingdom their butter, cheese, lamb, saw no virtue in courting Asian or other markets—'home' would buy all they could send forever and ever. When in later years the United Kingdom elected to join the European Common Market and abandoned New Zealand, it was a bitter blow. The death knell of Empire. New Zealanders truly felt betrayed; their long loyalty had mattered not a scrap. All that blood spilled fighting England's foes ... A fine thank you.

Luckily Helen had sufficient time to acclimatise to New Zealand and Wellingtonian life before she became pregnant; their first son, whom they called Roden David (the David after Helen's dead brother), was born on 1 October 1947. He was to be known as David, and his New Zealand birthplace was to prove a problem in the future.

Helen could not have been better suited to her public job, diplomat's wife, nor to her private job as a mother. Experience would teach her how to combine the two, but it was no hardship for her to give up the long-distance trips at Roden's side in favour first of pregnancy and then of motherhood. The residence had a staff and she could find babysitters, so she was able to continue her public duties whenever Roden was in Wellington. The Establishment liked her pleasant, calm style, even if it was a bit unusual to have a high commissioner's wife so young that she had her first baby in office, so to speak.

Once they moved into the residence in Cashmere Avenue, Khandallah (one of Wellington's choicer hill suburbs), they were able to entertain, to reciprocate. The district was replete with Indian names because a number of the original settlers had been British officers in the Indian Army, to whom it seemed natural to use Indian names for the streets, even the district.

They began to make friends too. Roden had become involved in the Wellington cricketing scene, and was delighted to discover that his brand of Rugby football, known as 'Union' to distinguish it from the professional 'League', was New Zealand's favourite winter sport. Most of his friends were fellow cricketing buffs; Helen found that she could make friends of their wives, as all of them were in some kind of senior public work.

Chief among his first friends was the new Governor-General of New Zealand, Lord Freyberg, V.C. A fascinating man, so big that his nickname was 'Tiny'. His family had moved to New Zealand when he was two years old, so he was commonly regarded as a native New Zealander. He had trained as a dentist, but he had an adventurous streak which led him to volunteer as a stoker on a freighter during a massive strike of stevedores and seamen. Rumour said he had landed in America and fought with Pancho Villa, but Roden states that Freyberg disclaims the story. Having eventually got himself to London, after all kinds of exploits so conflated they have passed into myth, he enlisted in Churchill's Brigade, which went to fight at Gallipoli in 1915. Before the troops landed he swam ashore towing a raft of flammables and lit a fire to delude the Turks into thinking that the British were landing in that spot; for this he was awarded his first Distinguished Service Order. Bernard Freyberg won two more D.S.O.s in Flanders, then followed them up with a Victoria Cross. One gathers that this kind of bravery was akin to Roden's—even in the thick of battle he could think and plan. Lady Freyberg was 'rather quiet, but very intelligent'.

The couple seemed to collect governors-general of New Zealand; two more of their close friends were destined to fill that august post as head of state without constitutional powers (not true, as Sir John Kerr was to prove later). The first of them was Sir Arthur Porritt, who was Sergeant Surgeon to the King and afterwards made a peer. Lord Porritt lived to be very old; when he last wrote to Roden, he was well into his nineties. The second, Denis Blundell, was also a great friend of the Freybergs. He became New Zealand's High Commissioner in London before he was the Governor-General; his wife, June, occupied a very special place in Helen's heart.

Roden's leisure activities were to crystallise permanently during his time in New Zealand—cricket, Rugby Union, fly fishing and duck hunting. His disability negated prone rifle shooting, but he took to the shotgun comfortably. Predictably, he was an excellent marksman.

He did try game fishing, had an exhilarating tussle with a 304-pound marlin, but again, lacking a leg made it difficult to sit properly in the fishing chair. When he brought his enormous catch ashore, some Americans were standing on the jetty.

'Wow! Going to have it stuffed?' asked one American.

'No. I suppose I'll just throw it away,' said Roden.

All the Americans looked appalled. 'Don't do that! Can we have it?'

'What for, to stuff?'

'To eat! It's great eating.'

Well, he deemed them crazy, but it takes all sorts to make a world, so he donated his beautiful marlin to the Americans. As Consul-General in New York City years later, he was to realise that swordfish steak is indeed great eating.

His whaling experience was less happy. A family of Italian extraction named Perano used to whale out of the Marlborough Sounds, a collection of fiordlike inlets on the northern coast of the South Island, just across Cook Strait from Wellington. As Australia bought whale oil from the Peranos, Roden thought that it behoved him to find out more, though negotiating with them took some time. They were suspicious of his motives. This could not have been due to public disapproval of whaling; that was for the future, it did not exist in the 1940s. Roden thinks their attitude stemmed from the fact that they were of Italian ancestry in a country which disliked non-British foreigners.

He succeeded in obtaining their permission to have a look, and at first was fascinated. The Peranos had a mother ship which appeared to be a converted tugboat, plus three high-speed chasers. Each chaser had a skipper and a harpooner in the bow at his gun.

'Thar she blows!' came the cry from the lookout.

There was a whale spouting in the channel. Everybody leaped into action, raced down the hillside to the boats, Roden sliding and slipping. He managed to board the last chaser. By the time they reached the spot another chaser had put a harpoon in the female, which Roden thinks had a calf. The male wouldn't leave her, swam around trying to protect her until they put a harpoon in him. He dived but eventually had to come up for air, grew very tired. Then they put a lance in just behind his head and exploded it, killing him.

Exciting, yes, but so sad. Though he can say he actually went whaling, Roden is on the whales' side. In one odd way it was a repeat of his experience with the marlin; the Peranos loved to eat whale meat. He could not bring himself to try it.

Though there has been great turmoil and much difference of legal and ethical opinion between the Maori and the Pakeha (the white man), the Maori has theoretically had the same rights as the Pakeha since the Treaty of Waitangi in 1841. Unlike Australia, which finally began to enfranchise the Aborigines in 1962.

But unofficially the Maori in Roden's day were discriminated against by some Pakehas, particularly by the police, who tended to hound them for drinking alcohol and poaching pheasant, wood pigeon and the like. It was not against the law for a Maori to consume alcoholic beverages save in situations where his own law forbade it—he (or she) could buy it and drink it as freely as any Pakeha. However, the police considered that Maori suffered from the 'firewater syndrome'—that is, that liquor adversely affected them more quickly, that they were more likely to be violent.

Quite why, Roden is not sure, but the Maori took to him, liked him enormously. He became particularly friendly with Maori who lived to the north of Gisborne, in the earthquake country of the North Island's east coast; the tribe made him an honorary member with the title of 'navigator of the Australian canoe' and the name Katara.[†] When David was born, they wanted Roden to call him Pine (peenee) after Roden's greatest friend in the tribe.

He would get a letter from Pine saying, 'Dear Katara, I know kumaras [a variety of sweet potato] must be scarce in Wellington. We have put a bag of them on the train for you.' Roden would send a letter back saying, 'Dear Pine, thank you very much. The kumaras have arrived and I know whisky must be short in your area. There is some whisky on the train going back to you.'

Maori custom forbade alcoholic liquors in the marae (the village centre), but there were occasions when this went by the board, as the police well knew. An important Maori died, so the police set up a road block outside the marae. The hearse was an open-backed utility truck with a wooden bench down each side, on which the chief mourners were sitting. The coffin sat on the truck tray between their feet. Checking the truck with a fine-toothed comb revealed no liquor, so the police waved the funeral party onwards. The truck drove round behind the back of the Maori meeting hall and the mourners lifted the coffin through a window. Then they lifted a very immobile mourner through the window. Once inside, they opened the coffin, removed the liquor and inserted the immobile mourner. The wake was terrific.

One particular Maori was known to be poaching wood pigeons, which were protected. The police stopped him at a road block many times, but they never found any wood pigeons. He concealed them in his utility truck's spare tyre.

The very great Rugby Union fullback George Nepia was a good friend to both the Cutlers, who once attended a dance with him and his wife. After the fun was well under way, Nepia very solemnly asked Roden and Helen to come with him, his wife and some others

---

[†] It meant 'sharp point', which isn't a bad name for a man with one leg.

to the place where the spirits of their ancestors lived—very sacred. On their best behaviour, Roden and Helen tiptoed into an utterly dark room. When the lights came on they were handed glasses of homemade sloe gin.

'To the spirits of our ancestors!' said George Nepia, and tossed the sloe gin down the way a Russian drinks vodka.

The second Cutler child—another boy—was born in Wellington on 5 December 1948. They christened him Anthony. Another son born in New Zealand, therefore a double problem for the future.

They did get home on leave during their six years in New Zealand; the sight of her grandchildren did much to reconcile Ruby to Helen, who was a more than good mother. Ruby missed Roden.

If Helen had been offered a choice between a quiet, domestic life and her public one, Roden thinks she would have picked the former, but her sense of duty was so strong that she never faltered in her attention to that public life.

She did say to him once, 'You know, if I had had *any* idea that I would have to give so many speeches to so many different groups of women, I think I would have stayed an old maid.'

The exchange rate altered during their term, which benefited Roden greatly; his two thousand pounds per annum were pounds Sterling (British pounds rather than Australian), so became worth more than the Australian pound. He also did well out of some shares he had bought, and could relax a little. His financial future looked rosy.

When the Cutlers left New Zealand in April 1952 (this time they sailed), Roden received a number of glowing valedictions from the New Zealand newspapers, which credited him in no small measure for the easier relations between New Zealand and Australia. Some of the friends the couple made there were to be lifelong.

There had been a change of government in New Zealand, from socialist to conservative; the Prime Minister when the Cutlers departed was Sidney (later Sir Sidney) Holland.

The government in Australia had also changed from socialist to conservative. Though Labor had been returned in September of 1946 with only slightly reduced majorities in the two houses, 1946–1949 under Ben Chifley's leadership were stormy. His Cabinet saw some changes: Beasley went to London as high commissioner without contesting the 1946 election, and Makin went as ambassador to Washington D.C. under the same circumstances. Francis Forde became High Commissioner to Canada, while Charlie Frost got the Ceylon high commissioner-ship. Thus did Chifley manage to move his own men into the important Cabinet slots: he had emerged from out of Curtin's shadow. His deputy was Dr. Evatt, still Attorney-General and External Affairs. Unfortunately for Chifley, Jack Lang won a seat in the lower house and took huge pleasure in needling him. The two Labor men detested each other. Menzies and Fadden in opposition played on Lang at Chifley's expense constantly.

Chifley fell on an extraordinary issue: the nationalisation of Australia's private banks. However, other factors worked against him too. Public servants had proliferated under Labor, and they continued to increase; the general populace tended to resent their pay and power, both of which were greater than in many other social groups. Chifley exacerbated this resentment by saying publicly that public servants were entitled to have political opinions. The iron rule had always been that a public servant must be apolitical in order to serve the government of the day with complete loyalty. But Chifley undermined that, even made it legally easier for a public servant to stand for elected political office.

Postwar inflation was very serious. Chifley believed that the way to control it was to endow the Federal Government with sweeping powers over prices, rents, interest rates, bank deposits, wages and other factors. The stumbling block was the High Court of Australia, which had the final say in any constitutional matter. Federal powers had been enlarged and strengthened to cope with a war situation, but there were signs that the High Court Bench felt it was time to strip Canberra of some of these powers. To counteract this High Court attitude meant the Australian Constitution would have to be changed, and that could be done only at referendum. As the people almost invariably said NO, Chifley sought other means.

The Banking Act of 1945 required private banks (that is, all banks except the six State banks and the federally owned Commonwealth Bank) to comply with new regulations; this they were extremely averse to doing. In 1947 the Melbourne City Council was ordered under Section 48 of the Banking Act 1945 to cease dealing with private banks. It decided to challenge Section 48 in the High Court. On 13 August 1947, the High Court found in favour of the Melbourne City Council—a colossal defeat for Chifley's ideas on economics and finance. After reading the opinions of the members of the Bench, the Prime Minister realised that the implications of their finding went far beyond Section 48. 'The High Court decision made it clear that, although the Commonwealth Parliament had by the Constitution been given power to legislate on banking, nevertheless a law which was clearly a law with regard to banking could be held invalid on other constitutional considerations,' Chifley said to the House.

There were two alternatives: to accept the High Court's judgement on Section 48 and wait for a challenge to the absolutely critical credit control Sections 18–22; or to go ahead and nationalise all private banks. After his Cabinet voted unanimously to nationalise, Chifley promulgated his nationalisation bill in the Parliament.

While the federal House of Representatives debated the bill, a conservative-dominated upper house in the State of Victoria forced a State election by blocking the budget. Victorians at the polls voted heavily against Labor, an ominous warning to Chifley, who did not heed it. After seventeen days of debate so heated that men came to blows, the nationalisation bill passed in the lower house and went to the upper house, which also passed it. The Royal Assent making the bill an Act was given by the Governor-General at the end of November 1947.

The private banks immediately challenged the Act's validity in the High Court of Australia. Leading the banking team was a Sydney K.C., Garfield (later Sir Garfield) Barwick. Leading the Government's team was the Attorney-General himself, Dr. Evatt. Many partisans of nationalisation have considered Chifley's giving Evatt the job as his prime mistake. Evatt had sat on the same Bench and made enemies on it, some of whom were still sitting (it was said two of them were determined to keep on sitting until Evatt was no longer Attorney-General, and therefore empowered to appoint their successors). For it is naive to cherish the conviction that judges are more than men; they too have emotions—and political feelings. As Robert Gordon Menzies said, 'There is no question that what we call constitutional law is only half law and half philosophy—political philosophy.'

When the case was heard in 1948 there were twenty-seven barristers involved, including ten K.C.s. Dr. Evatt did not endear himself to the Bench when he demanded the disqualification of two of the judges on the grounds that he believed some members of their families had shares in private banks. His request was disallowed. The hearings went on for weeks; Dr. Evatt himself addressed the High Court for a total of seventeen days. Judgement was handed down on 11 August 1948, and was in favour of the private banks. Barwick had fought his case on the hitherto rather overlooked Section 92 of the Constitution: 'On the imposition of uniform duties of customs, trade, commerce and intercourse among the States, whether by means of internal carriage or ocean navigation, shall be absolutely free.'

Chifley announced that his government would appeal the decision to the Privy Council's Judiciary Committee in London. The committee agreed to hear the case.

This time fourteen K.C.s led the legal ranks. Hearings ran for the thirty-six sitting days between 14 March and 1 June 1949, and the transcript numbered over 1,250,000 words. Dr. Evatt took fourteen days to present the case and eight more in replying to Barwick's case; Barwick (perhaps wisely) kept his presentation to a mere nine days. Two of the judges died during the hearing period.

The verdict was handed down in July 1949. It went in favour of the private banks and the overriding principles behind Section 92 of the Constitution. After studying the Privy Council's opinions, Chifley pronounced the nationalisation of Australia's private banks a dead issue. 'We will not do anything that is outside the Constitution.'

At the general federal elections held in December of 1949, Labor was defeated in the House of Representatives by the conservative coalition between Menzies' new Liberal Party and Arthur Fadden's Country Party. Control of the Senate remained in Labor's hands because only half of the sitting senators had served their full term;

it was a half-Senate election. This so constrained the Coalition in trying to govern that in 1951 Menzies, now Prime Minister again, successfully sought a double-dissolution election by convincing the Governor-General that the only solution was to dissolve both houses of parliament and start again. This had been done only once before, in September 1914, but from 1951 on, it was to become more usual. Menzies was determined that he would not be forced into the same kind of corner he had endured in 1940, with two independents holding the balance of power.

It was to be twenty-three years before the Australian people elected another socialist government. Labor's ranks were in total disarray, something more likely to happen in a political party whose individual members had very different ideas of what exactly constituted the party's political objectives, let alone philosophy.

For Roden, the change in the colour of Canberra politics made no difference; he continued to be the High Commissioner to New Zealand until a year after the 'double-dissolution' election of April 1951.

Menzies' first Minister for External Affairs represented one of the curious co-incidences which dot Roden's life; he was Percy Spender, the member for Manly. But in April 1951 he did not seek re-election; Roden's new boss was Richard Casey (to become Lord Casey and a governor-general of Australia later on). Casey had had an illustrious career which started when he won a Distinguished Service Order and a Military Cross during the Great War. His postwar job had been in diplomacy, as liaison officer between the British and Australian governments, after which he entered Federal Parliament and was Treasurer from 1935 to 1939. From 1940 to 1942 he was the Australian Ambassador to Washington D.C., and did magnificent, if sometimes thankless, work there. From 1942 to 1944 he was British Minister of State to the Middle East and a full member of the British War Cabinet; in 1944 he became Governor of Bengal, and in 1949 he went back into the Federal Parliament. There was little he didn't know about the ins and outs of diplomacy, though he lacked Evatt's entrepreneurship.

So it was Casey's department which recalled Roden in April of 1952—but for what job? There were four posts open: the Ambassador to Indonesia; the Ambassador at Large to South-East Asia with headquarters in Singapore; the Ambassador to Italy; and the High Commissioner to Ceylon (as Sri Lanka was then called). Though 'they seemed halfhearted about Italy', the one post Roden was assured he would not get was Ceylon. Which meant, of course, that he got Ceylon.

The previous High Commissioner to Ceylon had been Dr. John Burton, a protégé of the Doc's who rose to become the bureaucratic head of the Department of External Affairs before switching to the diplomatic side. Then he resigned to stand for parliament as a Labor member at the federal elections of April 1951, but was not elected. Neither Prime Minister Menzies nor External Affairs Minister Casey would have him back. As a result, the Ceylon High Commission had had no master for over twelve months.

Helen was pregnant with their third child, so Roden decided not to risk her or the baby's health by taking her with him; she would remain in Sydney with her parents, as would David and Anthony, until after the new baby was old enough to travel. The Morrises had moved to Bronte, further from Manly, but Ruby visited. She had grown to love Helen, and had quite forgiven her stealing Roden.

The object of their affections flew from Sydney to Colombo on a Constellation; the journey took two days.

For the second time in a row he was to find the Australian

diplomatic mission disliked by the national government, and the residence a shambles. The author will explain why the residence was a shambles first, by outlining the Colombo Plan.

This was Percy Spender's brainchild (in Canberra circles it was usually called the Spending Plan), and was the first concerted effort by Australia to join the South-East Asian community. Though its ultimate objective was to develop trade with South-East Asia, in 1952 it took the form of no-strings-attached aid, and became known as the Colombo Plan because it was first mooted there at a conference. The initial aim was to give Australian assistance to various South-East Asian nations to stabilise their economies and raise their levels of production. It also encouraged a traffic in students by offering financial help enabling them to attend Australian high schools and universities. Money, of course, was the principal form of aid, but in Ceylon, for instance, Australia established tuberculosis clinics (the disease was endemic there) and donated agricultural implements such as tractors.

Just prior to Roden's arrival in Ceylon there had been a Colombo Plan exhibition in the city—gorgeous displays of various grains, fruits, vegetables, medical gadgets, farm machinery, you name it. The valuable items were shipped back to Australia afterwards, but the dismantled exhibits of perishables were deemed not worth worrying about. So, since the residence was empty, these perishables were dumped inside it instead of being given away.

What Roden surveyed with sinking heart was a jumbled mess— rice, wheat, corn, sorghum and pulses were spilled everywhere, bags ripped open by visiting animals, sodden bits of fruit and vegetables splattered on walls, ceiling, floor. Over which every noisome thing in the world seemed to be crawling, darting or scurrying. The pooches (all bugs, including cockroaches) seemed about the size of canine pooches, and the skunklike odour of the civet cats living in the roof was nauseating. Sighing, the new High Commissioner about-faced and took a room at the Galle Face Hotel.

After three days of seductive comfort, the new High Commissioner about-faced and marched back to the residence; he had resolved that the best thing to do was to move in, suffer being bitten raw and crawled all over, hire some staff and get the place shipshape. After a gigantic orgy of cleaning and waving goodbye to trucks loaded with rubbish, the residence became more or less livable.

Morale had decayed at the high commission offices as well. The staff, Australian and Ceylonese, had abandoned all formality and wore what they liked to work, usually not enough. That soon changed. The white linen or cotton suits common throughout the tropics became mandatory; if no outsider were present, staff were permitted to take off their coats, but the moment a strange face appeared, coats had to go on again. This was a high commission and it must be a credit to Australia. Opposition was minimal; Roden gained the feeling that what everyone had wanted for some time was a firm hand at the wheel of this tiny ship of state.

Colombo in 1952 was the great crossroads of South-East Asia, much as Singapore was to become after airlines took over so much of what had previously been conducted on the seas. The harbour was a constant hive of activity as ships, both cargo vessels and ocean liners, docked to unload, sailed again. The P & O liners were nicknamed 'the fishing fleet' because the multitude of single Australian girls they bore were on the lookout for a nice tea planter husband. The main export was, of course, tea, but rubber was grown in the lowlands in commercial quantities also. Ceylon was famous for its sapphire gemstones—the traditional blue, but red and yellow sapphires as well.

This big, pear-shaped island had been known in the West for over two thousand years; as ancient Taprobane, it was visited each autumn by the Ptolemaic Egyptians and the Nabataean Arabs, who bought ocean pearls, pepper and spices there. The Tamils had invaded from southern India during the time of the Kings of Kandy; the Portuguese, the Dutch and the English had all established a colonial outpost there, and the population in 1952 was very mixed. There were Moors, Ceylon Moors, the Ceylonese (more properly, the Sinhalese), Tamils, a hybrid people of Dutch-Ceylonese origins known as the Burghers, and a goodly number of British, mostly tea planters living in the highlands. The Tamils were mostly confined to the north and east of the island, and provided the labour force for growing, picking, drying and packing tea.

Politically Ceylon was completely self-governing as a full member of the British Commonwealth of Nations; the Prime Minister when Roden arrived was Dudley Senanayake, but the minister with whom he dealt directly as Australian High Commissioner was Lionel Kotellawala, later Prime Minister.

Kotellawala absolutely refused to see him, an attitude which Roden discovered present at every official Ceylonese level. The Australian High Commission was not liked, and the White Australia policy was deeply resented. As when he had arrived in New Zealand, Roden proceeded with patience to combat Ceylonese mistrust and dislike by first doing some detective work and then tailoring his conduct to what he perceived as true diplomacy: loyalty to his country combined with political neutrality.

By far the most difficult obstacle to overcome was White Australia. In 1952 it was just beginning to come under universal international disapproval, though at home in Australia it was very much a force to be reckoned with. Labor supported it wholeheartedly, not surprising in a political movement having its roots in the trade unions, always jealous of the Australian's right to a job first, and convinced that foreign labour would be content with lesser wages and fewer fringe benefits.

White Australia was a nineteenth-century phenomenon which had emerged as a result of what was seen as excessive numbers of Chinese working the goldfields and Kanaka labour from the Melanesian islands working the sugar plantations of Queensland. Some of it originated from fairly altruistic motives—it was seen as a deterrent to slave labour. But there can be no doubt that most of it arose out of xenophobia and job protection. The character of Australian civilisation was perceived as purely European and, until Arthur Calwell commenced his massive program of encouraging non-English-speaking European immigrants in 1946, preferably British.

The phrase 'White Australia' was dropped from all official documents in 1945, but the general immigration policy remained one of exclusion of non-Europeans until 1973, when the Whitlam Labor Government adopted a policy of non-discrimination on grounds of race, colour or religion. Like so many policies, be they initiated by socialists or conservatives, once official they stayed official even after governments changed poles.

Having no doubt that White Australia was by far his biggest headache, Roden decided to tackle it head-on. Diplomatic double-talk or political beating-around-the-bush, he decided, only made matters worse. Once he had an ear to listen—any ear—he spoke about White Australia absolutely directly. He was a servant of the Commonwealth of Australia, and therefore honour bound to uphold Australian policies. It was the sovereign right of Australia to decide its internal organisation; on matters which affected its domestic situation, it could act as it thought fit provided that it acted within the Australian Constitution. However, provided that non-Europeans could cope with language barriers and manifestly different customs, traditions and attitudes, non-Europeans could and would be admitted to Australia.

He received some ministerial criticism for his candidness (not, however, from Menzies or Casey), but when, as was his right as High Commissioner, he issued resident's visas to a large group of Ceylonese, he was lambasted in the Australian press. Richard Casey backed him up unreservedly; the new immigrants came.

This forthright approach worked. Relations with Ceylon improved so much that when he left that country in 1955, Lionel Kotellawala gave him a farewell luncheon and presented him with a silver tray in the shape of Ceylon.

'How did you earn those?' asked the British High Commissioner. 'You've made history.'

Baby Richard was born in Sydney on 9 July 1952, and Helen was well enough to travel by August. Roden went to the airport to meet his family, brought them back to the residence, and produced a cake for afternoon tea which he had had the cook make in the shape of an aeroplane. Oh, it was so good to see them!

From that moment on the residence began to look and feel like a home, though getting rid of the civet cats in the roof was wellnigh impossible. They lived comfortably; staff were easy to find and usually properly trained. Helen was now the 'Lady', and had to learn the Ceylon way of doing things. The cook did the marketing, and added 10 per cent onto the total as a matter of course. If the Lady objected, he packed his things and departed in a huff; if the Lady let him get away with more than 10 per cent, he deemed her a fool and became unmanageable.

Everything was always in short supply, so the Cutlers would go to an official dinner or curry tiffin at another embassy or high commission residence and find themselves drinking from their own glasses, or using their own cutlery, or eating off their own plates. But everything would be returned, generally in the same condition it enjoyed at the time it had been borrowed. Such exchanges of diplomatic property were the province of the Ceylonese staff, who didn't ask permission, simply went ahead and did it.

'How amazing!' said one British gentleman to Roden when they encountered each other on the street, eyeing Roden's gorgeous orchid *boutonnière*. 'I thought I was the only chap in Ceylon who grew those orchids.'

'Where does my buttonhole come from?' Roden demanded of his 'boy' when he returned to the residence.

'Oh, I get it from another boy!'

The British gentleman's boy. Oh, dear.

Curry tiffin was a ritual. This occurred on a Sunday. The group gathered about noon after watching a game of cricket, washed down by beer. The pink gins began about 1.30 p.m., and continued until about 4 p.m., when everyone sat down to a banquet of curries with all the traditional side dishes—coconut, sliced bananas, poppadums, cashews and many more. The meal finished, everyone said thank you very much and went home.

The Colombo Cricket Club was a revered institution, and the Ceylon cricket team was world class, played in matches against the other British Commonwealth nations. Roden was in his element.

Since Colombo was the great crossroads, all sorts of people turned up there en route between Australia and England. Some of the Australian visitors were so naive they would arrive at the residence convinced that one of a high commissioner's duties was to feed them a slap-up meal. But more often they would come to the High Commission itself, distraught because they had been gulled into buying glass cats' eyes dug out of a road rather than the red sapphires they thought they were buying. Roden or his staff would ask them to leave the 'gems' and their addresses, then try—more often than not, successfully—to trace the rascally purveyor of cats' eyes and get the money back. For this kind of job a close relationship with the British officers of the Colombo police was essential.

The Cutlers had a constant stream of visitors, official and relatives. The Morrises came, Ruby came, and Aunt Dais came twice. That was a great joy, to be able to play host to these beloved people, take them on excursions and longer trips to see magical things. At Mt. Lavinia, which was about eight miles from Colombo, there were actually elephants which had been trained to play a game of cricket. Everyone loved the elephants, which were saucy, mischievous creatures always after buns or bananas. However, the last stage of an expedition to see the ancient murals at Sigiriya was frightening. The area was plagued by lethal wasps: one sting and you were dead. So cages made of insect screening dotted the route. When the wasps arrived, you got into one of these cages and stayed there until the wasps gave up and went elsewhere.

The Australian cricket team always called into Colombo if it were playing in England—or Ceylon. Naturally the cricket-mad High Commissioner entertained the players, which on one occasion proved a little difficult. The team had to leave because their ship was due to sail, but Lindsay Hassett (the captain) and Bill O'Reilly (one of the world's greatest bowlers) were having such a good time that they remained. O'Reilly spent his time talking to Helen, while Hassett concentrated on Roden.

Finally Roden said to Hassett very firmly, 'Look, I'm going to take you to the ship right now, because I refuse to keep you here for three more days until the next ship arrives.'

Hassett rose to his feet, drained his glass and threw it against the wall.

Helen's face was the picture of utter horror—only she knew how hard it was to replace a wine glass in Colombo.

The ship was in the roads, on its way out to sea. Roden took the two cricketers out in the agent's launch and made them jump from boat to ladder on the ship's side. They made it.

Bill O'Reilly sent Helen what Roden gleefully describes as a 'love letter'; Hassett never said a word.

Robert Gordon Menzies passed through for a couple of days on an overseas trip. Because the weather in Colombo was exhaustingly hot and humid, Roden took him up into the hills to a cottage belonging to Ceylon's Governor-General. The Ceylonese chief of protocol, Mr. Alfred, accompanied them.

When Roden suggested a visit to the local market, Menzies accepted with alacrity. There the Prime Minister spotted some cobs of corn, and insisted that they buy half a dozen, cook them for dinner. Mr. Alfred looked very disapproving. Over the meal, while Menzies and Roden poured ghee (clarified butter) all over their corn cobs and gnawed away with gusto, Mr. Alfred sat in stony silence, his corn untouched. To the chief of protocol, the whole act of consuming corn was clearly one that heads of state ought not indulge in. Dignity could not be maintained with a chin running butter.

Menzies looked at him, great prawnlike eyebrows wiggling. 'You know, Alfred,' he said gently, 'there's one thing about sweet corn—it does inhibit social intercourse.' And went on gnawing.

King George VI died in 1952; his elder daughter succeeded him as Queen Elizabeth II. A mere high commissioner did not rate an invitation to sit inside Westminster Abbey to see her crowned in 1953, but one with a Victoria Cross did. When Mr. and Mrs. Morris offered to stay in Ceylon to look after the three little boys (they were on their way to England), the Cutlers decided to go to the coronation. Because Mr. Morris thought it unwise of them to travel together, Helen left first by ship, and Roden by plane some days afterwards. Coming home they decided to risk flying together; it was no fun on one's own.

Then later, in 1954, the new Queen spent two days in Ceylon as a guest of its government on her way to Australia and New Zealand. Here Roden had the opportunity to meet her at last. To British peoples of the time her accession created enormous excitement. In these last days of the Empire's setting sun, with the world map steadily losing its pinkness, the idea of a second Elizabeth Regina generated dreams of a British rejuvenation, of a new and even more splendid Elizabethan Age. That was not to be, but in 1954 many hoped for it ardently. She was so young, so sweet and pretty! Forgetting that her namesake, the first Elizabeth, had been a tough, crafty, ruthless absolute monarch with bad teeth and a bad temper.

It was while he was in Ceylon that Roden had his only real quarrel with an Australian minister. Richard Casey was on leave when Menzies, looking after External Affairs, had to dash suddenly to New York for a brief time. So he left Senator John Gorton, not yet a minister, in charge of External Affairs ex officio. Gorton, in effect, was being given a trial run.

Some disgruntled person in Ceylon wrote to the minister and called Roden and his mission 'ugly Australians'. The person particularly criticised the fact that Roden had one of his staff

permanently occupied with Colombo Plan matters—an absurd
waste of the Australian taxpayers' money! 'All these people need
are shovels, so send them shovels and get them *working*!' Gorton
responded by sending Ceylon a shipment of shovels. The Cutler
temper, almost always under control, snapped; he sat down and
wrote a biting, 'very strong' letter to Gorton (later to be Prime
Minister). One of its chief points was that Gorton had not bothered
to consult either the High Commissioner or his mission about the
letter or the shovels. He had bypassed them as if they did not exist,
all on the say-so of someone who patently had no idea what
Australia was trying to do in Ceylon—and had a poor opinion of
Ceylon's people into the bargain.

'Have you seen John Gorton yet?' Menzies slyly asked Roden
when next he was in Canberra.

Gorton invited him to a cocktail party and was suitably contrite.

But it is interesting that John Gorton didn't get a ministry until
the very end of 1958—Navy, which wasn't a Cabinet post because
Menzies had adopted a new system in 1956: he admitted none save
senior ministers into Cabinet, which thus was smaller and much
easier for a prime minister to control. Only Gough Whitlam was to
revert to the full-sized Cabinet; all other governments since 1956
have used the Menzies system.

In fact, Gorton's career stagnated until Menzies retired.

Midway through 1955, Roden knew that Ceylon would shortly
be winding to a close. Where might he be sent next? Somewhere
quite difficult, he suspected. He never seemed to be posted
anywhere easy.

●

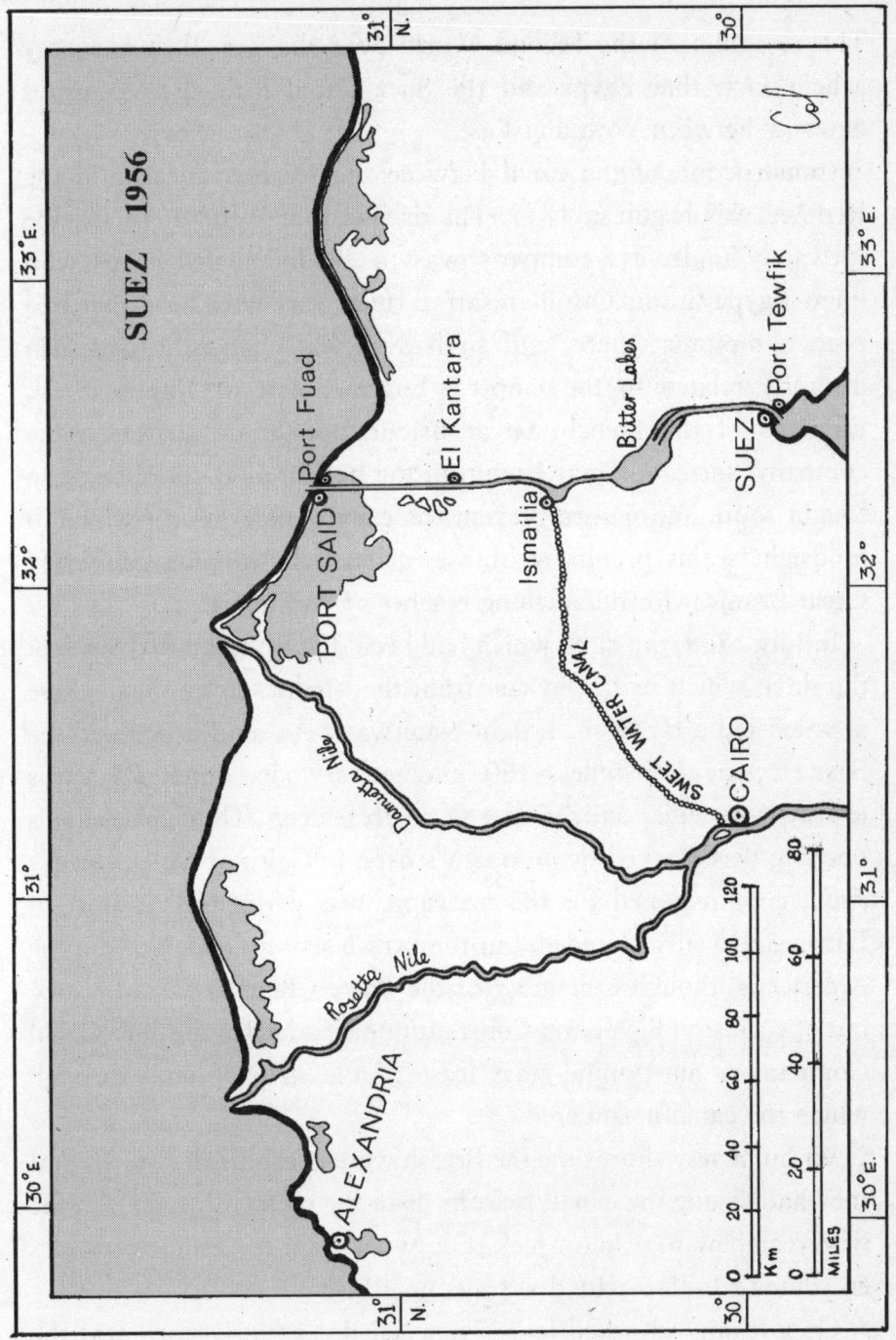

SUEZ 1956

Port Fuad

Port Tewfik

El Kantara

Bitter Lakes

PORT SAID

SUEZ

Ismailia

Nile

Damietta

SWEET WATER CANAL

CAIRO

Rosetta Nile

ALEXANDRIA

The cessation of the Second World War did not alter one very salient fact: that Egypt and the Suez Canal formed the natural gateway between West and East.

Construction of the canal between the Mediterranean and the Red Sea was begun in 1859. The driving force behind the scheme (privately funded as a company) was one Ferdinand de Lesseps, who knew Egypt and its Ottoman satrap rulers very well; his father had been a diplomat there, and so had he. By chance he was also distantly related to the Empress Eugenie, wife of Napoleon III, Emperor of the French. Great Britain bought no shares in the company. Instead, Great Britain in the person of Lord Palmerston fought tooth and nail to prevent the canal's excavation—which in hindsight seems peculiarly obtuse, given that shipping connected Great Britain with the farflung reaches of its Empire.

In July 1869, the ditch which had been dug from the Red Sea met the ditch which had been dug from the Mediterranean Sea. There now existed a far from straight waterway between Europe and the East. It was 100 miles (160 kilometres) long, about 75 yards (68 metres) wide, and 26 feet (8 metres) deep. The Suez Canal's opening was marked by an opera season in Cairo at which Verdi's *Aida*, commissioned for the occasion, was performed. A host of European royalty attended, but the British sent no one. Nor did the Americans, though a member of the Boston Board of Trade came out of curiosity. Egypt and Constantinople had given the Suez Canal Company a ninety-nine-years lease of the strip of sand through which the canal meandered.

Within a very short time the British were gnashing their teeth that they hadn't dug the canal; two-thirds of the traffic through it in the first year flew the Union Jack. Oh, woe! cried the Prince of Wales en route to India—why don't *we* own this?

Opportunity knocked in 1875, when Benjamin Disraeli was the

British Prime Minister. Egypt owned 44 per cent of the Suez Company's shares, and its Ottoman satrap ruler, Ismail Pasha, had borrowed millions to fund the riotously high living he considered his right. Desperate because his creditors were dunning him unmercifully, he offered Egypt's shares to a consortium of French banks, which hemmed and hawed a little too long. The moment he got wind of it, Disraeli dashed to Paris, borrowed four million pounds from Baron Rothschild and bought Ismail Pasha out, then sent a note to Queen Victoria: 'It is just settled; you have it, madam.'

The 177,000 shares Ismail Pasha had sold enabled the British Government to assume a number of seats on the company's board of directors. The Suez Canal Company was now a joint Franco-British enterprise operated by private banks in France on the one hand, and the British Government on the other. This meant that the British almost-half was in a far better position to marshal the military machine if the canal were threatened.

Egypt emulated the canal's fate when Ismail Pasha's debts became so enormous that the British and French got permission from Ottoman headquarters in Constantinople to take over and administer Egypt's finances. Though the existence of the canal created immense new trade and prosperity (particularly for Great Britain), from the moment Ismail Pasha sold Egypt's interest in it, it did virtually nothing to benefit Egypt, across whose sands it straggled. In this were the seeds of the Suez Crisis of 1956.

In 1882 the first in a number of Egyptian colonels with nationalistic ideas, Colonel Ahmed Arabi, tried to seize power. The British and French fleets moved in, but at the last moment Paris ordered the French fleet home. The British continued alone and the fate of Egypt was sealed, though there were to be many rebellions both in Egypt and the Sudan. Nominally ownership of Egypt was to continue to rest in Egyptian hands, but the reality was British.

The canal had to be protected. Not only was it a main artery of Empire trade and commerce; it was also a first-class strategic military prize.

In 1888 the canal itself became an international waterway allowing free passage of ships of all nations according to the Treaty of Constantinople. The canal garrison was to be British.

Another pact confirmed British dominance after the end of the Great War. The Treaty of Versailles formally recognised Egypt as a British Protectorate. To many Egyptians it was the height of insult for the Big Powers to declare that a country which had a national history as old as Man could not manage its own affairs, that these affairs were to be managed by a nation still in short trousers, if not in diapers.

With some degree of sensitivity the British decided to allow a constitutional monarch[†] in Egypt and return some aspects of government to the Egyptians. But they still controlled the Egyptian army and they still garrisoned the Suez Canal. Military headquarters were in Cairo.

In 1936 Egypt was given a nominal interest in the canal and a seat or two on the company's board of directors; Egypt was to share garrison duty, and a few Egyptians were given jobs in what would now be called middle management.

In the meantime, the importance of the Middle East—and the British position there—had increased a hundredfold thanks to vast deposits of oil in Iraq, Iran and Arabia.

During all this time the United States of America had not taken much interest in the Suez Canal, which lay far from American spheres of interest; the Panama Canal was its business, and it was sure Panama was as safe as houses.

[†] King Fuad, father of King Farouk.

The end of the Second World War saw the United States of America the world's most powerful nation. France was a ruin of twisted railway tracks, demolished bridges, civilian factions and governmental chaos, while the British were to endure drastic food and commodities rationing until 1952, and even then rationing did not entirely cease. By default, the U.S.A. was more or less compelled to enter the world arena. Early on it realised that the U.S.S.R. was going to enter the world arena too, and ideologically the two superpowers were poles apart. Though the Entente Cordiale existed between France and the United Kingdom, both these powers had to understand that they no longer dominated global affairs. And that hurt. The Cold War came into being; so did the threat of nuclear holocaust. The old generation was tired and the new generation disillusioned.

When Dwight D. Eisenhower was elected President of the U.S.A. late in 1952, the American crusade against communism became two-fold: at home was Senator Joseph McCarthy, and abroad was John Foster Dulles, the Secretary of State. And by 1956, things had become so topsy-turvy that the U.S.A. was to find itself supporting Egypt against its old ally, the U.K.

The British relationship with Egypt after the Second World War was worse than uneasy. The 60,000 British troops stationed around the canal were far in excess of the number permitted by the 1936 agreement, and Jewish immigration to Palestine was deemed by the Egyptians to be London's fault and no one else's.

In 1945 the Arab League came into being and Egypt joined it, allying itself with Syria, Jordan, Iraq, Saudi Arabia and Yemen. The threat of an emerging Jewish state in Palestine had caused the formation of the Arab League, and Israel was to hold it together. But what it needed in its early years was one strong man.

Egypt itself was titularly ruled by the luxury-loving King Farouk, who was seen by his people as no more and no less than a British vassal. An un-Arab. Nationalistic Egyptians, who had suffered him since before the war, regarded him with contempt and loathing. In lieu of having anything better to do, he confined his interests to gourmandising and pornography.

In 1946 workers and students attacked British property and persons in Cairo and Alexandria; Moscow promptly got into the act by demanding that Egypt be 'liberated'. As the current British Government was a socialist one, Clement Attlee agreed to withdraw all British military personnel from Egypt and the canal zone by September of 1949. Then it all fell apart over British sovereignty in the Sudan, which the U.K. declined to abandon. Nor did the Sudanese want to be a part of Egypt. When Egypt appealed to the United Nations, that body (including the Russian delegation) refused to let Egypt annex the Sudan. The Sudan was to have self-government, said the U.N.

In an attempt to prove that London was not encouraging Jewish immigration into Palestine, the U.K. tried to restrict these many thousands of Jewish refugees from Europe. The result was a wave of terrorism and sabotage. The U.S.A. tended to support the emerging Jewish state. So did the U.S.S.R. Thus in 1947 at Lake Success, New York, the state of Israel was born. Within a week of Israeli independence the Arab League invaded—and was soundly defeated.

The Egyptian segment of the Arab army was even more angry at its own government in Cairo than at Israel. Among its middle rank officers was Gamal Abdel Nasser, a member of the Free Officers movement dedicated to abolishing the corrupt Egyptian regime and King Farouk. One of their avowed targets was the 80,000-strong British garrison on the canal. Yes, there were now 20,000 more.

Attlee lost power in October of 1951; Winston Churchill was Prime Minister again. His Foreign Secretary was the sophisticated, handsome, slightly withdrawn Anthony Eden. Along the canal the British troops were now literally at war; after they attacked the Ismailia police station, Egyptian nationalists set fire to British and other foreign-owned property in Cairo. King Farouk and his ministers were impotent, but Churchill finally decided that the British troops would stay to guard the canal. Cairo would just have to burn.

Nasser's main problem was his junior status. All his fellow members of the Free Officers group were majors or captains, even lieutenants, while he himself was a mere colonel. They needed a figurehead—and found one in Brigadier Mohammed Naguib, who was elderly and extremely partial to Scotch whisky, therefore (they thought) easy to control. Naguib had natural charisma; Nasser had to work at it.

The ensuing revolution was relatively bloodless. King Farouk was sent into permanent exile and his government was sacked. It then turned out that Brigadier Naguib was not malleable after all. As he thought the proper place for an army was in the field, he appointed civilians to government, including the prime ministership. This did not sit well with the rest of the military junta, which was further incensed when these civilians did little to redistribute land, in the ownership of a tiny, immensely wealthy minority. As the discontent mounted, Naguib assumed the prime ministership himself—the people loved him—and gradually usurped more power. He appointed a board to study the operation of the Suez Canal, which had sixteen more of its ninety-nine-years lease to go. When the lease ran out, the canal would finally belong to Egypt. Naguib was content to wait.

In February 1953 the Sudanese problem resolved itself. London and Cairo jointly agreed that the Sudan should have immediate independence, and be left to choose for itself whether it would join

Egypt later (it chose to remain independent). Naguib began to look like a decent sort of man to London; hopes rose that all might yet be well.

Worried about growing Soviet influence in the Middle East, John Foster Dulles stuck his oar in by visiting Cairo early in 1953. His aim was to try to convince Naguib that a British presence along the canal would form a buffer between Egypt and the growing Soviet menace. Naguib did not give him a direct answer, simply requested American armaments. When Dulles left, he was under the impression that if only the British would withdraw their troops from the canal, Egypt might join his embryonic brainchild, the Middle East Treaty Organization.

A year later, in February 1954, Nasser moved to wrest Egypt from Naguib by forcing him to resign, but Naguib was just too popular; three days later he was back. In April the two men divided up the power, with Naguib as President and Nasser as Prime Minister. By November, Nasser knew what he had to do. He popped Naguib into a comfortable villa on the outskirts of Cairo and gave him all the Scotch whisky he could drink.

Son of a post office worker and a coal merchant's daughter, Gamal Abdel Nasser was born in 1918. He suffered greatly from Egyptian reluctance to admit those of low birth into the bureaucracy and the officer corps. Despite his having passed their entrance examination, the National Police Force turned him down because of his lowly origins. Thanks to the fact that governmental policy had changed, in 1937 he was admitted to army officer school.

Tall and well built, he was an imposing man who learned the hard way how to please the masses. In private life he was most abstemious, and he had an intense mistrust of personal wealth. As clever as he was ambitious, he pored his way slowly through English-language newspapers and cultivated an educated air.

Negotiations on a settlement of the canal dispute resumed, but if the British had hoped that an amicable solution of the Sudan matter augured well, they were soon disenchanted. Nothing less than complete evacuation of all British troops from the canal zone would satisfy Nasser, nor would he consent to free navigation. No Israeli ship or ship bearing cargo for Israel could use the waterway.

In July 1954 the British began to crumble. They decided to transfer their Middle East military headquarters from Egypt to Cyprus. This permitted a phased withdrawal of British troops from the canal zone. Nasser was assured by London that by June 1956 the last British soldier would be gone.

The British concessions emboldened Nasser to start making friends abroad among 'non-aligned' countries, particularly Muslim ones. Dissidents at home shot at him—and missed— which turned him into a demigod to many Egyptians who had wondered. After he attended talks in Indonesia and announced that Egypt would adopt a policy of 'positive neutrality', his demigod status bloomed. Now he could take on the role of chief spokesman for the Arab League. And that meant that both Washington D.C. and Moscow started to court him.

While all this was going on, Israel had produced David Ben-Gurion, another man who mistrusted the British deeply. The one, Ben-Gurion, had perforce to manipulate an internal political web that wheeled in a circle from left of Karl Marx to right of Genghiz Khan. The other, Nasser, was uncomfortably aware that as the head of a military junta he was vulnerable to overthrow by an even younger and more ambitious colonel than himself; his answer was to develop his own army of secret police and informers.

The first five years of Israel's existence under Ben-Gurion were desperate. The Arabs never ceased to plague Israel, while Israel always retaliated. But after Ben-Gurion retired in November 1953, his place as Prime Minister was taken by a man inclined more to the negotiation table than violent reprisals. Moshe Sharett began to communicate secretly with Nasser by devious routes, and while this went on the border situation quietened a little. It would seem that these furtive dickerings were sincere on both sides.

What drove Sharett out and brought Ben-Gurion back were the shifting sands of British, Soviet and American actions and policies in the Middle East. This was particularly true of the Americans, for under Eisenhower policy swung away from Truman's pro-Jewish stance and tried to quiver in the centre of the dial. Nothing really mattered save containment of the U.S.S.R.

We would probably live in a more serene world if its leaders could divorce themselves from their emotions, but such is not the case. As with the history of the Australian Labor Party, so too the political history of the postwar globe. Anthony Eden and John Foster Dulles detested each other. The Soviet Foreign Minister, Vyacheslav Molotov, trusted nobody and loathed everybody. And in 1954 the antipathy between Eden and Dulles grew worse and worse. Neither man was prepared to listen to what the other was saying. There were diplomatic injuries in which Eden was perceived to have let the U.S.A. down.

Then Dulles' eagerness to get the Middle East to pull as a team began to evaporate—at precisely the moment when British enthusiasm waxed, thanks to the Baghdad Pact between Turkey and Iraq early in 1955. Since Dulles had been applying pressure for a long time, the U.K. announced that it would sign the Baghdad Pact, sure that Dulles was going to commit the U.S.A. as well. But Dulles didn't. Nor would France come to the party. London was out on a limb that everyone seemed intent on sawing through.

Moreover, the Baghdad Pact convinced Nasser that the British would never withdraw from the Middle East. India, self-proclaimed leader of the non-aligned nations, castigated the U.K. loudly, and the U.S.S.R. was quick to follow suit. Soviet criticism was harsher than of yore because Malenkov, a moderate, had fallen; his place was taken by Nikolai Bulganin, who was a front-man for Nikita Khrushchev. Khrushchev and Foreign Minister Molotov began to step up the Cold War and amass nuclear arms. The world shivered.

The guard was changing in another place too. On 6 April 1955, an old and ill Winston Churchill retired. He passed the prime minister's torch to Sir Anthony Eden, who had been waiting for the job for a long time. Too long, perhaps. Though he was to live for another twenty years, a series of major operations in 1953 had left him debilitated and weary. Never possessed of Churchill's millstone endurance, Eden was inclined to flag. He lacked toughness, decisiveness, ruthlessness.

As if all this were not enough, Israel raided Gaza. Nasser immediately increased the size of the Egyptian army and started shopping for arms. Thanks to Algeria and Indo-China, France had none to sell; any surplus was going to Israel. Nor was Nasser a favoured person in Paris, where he was blamed for the Algerian insurrection. London was willing to assist Egypt—on the condition that Nasser sanctioned the Baghdad Pact. Which he could not do if he wanted to remain dominant in the Arab League.

So he petitioned Washington D.C., which asked him for a shopping list. He sent a modest one. No one bothered to look at it until May 1955, when Nasser finally got an answer. Yes, he could have arms—but only if he paid cash on the spot. He declined.

For in the meantime he had found an easy-credit source of military equipment: Czech. That is, Soviet arms aid. He notified Washington D.C. and submitted another modest list. The Americans did nothing; Dulles was convinced Nasser was bluffing as well as blackmailing. Then intelligence started coming in that

Nasser may have been blackmailing, but he certainly wasn't bluffing. He was getting what he wanted from the Soviet bloc—and his shopping list was yards longer because Egypt's credit rating was immaterial.

By August, London and Washington D.C. were galvanised. Oh, oh! Nasser was thick with the Russians! Emissaries from the U.S.A. were received coldly in Cairo and sent home cheerless. The arms deal with Czechoslovakia was going through to the tune of $250 million—ten times more than he had asked of the U.S.A. Soviet technicians and arms were arriving in Cairo, and Nasser was sending army officers to Moscow for training. This arms deal with Egypt was the first the U.S.S.R. had concluded with a non-communist country. And there were hints that internal troubles were coming to a boil within the communist enclave. Tito's Yugoslavia had seceded from the Soviet bloc and went its own communist way; Albania was to follow. Hungary was rumbling. Poland was too.

Eden attempted to counter the Egyptian-Soviet arms deal by wooing King Hussein of Jordan into joining the Baghdad Pact, but when Hussein, British educated and an Anglophile, indicated that Jordan would be interested, the King's own subjects—and ministers—protested so strongly that Hussein hastily backpedalled; even so, his credibility in Jordan was damaged. All he got out of it were ten state-of-the-art British fighter planes.

Israel took the Egypt-Soviet arms deal as an indication that Nasser was girding his loins for war, and put its own economy and troops on a war footing.

And then there was the vexed question of the Aswan Dam. The 1950s constituted the height of dam building; put in a dam and all would magically be right—no unregulated floods, a vast reservoir of water against poor rainfall, the right amount of water for irrigation. To Nasser, damming the Nile River in the area of the First Cataract seemed the answer to Egypt's precarious economy. Production of food, he calculated, would rise by 90 per cent. There would be no cotton crop failures to prevent foreign money flowing in to buy Egyptian cotton. But a dam at Aswan was a major undertaking, a gigantic project requiring multi-millions Egypt just did not have to spend.

First he approached the Germans, but by the end of 1953 they realised the scheme was too big for them, and bowed out. In 1955 Nasser asked the World Bank for part of the money to fund it. As he outlined his plans to bank officials, they were to consist of two stages. The first and far cheaper stage (it would cost a mere $70 million) was the planning, drafting and preliminary engineering, and it was to be funded by the U.S.A. and the U.K. The second stage was the building of the dam itself, five years down the track; half of that $400 million was to come from the Americans and the British, and the other half, he hoped, would come from the World Bank.

The Americans and the British were suddenly eager to finance Nasser's dream because of the Soviet arms deal—especially after they learned that Moscow was offering to pay for the building of the dam itself. So by November 1955, Nasser had been assured of the American and British money—provided, that is, that the World Bank agreed to lend its share. And provided that Nasser tempered his commitment to the U.S.S.R.

But when King Hussein of Jordan abruptly fired Glubb Pasha, the British general in charge of the famous Jordanian Arab Legion, Eden blamed Nasser. The British dilemma over Jordan increased after it became clear that both Saudi Arabia and the U.S.S.R. were happy to replace the British subsidy to Jordan. Yet Eden seems to have done nothing to bridge the ever-widening gap between the

U.K. and King Hussein, who was simply trying to stay on his throne. By March 1956 he was still, he said to the House of Commons, unable to formulate a policy anent Jordan. Ever and always at the back of Eden's mind loomed the malign spectre of Gamal Abdel Nasser, who was first 'the new Mussolini' and then 'a petty Hitler'. Eden no longer wanted Nasser neutralised; he wanted him destroyed.

Whereas John Foster Dulles believed that fair words and a lot of American dollars would woo Nasser into the free Western fold. He was not a communist, rather a nationalist who was determined to rid Egypt and the Middle East of the British colonial presence—a sentiment any American tended to view kindly—been there, done that. Besides which, British activities in the Middle East and French ones in Algeria (Tunisia and Morocco were to gain their independence, but Algeria was a different matter) meant that British and French participation in the North Atlantic Treaty Organization (NATO) was less than both Dulles and Eisenhower wanted. They were spilling their seed upon the sand.

A meeting in London between Eden, Bulganin and Khrushchev in April 1956 did not go well. The British Prime Minister told the Russians bluntly that in order to keep the oil flowing from the Middle East to the U.K., the British would go to war if they had to. This plain speaking astonished the Russians, who had expected a more cringing attitude. They then had to listen as Eden outlined an East-West embargo of armaments to any country in the Arab-Israeli sphere. As if all this wasn't enough, when they attended a dinner hosted by the British Labour Party (in opposition), it ended in a brawl over the fate of some eastern socialists held in Soviet gaols.

'Bulganin can vote for Labour if he wants, but I'm voting for the Tories,' said Khrushchev on the way home.

But in May 1956, Nasser blotted his American copybook with a vengeance: he formally recognised Communist China. To Dulles that was unforgivable, as Communist China was top of his hate list. What prompted Nasser to acknowledge Peking was probably intelligence that the Soviet Union was going to join an arms embargo in the Middle East—but France was still selling arms to Israel. Therefore if Soviet aid to Egypt stopped, whereabouts would military aid come from? The answer was Communist China, not then a member of the United Nations. Undoubtedly he knew that Peking had no arms to sell, but mentioning the place was a good way to ensure that the Soviet aid kept coming. What he did not appreciate, it seems, was the depth of Dulles' loathing for Peking. Colonel Nasser would have to learn that painfully.

The loans to build the Aswan Dam were contingent upon each other. The British would not contribute if the Americans and the World Bank did not, and the World Bank would contribute only if the Americans and British stumped up their shares. Even in May 1956 both the British and the World Bank confidently expected that Dulles would tender the American share.

There were problems on the American home front: Egyptian cotton cut into the American share of the cotton market; it was an election year and Eisenhower wanted a second term; Republican administrations were not famous for spending money; and Congress hated long-term financial commitments, especially to foreign places which were displaying affection for communists. So Congress offered Dulles a choice: aid for Tito, an outright communist, or aid for Nasser, a communist flirter. Dulles chose Marshal Tito. Divide and conquer every time.

By late June the last British troops were off Egyptian soil and the Soviet Union was renewing its pledges of arms and low-interest loans to pay for the Aswan Dam. Nasser's intelligence network had informed him that the Americans were going to renege, so he sent an emissary to Washington D.C. under instructions to inform Dulles that Egypt would do everything the Americans wanted. It took Dulles until 19 July to inform Ambassador Hussein that there was no deal. The U.S.A. just could not be sure that Nasser would honour his promises.

Colonel Nasser got the news on his way home from Yugoslavia, where he had been conferring with Marshal Tito and Pandit Nehru, Prime Minister of India. The chips were down, but he would play his hand. On 26 July 1956, he nationalised the Suez Canal. The fourth anniversary of the expulsion of King Farouk.

The stage was set for the Suez crisis.

'Egypt? Oh, no!' cried Helen when Roden told her that he had been informed from Canberra that he was go to Cairo as Her Majesty's Australian Minister to head the legation in Egypt. The post was not ambassadorial because protocol demanded that two nations should each have diplomatic representation of like kind; Egypt at that time had a legation in Canberra, so Australia had a legation in Cairo.

The date was mid-July 1955 and things were already looking grim in Egypt; the Baghdad Pact had been signed, Sir Anthony Eden was Prime Minister, Khrushchev and his front-man Bulganin were in power in the U.S.S.R., and Nasser was shopping for armaments as well as funds to build the Aswan Dam. Even in Ceylon, the papers regularly featured Egypt in the news. Ceylon was also beginning to feel a little sympathy for Egypt and Nasser.

This was the only moment when Helen was ever to betray alarm or dissatisfaction on being told of her next destination. Whenever the couple moved, she said goodbye to the old post and the good friends, packed up, occupied the next residence without complaint and buckled down to transforming it into a proper home without spending too much of Australia's money. No better wife for a peripatetic diplomat could have existed. But she wasn't very happy about going to Egypt, though after that unguarded exclamation of dismay, she shrugged philosophically and started the packing.

They had already discussed the children's futures. David and Anthony were getting a little too old to continue attending local schools wherever they went, and the days of top schools for diplomats' children, at least in Asia, had not yet arrived. The British tradition throughout the East was to send offspring to be educated in England. But ought the Cutler boys go to school in England or Australia? Time they had at least one stable aspect to their lives. Maybe because so many local children went, the air fares to England from Asia were less expensive; while Roden's salary was excellent, he had three boys to educate, all of whom would wind up boarding. Not a problem for them; they understood why.

Roden and Helen decided on England because the diplomatic lottery favoured that as the cheaper destination. In Asia return fares would be paid by the Government once a year; minor breaks would have to be a personal expense, but the Cutlers felt strongly that the boys should join them for every vacation.

But in the meantime they sailed for Suez with all three boys; Cairo had good schools. Eerie for Roden to dock at Suez, see the canal he knew so well. In and out of Egypt; always on duty and perhaps never without some kind of danger. It was 26 July 1955—the third anniversary of King Farouk's expulsion from Egypt.

The First Secretary, Nick Parkinson, wasn't there to welcome them; his wife was most unwell. Someone else drove them to Cairo through the heat of the day. A bottle of Coca-Cola cost the Egyptian equivalent of threepence—very expensive—but the boys loved the thought of drinking Coca-Cola in a strange land.

The residence came as a wonderful surprise. Cool, airy, spacious, beautifully furnished. Helen looked much happier as she explored the first official house she didn't need to have rewired or replumbed or repainted or deloused or disinfected—or all five. The Legation ran the width of the block. One entered the chancellery from a main street in the north part of Zamalik Island (an elegant Cairo suburb), whereas one entered the residence from a more minor street behind. Ceiling fans whooshed gently, polished brass gleamed, the courtyard between chancellery and residence was the most delightful garden— oh, heaven! How different from Wellington and Colombo!

Leaving Helen to prowl the upper floors, Roden went down into the residence basement, where he discovered, a sinking feeling in the pit of his stomach, that one room contained a veritable armoury. Sub-machine guns, ammunition, even cans of petrol. He then went on another and more thorough tour, face set, eyes going everywhere. He hadn't worn that look since Syria.

'This is ridiculous,' he said afterwards to his assembled senior staff. 'There are far too many doors and windows to hope to hold this place successfully. Which turns weapons into a liability, not an asset. If we keep them, we might be tempted to use them, and we'd be dead in a hurry. Nasser's not a fool, he wants to keep his international image as irreproachable as he can. Our diplomatic status is better protection than this stuff. Send it back to the British on the canal. At once.'

This was mid-1955. There were still British on the canal.

His staff briefed him on the situation, after which Roden presented his letters of credence to Colonel Gamal Abdel Nasser.

'A big man, always smirking,' Roden describes him.

Cairo seethed with suspicion of and antipathy to Westerners, and the Australians were deemed a minor offshoot of the British; neither Nasser nor his Young Turks ever accepted invitations to receptions or dinners hosted by Westerners, though as a minister Roden always issued invitations.

He had little chance to say much during that initial audience with Nasser, who dominated the conversation completely. What Nasser seems not to have understood is that his auditor was a veteran of this part of the world; he would have done better to keep his mouth shut. Much has been written about Nasser's command of English, of the way he devoured every English-language newspaper he could get his hands on, but Roden insists that in actual fact his grasp of English was not good. His long harangue was a repetitive jumble of meaningless words and phrases, the kind of thing one might memorise without truly grasping its import. When Roden did have a chance to speak, Nasser's replies betrayed the fact that he had not comprehended. As Her Majesty's Australian Minister spoke the kind of clear English usually called 'international English', he should have had no trouble comprehending.

Cairo crawled with police, secret police, spies and informers. No matter where the Westerners congregated—at an embassy, a club, a restaurant, an office—the police and other more furtive types would be outside, making notes of every person who went in, writing down the car licence plate numbers.

Since no Westerner with a soupçon of intelligence could have failed to see all this observation, there were certain places only where men spoke freely to each other. The Gezira Club was the main gathering place for diplomats, British expatriates and all sorts of Westernised foreigners, and it was here that most information changed hands. Nobody who went to the Gezira Club had any time for Nasser, but some at least of the servants were in his pay—there were eyes and ears almost everywhere. So lots of people jogged on

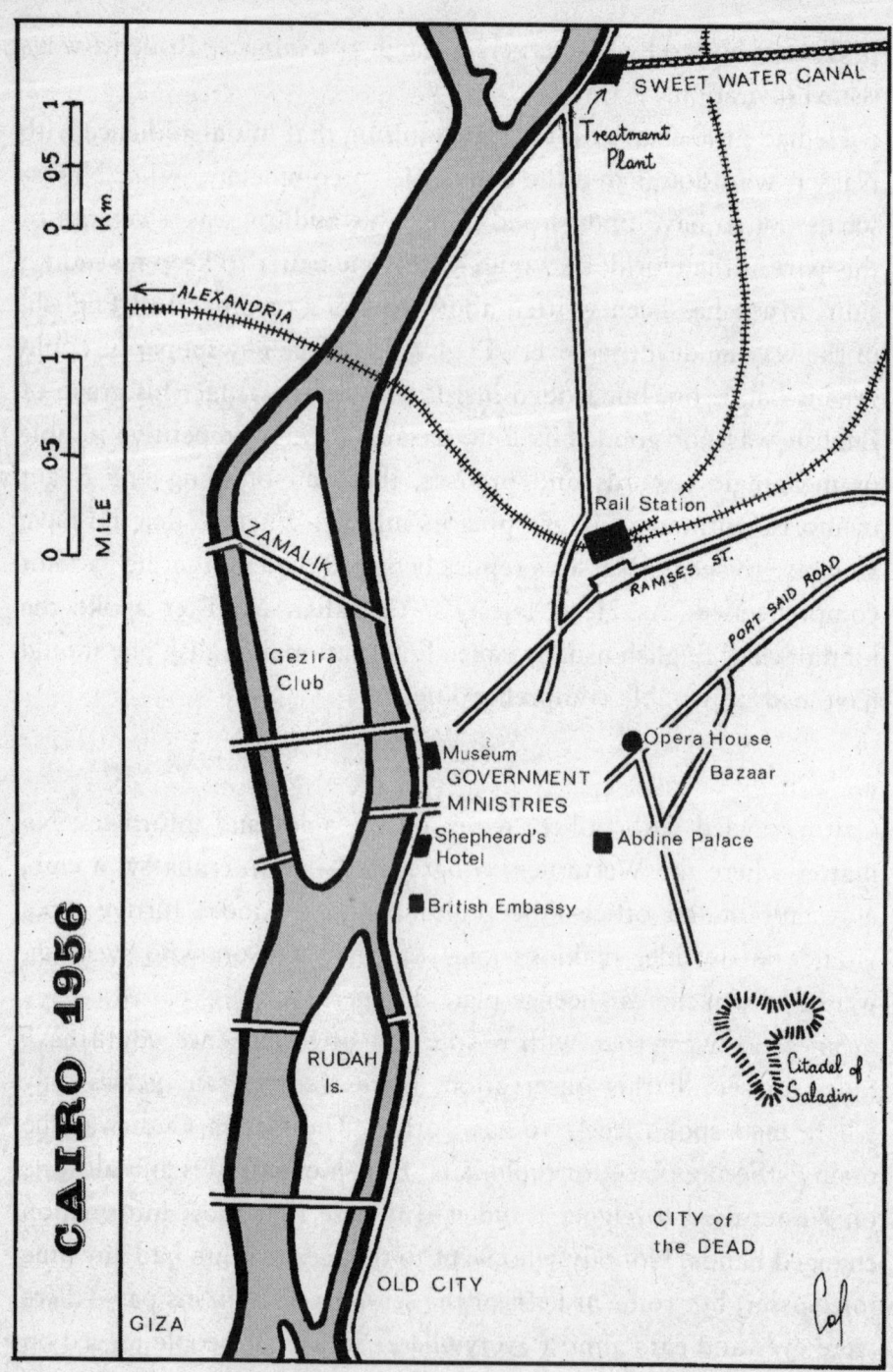

SWEET WATER CANAL

Treatment Plant

ALEXANDRIA

Rail Station

RAMSES ST.

PORT SAID ROAD

ZAMALIK

Gezira Club

Museum
GOVERNMENT
MINISTRIES

Shepheard's Hotel

British Embassy

Opera House

Bazaar

Abdine Palace

Citadel of Saladin

RUDAH Is.

CITY of the DEAD

OLD CITY

GIZA

CAIRO 1956

Km

MILE

the exercise track, pretended to puff and stopped in groups to recover; mornings usually saw people in the swimming pool, treading water in clusters in the middle as if having a wonderful time. It was during one such discussion that Roden found out how Nasser had managed to dispose of Naguib so nicely and bloodlessly; the world knew nothing of Naguib's addiction to Scotch whisky. Of course he drank himself to death.

Even in the residence one had to be careful, though Roden was to find as time went on and the situation deteriorated that his staff in the residence were very loyal. After he advised them to get out before they landed in gaol, they elected to stay—but not to spy. On the chancellery side it was more difficult. Someone would walk into a room to find a strange Egyptian there with the telephone receiver in his hand—ooops, just making a call! They assumed the phones were tapped. All private talk at the residence or chancellery had to take place on the flat roof in the open air, and even then the conversationalists made sure that they were on the correct side of the roof. Right next door was a large structure Roden nicknamed 'The Chummery'; it housed all the unattached staff from the Russian Embassy. Luckily in 1955 and 1956 listening devices were not as sophisticated as they were to become later. They were the age of the vacuum tube, not the transistor, so electronic apparatus was cumbersome. Australia did not run to radio transmitters, not surprising when the Canberra public servants had made sure that no diplomatic staff in the tropics had air-conditioned cars because the Canberra public servants were not issued with air-conditioned cars. A small point which still irks Roden, remembering Ceylon and later Pakistan with an artificial leg attached to a sweating, infection-prone stump. So, not having a radio transmitter, the chancellery had to encode all messages to Canberra and send them through the Egyptian post office system—which refused to send anything in code. Roden's answer was to send everything in plain

English; he and his senior staff simply included references which they hoped those in Canberra interpreted the right way. Telephone calls had to be in plain English too.

There were visitors before Egypt grew too perilous. The chairman of P & O called in to say hello when passing through; Roden had met him in Wellington, and he had sailed with Helen to Sydney when she went to Mim's wedding in 1949. A Scot, the chairman was convinced that Nasser would leave the canal alone; the Egyptians just didn't have the technical know-how to operate it.

'It isn't Panama,' said Roden, disagreeing. 'What's really to operate? If their pilot did run a ship aground, the ground's sand. Harmless. Besides which, any ship's captain can pilot his own way through Suez.'

Arthur Fadden, now Deputy Prime Minister and Treasurer, paid a visit on his way to a monetary conference in Europe. In those days of the Constellation people preferred to sail—and Suez did cut a big slice of time off the journey.

The Cutlers had bought a brand new Buick, a beautiful car, for their own use; AUS 1 was an Austin limousine that looked a typical diplomat's car, chauffeur, glass partition, mast for the Australian flag. So Helen got herself around by driving the Buick, and set off with Lady Fadden (Fadden had been knighted in 1951) for a day's pleasurable shopping. It was left to Roden to entertain Sir Arthur.

He was generally regarded in Australia as a bit of a buffoon, but he was much cleverer than people realised. A good brain and a streak of shrewdness to boot. Roden remembers that when the main speaker at a Legacy function in Canberra fainted, Fadden got up and kept the audience entertained by reciting reams of Banjo Paterson's doggerel poetry extremely well.

'Where are we off to?' Fadden enquired as AUS 1 glided out of the residence gateway.

'Cairo museum.'

'Oh.'

In 1955 the ground floor of the Cairo museum was wall-to-wall sarcophagi, hundreds of dreary stone coffins.

'What's all this about?' Fadden asked, gazing around.

'These are the coffins of ancient Egyptians. Sarcophagi.'

'Is this all there is to see?'

'No, minister. What we're really here to see are the contents of Tutankhamen's tomb—his chariot, chairs, sarcophagus, jars, ornaments—an absolute treasure.'

'I do *not* want to look at these—these sarcophagi! Let's get out of here,' said Fadden.

'But you really should see Tutankhamen, minister!'

'No! Let's get out of here.'

They got out of there.

What on earth was he going to do to entertain a man with scant interest in antiquities? By the time they reached AUS 1 he had made up his mind. 'Jean,' he said to his Cypriot driver, 'take the flag off the car, please.'

'Why are you doing that?' asked Fadden.

'Because, minister, we are going into the red light district, and I do not want Nasser's informers reporting that two Australian ministers were seen stopping at Annabel's.'

'Now that's more like it!' said Fadden, face lighting up.

As AUS 1 made its stately way into sleazier and sleazier alleyways, Jean regaled the two ministers in the back seat with stories about every brothel and bar they passed.

'How do you know so much, Jean?' asked Roden, intrigued.

'Your Excellency, I was a taxi driver in Cairo right through the war, and I had to take all the Australian soldiers here.' He grinned reminiscently. 'Even generals.'

Sir Arthur looked and looked and looked (Roden assures the author that he didn't touch). On the way back to the residence he sighed happily. 'This has been a wonderful morning!' he chortled. 'Wait until I get home and see my mate Rankin!' General Rankin.

Roden's stump had been troublesome since shortly after he had arrived in Ceylon, and even though the air in Cairo was less humid, it continued to look and feel nasty. The Colombo doctors had told him sternly that he ought to go to London and consult the brilliant plastic surgeon Archibald McIndoe, a New Zealander.

When the Cutlers left by ship for London in November 1955, Nasser was in the midst of petitioning the World Bank for part-financing of the Aswan Dam, sure that if he were successful the Americans and the British would put up the rest of the money. The number of unattached Russian males in The Chummery next door had swelled, and was to go on doing so. Notes compared at the Gezira Club had revealed that Czech matériel was beginning to flood into depots strategically located between Cairo and the canal, steadily emptying of British troops. But there seemed no immediate danger, no real reason not to go to London when Roden's legation staff were excellent.

Archibald McIndoe turned out to be a grumpy, churlish sort of man with scant interest in amputated limbs. 'Take yourself to Queen Mary's at Roehampton and see them,' he said.

At the time Queen Mary's Hospital, Roehampton (in south-western Greater London), was a veterans' institution.

'What you need is a new and better artificial limb,' they said, and proceeded to make him one which was indeed a vast improvement on the old model.

The damply chilly beauty of London in late autumn was a pleasant change from Cairo's relentless heat, but the family did not linger. They sailed on the *Stratheden* and had Christmas at sea. The boys loved that. David was now eight years old, Anthony seven, and Richard a three-year-old explorer type, curious about everything. Roden was thirty-nine, and Helen was thirty-two. The boys adored their father, though as yet they had no appreciation of Victoria Crosses or senior diplomats. They had never lived in Australia, but one of the few advantages of this foreign lifestyle was that Dad usually got home for lunch; they saw more of him than most children did of their fathers. Their interests were, as normal for little boys, more towards outdoor activities than the schoolroom, though Anthony was apostrophised 'a brainbox'. Their mother took an intensely personal role with them; they rarely suffered the fate of a lot of children whose parents have limousines at their disposal, always shunted off with a chauffeur. Helen had her Buick, and drove them to and from school herself. It was, besides, becoming provocative to sail around in AUS 1—Nasser had, mostly through the stream of Arabic-language invective Radio Cairo emitted constantly, inflamed the populace against Western fat cats. Wherever one went in Cairo, one could see the charred ruins of buildings in foreign ownership.

In this steadily mounting atmosphere of hatred, and having literally just got off the ship from London, Roden found himself invited to a dinner given by Nasser in honour of Marshal Tito and the second of his three wives, Madam Broz. He was desperately tired thanks to the stump and the new tin leg, but didn't dare not attend. The drinks were either unchilled water or nauseatingly sickly-sweet cordials at this Muslim affair; Roden decided to leave after everyone rose from the dinner table, having waited long enough to observe courtesy. Halfway down a corridor he was grabbed by guards and manhandled into a room, wherein he was detained for some time. His mistake had been to go before Nasser and Tito; if he had planted a bomb, the guards were determined he would die too.

Tito himself hosted a dinner at the Abdine Palace, where he was lodged, and Roden was invited; they had met previously in Ceylon, and Tito remembered him well. Another war hero. Mercifully Tito provided alcoholic and chilled drinks. What Roden noticed were the exquisite surroundings and the fabulous tableware. All of it had belonged to King Farouk. Owning the temperament of a mendicant friar, Nasser had plundered nothing, simply kept Farouk's palace for guests like Marshal Tito.

Roden deemed Tito a very handsome and extremely impressive man whose wife was equally formidable. An interesting couple, especially given that Tito had consistently defied Stalin and lived to tell of it. Understandable that he had managed to unite the perpetually confrontational assortment of little states called Yugoslavia; understandable too that after his death Yugoslavia began to unravel. Blood feuds fuelled by differing religious beliefs mean nothing save trouble.

Egged on by Khrushchev, Tito was busy forming a body of non-aligned nations, the chief of which was Pandit Nehru's India. Egypt was also a member. It was very important that India be kept on side, as India's fate was inextricably bound up with the fate of the Suez Canal. The Indian Foreign Minister was Krishna Menon, whose London barrister background enabled him to orate in the most Ciceronian of manners. He hated the British, and drew a great deal of attention from the world press.

While the international wheeling and dealing went on, Roden and Helen took the opportunity to visit the Egyptian shore of the Red Sea, where the boys were hugely pleased to discover they had to camp. Roden had bought the camping gear in London because he and Helen were anxious to see as much of Egypt as they could, and hotel accommodation at the time was risky. Top of the list was an expedition down the Nile before the dam went in, but they were not to fulfil that ambition until the 1980s. Too late to see Abu Simbel as it had been, too early for the Egyptians to admit that the Aswan Dam had not been such a brilliant idea.

Three other purchases were made in London: a magnificent Evans shotgun and two Webleys, a .38 revolver and a .22 air pistol. Together with some others, Roden had acquired the duck hunting lease of a big swamp around the base of the Nile delta not far from Cairo, hence the shotgun—which he was never to use because the real trouble began before duck season. The air pistol in the hands of a good shot was all he needed to wave at people; Roden was not enamoured of killing, nor had he done much—if any—of it while earning that Victoria Cross, save by lobbing projectiles. The revolver had a different purpose. It was there to use on himself and any others, including his family, if rape and death by torture became inevitable.

Interestingly, under the new Australian gun laws, in 1998 Roden was deemed too old to renew his licence for the Webleys—an extraordinary insult in the author's view. It looked as if these historic weapons would be destroyed, but luckily a collector acquired them—perfectly legally—and they remain Cutleriana. The air pistol has been fired, for Roden used to take it up on the Legation's roof and pot at a target paper, but the .38 revolver has never been fired at all.

As 1956 began to hurtle towards its inevitable outcome, the

situation in Cairo grew tenser. Some diplomatic circles were so apprehensive that the heads of embassies or legations departed, never to return. Nasser was now using what Roden describes as 'rent-a-mobs', which he would turn loose to give the Westerners a fright. A past master of the war of nerves, he preferred this kind of technique to armed aggression.

Nasser was not, says Roden, entirely happy with the Russians, who had a tendency to want to take over whatever they could. Nor did his returning pilots and army officers rave about their stays in the U.S.S.R. Well aware that he was viewed by Moscow as a simple catspaw, he bided his time and continued with some sincerity to woo American and British aid. Of course he was hoist on his own petard; his fierce hatred of colonialism insisted that the British had to go, but he was quite intelligent enough to realise that Soviet imperialism was of the colonial kind also. And his lack of foreign exposure ensured that he did not for one moment appreciate, for example, the phenomenon of the United States of America in a presidential election year with an incumbent president seeking a second term. It was his bad luck too to have to deal with John Foster Dulles who, if he had had his way, would have burned all communists at the stake. Egypt was broke, he had to lift the economy and improve the lot of the peasants, and among the latter he was adored. But his personal equipment for gauging Western reactions was sadly lacking. Tito knew how to do it. Nasser just did not. While Nehru and Krishna Menon meddled. To compound his woes, he had the new state of Israel on his northern border, with the old lion, Ben-Gurion, roaring.

1956 was also the centennial of the creation of the Victoria Cross, and it was to be celebrated by gathering every living V.C. winner together in London on the 99th anniversary of the first award ceremony, 26 June. Australia was paying the fares of all its Victoria Cross winners and their wives, and Roden was determined to go. This time, however, it would have to be a quick visit. He and Helen would fly.

They hired a highly reputable nanny to look after the boys (she proved lax), and left for London as the last British troops were quitting the canal zone. Nasser was waiting to hear from Dulles about the loan money, anxious because early intelligence kept telling him that the U.S.A. was going to renege.

The celebrations were all that any Victoria Cross winner could have hoped for, but were especially happy for Roden, who was one of the few the Queen singled out on parade to speak to personally. Buckingham Palace gave a reception, there were other events, and a visit to Roehampton about the leg. On the way back to Cairo they couldn't get out of a tour the Australian Government had arranged for their V.C. winners to the Australian war cemeteries. Roden remembers the row upon row upon row of graves at El Alamein—over two thousand of them—and the ages of the dead soldiers: eighteen, nineteen, twenty. Some simply said, KNOWN UNTO GOD.

'Nobody wins a war,' he says sadly. 'Oh, they're a waste! Of resources, money and the flower of a country's young men. Most especially that.'

After Nasser nationalised the canal things got a lot worse. The mobs were more prevalent and more violent, took to throwing stones at big foreign cars. Of all the diplomatic missions Roden was least impressed with the Canadians, who, he says, couldn't get their act together. The head of their diplomatic mission was the son of missionaries in Japan and had witnessed the Japanese atrocities during the Second World War at first hand. Undoubtedly he set the Canadian diplomatic mood, further complicated because loyalty to the mother country said they ought to be pro-British and pro-French, but on the other side of the border was Uncle Sam, who had a lot to say about what Canada did and did not do. The upshot of this was that right about when the Canadians ought to have taken over British duties after the Egyptians shut down the British Embassy, their mission head went up onto a roof and jumped off it, killing himself. Rudderless, the Canadians became quite incapable of acting decisively.

In London the heads of the twenty-two nations which used the Suez Canal had gathered to debate the next logical move. These meetings went on until 23 August, at which moment—and at the suggestion of Dulles—eighteen of them decided that an international organisation should administer the canal. But four—the U.S.S.R., India, Indonesia and Ceylon—voted NO. Despite the four negatives, Sir Anthony Eden insisted that a delegation from among the eighteen affirmatives should seek an audience with Nasser and persuade him that this peaceful solution was face-saving enough to be palatable. One of the delegates in London was the Australian Prime Minister, Robert Gordon Menzies. Eden wanted Dulles to lead the mission himself, but Dulles wanted the leader to be someone less noticeable—a strong man, yes by all means, but not an international big shot.

A C.I.A. (public) source in the author's possession says that Menzies volunteered to lead the committee, but as the same source twice calls him Australia's Foreign Minister (he was not, Richard Casey was), its accuracy is doubtful. On the other hand, Roden is emphatic that Dulles approached Menzies and asked him to take the job, and that Menzies was somewhat reluctant. The latter version is more likely; Menzies was fond of his creature comforts.

Nasser agreed to see the committee on 3 September; it consisted of Australia (with Menzies as chief spokesman), Iran, Ethiopia, Sweden and the U.S.A. (the last headed by a mere assistant secretary, Loy Henderson). Then Egypt flatly refused to provide a place wherein the committee could meet. The British said they were unable to help, and the Americans promptly followed suit. The French ambassador had already packed up and departed. It ought to have been the Canadians next, but they were in such disarray that the lot fell upon Australia (New Zealand had no diplomatic mission in Cairo). Roden said it could meet in his Legation's residence, but on one condition: that the Americans provide a guard of U.S. Marines for both sides of the Legation. This having been agreed to, he went ahead and set the machinery in motion.

Loy Henderson was to stay at the American Embassy and the others elsewhere, while the Australian residence inherited Menzies, Sir Allen Brown (public service chief of the Prime Minister's Department), and Menzies' aide, Hugh Dash.

Roden met them at the Cairo airport with AUS 1 and another car, aware that Nasser would rent a mob for the occasion. Knowing a back way out, he hustled Menzies, Brown and Dash away from the mob spilling onto the tarmac. Menzies found himself unceremoniously bundled into AUS 1, Sir Allen after him; Dash went in the second vehicle with the luggage. AUS 1 sported one Egyptian on its roof and another on its bonnet; dozens of hands were plucking frenziedly at the door handles.

'Go, go!' snapped Roden to Jean the driver. 'Don't stop for anything!'

Ex-taxi drivers love that kind of order. Jean punched the accelerator and the car shot forward. Those hanging onto it were thrown off, and the mob was left far behind.

En route to Zamalik, a very shaken Prime Minister filled Roden in on what the British Foreign Secretary, Selwyn Lloyd, had told him. Eden, said Menzies, had no expectation whatsoever that the committee would succeed, but Selwyn Lloyd was even more gloomy. He had told Menzies that Nasser was such a wily charmer that the committee would end in singing Egypt's praises to the skies. Roden thought Eden right, but Selwyn Lloyd wrong, and proceeded to tell Menzies that Nasser did not understand English nearly as well as he pretended to. Nothing the committee said would sink in, yet Nasser was too far into his I-understand-perfectly act to climb down via an interpreter. After the meetings he would confer with minions whose grasp of English was good, but that was not the same thing as listening properly himself. Menzies was inclined to demur, sure that Selwyn Lloyd would know beyond any doubt.

'Look,' said Roden, 'talking to Nasser is like going to Flinders Street railway station and reading the advertising hoardings for information about train departures. As for charming—rubbish! He's just devious and unreliable. Whatever you discuss with him—whatever he says to you—make sure it's down in writing.'

1956 was not endowed with pocket-type recorders; recorders then were bigger than briefcases.

'I'll put everything in writing,' said Menzies.

'How is Sir Anthony?' Roden asked then.

'A sick man, Ro, a very sick man.'

'Will he invade?'

'He hasn't made up his mind. Doesn't seem able to make up his mind. The difficulty is that the British public thinks it's an authority on Egypt because so many were through here during the war. It thinks invading will be like falling off a log.'

'Has Churchill been consulted?'

'Yes.'

'And what does he say?'

'That if there is going to be an invasion, it must be a very sudden and ruthless strike at Alexandria and Cairo as well as Port Said and the canal.'

'He's right, Prime Minister. Cairo is vital because of the sweet water canal. There's no point in taking Suez if the troops have no sweet water to drink. The sweet water canal is the key to the whole enterprise.'

'Everyone in London says the Egyptian army is hopeless.'

'I don't agree. I know during the war we tended to despise the Egyptian garrisons in places like Mersa Matruh—they'd head for the hills before the air raid sirens went off. But they're not like that now. Better trained and much better equipped—and they're fighting on their own soil for their own soil. I believe the Egyptians will do better than London thinks,' said Roden.

They arrived at the residence to find the U.S. Marines on guard, extremely smart and impassively square-jawed.

Helen had already encountered them, and wasn't very impressed. When she tried to drive her Buick into the legation grounds, she was halted and detained.

'Sorry, ma'am, this is off-limits.'

'What do you mean? I *live* here!' she cried.

'Sorry, ma'am, I need to see a permit.'

'I don't have one! In fact, nobody even told me about this! I insist that you let me through immediately—I'm the Australian Minister's wife!'

The matter was sorted out in short order, but when Roden walked in with his share of the committee, Helen was still upset. Not at the guards, who were doing their duty, but at the fact that no one had remembered to inform her what was going to happen— or issue her with a permit. Her nerves were a little raw; when you have three little boys, the sight of square-jawed professional troops is frightening. Especially when you realise that they're protecting you.

She was, besides, heavily pregnant.

Menzies loved her and greeted her with delight. But also with dismay.

'What on earth is Helen still doing here?' he demanded.

'Well, Prime Minister, I've been encouraging my Australian staff with families to leave, but I didn't want a panic. The calmer and more casual an evacuation is, the less notice anyone Egyptian will take of it. You've just experienced an Egyptian mob, so you know what I mean. I want my people out, but it seemed to me that if my own wife and children were still here, they'd go looking easy and relaxed. You have to bluff, Prime Minister. I discussed it with Helen, and she agreed with me.'

'She has the strongest sense of duty of any woman I've ever known,' said Menzies with sincere admiration. 'A treasure, Ro.'

'I agree, Prime Minister.'

'But get her out, man! And soon, please!'

Evacuation of diplomatic staff had become advisable for all those missions which belonged to the eighteen affirmative nations involved in the London conference. Paradoxically, the Indian ambassador in Cairo was very useful and very willing to pass on any news he had—which was considerable, as both his prime minister and his foreign minister were politically intimate with Nasser.

The discussions with Nasser began the next day, 3 September, and Menzies at the end of it was cautiously optimistic. Though his biographers were to state later that he wasn't in the slightest bit fooled by Nasser, Roden listened to a man who thought Nasser was 'probably all right'. Like so many others, Menzies was convinced Nasser's grasp of English was excellent. But he hadn't neglected to have every word taken down; Menzies had won his fortune and his formidable reputation at the Bar acting for trade unions, very touchy clients.

Then during the night (Washington D.C. was some hours behind in time) Dwight D. Eisenhower spoke at a press conference and shot the committee down in flames. Using traditional lawyer's tactics, Menzies had striven to put a doubt in Nasser's mind, to the effect that force would definitely be used if an international body were not appointed to administer the canal. Now the American President was quoted as saying that the U.S.A. would not condone any military intervention in Egypt; another way than force would have to be found. Peacemakers got votes. Warmongers did not.

There were to be two more sessions, but they came to nothing. On 9 September the President and Prime Minister of Egypt, Colonel Gamal Abdel Nasser, dismissed the committee disdainfully. Menzies had had one private interview with Nasser, but the American, Loy Henderson, had been granted five such.

The telephone had been quite busy. When Dame Pattie Menzies discovered that Helen was close to term with her fourth child, she urged Helen not to make the long flight home to Australia, but to go to London instead, where the Australian High Commissioner's residence at Hyde Park Gate was vacant. After talking it over with Roden, Helen decided to risk the flight to Australia. The airline agency representative in Cairo, when approached, said cheerfully, 'Oh, we've had worse things happen on planes than babies being born!' These days, of course, no airline would willingly accept an eight-months-pregnant woman as a passenger.

The Swedish diplomat who had served on the committee had

brought his wife with him, and asked Menzies and Roden to dine with them at Shepheard's Hotel the night before they were to return to London. As Menzies was a bit on the glum side, Roden thought the excursion might cheer him up, so they accepted.

Having ensconced the distinguished party at the best table, the head waiter smoothly suggested the prawns.

'Oh, I love prawns!' said Menzies, starting to smile.

'*I'll* have the soup,' said Roden loudly.

'Prawns for me,' said Menzies firmly.

'Prime Minister, the soup here is really delicious! *Do* have the soup,' said Roden, fixing Menzies with a steely eye.

'In this climate? Prawns,' said Menzies. Who consumed his prawns with great relish.

Roden passed the best guest suite the next morning on his way down to breakfast and encountered a very slow and seedy-looking Prime Minister tottering into the corridor.

'I've got it!' Menzies groaned. 'See there's plenty of paper in the toilet, would you?'

In fact, the Prime Minister was quite sick. Roden went to the kitchen and told the cook to make plenty of arrowroot gruel. As soon as it was ready he bore a bowl of it upstairs.

'*Arrowroot?*' gasped Menzies. 'I refuse to eat it! I *hate* the stuff! Take it away!'

'Eat it, Prime Minister.'

'I will not!'

'You really should.'

The Menzies temper snapped. After telling Roden what he thought, Menzies ordered him out of the room.

Sir Allen Brown and Hugh Dash were gathered in the breakfast room, and had been told the dire news.

'It's your turn,' said Roden, handing the bowl of arrowroot to

Brown. 'He won't admit me again, but he's got to eat this.'

Off went Sir Allen bearing the bowl. Back he came bearing the bowl. He and Roden turned their glittering eyes upon the shrinking, horrified Dash.

'No, not me! I won't do it!'

They marched Hugh Dash up the stairs with the bowl of gruel and pushed him through Menzies' door. Menzies eventually gave in and ate his arrowroot.

Aside from arrowroot, he was a good guest. He would sneak into the boys' bedroom and talk to them, give them money to buy cricketing gear; David and Anthony were on the Gezira Club under-tens cricket team. To Helen he was extremely considerate and tender—and very anxious to see her safely away.

Children sense things, no matter how sheltered from events they might be. Somehow all the boys knew that Mummy was in danger, that they had to go home in a hurry to make sure she was all right. On Richard, the youngest, this had a peculiar effect. He fell off the little tricycle he was pedalling around the garden and said he couldn't walk. The doctors found absolutely nothing, but Roden had to carry him onto the plane two days after Menzies had departed.

Helen and the sobbing Richard sat on one side of the aisle, Anthony and David on the other. Why wasn't Dad coming too? Richard wanted to know. Home to him was where his parents were.

Said David to Anthony, rather audibly: 'Well, there's one good thing—we won't have an Egyptian brother now.' They thought a baby born in Cairo would wear a fez, djellabah and sandals. But they never doubted for a moment that it would be a brother.

When Helen's plane landed at Karachi, it was met by an ambulance and a full obstetrical unit, thanks to the Pakistani ambassador in Cairo; Roden and Helen were very well liked in Cairo diplomatic circles, but somehow the Pakistanis were always special.

Mark was born in Sydney a little less than a month later, on 13 October 1956. The Cutlers now had four sons. Prime Minister Menzies insisted on being Mark's godfather.

Hungary had been in turmoil for some time, but in the middle of October what had been scattered riots and mutterings flared into a strong and open rebellion against communist repression and the Soviet colonial overlords. Early in the year Khrushchev had made what in retrospect he must have realised was a blunder by admitting to a select few that the rule of Josef Stalin had not been all beer and skittles. The Russian people were not informed, but the papers circulated abroad and were seized on by the nations of the eastern European Soviet bloc as well as by Westerners. His admission was seen as a sign that Soviet solidarity was breaking apart, and that perception emboldened certain countries ruled by a Soviet-oriented Communist Party to think that they could forge their own version of communism. As Tito had.

In Poland riots and revolt broke out in Poznan, but as the Polish Communist Party never lost control of the political and bureaucratic apparatus, Khrushchev was able to conciliate the Poles by letting them have a less inflexible, less Soviet brand of communism. A necessary concession; the U.S.S.R. was suddenly fearful that if the Poles and the Hungarians revolted simultaneously, the whole fabric of Soviet-dominated eastern Europe might fall to shreds.

Hungary went further than Poland did. By late October the Hungarian Revolution had achieved its purpose; the Communist Party leader, Erno Gero, was ejected together with his minions and then replaced by Imre Nagy, who was sensitive enough to popular

Ruby Daphne Cutler (nee Pope), Roden's mother, photographed in 1915, the year of her marriage.

Arthur William Cutler, Roden's father, also in 1915.

Ruby, Arthur and family, 1927. Children, standing from left: Roden, Rob, Geoff and, in her mother's arms, Doone.

Lieutenant A. R. Cutler, 2/5th Field Regiment, A.I.F., carried towards Yerate by French prisoners of war. The regimental medical officer, Captain Adrian Johnson, is on the right and Sergeant Jack Robinson is on the left. French shells explode on the road in the background. (*Photo courtesy of the Australian War Memorial.*)

Admiralty House, Sydney, 1941 on the day of Roden's investment with the Victoria Cross. From left: Doone, Ruby, Roden, Aunt Dais and Rob.

Roden with Lieutenant Colonel Clyde Ingate (left) and the Governor-General, Lord Gowrie, V.C. (centre), at Admiralty House.

Prime Minister John Curtin with General Douglas MacArthur, Commander-in-Chief of the Allied Forces in the South-West Pacific area and Commander-in-Chief of U.S. Forces of the Far East Command. (*Photo courtesy of Murray David Publishing.*)

The Right Honourable Herbert Vere Evatt; along with John Curtin, one of Roden's two 'Labor fairy godfathers'. (*Photo courtesy of Murray David Publishing.*)

Sir Robert Gordon Menzies, Prime Minister of Australia 1939–1941 and 1949–66. (*Photo courtesy of Murray David Publishing.*)

Lieutenant Helen Morris,
1944

Roden and Helen
on their wedding
day, 28 May 1946.

Aboard the aircraft carrier H.M.A.S. *Sydney* in Colombo, Ceylon, 1953, carrying the Australian contingent to the coronation of Elizabeth II. Roden, High Commissioner for Australia (centre, in dinner suit) and four other Victoria Cross winners from World War II, from left: Sergent R.R. Rattey, Private R. Kelliher, Private E. Kenna and Private F.J. Partridge in the cabin of Brigadier D.A. Whitehead (to the right of Roden). (*Photo courtesy of the Australian War Memorial.*)

At the Australian Residence, Cairo, 15 August 1955. From left: Roden; the Egyptian Chief of Protocol; N. Parkinson, First Secretary; and S.D. Shubart, Commercial Minister. (*Photo courtesy of the Department of Foreign Affairs and Trade.*)

Roden and the Vice Consul, Alan Fogg, leaving the train at the Libyan border on 12 November 1956, following the breakdown of diplomatic relations between Egypt and Australia. (*Photo courtesy of the Department of Foreign Affairs and Trade.*)

Don Walker, Commercial Secretary, and Michael Cook, Third Secretary, under guard while waiting to cross the Libyan border. (*Photo courtesy of the Department of Foreign Affairs and Trade.*)

First meeting between Joan Goodwin and the Cutlers, August 1963 in New York. From left: Joan, Helen, Mark, Roden, David, Anthony (Richard absent).

The Cutlers outside Government House, 1972. From left: Richard, Anthony (with Khyber), Roden, Helen, Mark (with Taimyr) and David.

Roden and Helen at Government House, 1977. (*Photo courtesy Government House, Sydney, Historic Houses Trust of New South Wales.*)

Governor of N.S.W. *Top left*: Taking the guard's salute at the opening of the New South Wales Parliament. *Top right*: Roden receives a sprig of rosemary from a young admirer and Legacy ward on Anzac Day 1969. *Bottom*: The Cutlers with Her Majesty Queen Elizabeth II, Prince Philip, Princess Anne and Prince Charles, 1974. (*Photos courtesy Government House, Sydney, Historic Houses Trust of New South Wales.*)

Roden and Joan at An Evening with Australia's National Treasures, Sydney Town Hall, 18 February 1998

feeling to proclaim Hungary a neutral state about to own a multiparty, democratic form of government. Russian troops arrived after Gero appealed to Moscow for help. Nagy responded on 1 November by appealing to the United Nations.

On 4 November the full Soviet military catastrophe rolled into Hungary and proceeded to put the rebellion down with characteristic ruthlessness. The free Hungarians fought back heroically, but to no avail. David could not conquer this Goliath. The Moscow puppet Janos Kadar was installed in Budapest, and the threat was over.

But all of this took time, and that time was in synchrony with events in Egypt. Some authorities say that it was Suez took the world's attention away from Hungary, others that it was Hungary took the world's attention away from Suez. Certainly for the Western press it was a torment—which country do we feature today? Do we cover the debates in the U.N. General Assembly, or in the U.N. Security Council? For Suez and Hungary occupied one or the other exclusively.

What one can be certain of is that Hungary and Suez were like two people colliding in the dark. Looking back through the years improves clarity, the historical perspective; but in November 1956, things just exploded at the same moment in two different places and for two different reasons. Because invasions are not procedures that can be assembled in days or weeks—especially by two allies as disparate as the U.K. and France—one cannot possibly credit the British and the French with seizing the moment to act in Egypt while Hungary burned and bled. The U.N. was in a furore—what to do where? Naturally nothing was done anywhere.

Just after the committee's failure the French Prime Minister, Guy Mollet, and his Foreign Minister, Christian Pineau, went to London to see Anthony Eden and his Foreign Secretary, Selwyn Lloyd. Lloyd had cabled Washington D.C. to say, with some exasperation, that while America disagreed with every alternative Eden and Mollet had come up with, it wasn't offering any of its own. John Foster Dulles had brainstormed up a Canal Users' Association to be administered by the five countries which had formed the committee—Australia, Ethiopia, Iran, Sweden and the U.S.A.—but he wanted the canal's revenues to be paid directly to the collectors on the canal, which meant Egypt and Nasser. This was unacceptable to Eden and Lloyd, but the two Frenchmen took it as an insufferable insult. Mollet and Pineau returned to France determined on a military solution. But Eden still shrank from using force unless he could persuade the Americans to condone force, so he talked hard and managed to restrain Mollet.

Eisenhower held another press conference on 11 September. 'This country will not go to war while I am occupying my present post unless Congress ... declares such a war ...' After which Dulles told the press that he thought Nasser less likely to approve the Canal Users' Association than the proposals put forward by the five-nation committee. An odd thing for a man to say when the Canal Users' Association had been his own idea. On 15 September in Cairo, Nasser called the Canal Users' Association an excuse to make war on Egypt, and on the 17th the Soviet chairman Bulganin sent Eden a letter warning him not to use force against Egypt.

Eden and Mollet ordered all canal personnel to leave; six hundred pilots, engineers and technicians promptly departed, which left Egypt with the onus of operating the canal. *That* would teach the 'Gyppos' a lesson! They'd bungle it for sure.

Roden had told the head of P & O that he didn't think the Egyptians at all incapable of operating the canal, and in London the odd naval officer or spook said the same thing, but they were voices crying in the wilderness.

Until reports vindicated them; traffic was moving through Suez pretty much as it had before—a trifle on the slow side, perhaps, but without ships running aground or colliding with each other. Anglo-French intellectual snobbery looked exactly that. The 'Gyppos' were not so dumb after all.

Even so, under continuous pressure from Dulles the Suez Canal Users' Association was born—without solving the vexed question of tolls. It was a joke; everyone knew it. Countries started to withdraw, including Japan, Pakistan and Ethiopia. India had refused to join from the start, but sent an observation group to report back to Nasser. Eden and Mollet decided to appeal to the U.N. Security Council, which agreed to discuss the matter on 5 October.

Dulles gave Eden and Mollet little hope that they would get American support: first he stated that the U.S.A. would remain aloof from 'colonial problems', then he commented that the Suez Canal Users' Association 'never had any teeth'. His idea, but why did he keep knocking it down? The dig about 'colonial problems' really got under Eden's skin; he threw the piece of paper containing it away and said between *his* teeth to Anthony Nutting,[†] 'And now what have you got to say about your American friends?'

Colonial problems were everywhere in 1956, as a matter of fact: Malaya, Kenya, Egypt, Cyprus. The Mau-Maus in Kenya and the communist insurgents in Malaya were too unimportant and far away in Egyptian terms to interest Nasser, but he and Tito took pleasure in encouraging the Greek Cypriot leader, Archbishop Makarios. Though Makarios had been put in detention on one of the Seychelles, the EOKA terrorists were fighting the British bitterly when the troops started moving to Cyprus in August to man Operation Musketeer (the code name

---

[†] Nutting was the junior minister assisting Selwyn Lloyd in Foreign Affairs.

for the invasion of Egypt). Malta, a thousand miles away, had to be used as well as Cyprus.

Discussions at the U.N. Security Council in New York went well; Nasser's Foreign Minister, Dr. Mahmoud Fawzi, sounded truly anxious to conclude a peaceful agreement. Still timid about American intentions, Eden and Lloyd were inclined to go along with a deal, but Mollet and Pineau were thirsting for Nasser's blood. It was he and his disciples fanning the flames of revolt in Algeria; eliminating Nasser was a springboard to victory in Algeria. Nor did the two Frenchmen care much what the U.S.A. thought.

They started wooing Israel. The contact talks went back to mid-September—might Israel be interested in joining a Franco-British strike against Egypt? David Ben-Gurion took a little time to make up his mind, then on 23 September his Defence Minister, Shimon Peres, told the French that Israel was probably a starter. Israeli forces would move on the canal and on the Egyptian fortresses guarding the Gulf of Aqaba. Peres passed the news on to Ben-Gurion and General Moshe Dayan that he thought the French were prepared to move on Egypt alone if the British kept on trying to placate the U.S.A. France had been assisting Israel for some years, and Ben-Gurion trusted the French. He could not trust the British, who had too much affection for Jordan.

While the Security Council meeting in New York was getting under way, Israel's Foreign Minister, Golda Meir, Moshe Dayan and Shimon Peres were in Paris talking to Pineau and handing over an armaments shopping list. If Eden, still in London, knew of this Franco-Israeli alliance, he did not inform Selwyn Lloyd in New York. So while Selwyn Lloyd looked for an alternative that would please Washington D.C., Pineau after he arrived displayed boredom with the proceedings.

Israel stepped up its raids against Jordan, and Eden had a new torment: how could he reconcile British commitments to Jordan with British necessity to keep Israel friendly? When hostilities along the border ceased, he breathed a sigh of relief. Then an anti-British, nationalistic government took over in Amman, and Jordan signed a military pact with Syria and Egypt.

Eden by now had more or less made up his mind; Mollet's had been made up for weeks. They would go for war, which meant that a little diplomatic sabotage had to be wreaked on the six-point agreement that looked like being approved by the Security Council. New orders were issued to Lloyd and Pineau, who tacked a few provisos onto the end of the draft agreement with predictable results: the U.S.S.R. exercised its veto. The U.N. Secretary-General, Dag Hammarskjöld, was deputed to meet with the potential belligerents in Geneva on 29 October.

The French and Israelis formulated a military plan involving an Israeli blitzkrieg-style strike across Sinai towards the canal and Aqaba; when the Israeli forces were almost to the eastern bank of the canal, French (and, hoped Mollet, British) forces would occupy Port Said, Ismailia and other key areas along the waterway. Radio Cairo and Nasser would have to be silenced.

Still sweating over Jordan and the U.S.A., Eden arrived in Paris with Selwyn Lloyd and agreed that the British would come to the party. Trained in diplomacy rather than in law, Eden was not a politician; he had no taste for in-fighting and the other trappings of political manoeuvring. *How* could he involve the U.K. in the Franco-Israeli scheme without making the world think that he was an unashamed warmonger, a colonial Big Brother out to crush all nationalistic opposition? Krishna Menon's would be the first and loudest voice. He delivered his solution on 16 October: Israel would invade, and the U.K. and France would hastily step in to occupy the canal zone and keep the Egyptians and the Israelis from each other's throats. That way, the British would simply appear as adjudicators.

Ben-Gurion was livid. So Israel was to take the entire blame for aggression, eh? Typical! Nor was Moshe Dayan impressed with Selwyn Lloyd when the three conspirators met secretly at Sèvres on 22 October. The British Foreign Minister treated Ben-Gurion and his colleagues with frozen disdain, would not sit in the same room with them. The French had to run back and forth between the British room and the Jewish room.

On one point the Israelis were in complete concord with the British: the attack should not commence until after the American presidential elections. But the French wouldn't consent to wait, and France carried the day. The Israeli attack would jump off on 29 October; the U.K. and France would issue an ultimatum the following day that both sides must refrain from entering the canal zone, and twelve hours after that the British and French troops would move to occupy the canal zone. British honour would be upheld. All that kept Ben-Gurion in the scheme was the hope that its outcome would make the Israeli borders safer, that the cherished port on the Red Sea would be theirs at last, and that victory would provide a powerful basis for negotiations with the Arab League.

In Cairo the situation at the end of September was tense. The U.K. had issued instructions that the hundred-strong staff at its embassy was to be reduced to twenty; Australia told Roden to get his staff down to four including himself. British ambassador Sir Humphrey Trevelyan knew absolutely nothing about the coming military action, so his staff dallied until it was too late to get anyone out, from the local employees and their families to the British and their families. If anything more than everything undid Anthony Eden, it was the absolute secrecy which prevailed from Whitehall to Foggy Bottom. No one knew who might have tried to talk the Prime Minister around.

Some of Roden's people had already gone, but he acted on these new orders immediately. Whom would he keep? The Commercial Minister would have to go on leave. Definitely Nick Parkinson, who had a young family. In the end he kept the Consular Clerk, Alan Fogg, in case there were visas or other consular matters to attend to; the Third Secretary, Michael Cook, who was on his first post after serving his cadetship; and the Commercial Secretary, Don Walker, who had been a warrant officer class one in the North African campaigns—a tough, resourceful man, handy in a pinch. Roden's own secretary was a young and very attractive Australian woman, Virginia O'Neill, and for a while it didn't seem as if she would get out at all. Then she used her feminine charms to cajole the American Embassy into taking her, and went out with them.

Roden had delivered the five-nation committee's report to the Egyptian Foreign Minister, Dr. Mahmoud Fawzi, as soon as it was typed up. Menzies had heeded Roden's advice and put everything on paper. Though the chore of delivering it was difficult; it was done in the middle of the night and involved a long drive over a rough track to Fawzi's desert villa.

All dispensable files were destroyed early on; only the papers Roden felt he had to keep until the last moment remained. The Chummery next door was overflowing with young Russian men, as fifty Soviet water pilots had arrived to help the Egyptians handle shipping through the canal.

Of course he had the news from Sydney that he was the father of another boy; that was an enormous relief, freed up his mind to deal with the rapidly disintegrating situation in Cairo. Though he knew nothing, somehow he knew everything. Trouble was on its way and it was not going to be long in arriving. The British were going to invade, he knew it in his bones. Nor was he surprised when the BBC broadcast news of an Israeli attack.

Roden considers that the Israeli strike across Sinai on 29 October was not given anything like enough Anglo-French support: 'Britain and France should have provided all the under-the-lap help possible to Israel while proclaiming non-involvement.' British and French troops were supposed to land in the canal zone twelve hours after the day's grace ultimatum calling for an Israeli cease-fire: that would have seen them on the ground on Wednesday, 31 October. But there were to be no Anglo-French troops on the ground until 5 November. Israel went it alone.

The Israelis did very well despite going it alone. After a feint into Jordan, they were within thirty miles of the canal a day later, and moving steadily towards Aqaba. The outmanoeuvred and shattered Egyptian army wandered the desert in confusion.

Ben-Gurion and his general in the field, Moshe Dayan, had their own agenda. They would be content with extending their borders into Sinai and with freeing up Eilat, the port at the head of the Gulf of Aqaba. At which moment they would sit tight, whether the British and French were with them or not.

The problem was British, not French, and was not limited to Eden; the British chiefs of staff didn't like the invasion either. Two-thirds of the soldiers were British, two-thirds of the equipment was British, and two-thirds of the planes were British. A French battleship, five British and French aircraft carriers, some cruisers and destroyers made up the naval force.[†] Operation Musketeer had

---

† The French battleship was so dilapidated that it had only one working gun turret. Then orders came that no shell bigger than 4.5 inches (112 mm) was to be used, which meant that the only vessels in the fleet with guns small enough to fire were the destroyers.

called for a full invasion of Egypt from Alexandria to Port Said and down to Cairo, but in the end London decided to concentrate on the canal itself—at Alexandria all they needed was the airport. And before any ground forces went in, every military installation—and Radio Cairo—must be bombed out of existence. Without harming any Egyptian civilian. So the Anglo-French attack when it came was an air attack limited to 1,000-pound (500-kilogram) bombs, far too small to destroy military targets quickly and effectively.

Eden was not a cool commander-in-chief like Churchill, really absorbed in strategy and tactics. He breathed down the necks of his high command, but in gasps. Even then, the air attack did not begin at dawn on the last day of October, as originally planned. A frantic message had come to the Royal Air Force that the Americans would be using the airstrips all day to evacuate their citizens, so the raids began at dusk.

The moment the ultimatum to Israel (it said little about Egypt) was issued, the world woke up to what was going on, and the reactions ranged from sheer incredulity to roaring rage. Rumour had it that Eisenhower got on the phone and served Eden an unparalleled dressing down, but neither gentleman mentions it in his memoirs. India screamed; Moscow ordered Israel to cease and desist, and forbade either the U.K. or France to engage in any military actions on Egyptian soil—or over it.

The bombing began anyway, and it was effective enough as it continued for the next several days. The Egyptian air force was destroyed on the ground, but no one seems to have known whereabouts Radio Cairo was, so it lasted almost until the end, with Nasser exhorting his people to fight, fight, fight! The author finds it fascinating that the U.S.S.R. removed all its planes and pilots immediately to remote bases in southern Egypt and Arabia. Doesn't this indicate that Moscow was not nearly as sure of itself as its tone in letters and broadcasts suggested?

Together with Sir Humphrey Trevelyan and the friendly Indian ambassador, Roden went up onto the roof of the British Embassy and stood watching the bombs falling on Cairo airport, which was soon reduced to craters interspersed with heaps of twisted wreckage.

Sir Humphrey was still in shock. 'London said they'd send an aircraft from Nicosia [Cyprus] to pick us up—your lot too, Ro—but they can't very well do that if they bomb the airport, can they?' Good question.

From the moment when London and Paris issued their ultimatum to Israel on this last day of October, Trevelyan had been in much urgent discussion with Nasser and Dr. Mahmoud Fawzi. Then on Saturday, 3 November, Nasser broke off diplomatic relations and shut the British Embassy down. A hundred people, including Egyptians, were barricaded inside, and no one had thought to stock up on food.

Roden learned of it from two Swiss diplomats on Sunday morning; the Swiss were very anxious and most concerned that the British Embassy was under armed guard, completely cut off.

As Roden's instructions from Canberra were to do everything in his power to prevent Egypt's breaking off diplomatic relations with Australia, he ought by rights to have ignored the plight of the people inside the British Embassy. But there were principles involved, and Roden on a matter of principle is unbending. He and his three remaining staff were all living in the residence, and had plenty of food as well as emergency water rations in case the supply were to be turned off.

'Don,' said Roden to his Commercial Secretary, 'go to our wholesalers in the bazaar and load the Buick up with every bit of food you can—flour, tinned stuff, powdered milk for babies—and plenty of whisky. Here, pay cash.'

Roden himself took Jean and AUS 1 and drove to the market in Zamalik where the legation bought its meats, vegetables and fruits. There he paid cash for a whole side of beef, several whole sheep, hardy vegetables and whatever else he thought might be welcome. While this was going on a crowd gathered, followed by the inevitable rabble-rouser, who began to urge the Egyptians to stop the Western pig buying up all the food. Discretion, thought Roden, was the better part of valour; the car was stuffed with provisions. He jumped in beside Jean and they set off for the British Embassy.

Cutler's luck was still alive and well; he recognised the captain of the Egyptian guard as a fellow he had had dealings with—quite pleasant dealings—on several occasions. Don Walker drove up in the Buick with a similar tale of a similar mob in the bazaar, but he too had a carload of food.

'Don, start getting the food through and over the fence as fast as you can while I distract the guard—and start with a bottle of whisky. They must need a drink badly in there.'

No matter how strong feelings of national pride and hatred of the colonial overlords might be, it is very difficult for a man in a soldier's uniform to dominate an immensely tall and authoritative figure well known throughout Cairo as a Victoria Cross winner, and also very well liked. So the captain smiled and prepared to have a conversation in rudimentary English, which many urban Egyptians spoke. Don Walker was frantically hurling things over and through the fence while word spread inside the British Embassy grounds and people came flocking to bear away the food and handle with tender care those precious bottles of Scotch.

'No!' the captain cried when he realised what Don Walker was doing. 'No!'

The other soldiers tensed, brought their arms to bear.

'Oh, come, come,' said Roden gently, face smiling but eyes stern. 'I'm not passing any guns, just food. There are people inside who'll starve if they don't eat, and quite a lot of them are your fellow countrymen. It's not their fault that they're British employees, they have families to feed. You can watch everything that goes in—look at it and feel it if you want—but it really must go in, you know.'

The captain dithered, wavered. And all the food was passed inside. With a broad smile and a clap on the captain's shoulder, Roden and his cohorts departed back to their residence.

Where he interviewed his own Egyptian staff and advised them to leave; the legation bodyguard, an Egyptian, had already been hauled away after being severely beaten. But they refused to go. The butler was an Iraqi who was adamant that the British would win because the British always did. So Roden had Alan Fogg prepare immigration visas to Australia for all of them; the majority did indeed emigrate and become Australian citizens.

The Swiss Embassy had indicated that it would be the neutral 'protection mission'; Roden talked to them on the telephone and arranged that those in distress should be received if they came pleading for help. Save for arresting the bodyguard, the Egyptians had made no move to restrain or restrict the movements of the four men left inside the Australian Legation. Though, Roden felt, it was only a matter of time.

Menzies had previously agreed to the British request that Roden be briefed on the British intelligence network; it was now his duty to gather all the information he could and pass it on to London. Not his cup of tea, but he proceeded to do the job with his customary thoroughness. Nasser had a huge secret police force, and it was beginning to crack the British network. The main man working for the British was a Cypriot named Zarb, who ran a business as a furniture removalist and contracted to all the diplomatic missions. Very handy. The new chief of British intelligence in Cairo ('there's always someone in every mission who does a bit of polite spying') never met poor Zarb, who was arrested just before they were due to make contact.

With no radio transmitter, any information Roden did manage to gather had to be sent from the Zamalik post office in ordinary English. He and his three companions used to work out oblique ways of saying things—innocuous on the surface, significant underneath. The last cable they managed to send—no telephone calls outside Cairo!—concerned Nasser's movements. Opposite the Australian Legation was Princess Shulfikar's palace; she had been the first wife of old King Fuad, but not Farouk's mother, and she had recently died. Nasser had been staying at an army base; when the bombing became too accurate he and his Young Turks moved into Princess Shulfikar's palace. Of course Roden had pointed the building out to Menzies during his committee visit, so the cable wandered on about admired edifices and A Certain Person's regard for his own hide. It ended, 'Who protects who?'

'You can't say that!' said Michael Cook, very young and correct in those days.

'I certainly can. Mr. Menzies will interpret the last bit as my way of saying that we're hanging on and we'll be all right.'

On Thursday, 1 November, the United Nations General Assembly passed a resolution calling for a cease-fire in Egypt and 'a halt to the movement of military forces and arms into the area'. It passed 65 for, 5 against. The five who voted NO were the U.K., France, Israel, Australia and New Zealand. The U.S.A. was one of six nations which abstained.

On Saturday, 3 November, Sir Anthony Eden announced in London that the U.K. rejected the General Assembly's resolution calling for a cease-fire.

By then the U.S. Sixth Fleet was patrolling the sea approaches to Egypt, where the Anglo-French fleet was sitting offshore sending and receiving fighter planes and light bombers; the heavy bombers were using Alexandria airport. And the troop transports, many of them wallowing landing craft, were en route from Cyprus. The co-commanders of the invasion were the British Sir Hugh Stockwell, who had once been a jackaroo in the Australian outback, and the French General André Beaufre. After the invasion forces had been despatched from Cyprus, the two commanders received new orders: don't touch anything in Egypt except the actual canal zone! Beaufre in particular was furious. 'This is a police action, not a war!' he cried.

For a few tense hours the American Sixth Fleet behaved as if it were going to open fire on any troop vessels which attempted to run its gauntlet, but when British and French activity continued, the Sixth Fleet drew in its horns and hung around to watch.

The landings were by paratroopers and infantry around Port Said and Port Fuad, and went relatively smoothly save that French troops occupied Port Fuad quicker than expected, and were bombarded by the British ships. Orders which had to be translated from French into English or vice versa stalled communications.

When Port Said and Port Fuad fell into Franco-British hands, Nasser scuttled a total of seven ships and blocked the canal at either end; the waterway was to be out of action for over six months. This was something Nasser had been reluctant to do; he needed the Suez tolls desperately. The invasion moved towards El Kantara and Ismailia, meeting little resistance.

Resistance was to come from London, where Eden found himself in the centre of a vast storm. The Labour Party Opposition was so angry—even its leader, Hugh Gaitskell, had been kept in the dark—that the House of Commons resembled an Egyptian mob on the loose. Newspaper editorials were not all favourable, nor, as it turned out, was the man on the street. For the first time in Soviet history, foreign embassies were the scene of angry demonstrations—probably with the Kremlin's consent. The pound Sterling had been sliding since September, and now the run on it was terrifying; a part of it was with U.S. Treasury consent. News arrived that the Syrians had blown up three pumping stations on the oil pipeline from Iraq to the Mediterranean, and the Americans would not promise to supplement British and French oil shortages with oil from the Western Hemisphere. Both the U.N. General Assembly and the Security Council had sat all weekend and were still in session.

What broke Eden was the communication from Moscow. Various versions were sent to Washington D.C., London, Paris and Tel Aviv. The one to London—similar to the one to Paris—said in veiled language that if a cease-fire were not called immediately, some powerful nations might have the ability to strike at London without mounting an invasion; that there were such things as rockets and nuclear warheads. Konrad Adenauer, Chancellor of West Germany, was in Paris when Mollet's note from Moscow came through, and said that while it may be debatable that the U.S.S.R. could reach the U.K. or France, missiles could certainly fall on Berlin. He urged Mollet to give in. Eden was already urging Mollet to give in, for he had in all but name. There were experts in M.I.5 and other British intelligence networks who said that the Soviet Union did not have that kind of capability, but the confirmation of this Eden so desperately wanted from the C.I.A. was not available; the Americans had virtually broken off relations with the British and French. Eisenhower's mood had not cooled down very much, and

John Foster Dulles was in hospital. He had collapsed suffering from abdominal pain, and not because of stress; exploratory surgery revealed stomach cancer. It wasn't to put him out of the arena for good. 'That cold, gray man', as Golda Meir was to call him, was back in the Secretary of State saddle by 13 December. Far too late to have had much of a voice in the Suez Crisis.

In Tel Aviv the Moscow note infuriated Ben-Gurion, not so much because it threatened nuclear retaliation, but because its tone was crude, blatantly insulting; Jews didn't have the clout to command delicate handling. Just bludgeon them. But Ben-Gurion had no intention of being bludgeoned by anyone. As far as he was concerned, he had what Israel needed already, and the Israeli war was over. The Gaza Strip was in Israeli hands, and so was the Gulf of Aqaba when the great Egyptian fortress of Sharm-el-Sheikh athwart the narrow entrance to the gulf fell into Israeli hands; Eilat, at the top of the gulf, was now their Red Sea port. He was happy to obey a cease-fire, but he was not about to withdraw.

Eden bowed to the inevitable and issued formal instructions for the British to get out of Egypt on the night between Tuesday the 6th and Wednesday the 7th of November. Mollet and Pineau had tried, filled with anguish, to persuade him that now the operation was a fact they had nothing to lose but much to gain by finishing it and Nasser. Eden refused. The British would be told to withdraw, and since the force was two-thirds British, France had no alternative other than to do the same. 'Our mountainous elephant has given birth to a mouse!' wailed General André Beaufre.

Early in the daylit morning of Wednesday, 7 November, Roden was summoned to the Egyptian Foreign Office to see the head of the department rather than the minister.

'Don, I don't want to risk using Jean. Would you take me?' Roden asked Walker, whom he liked very much—and trusted in any sticky situation.

The interview was conducted in French and was therefore a halting one for Roden, but the two men managed to understand each other. He was extremely sorry, said the Egyptian bureaucrat, but Egypt was breaking off diplomatic relations with Australia, which had voted the wrong way in the United Nations.

'Thank you, I appreciate your courtesy,' said Roden, getting up. 'It is time to go, with the British a few miles further down the canal than Port Said.'

The Egyptian gasped, went pale. 'How do you know that?'

'The BBC news,' said Roden, looking surprised.

The moment he got back to the car he snatched the flag off AUS 1. 'Put your foot down and get us home!' he said.

Walker, who never panicked, did as he was told.

As soon as they reached the legation chancellery the work began. All papers, passport blanks, code and cipher books were torn up and burned; remained only the Australian seal, which proved impossible to destroy. But by dint of hammering, gouging and sawing, they finally managed to deface it sufficiently to render it unusable.

They just beat the Egyptian police, who arrived in force to lock the four men in the residence. The local staff were arrested and taken away, though, as previously mentioned, most of them managed to reach Australia, where Roden found them jobs.

While they were in the residence they could hear and sometimes see the police taking the chancellery apart; the residence was also searched. Nothing, nothing, nothing!

From now on they would just have to sit it out and see what happened; they were a little apprehensive, but by no means stewing.

It might be prison, but it wouldn't be the firing squad, and even prison was unlikely. Nasser was being very careful of his international image, and was quite sophisticated enough to realise that atrocities would not enhance it. Like many foreigners exposed to the punctilious correctness of the British, he was imbued with a desire to be seen as no less than his old masters. If there were risks for the four men, those risks involved worked-up mobs or over-zealous underlings. Roden's opinion was that if they behaved themselves, did no rash acts of pointless heroism, they would be all right. Though it would have been nice to walk in the garden. Off-limits, alas.

The planes were still zooming overhead. At one stage before they were locked up they had heard the unmistakable rumble of armour coming into Cairo and therefore away from the canal zone; Roden did not make the mistake of thinking the tanks were British. The Egyptian army was on the run. He was not to know for some time that Eden and Mollet had called the invasion off; when he did, he wasn't very surprised, though he was disappointed. The venture was half-baked anyway; without the sweet water canal, the troops would have been in trouble quickly. It should have been all or none.

On Tuesday, 6 November, two important things had happened: Dwight D. Eisenhower was resoundingly re-elected the President of the United States of America (though Congress went to the Democrats, which meant an antipathetic legislature for at least two years); and Evening Peal won the Melbourne Cup, Australia's most famous horserace. Roden's recollection of dates during the Suez crisis usually goes, 'two days before the Melbourne Cup' or 'the Sunday after the Melbourne Cup'. Handy thing, the Cup.

A car came to fetch them from the residence in the early hours of Sunday, 11 November. Each man was permitted one small suitcase only; Helen had taken a few things with her, but most of what they owned had to stay behind. Though residences are funded by governments, their occupants always have many of their own things there as well. With Roden went his air pistol and the Webley revolver. The air pistol had not been fired in anger, the revolver had not been fired at all. The shotgun, a pride and joy, remained in Cairo. In Bardia, across the Libyan border, Roden had tried to persuade External Affairs in Canberra to ask the Swedes to look after the Australian Legation, but someone in his wisdom gave the task to the Canadians, who were still in such disorder that what wasn't looted was mutilated or defaced. Thanks to the Canadian Foreign Minister, Lester Pearson (who was awarded the Nobel Peace Prize for his efforts), Canadian stocks were to rise considerably in the aftermath of the Suez Crisis.

The staff of several diplomatic missions were loaded onto a train at the Alexandria platform, though precisely where they were going they didn't know. Only one diplomat came to see them off, the Dutchman Berend Slingenberg, whom Roden was to meet in New York years later. They became great friends. The train was jam-packed and had no refreshment facilities; senior diplomatic staff had money, but many of the passengers had none to buy food or drink at one of the many pauses along the way.

First Alexandria, a hundred miles north-west of Cairo; then a very familiar journey for Roden—they were heading for Mersa Matruh. He had deemed those journeys awful enough, with their hard wooden benches and lack of other comforts, but this was the Train to Hell. Before it reached Alexandria the toilets were hopelessly blocked and overflowing; by El Alamein the carriage floors were awash in urine and faeces, and it only got worse as the hours dragged by on this four-hundred-mile trip. The train was slow, assistance nil. One of those odd occasions when no air-conditioning was a blessing; the windows could be opened, which let out a little of the stench and permitted people to lean far out, inhale sand and soot.

Mersa Matruh looked even sadder and more tattered than in his days there in 1941. No international socialites would dream of visiting it. Then came Sidi Barrani, another whistle stop on the long British-German-Italian battle trail. And finally the end of the line at Salum, on the Libyan border. These were times before Gaddafi, of course; the Libyans then were very friendly.

Roden had travelled with the British ambassador, Sir Humphrey Trevelyan. Once off the train they had to walk half a mile to the actual border, but on the other side of it some British officials were waiting with cars. The ride into Bardia was heaven, but the airport was in Tobruk, a hundred miles further on. At least it was done by car. Roden travelled with Sir Humphrey Trevelyan and the British Consul-General in Libya. Tobruk, where a part of the Australian Seventh Division had sat it out for months.

The airport was frenzied chaos. Though the senior French diplomats had departed well before the action commenced, the junior French were on the Train to Hell. There were two planes to London and one to Paris—not nearly enough transport. Nor were the British and French counter staff obliging. Everyone had to be weighed—not unusual in those days—and Roden was a big man. Not fat, just big. Odd! He didn't weigh very much at all! Then the BOAC counter clerk looked down and saw Michael Cook's foot poked under the edge of the scale. He was very angry.

Eventually the four Australians were put on one of the two London-bound Constellations, to find the plane absolutely stripped—another nightmare journey, spent like paratroopers. The cabin staff were snooty and clearly resented this impromptu flight. Of the two toilets aboard, one was for men and one for women. The queue to the men's was endless; many of the refugees had caught some sort of Delhi belly. Roden was fine, but as there were extremely few women present, he nipped into the women's toilet. When he emerged the steward was waiting, foot tapping. How dare he use the women's toilet! Being a gentleman to his fingertips, Roden did not tell the author what he replied.

In London they received their orders. Don Walker was to stay briefly in London, the others were to fly home. That was a happy reunion! At Sydney airport Roden felt something wrapping around his leg: Anthony, who wasn't going to let go of Dad again.

The family in Australia had gone through a terrible time. As soon as Helen had settled into the new Morris house at Bronte Beach, she sent David and Anthony to Scots College, a private boys' school in Bellevue Hill. Things weren't too bad until after Mark was born, when the Suez situation began to occupy a lot of space in the newspapers. Naturally Roden's name was mentioned, and much was made of it because Australians in Cairo were in short supply—at least, newsworthy ones. Then about that moment, Roden was no longer able to telephone Australia.

The boys at Scots started to tell David and Anthony that their father was bound to be killed—Nasser was killing *everybody*! Maybe he was dead already. Small boys are thoughtlessly cruel. Their mother and all three grandparents tried to reassure the boys, but both of them remained grief-stricken and frantic.

If it had not been for Aileen Slim, wife of the Governor-General of Australia, Sir William Slim (he of the Tenth Indian Division), Helen would have known nothing. But Lady Slim had her husband enquire every day of Menzies and Casey what was going on in Cairo. Then she would pass what she gleaned on to Helen.

A Canberra newspaper published an irate article which said

Australia's minister in Cairo was grossly derelict in his duty—he wasn't doing a darned thing! At the time of the article, Roden and his three cohorts were locked up in the residence.

The joy when the tall, familiar figure limped across the Mascot tarmac, beaming and waving! Oh, he was safe!

He had returned to Australia at the end of November 1956, by which time the shock waves of the Suez Crisis were subsiding. Ill and broken, Sir Anthony Eden resigned as Prime Minister of the U.K. on 9 January 1957. He was succeeded by Harold Macmillan, who had to sort out the pieces and try to stick Humpty-Dumpty together again. Bigger powers had nudged the U.K. off the centre of the world stage. The same could be said of France, which, under Charles de Gaulle, was to give Algeria independence. Israel stood pat, fired no shots at Egypt but refused to withdraw either. When the Canadian Lester Pearson engineered the first U.N. peace-keeping force, it could take itself home because the U.N. was caretaking its gains—and Israel had bought time to prepare for its next slug at its neighbours in 1967. As for Gamal Abdel Nasser, his was the diplomatic and psychological victory, though his military machine was revealed for all the world to see as third-rate.

Nasser's instincts proved right; climbing into bed with the U.S.S.R. was a poor answer to his country's problems. The age of the too-big-for-Suez supertankers was just around the corner, so canal revenues never did do what he had hoped they would. After the Six Day War against Israel in 1967 the canal was closed for eight years. And as he had known, Soviet aid was not gratis. The cotton crop had to pay the interest on loans for matériel and the Aswan Dam, which left nothing in the larder for Egypt. He had tried with all his might to evict the colonial overlords while maintaining his alignment with the West. He achieved the eviction, but he alienated the West. Alas, he had oil to the right of him and oil to the left of him, but none in the sands of Egypt.

The real victor of Suez was Israel; the Russian bear might show his fangs and roar, yet time was to prove that even the biggest bears grow old and toothless. If the Franco-British elephant did give birth to a mouse, that mouse was nonetheless to alter the political Middle East permanently. Elephants, lions, cobras, doves, hawks, bears, donkeys, mice: Suez really was a zoo.

Roden had not been due back from Cairo for another eighteen months, so there just was not a diplomatic post available to give him. The best Richard Casey could do was to employ him in the national capital until a suitable job did come up. Sorry, but that was the situation.

'In which event,' said Roden, 'I'd like to stay in Australia for two years. My children don't know their homeland.'

'There's a SEATO conference coming up in Canberra,' said Casey. 'You can start by acting as its Secretary-General.'

SEATO (the South-East Asia Treaty Organization) was a John Foster Dulles brainchild of 1954 vintage. Dulles seems to have been addicted to acronyms, though his SCUA (Suez Canal Users' Association) was more usually known as 'SCRUYA'. Certainly SEATO lacked some significantly large South-East Asian teeth— India, Ceylon, Malaya and Indonesia did not belong to it. The members were the U.S.A., the U.K., France, Australia, New Zealand, Pakistan, the Philippines and Thailand, and it extended to cover Cambodia, Laos and South Vietnam. These last three 'protect- orates' were to lead to Australia's participation in the Vietnam War. SEATO's aims were the usual ones: to recognise the sovereign equality of all member nations; the self-determination of peoples; and to promote economic development and wellbeing within the ranks.

To his delight, Roden learned that Casey had given him Nick Parkinson, of Cairo days, as his right-hand man; Nick would appreciate Roden's burning desire to run the best and smoothest SEATO meeting yet. The last one, held in Pakistan, had not been bureaucratically satisfactory; minutes of each day's proceedings, for example, were not delivered for a month, which meant they did not appear until well after the conference was over. Though it was disappointing to understand that he would not participate in the SEATO conference as a diplomat, he was determined to show his executive skills to men like Dulles, who would be attending; as a veteran of Suez, Roden had little love for Dulles. The Americans had such a reputation for efficiency—well, after this SEATO conference, so would Australia.

No ends were left untied. The meetings were to be held in Parliament House itself, as the Parliament was in recess: the diplomatic delegates were to convene in the green-hued House of Representatives, and the military delegates in the crimson Senate. Of course this was the old, low-profiled, white Parliament House built in 1927 as a temporary structure; it did quite deedily for over fifty years. One rather grumpy senator protested bitterly at the thought of a SEATO military man seated in his seat, but Roden smoothed his feathers and they became good friends. Not all Australian politicians condoned SEATO.

Rooms were reserved—and paid for in advance—at the best hotels from the night before, as some of the delegations were due to arrive early in the morning. The heads of most missions would be housed in their embassies, but, as is the wont of important men attending important meetings, they came with entourages, some members of which were important in their own right. Essential then that they should be able to move straight into their hotels. This went smoothly save for the Pakistani delegation; the U.S. air force crew of

Dulles' flight had been accommodated at the R.A.A.F. base nearby, but they didn't like the standard of living there, so they went to the Canberra Hotel and wheedled a susceptible female clerk on reception into giving them the Pakistanis' rooms. Roden had met the Pakistanis in person and conducted them to the hotel—to find their accommodation gone, though it had been prepaid. The author has never seen Roden annoyed—nor, candidly, does she want to! Suffice it to say that the fur flew in all directions. Dulles' air crew were summarily ejected, cleaning staff were galvanised, and the weary Pakistanis were tenderly inserted into their rooms in short order.

Having ensured that there would be no indignant occupants of Parliament House to challenge the delegates, Roden thought it would be appropriate to arrange that liquid refreshments be laid on free of charge. So he went to the Parliament House barmen and instructed them to bill External Affairs for SEATO drinks.

'What?' gasped Richard Casey. *'Free drinks?'*

'Yes, minister,' said Roden firmly. 'It will keep abrasiveness to a minimum if they can get a lemonade free of charge any time they feel like a lemonade.'

The Australian ministers, particularly Athol Townley, teased Roden to buy them a drink for ages afterwards.

SEATO was discussing a very mixed bag at that meeting, but the main item on the agenda concerned assembling an effective program of defence in case of Communist Chinese aggression.

Touchy subjects like this, Roden reasoned, made it vital that the delegates have their minutes immediately; he and Nick Parkinson went to painstaking lengths to ensure this. They started at the Government Printing Office, where they arranged that a staff should work through each night. Hansard stenographers took down every word, and at 6 p.m., when each day's doings were concluded, the Government Printing Office produced a rough draft to send to each delegation for vetting. Once vetted, the Government Printing Office produced perfectly printed minutes which were laid at each delegate's place the next morning. Dazzling, thought the delegates. All of them save one, in fact, were so delighted that the corrected draft was back in no time; the exception was Dulles, who, Roden suspects, was either too sick or too lazy to get down to it, with the result that his draft was always the last to be returned.

'I'd be hopping from one foot to the other, except I only had one foot to hop onto,' says Roden, grinning.

While the conference was winding down President Magsaysay of the Philippines died, and Vice-President Garcia, who was the Philippines SEATO delegate, was frantic.

'Minister,' said Roden to Richard Casey, 'he's desperate to get home because he thinks there's a fair chance of his becoming president if he's on hand. We can do with a friend in that country, so I would appreciate it if Australia could provide a plane to get him home at once.'

Casey saw the sense of that and arranged it, with the result that Garcia did become president, and did feel warmly towards Australia during his time as president.

The SEATO conference was pronounced a great success; Roden received much praise from the delegates, particularly from Sir Alec Douglas-Home, the British delegation head, and from President Garcia of the Philippines.

Arthur (later Sir Arthur) Tange was the Secretary of External Affairs. Upon SEATO's conclusion, he had nothing to offer Roden except Chief of the Consular and Protocol Division.

'A wearisome and rather dull job,' is how Roden describes it.

He had been created Commander of the Order of the British Empire (C.B.E.) at the end of December 1956, he thinks because, among other things, he shoved that food through the fence of the

Cairo British Embassy. A memo he was shown years later in New York was very glowing. So he was now Roden Cutler, V.C., C.B.E.

Among the duties of the consular and protocol head was that of determining how far and to what extent consuls could claim diplomatic privilege. Fortunately Roden knew some of them from his earlier diplomatic jobs, which was a help—diplomats can be touchy over privilege.

The most unpleasant incident happened during the state visit of Prime Minister Kishi of Japan.

Ambassador Suzuki of Japan, accompanied by Jim (later Sir James) Scholtens, came to see Roden. Scholtens at that time was hospitality officer of the Prime Minister's Department. Suzuki was there to discuss the coming state visit, and the conversation went well until he said that Kishi wanted to lay a wreath at the Australian War Memorial. Oh, dear! Not politic in 1957, a mere twelve years since the end of the Second World War and a time when many Australians would not buy goods made in Japan or under a Japanese brand name.

'Your Excellency,' said Roden, looking Suzuki straight in the eye, 'you know as well as I do what feelings are in Australia at this time. The best I could do for you would have to be ex officio, not in the program of events. If your prime minister's motorcade were to pass by the Australian War Memorial on its way from the airport, the Prime Minister could stop and lay a wreath—provided, that is, that I can get permission from Mr. Menzies and from certain bodies like the R.S.L.'

'I understand perfectly,' said Suzuki, bowing.

The National Secretary of the veterans' R.S.L. was William (later Sir William) Keys, whom Roden knew. Roden rang him and asked if he would lend his support. Keys thought for a moment, then said yes. Roden then rang Menzies and told him that the R.S.L.'s national secretary had agreed: would he too? Yes, said the Prime Minister.

But the news leaked to Richard Casey in External Affairs before Roden had a chance to contact him. Casey was furious.

'Cutler, what *have* you done?'

Roden explained, including the fact that Keys and Menzies had lent their support.

'Well, I'm going to get in touch with Mr. Menzies straight away and tell him it must be cancelled!'

Menzies preferred to back Roden.

Someone leaked the unofficial visit to the Australian War Memorial, with the result that Prime Minister Kishi of Japan was bombarded by a shower of leaflets describing Japanese war atrocities as he stood by the long pool. Bill (later Sir William) Yeo, head of the New South Wales R.S.L., screamed blue murder about the visit.

Aside from this one incident, Richard Casey was a gentleman who strongly supported his staff in External Affairs.

'He wasn't perhaps as brilliant as some ministers were in that portfolio, but he was always very decent and dedicated, even a little oldfashioned,' says Roden.

Casey and his wife, Maie, were to become good friends of the Cutlers', though for a horrible moment Roden thought he might have alienated Maie Casey's affections forever during the SEATO meeting. She was standing next to him during a reception when she admired Garcia's Filipino blouse, contemplated getting one for herself.

'The trouble is, Mrs. Casey,' said Roden, not at his diplomatic best, 'that it's so transparent I don't think it would look good on you.'

She forgave him.

Two more, less boring, jobs filled out those two years Roden had requested in Canberra. The first was as head of the Europe, Africa and Middle East section of External Affairs, and the second was as head of the South and South-East Asia section. The third section, the Americas and the Pacific, he never had much to do with. Both these jobs meant he was back on the political side, which he much preferred. As head of the section, it was his task to gather and disseminate all political information, make sure all embassies and high commissions in his area were properly instructed, and keep all relevant Australian ministers au fait with whatever was going on.

On the domestic front, these two years in Canberra were a treat. Though they had wanted to buy a house, the only one they liked was too expensive, so they ended in renting. David and Anthony went to Canberra Grammar School. Richard was sent to its junior school, where he struggled with his three Rs. After Colombo and Cairo, the combination of Australian life and starting proper school was very difficult; it took time to settle down. All three boys were bright and co-operative, nor were they ever to be 'problem children'. Mark, of course, was a baby, yet not too young to know the sound of his father's car coming home for lunch; he would jig up and down in his high chair and make a great fuss of Dad when he walked in. The elder boys bicycled to school, where there were plenty of chances to play cricket and Rugby Union football.

They visited the Morrises and Ruby in Sydney and went to Port Stephens for holidays, as the Morrises had a cottage there. The Snowy Mountains were near enough to Canberra to permit a day's outing whenever some snow fell. To children whose life experience had mostly been tropical, snow was huge fun.

Time for a Cutler family bulletin.

When Geoff was discharged from the R.A.A.F. he went back to university, but not to continue with Economics; he chose Medicine and became a surgeon. Rob did Dentistry. And Doone married, not happily. Though the union was to last until her husband died, it became an on-again, off-again affair because of his alcoholism. The old injuries meant that she never had children. Obliged to support herself financially, she opened a dress shop, Isabel's, in Chatswood on Sydney's exclusive North Shore, and proved an excellent businesswoman. Sir Garfield Barwick's wife bought her clothes from Doone. Bob Milligan went back to Tasmania after demobilisation and ran his father's kitchen utensils and appliances store for a while. He married a Tasmanian girl, sold the store and went into the State public service. Ruby loved the two years Roden and his family spent in Canberra, and adored her grandchildren. Maybe in one way having her sons to herself was best, but there were definitely compensations. Just as she had adjusted to Helen's advent, she adjusted to the advent of Geoff's and Rob's wives too.

There also came a final parting: after a valiant battle against cancer, Aunt Dais died while Roden and his family were in Australia.

For Roden and Helen, life in Canberra was busy. At least four nights of the week would see their attending some diplomatic or governmental function, which meant quite a load for Helen to carry. The boys had to be fed before she left, something she insisted on doing herself; she had a lady to do the heavy cleaning and a babysitter for these evening affairs, but did the rest herself. So much a part of Roden's professional sphere, at no time in her life was she ever salaried or given an allowance of her own. At no time in her life did she ever complain about that, though dressing was costly. This last was not a fault; it was a necessity. Meeting the same people doing the same rounds meant a certain amount of variety in her wardrobe was essential. To appear in the same garb reflected badly on Roden, who might be apostrophised as stingy: as he was not, one dressed. But she was knacky and canny, looked Dior without wearing Dior.

At the beginning of 1959 the new post came through. Roden was to go to Pakistan as High Commissioner. Minister Casey wanted to keep him in Asia, where he wanted to be anyway.

The only snag was that he had just been elected President of the Australian Capital Territory R.S.L. Now he was obliged to stand down. Only one member objected.

The family sailed in January 1959. Colombo was a port of call, not a destination, but it was to become a temporary destination when word arrived that the outgoing High Commissioner of Pakistan, Major-General William (later Sir William) Cawthorn, was proving difficult to dislodge. He had been a soldier in Pakistan and was very attached to the people as well as the place; now that his term was ended, he was very reluctant to let go.

Thus the Cutlers moved into the Colombo residence, vacant at the time (save for the civet cats), and had to contend with a great deal of local joy at their return. Everyone assumed Roden was back as High Commissioner in Ceylon! People flocked to welcome them, marvel over the boys, beam at Helen, pump Roden's hand. Then would come the disappointment as each visitor learned the Cutlers were simply en route to Pakistan.

They were there for twelve days before orders came to fly to Karachi. The second house boy in the Colombo residence dated back to Roden's time there, and when they left he handed Roden a packet of Ceylon rupees.

'Please, master, get them to my relatives in India!'

'But I'm not going to India, I'm going to Pakistan.'

'Yes, master, I know. But I also know that you will manage to do it,' said the Tamil second house boy with complete confidence.

So there he was with a packet of Ceylon rupees and the address of the relatives in Indian Tamil country.

He wrote to Don Walker of Cairo days—Walker was now Trade Commissioner in Bombay—and asked him to help.

'I'll put the Ceylon rupees in my bank account, transfer the equivalent in Australian pounds to your bank account, then you take the equivalent in Indian rupees and make sure it gets to the right family in the right village.'

And thus were the rigid currency regulations overcome. Don Walker took the trouble to drive personally to the village and hand the money over to the second house boy's relatives. The second house boy was delighted.

'Thoroughly illegal,' says Roden, 'but what do you do when people trust you so much and believe in your ability to get things done? You can't say no.'

Perhaps governments do not consider the winning of such lowly friends important, but the author understands Roden's way of thinking: that *every* action of the 'navigator of the Australian canoe' matters, and that a friend for Australia is a friend, be he the new President of the Philippines or a Tamil house boy. Word of mouth is grossly underestimated, and the doings of the mighty are always under the microscope of the lowly. Power can blinker, even blind; but Roden's vision was never clouded by it.

The High Commissioner's residence, Bath Island, was halfway between the city of Karachi and the waterfront of Clifton, and it was a good house of three storeys. A wide ledge ran all the way around the middle floor, which the boys were to find extremely convenient; they could sneak out a window and walk the ledge to see what was going on at a party.

No one in the family—especially Roden—was sorry that Pakistan was less exciting than Egypt. Though the times were interesting: Pakistan as a nation had come into being on 4 August 1948, as West Pakistan (adjacent to Afghanistan) and East Pakistan (Bengal) with the huge nation of India dividing them. A situation which eventually was to see the emergence of Bangladesh in 1971. In 1959 the new country was still settling down, though Roden believes that if the British Raj did nothing else, it did endow both India and Pakistan with a basis for law, government and commerce. Pakistan seemed more rational in its international relationships than India, particularly with regard to the British Commonwealth of Nations. India loved to create a stir, whereas Pakistan preferred the subtle approach. Nor was it as aggressive; sheer numbers made India think of itself as a world power. The situation between India and Pakistan was as tense then as it is now, however, and that kept the High Commissioner on his toes.

There were still many signs of 'the division' of 1948, including a gigantic refugee camp on the outskirts of Karachi wherein lived many of those who had fled from India. Sanitation was a nightmare. During a dinner party which Roden attended, one of the serving staff suddenly began to scream frantically—hair raising! After the horrified guests had calmed him down, a Pakistani got the story out of him: his relatives had been on a train leaving India when it was attacked by Indian militants who had murdered every one of them. He had received the news during the dinner. This kind of thing was still happening.

High commissioners do not present letters of credence, but rather a simple letter from the Prime Minister.

Mohammad Ayub was President of Pakistan, and accepted Menzies' letter a little wryly. 'Oh, yes, I know your prime minister has recommended you because he thinks very highly of you, but *I* think you've been sent here to intimidate us.'

Despite this dismaying intelligence, Roden was to get on very well with Ayub Khan, and Helen with his wife, Begum Ayub.

Perhaps one of the most daunting aspects of Pakistan for Helen was purdah; wives in this Muslim nation were often excluded from public affairs, including luncheons, dinners, receptions. In Karachi it was not as bad as in other places, but to some extent Helen was obliged to live apart from Roden's professional world, enter the world of the women instead. Not without its entertaining side; the gossip was extremely lively and ranged across the full gamut from political scuttlebutt to fashion, so sometimes Helen could gift Roden with snippets of information he might otherwise never have discovered. English was generally spoken by educated Pakistanis, female as well as male.

Though Richard, attending a school run by nuns in Clifton, became very fluent in Urdu. English was the language of the classroom, but in the playground it was Urdu. David and Anthony were sent to school in England at last, to a preparatory school before they would enter Rugby. Not a happy choice, as it turned out; the headmaster had changed since Roden had first chosen the establishment, and the new headmaster was not fond of colonial boys. The food was grim, and Anthony was beaten with a cricket bat for some minor transgression. David was the quiet one of the four, a cautious fellow with a soft side, which meant he was easily hurt.

The family did have some fascinating experiences in Pakistan before the two elder boys went off to England, though it was Mark who had the chance to visit the British-established principality of

Swat, in the far north of the country. The ruler of Swat went under the title of the Wali of Swat; his son and heir was the Waliahed of Swat, and he happened to be married to President Ayub Khan's daughter. So when Roden, Helen and Mark were staying in a rest house (a kind of small, unlicensed hotel) in Malakand, Roden received an invitation to dinner with the Wali and Waliahed of Swat. Mrs. Cutler, said the messenger, was also invited.

'Are you sure?' asked Roden.

'Yes, sir.'

Off they went, to discover that Helen was the only female present. An extraordinary distinction which made Helen feel most uncomfortable.

Swat itself was remarkably well developed and less poverty-stricken, less barren than much of Pakistan. ('Frankly, I don't know what many of them lived on.') The area grew a lot of fruit and was filled with seasonal workers who came down from the Hindu Kush in winter. In Chitral, to the north of Swat again, the only local industry seemed to be the opium poppy; the poverty was appalling.

There were a couple of odd incidents with the Americans, and they may have been related if the Pakistan Government actually did know what was going on in Peshawar (it denied all knowledge).

The first concerned the sale of Australian wheat. Pakistan had signed a contract to take Australian wheat to the value of one million pounds—a lot of money in 1959. Then Roden heard a whisper that the Pakistanis were going to renege on the contract, as they had been offered a great deal of very cheap, U.S. Government-subsidised wheat.

'You'd better have our ambassador in Washington check,' said Roden, telephoning Canberra.

Sure enough, enquiries revealed that Roden's rumour was right.

'I'll beard the Pakistani Minister of Finance in his den and demand that he honour the contract,' said Roden.

Canberra had a conniption fit at the very idea—no, no! The Australian Government didn't dare offend Pakistan!

'Nonsense, it won't offend,' said Roden. 'My reading of most governments—including our own—is that they like to be stood up to. Crawl, and they despise you.'

Roden was correct. The Pakistani finance minister honoured the contract and presented Roden with a cheque for one million precious pounds. He then requested that he and Roden get onto a first-name footing; the two men became good friends.

The second incident was more mysterious. Suddenly Peshawar, the city near the famous Khyber Pass, seemed to be swarming with Americans, as was Karachi with more Americans en route to Peshawar.

'What are you lot doing up there?' Roden asked the American ambassador, his curiosity burning to know.

'Not a thing!' was the airy reply.

'I hope you don't mind my asking?'

'It's never the questions are embarrassing, only the answers.'

There was a summit meeting due to be held in Paris around the middle of May between the U.S.A and the U.S.S.R. The year: 1960.

On 5 May Nikita Khrushchev told the Supreme Soviet that an American spy plane had been shot down over Sverdlovsk on 1 May. On 7 May he revealed that the pilot, one Francis Gary Powers, had parachuted to safety and was in custody in Moscow. Powers had testified that he had taken off from Peshawar in Pakistan in a plane called the U-2—a flimsy, gliderlike craft which flew fairly slowly at 490 miles per hour, but at an altitude of 70,000 feet (21,000 metres)—beyond the range of Soviet anti-aircraft gunfire, it was fondly believed. Not so! His mission was to fly over the U.S.S.R. via the Aral Sea, Sverdlovsk, Kirov, Archangel'sk and Murmansk before landing at Bodo airbase in high Norway. Powers then admitted that his employer was the C.I.A.

The U.S. Government denied that there had ever been any spy mission, though it admitted that a U-2 plane may have accidentally flown over the U.S.S.R. That wasn't good enough for Khrushchev, who sent protest notes to Turkey, Pakistan and Norway; all three countries denied any knowledge of spy flights, U-2s and the C.I.A.

On 16 May Khrushchev demanded that all flights over Soviet territory cease forthwith, and also demanded that the U.S.A. apologise. Otherwise—no summit. Nearing the end of his second term as president, Eisenhower promised that Soviet airspace would be sacrosanct, but wouldn't apologise. The U.S.A. knew absolutely nothing about the matter. The summit meeting did not take place, and the Cold War's temperature dropped a few degrees.

In 1960 a new state was born: Somalia, in East Africa. A great many national representatives were invited to attend the celebrations, and Roden got the Australian guernsey. He flew on Lufthansa to Nairobi in Kenya, where the fun began. The flight to Mogadishu was courtesy of East African Airways, and the plane was overbooked. When Roden climbed aboard he found a gigantic Arab in his seat, sporting a businesslike dagger. Oops! Some airline officials charged into the melée and threw the Kenyan Minister for Immigration off the plane. As he refused to disembark without his luggage, the plane was held up for what seemed like an eternity. When it did land in Mogadishu everyone was already muttering that they'd better see about making sure they had plane bookings out. With the result that there was a rush on the ticketing counter the moment people spilled out of the arrival area.

Mogadishu was tiny, possessed a total of about one kilometre of sealed road; beyond that was the desert, in which dwelled lions, sheep, cattle and small bands of nomads who made and hoped to sell a kind of curved Arabian dagger. All the hotel accommodation came as prefabricated modules in enormous containers from Italy; one would be in one's room preparing for the day's or the evening's events when someone would run in carrying taps or toilet roll dispensers and proceed to affix them. Going to breakfast was an adventure. There was neither table service nor a buffet spread. Roden appeared holding a plate loaded with food.

'How did you manage to get that?' gasped one hungry diplomat.

'I went into the kitchen and cooked it.'

The mood was optimistic and the Somalis really tried to do their best, but it was not difficult to sense that independence for poor—literally as well as metaphorically—Somalia was going to be troubled. 'Nothing overt, but there were rumbles beneath the surface,' says Roden.

The British representative was Cabinet minister John Profumo, afterwards to become embroiled in the Christine Keeler scandal. Roden thought him a pleasant enough man, and his wife, the actress Valerie Hobson, one of the most impressive women he had ever met.

After four days the festivities were over; everyone flew back to Nairobi with allocated seats. Unfortunately the moment the plane lifted off from Mogadishu airport, the steward and his staff got stuck into the contents of the bar and drank with great glee all the way to Nairobi. After that it was Air India and a seat next to Valerie Hobson. An absolutely charming woman.

Helen hadn't gone to Somalia with him; four-year-old Mark was best not catapulted into potentially bizarre situations. She stayed at

Murree, in the hill country north of Rawalpindi, where Roden had successfully done battle with the Canberra bureaucrats over obtaining a commodious Australian High Commission house.

The need for official accommodation so far north had arisen because Pakistan had decided that Karachi, festering in the humid heat of the seashore and possessing all the inconveniences of a huge city, was not an appropriate capital for the new nation. It would build a new capital in more salubrious climes and call the town Islamabad. As Canberra was one national capital the Pakistanis admired tremendously, they asked Roden to give them all the plans and schemes involved in the creation of Canberra.

'I told them they were mad to isolate their bureaucrats in a place they could call their own,' says Roden, 'but they wouldn't listen.' So he went ahead and got the requested data, which was mountainous. 'If this lot doesn't convince them not to go ahead with Islamabad, nothing will!' said Roden to himself. But for better or for worse, Islamabad was built.

Murree was more or less right next door to the site of the new capital. Roden found an ideal house adjacent to the Pakistan president's house, but the Canbera official in charge of Pakistan said that they had already found a house elsewhere. As it was neither as good nor as convenient as the one Roden wanted, he hammered away until the official crumbled—and snatched the house out from under the noses of the Americans, who had also had their eyes on it. And here Helen and Mark spent much of their time, for it was indeed a far kinder climate than Karachi. Roden would work from Monday to Friday in Karachi, then fly up to Rawalpindi to join his family for the weekends. Always a fan of Rudyard Kipling, Roden loved this part of Pakistan, scene of so much that Kipling wrote about. The four Cutler sons in their turn were to love Kipling.

'Walk with Kings—nor lose the common touch.' That line from Kipling might have served as Roden's motto.

But in 1961 he had been in Pakistan for two and a half years, and he knew it would soon be time to go. Robert Gordon Menzies was holding the portfolio of External Affairs as well as Prime Minister when the cable came through asking him if he would like to go to New York as Australian Consul-General. It was couched as a request rather than as an order, for it had its down-side, as Menzies knew. While it carried no reduction in salary or status, it meant that he would not be on the political side of diplomacy, as was a high commissioner or ambassador.

'What are you delaying for?' asked Helen three days after the cable had come. 'You know you have to give an answer.'

'Yes, dear, but I'm not very keen to be on the consular side. Except that New York is a place we know and we'd be very comfortable there,' said Roden.

'I would like it very much,' said Helen quietly.

Well, the good Lord knew that life was sometimes very hard on Helen in Asia and the Middle East, between non-air-conditioned cars and residences, civet cats, armies of crawlies, the threat of tropical diseases—and purdah. Her sacrifices for him were legion. Time to make a sacrifice for her. He cabled Menzies and said he would take the post.

They had a little while in Canberra between Karachi and New York, including a quiet lunch with Menzies and Dame Pattie at the Lodge. Menzies made it clear that he understood the drop in title was considerable enough to warrant Roden's refusing.

'My attitude, Prime Minister, is that I am a servant of the Australian people and I will do whatever their government wants.'

●

The new post turned out to be no sinecure; the author suspects that whenever a diplomatic mission had got itself into a mess, the Australian ministerial answer was to send Roden Cutler. There had been no consul-general in New York for some time, and the previous one, Josh Francis, had been Minister for the Navy before that. It was a post usually given to an ex-minister, as was the ambassadorial slot in Washington D.C. That was held by Howard Beale, also one of Menzies' ex-ministers, and a man with whom Menzies did not see eye to eye. On one memorable occasion during an election campaign, a journalist asked Menzies if he had a job for Howard Beale.

'Well, I'm thinking of creating a Ministry of Antarctica and giving it to Beale,' said Menzies.

The news of Roden's appointment seems to have had the same effect on Howard Beale that it had had upon President Ayub of Pakistan: Cutler was there to intimidate him. Upon receipt of Roden's courteous letter informing the Australian ambassador that he had arrived, that he would co-operate completely, comply with the minister's wishes, and would like instructions as to what Mr. Beale would like him to do, Howard Beale let the new Consul-General know what was expected in no uncertain terms. First and foremost, there was to be *no* poaching on Beale's diplomatic preserves—he and nobody else would handle the political side of things. If he was in New York, his car would fly the Australian flag, but Roden's would not. Roden was to confine himself absolutely to consular business. Understood?

A little taken aback, Roden set out to allay Beale's fears. At first the ambassador would arrive in New York upon any occasion he thought might see Roden intrude onto his patch, or that he felt was too important for a mere consul-general. Gradually he settled down, but he watched Roden like a hawk. If Roden had to give a speech at a function Beale had deputed, then Beale wrote the speech himself and insisted that Roden simply deliver it. Roden confesses that he was sometimes naughty and altered it to his own phraseology.

Though Beale was a mediocre speaker, he wrote superbly well; after he retired he wrote for the *Sydney Morning Herald* and the *New York Times*, among other fine newspapers.

On the consular side, Roden found himself in charge of seven different departments, all part of Canberra departments and staffed by Canberra bureaucrats on 'temporary foreign duty'. This gave them unsuspected advantages over their boss, the Consul-General, who had to pay his children's air fares to their schools, be those schools in Australia or in the U.K., whereas the bureaucrats had the fares paid by the Australian Government.

There were departments entitled Treasury, External Affairs, Auditor-General, Procurement, Customs, Trade, and News and Information, and he was in charge of all of them. Which, since he insisted upon being kept informed and consulted by all of them, did not sit well with the New York based heads of these seven consular institutions. They were accustomed to running their own little empires, and resented what they considered his tendency to rubberneck. But Roden did not intend to be run; he would do the running. Among the least co-operative among these section heads was none other than a cousin of Menzies'. Which didn't impress or intimidate Roden Cutler.

The job was actually a very heavy one, as the New York mission was the second-largest in the Australian diplomatic hierarchy; only London exceeded it in size. There were several Australian consuls— in Chicago, Los Angeles and San Francisco—but Roden's office was responsible for affairs in thirty-two of the then forty-eight American states. He was also the chief accounting officer for the United States of America, Canada and the Caribbean area—which meant that he paid the salary and expenses of, among others, Howard Beale. In practical terms Roden didn't intrude upon the missions in the three other American cities, but he was obliged to visit them from time to time, and have Auditor-General's scrutinise their books. Once all his accounting was done, Canberra then checked Roden, but never queried his decisions.

The Consulate was in the R.C.A. Building at the Rockefeller Center and the residence was on Fifth Avenue at 87th Street (an apartment building which also housed a couple of Rockefellers). The residence was a typically large Fifth Avenue apartment—four bedrooms, a living-reception room, a dining room seating sixteen to twenty people, a TV-rumpus room, a study, bathrooms and a laundry. The cook was a jolly Jamaican woman with whom Roden still maintains a friendship; the chauffeur (by name of Charles) was a grumpy sort of fellow who didn't appreciate extra duty.

For Helen the New York posting was a joy. She chummed up with several women quickly, though her best friend was Dorothy Hammerstein, the Australian wife of the lyricist Oscar Hammerstein. David, Anthony and Richard were all at school in England—the two older boys were now able to enter Rugby—and Mark went to a small junior school run by the neighbourhood's Episcopalian church. This church rejoiced under the curiously fundamentalist name of The Church of the Heavenly Rest, which the local Episcopalians changed to The Church of the Celestial Snooze.

The Cutlers made a number of good friends: David Rockefeller, Chauncey Stillman, Floyd Blair, Amos Peaslee, the Austrian-American John Leslie. And wives, of course. Nelson Rockefeller, Governor of New York at that time, had a particular affinity for Australia because his son went missing in New Guinea.

David Hay was the Australian ambassador to the United Nations; Roden was asked to do the Fifth Committee, which was the financial and administrative committee of the United Nations, and was one of five seniors appointed as the Australian U.N. General Assembly delegation. With David Hay he got on very well. They both suffered the same peculiar distinction, which was to receive no financial help in educating their children in respect of air fares. Be it school in Australia or in England, as 'permanents' they had to find the air fares themselves. Though both men were on good salaries, the expense of keeping several children in boarding schools and paying their air fares at least once a year for vacations was more than either man could manage. Snobbery wasn't the operating motive. Simply, they wanted stability of schooling for their children, as they were forever moving around the world. England was usually a little cheaper; the long journey to and from Australia meant more expensive air fares. Eventually this predicament was to result in both Hay and Roden asking for transfer to some area wherein they would get relief—Asia or Europe, both of which saw the permanent heads of missions given air fares. A peculiar and unnecessary distinction, surely, but one which did exist in the 1960s.

About John F. Kennedy, Roden is ambivalent, though Helen liked him enormously. Too much of a womaniser for Roden's taste; he is austere in such matters and cannot understand why men or women fail to govern their basic urges. Though Roden gave him top marks for overcoming the obstacles in his path, particularly Catholicism. One small step towards an American president of any creed, any colour, either sex. 'He brought a flash of hope and faith in the future—a feeling that America was going somewhere. And he understood what Americans wanted, he appealed to the young and the underprivileged. A very capable man, though I couldn't like his style of oratory—too Ciceronian—you know, things like "Ask not what America can do for you, but what you can do for America." He had his thousand golden days, but if he hadn't been assassinated I think the gilt would have worn off his gingerbread.'

One of the stories circulating when Roden was Consul-General in New York went to the effect that Franklin Roosevelt proved a man could be president for as long as he wanted, that Truman proved anybody could be president, that Eisenhower proved a president was not necessary, and that Kennedy proved a president could be dangerous.

He had met Richard Nixon in Colombo, did not care for him. But Lyndon Baines Johnson he knew better than either Kennedy or Nixon: 'Ruthless and very devious. He had no sense of guilt at all and considered his own progress and future ahead of everything else.' In other words, a consummate politician.

One of Roden's best friends in the U.S.A. was the Pakistani ambassador in Washington D.C., Ghulam Ahmed, always known as 'Gee Ahmed'. Gee Ahmed invited Roden, Helen and Mark down for the weekend during the late Fall of 1963. They set out, Roden driving, and made the journey to Washington D.C. Next day, Friday 22 November, Gee Ahmed had a luncheon in their honour. It was a leisurely affair, very pleasant, until a Pakistani servant bore a silver tray to the ambassador, who took a note from it, read the few words it contained, then shook his head and muttered, 'Oh, she must be mad!'

He fell silent; so did the table, wondering at his pallid face, shocked expression.

'What's wrong, Gee?' asked Roden.

'My receptionist says that President Kennedy has been shot and assassinated passing in front of a book store in Dallas.'

The guests sat stunned until Roden asked if someone could turn on a television. And there it was. Lunch forgotten, they gathered in front of the television and watched, appalled, horrified. The end of an era, the beginning of a mystery. Though Roden firmly believes that the Warren Commission gave a proper decision.

There were 110 people on the staff of the Australian Consulate in New York, and room was very tight; one thing Roden achieved was the acquisition of a little more space. Customs was a queer section which involved much dickering between the Australian authorities and the American authorities, particularly in the area of quarantine. A member of the American press alleged, for example, that a carton of Australian beef contained kangaroo meat. On another occasion a shipment of canned pineapple from Australia was sprayed by the American Customs people with a gooey, sticky substance which ruined its marketability. But the big headache was Procurement. What did the Australian Government buy from the U.S.A.? The answer in the early 1960s was—arms and military equipment. Destroyers, planes, capital stuff. The annual bill could run anywhere from one hundred to three hundred million pounds, a considerable slice of the Canberra budget. Responsibility for making these purchases and paying for them rested with Roden and his Procurement section, and it was never easy. The Americans hated dealing with Procurement.[†]

After Paul Hasluck took over from Garfield Barwick as Minister for External Affairs in April of 1964, things worsened. Hasluck had no ability to communicate, nor any real leadership qualities. To

---

[†] 'Procurement' to an American meant buying a prostitute, so to sell armaments to 'Procurement' made them feel like whores.

Roden, a good deal of his time seemed to be taken up in complaints about the Salvation Army, which Hasluck felt had treated his father (a Salvationist) badly. He was to remain in External Affairs until 1969, when, knighted, he became Governor-General of Australia after Richard, Baron Casey, stepped down.

So it was to Hasluck that David Hay and Roden Cutler of the New York Australian missions tendered their ultimatum: a new post with some air fare relief, or resignation from the service. Hasluck bowed to the inevitable and offered both men the requested change of post. Roden was to choose between Burma and The Hague. Though Burma was where he wanted to go, he decided on The Hague because it was so close to the boys in England. Channel-hopping could be done in both directions.

In the meantime, things had been happening in New South Wales, long a Labor purlieu. The Liberal-Country Party coalition under Robert (formerly Robin) Askin won power in 1965, ending twenty-three years of Labor Party rule. The term of the Governor of New South Wales, Sir Eric Woodward, was due to expire, and he had been a popular figure. But the new Government felt like a change in all directions. This was the oldest and the most prestigious of the six State governorships; the first Governor of New South Wales had been the founder of the European settlement in the Australian continent, Captain Arthur Phillip, and among the luminaries who had borne that title were men as disparate as Lachlan Macquarie, Captain William Bligh (who had two further mutinies during his term as governor), the Earl of Jersey and Sir Philip Game. It was a full vice-regal appointment, and in the absence or indisposition of the Governor-General of Australia, the Governor of New South Wales was one of the six men who could be sworn in as his substitute.

The new governor, Askin and his associates decided, would have to be a very special person indeed: someone whose name many people would recognise easily, someone whom Labor, very chagrined at being in opposition after so long a time, could not criticise or cavil about. A man of the people whom the people knew. Preferably an acknowledged hero, but one without the taint of wealth, privilege, an aristocratic background. A success story, but by the bootstraps.

Before the Cutlers left New York to return to Canberra in June of 1965, William McMahon, Minister for Labour and National Service (his nickname was 'Billy the Leak' because he could never keep his mouth shut), called on Roden and astonished him by asking if he wanted to be Governor of New South Wales.

'If you do, I can fix it,' said McMahon.

As this came like a bolt from the blue, Roden was cautious in his reply; he didn't think McMahon (later Prime Minister) had that kind of clout. So he made no mention of it to Helen.

Back in Australia again! And, such were the vagaries of External Affairs regulations, David, Anthony, Richard and Mark were flown home at government expense for their (English) summer vacation because Dad was in Australia. Since he had been officially informed that he would be Australian Ambassador at The Hague, the boys would be flown back at government expense as well. American postings, one might be pardoned for assuming, were best filled by people who had no children to educate.

Helen rented a good apartment in Sydney, though Roden had to spend time in Canberra. But Sydney meant family, a precious chance to spend time with the Morrises and Ruby, so Roden flew to and from Canberra and did his business there with despatch.

Dutch rule in western New Guinea had ended in September 1962 (the year the Australian indigenes, the Aborigines, finally began to receive the right to vote), but there was still a lot of Dutch money in West Irian, as it was now called. Because he was to be Ambassador at The Hague, Roden was selected to visit West Irian and report back to Canberra on how the handover was going.

Of more import to him personally was a summons from Robert Askin, Premier of New South Wales. Thanks to Bill McMahon, Roden was able to fence his way through the wary conversation, during which the real subject, the governorship, was never mentioned. However, he was able to tell that his answers satisfied Askin, and that he might indeed be in the running for this august position.

The thing was, did he want it? He had turned forty-nine, a decade below the usual age at which men became governors; there would be, therefore, at least a decade left for him in the side of diplomacy he loved, the political side. But self-indulgence could only go so far. This Australian winter of 1965 saw him with sons aged seventeen, sixteen, fourteen and nine; two would soon be going to university, one had four more years in high school, and Mark another eight or nine years of schooling. To be back in Australia, comfortably situated, would offer them a great deal more stability—and a chance to experience their homeland. His own mother was eighty-one, and Helen's parents were not young either. How much higher could a man without political ambitions go than to be the Governor of New South Wales? Only one rung, really—Governor-General of the Commonwealth of Australia, and at his age there was even, perhaps, time for that later on.

Roden's first cousin, Charles Cutler (whose father had been Roden's father's partner in the property outside Blayney), was Deputy Premier and leader of the Country Party of New South Wales. No sooner had Roden been interviewed by Askin than cousin Charles telephoned and asked to see him. They met at the Royal Automobile Club, where Charles informed Roden that if he wanted the job as Governor of New South Wales, it would be his. The only stumbling block was the fact that Roden was first cousin to the Deputy Premier.

This fact made the appointment a ticklish one because the Australian press was traditionally more in love with socialism than conservatism; if the journalists got wind of it, any among them with political axes to grind could shoot the appointment down. They were well aware of their people-power and were not averse to using it.

'But I have no politics,' Roden said. 'I'm a true servant of the people and I believe in being loyal to the government of the day, not to a political creed.'

'Try telling the newspapers that!'

Askin had consulted three people: Paul Hasluck, Richard Casey and Henry Bolte (Premier of Victoria). Interestingly, he did not approach Sir Robert Gordon Menzies, who had become a Knight of the Thistle in 1963. Casey, about to be ennobled and Governor-General, gave Askin a glowing report. So did Bolte. ('I liked Henry—blunt and definite. The worst thing he did was to hang Ryan.') Hasluck was not so enthusiastic, but he lent his support to the scheme; perhaps he thought this was a good way to remove Cutler from his own bailiwick. But, said Hasluck, Cutler ought to go as instructed to The Hague and take up his ambassadorship. That would remove him from journalistic eyes and permit the appointment to happen before the press could work itself into an anti-Askin fury.

Wheels within wheels! Roden confided in two people only: Helen and her father, who was very close-lipped. As he was due for a considerable amount of leave, Roden decided that en route to The Hague he would take his four sons to Syria to see whereabouts Dad had won his Victoria Cross. It was summer in Syria, of course, but that didn't slow the sightseeing party down, though it did lead to some digestive upsets among the boys. Balate Ridge outside Merdjayoun had become, of all things, a tourist trap! The boys were most fascinated by walking around the area where their father and Lance-Corporal Williams had stolen away with their boots tied around their necks. They visited Wadi Damour and saw the place where Roden had lain for twenty-six hours; for Roden this trip to the past was a little grief-stricken. But there were happier excursions to places like Damascus and Baalbek. Ascalon, a mud-brick village in 1941, had become a dirty, overcrowded city of sullen-faced people. Later they learned that a thief had had his right hand amputated in the public square on the day they were there.

They arrived in London in time for the boys to return to school; the headmaster of Rugby had advised Roden not to enter Richard there because of David and Anthony, so Richard went to Worksop College. Mark, who had started boarding at the end of his father's time in New York, went to Bilton Grange preparatory school, from which he could enter Rugby or some other senior school.

As a matter of courtesy, one of Roden's first stops in London was the Australian High Commission, where Alec Downer was ensconced. A pompous and very status-conscious man, he kept Roden waiting in the anteroom for a long time before deigning to admit him to the inner sanctum. There he purred over a cup of tea and the fact that he was to be created a Knight Commander of the Order of the British Empire (K.B.E.). Rub it in, thought Roden, rub it in!

And the same old story. London saw a six-week hiatus in the move to The Hague. The outgoing Ambassador, Walter Crocker, refused to leave! So it was nearing Christmas of 1965 before Helen,

Roden and Mark settled into the embassy residence and Roden finally presented his letters of credence to Queen Juliana of the Netherlands.

She was far more fascinated with the fact that Richard Casey had been appointed Governor-General of Australia. 'Isn't that rather odd?' she asked Roden. 'He's an Australian, and I was under the impression that the governors-general were always Englishmen sent out for the job.'

'Not always, ma'am.'

The Cutlers' effects arrived, but they did little unpacking; as far as they knew, they would be returning fairly quickly, as Sir Eric Woodward had already stepped down from the governorship.

Sometimes when Roden finished for the day it was early enough to permit a stroll; he would ask the chauffeur to bring Helen in with him, then the two of them would walk the beach well rugged up against the damp cold, pleasantly alone. Living in an official residence makes solitude somewhat difficult.

On this particular evening they returned to the residence and sat down to dinner. Suddenly the butler gasped.

'Oh, Your Excellency, I forgot! Buckingham Palace rang and asked if you would contact them.'

'We understand,' said Queen Elizabeth's private secretary, 'that you have been nominated as Governor of New South Wales. Do you wish to accept the position?'

'Yes, sir, I do.'

'Then Her Majesty feels that you should be knighted before you return. Could you come to London, please?'

Off they went, though Roden didn't mention the knighthood to Helen, who simply thought he was going to 'kiss hands', as an ambassador from a British Commonwealth country does. The Queen saw Roden privately while Helen waited outside. A decade younger than Roden, at that time Elizabeth II was a woman in perfect bloom, assured, attractive, relaxed. No longer the sweet and pretty girl he had met in Colombo, she had yet to face her tormented years.

After some conversation about the governorship, she said, 'I'm going to knight you. I know you have been informed of this, and I understand you're taking the name Roden rather than Arthur.'

'Yes, Your Majesty.'

A cushion had been placed nearby and due consideration had been taken of his missing leg, for it was sufficiently high off the floor to enable him to kneel without much awkwardness.

The Queen touched him on the right shoulder with a sword, but she does not say, 'Arise, Sir So-and-so.' After she hung the ribbon of his order around his neck, he rose of his own accord. A most emotional, uplifting experience. They crossed the study, sat down, talked a little. Then the Queen pushed a buzzer.

An equerry opened the door, bowed and said, 'Your Majesty, Lady Cutler.' Helen walked in, eyes wide.

The Queen chuckled. 'The bombshell's dropped, I see!'

'Yes, Your Majesty.'

They were then formally congratulated and dismissed. As they turned to leave the Queen held out the star of his order. 'You'll want this,' she said, handing it to him.

Roden might have been pardoned for thinking, Eat your heart out, Alec Downer! Downer's Order of the British Empire was lower grade than Roden's Knight Commander of the Order of St. Michael and St. George. He was Sir Roden Cutler, V.C., K.C.M.G., C.B.E. How strange and wondrous, the turns a life can take. In Gaza he had told Mollie Nalder that he would probably wind up selling matches on the concourse at Wynyard station. And at that moment he had genuinely believed what he said. If Mollie Nalder had said he was more likely to become a knight, he would have laughed.

On their return from London, Richard presented them with a little note saying, 'Welcome home, Sir Roden and Lady Cutler!'

David, Anthony and Mark came from school on Richard's heels, and the whole family had a splendid Christmas and New Year in The Hague, skating on the ponds, throwing snowballs. Home had always been where Mum and Dad were; now home would be Sydney too.

When a man is knighted he may ask the Royal College of Arms to design a coat of arms for him. His input is required in matters like the contents of the escutcheon (the shield), its supporters, and the motto. The Commonwealth of Australia's escutcheon supporters, for instance, are the emu and the kangaroo. As one supporter Roden chose a kangaroo, which, as he had assumed a vice-regal office, has a coronet around its neck. But his other choice of supporter has puzzled many: a crocodile. He says he selected a crocodile because in ancient Egypt it had been a god, Sobek, and in curious ways Egypt had been lucky for him. But the crocodile is native to Australia too. Roden's has a sprig of wattle in its jaws. His motto is UNDIQUE SERVIRE (service in all places).

Poor Queen Juliana of the Netherlands was truly bewildered. 'It must be becoming the custom to appoint Australians governors-general and governors,' she said.

Two airlines got into a little bit of a squabble over who should look after Sir Roden and Lady Cutler on the way from Amsterdam to Sydney via London. Originally booked to go on KLM, Qantas decided the new Governor belonged to it, with the result that two of the Cutlers' suitcases were lost, never to be found. Not much of a tragedy, one might think; yet it was an enormous tragedy for which Roden finds it hard to forgive KLM. For in one of the suitcases was the Rolex watch which Ruby had saved so hard to give him, and which he had run back to retrieve under machine gun fire at Merdjayoun. So somewhere in Europe someone is wearing—or has thrown away—one of Roden's few material treasures.

GOVERNOR

Sir Roden, Lady Cutler and their four sons flew from London to Brisbane; Roden's setting foot on New South Wales soil was a formal affair not best undertaken by six people weary from a long plane ride.

In Brisbane they were welcomed by the Governor of Queensland, Sir Henry Abel Smith, and his wife, daughter of Princess Alice (a member of the Royal House of Windsor). Sir Henry was full of advice for the novice Governor, and had strong convictions about gubernatorial uniforms; he had designed his own, and thought Roden should design his. Roden's mind, however, was far more preoccupied with what would happen in Sydney on that first day in office.

He had been in touch with Sir Kenneth Street, Lieutenant-Governor of New South Wales, and arranged that all their close family would be waiting in a private room at Government House.

'And,' said he to Sir Kenneth on the phone from The Hague, 'a reception for two hundred guests following my swearing-in.'

'Tch!' clucked Sir Kenneth. 'That will be very expensive.'

'Don't worry, I'll pay for it myself.'

'Do think about it first! *Very* expensive!'

'Hang the expense, it's what I want,' said Roden firmly. 'I'll send you the invitation list.'

They flew from Brisbane to Sydney on an R.A.A.F. plane loaned to the state by Sir Robert Menzies, and landed at Mascot to find the skies overcast, rain threatening.

It was very formal; Roden wore a top hat and a morning suit complete with decorations; Helen a good dress, hat, gloves, and the four boys suits. They were greeted by Premier Robert Askin and a Royal Australian Navy guard of honour, which Roden had to inspect. Then it was into a Rolls-Royce (the Rollses were owned by the Federal Government, which leased them to the States for royal visits, the arrival of new governors and the like) to make the drive into the city of Sydney.

'Good on you, Ro!' a familiar voice shouted at the airport; Bill Courtney, his old battery commander from Syria, had gone to Mascot just to show his approval.

By the time the cavalcade reached the Sydney Town Hall it had begun to drizzle, but that didn't blight proceedings in the least. The Lord Mayor was an old friend (amazing how many of his old friends had made good!), John Armstrong, who formally welcomed the new Governor, presented him with a screed calligraphed on vellum, then listened as Roden replied. A large crowd had gathered to watch despite the rain, and Roden could see more people lining the route onwards to Government House. An open Rolls had been provided for the journey, but because of the rain Roden and Helen were offered the closed one instead.

'No, we'll go in the open one,' said Roden.

How moving. People had actually turned out to cheer him! For the second time in his life, Roden Cutler was made aware that Sydney loved him. An earlier governor had told Roden that the day he assumed office was one of the worst in his life, but for Roden, it was one of the very best.

At Government House there was a guard of the New South Wales

Mounted Police to inspect, splendid fellows on tall, matching bay horses so well trained they were completely still.

Inside at last, a little wet, but none the worse for wear. And this was to be home, this beautiful sandstone castle set in a wealth of lawns and gardens behind and not far from Bennelong Point, from which the ugly old tram depot had been removed; one could already see the new Sydney Opera House beginning to rise.

The two families were waiting within the Governor's study: a proud and beaming Ruby, Doone, Geoff, Rob, and their spouses; Mr. and Mrs. Morris and Helen's psychiatrist younger sister, Mim, with her son. Who could ever have guessed it? My son, the knight-Governor. My daughter, Lady Cutler.

Then it was into the ballroom, where the Chief Justice of New South Wales, Sir Leslie Herron, waited to administer the Oath to the new Governor. Perhaps to some taking the Oath might have been a glib and facile lip-service, but Roden Cutler was very, very serious. He undertook to do right by all manner of people without fear or favour, and swore allegiance to Her Majesty the Queen. Upon a book he believed sacred, the Bible.

'You know, one has so many little prejudices and crotchets,' he said to the author, 'that the Governor's Oath is very taxing. Without fear is easy enough, but without favour—ah, that's so difficult! But I swore it, and I did my level best to live up to it, always.'

Sworn in, he gave a short speech, choosing to dwell upon his personal favourite Governor of New South Wales, Lachlan Macquarie (1810–1821), who may truly be said to have laid the foundations of freedom in this convict dumping ground, and who commissioned the convict architect, Francis Greenway, to produce the first really imposing buildings in and around Sydney.

Protocol demanded that the new Governor seat himself upon the Throne Chair. ('A most uncomfortable thing, I must say, of some ancient vintage.') After which he was free to move among his two hundred guests and have a much needed glass of champagne himself. One of the judges' wives whispered to him that the press were outside, hoping for an interview; Roden, Helen and the four boys trooped down to the fountain area of the grounds, had their pictures taken and talked to the journalists, very friendly.

A snack lunch was followed by a seemingly endless array of delegations, associations, leagues, fellowships, committees, all sorts of organisations wishful of paying their respects.

Being curtsied to was not quite as much of a shock as it might have been had Roden and Helen not come from Holland, where the custom was for all young women to curtsy to their seniors. But it was strange, not something which swelled the ego; in time, of course, they grew quite used to it.

The last official ceremony was the laying of a wreath at the Cenotaph in Martin Place. For Roden and his tin leg, an absolutely exhausting day, yet not a day he would look back on with regret. And they were accustomed to moving into new houses, sleeping in different beds, coping with new conditions.

It was a time of changes, actually. On St. Valentine's Day, 14 February, Australia officially adopted decimal currency. There had been acrimonious argument as to what the new notes would be called; Prime Minister Menzies had wanted desperately to christen the major unit the 'royal', but the public outcry had been so vehemently against him that the decimal notes were finally termed 'dollars'. Unlike the U.K., which simply kept its pound and subdivided it into one hundred pence, the Australian dollar was worth ten old shillings, half a pound, and that was subdivided into one hundred cents.

It may not be so surprising, then, that on Australia Day, 26 January 1966, Sir Robert Gordon Menzies resigned from office and the Federal Parliament. He still holds two records: prime minister for the longest consecutive period, and prime minister for the longest total period. 1939–1941 and 1949–1966. Of the 31 years and 5 months he was a Member of the House of Representatives, 18 years and 5 months of them were as Prime Minister. At the time of his retirement he was seventy-one. A prime minister one either loved or hated. No one was indifferent.

So the commencement of Roden's governorship was also the end of two eras, that of the pound and of Sir Robert Menzies. The new Prime Minister was Harold Holt, who had been Menzies' Treasurer.

Government House had not really been lived in for some time. Sir Kenneth Street had tried to live there, but he moved out well before Roden and Helen arrived. The place was existing on a skeleton staff, the roof badly needed repairing, the cellar was damp, the bathrooms inadequate for a family with four children at home, and the tower, which at some time had been stuccoed, was losing its coat of plaster.

When Roden insisted that the tower be converted back to sandstone blocks, the bureaucrats yelped at the cost.

'Rubbish!' said Roden. 'This is the house of the people of New South Wales, it's built in sandstone and it has to be kept in sandstone. Cost is a relative thing.'

The tower went back to sandstone. It had gargoyles to disguise the gutter-pipe outlets, and one of them was missing; the new gargoyle was copied from the dragon on the Governor's coat of arms.

Things like removing the damp from the cellar were minor, but the absolute emptiness of the cellar was a disaster. The Government House butler, unsupervised for months, had drunk the lot. As he was inebriated by 11 a.m., he departed very quickly after the Cutlers moved in. Which didn't rectify the emptiness of the cellar. At first Roden had to send one of the staff out to buy whatever was needed each time a function occurred, but filling the cellar was vital. He called in Geoffrey Penfold Hyland, asked him to look at the cellar and recommend what wines should be put down. The wine king brought his winemaker, Max Schubert, who had developed Grange Hermitage. Then the pair invited Roden to the Penfolds warehouse at Tempe, gave him lunch and various wines to sample. At the time there was some dislike of Grange Hermitage; Schubert had produced it by continuing with an error in the fermentation process which the French had eliminated. Some Sydney oenologists of the period condemned the wine, but Douglas Lamb and others considered it brilliant. So did Roden, who chose it as G.H.'s basic red. Douglas Lamb was asked to provide his list of French champagnes. One hundred dozen bottles of wine were laid down, the champagne added together with Scotch, gin, vodka, cognac and other spirits. Finally Roden felt as if he could face his guests with confidence in the quality of the G.H. liquor.

'My bank account looked pretty sick after my first month in office, but it had to be done,' says Roden. Yes, he paid for it himself. Once the cellar was filled, whatever was consumed out of it on official occasions was replaced at government expense, but careful accounts were kept so that no one in the Premier's Department could accuse the Governor of having the people of New South Wales pay for his evening aperitif or after-dinner cognac.

Funding was fairly complicated. The State paid for functions which had been officially sanctioned, usually by the Premier's Department. Private dinners or receptions the Governor paid for.

The accounts were subjected to close scrutiny; one Arabian royal visitor asked for a box of cigars to be placed in his room, but when the bill for it was submitted to the bureaucrats, they were very loath to pay, though the guest was an official one—that is, the State government had requested that Government House put him up. Guests not billeted at G.H. by the Government were Roden's financial responsibility. Most guests, of course, were official visitors to New South Wales.

His salary was about $20,000 and was tax-free; his expenses were not a set sum but depended upon how much entertainment G.H. was requested to do; expenses were also tax-free.

'I never made any money out of being Governor, but I did have a lot of fun,' says Roden.

He and Helen had agreed that as the representatives of the people of New South Wales, they should present their official guests of all kinds and however brief their visits with a style of hospitality which reflected well on the State.

'There had been quite a lot of skimping in the past, and we felt that was shabby,' says Roden.

The upkeep and running of G.H. was largely funded by the State—gas, electricity, water, wages, linen, air-conditioning. The Governor's private secretary, aide-de-camp, chauffeur and Helen's secretary were public servants paid by the State, whereas the chef, butler, housekeeper and other domestic staff were paid privately by Roden, who was refunded by the State. The Governor had a limousine (an old Austin Princess at first, then a second-hand Rolls), but Helen's car was bought and maintained at Roden's own expense. Save that registration was gratis: it too bore a Crown. All food, liquor, petrol and similar items Roden paid for unless they were for official purposes. His first uniform he paid for himself, but those which followed were paid for by the State.

His superannuation had been Commonwealth public service, which of course ceased; after five years as Governor he received

Governor's superannuation, and after ten years as Governor it became maximum; as it is equal to the superannuation of the Chief Justice, its value has increased enormously over the years since Roden retired. His financial rewards for the fifteen years he spent as Governor of New South Wales happened after he retired, and he is grateful for their generosity.

His views about what the job should consist of were strong and positive. Though in one respect he and Helen agreed that they should move back in time a little, observe protocol, in another way they relaxed many of the customs. To the Cutlers, proper protocol didn't mean stiffness and haughtiness; it meant giving people enough room to get used to each other and the vice-regal couple without a lot of back-slapping and artificial bonhomie.

'Proper protocol is what I would call natural courtesy.'

Their chief objective was to get to know as many of the people of New South Wales as they could, find out what people were doing and thinking. Not just community leaders and not just those with social prominence, but people from all walks of life, all creeds, all races. So they were careful to mix their guest lists for the more formal occasions and vowed that they would not fall into the trap of having a standard guest list—the kind of thing which is passed on from one tenant of an office to his successor, ensuring that the faces around the dinner table should always contain a certain number of familiar ones—those the hosts know share similar opinions, similar goals, even similar pedigrees.

'It's so nice to come to Government House and have dinner as it was in the old days,' said one lady guest not long after the Cutlers arrived. 'You know, ladies withdrawing after dessert, men lingering around the table for port and cigars.'

Neither of the Cutlers saw this tradition as sexist or old-fashioned. After spending several hours together, they thought it proper that at one stage of the evening the men should have a chance to talk about what interested them exclusively, and that the women should have the same chance. At the end of half an hour, the men would rejoin the women to wind up the evening.

'Egalitarianism,' says Roden, 'doesn't really help establish true human equality. Familiarity can breed contempt, and reduction to the lowest common denominator doesn't improve relations between people at all. In some jobs and situations, a visible manifestation of authority is absolutely necessary.'

One of Roden's ways to make contact with people was through speeches, which he seldom composed and delivered in a formal way; he continued to do as he had from the time when he had been the State Secretary of the R.S.L. in 1942—feel out the audience and then decide on the kernel around which his speech would grow; his other technique was to walk and think. At most he had two points to make, though he was happier with one. The words he used and the manner in which he spoke the words he decided on his feet. If he had a philosophy about his speeches, it was to try to look for what people had in common, rather than what divided them.

'Sincere people believe completely in what they are doing, and they have no control over what religion, race or social condition they are inflicted with at birth. It's very important to remember that. It's also very important to remember that people have things in common too.'

On two occasions he made quite a stir with speeches delivered to the veterans of the R.S.L. The first occasion was in 1967, when he informed the members that they had either to expand or to wither on the vine. What he advocated was the admission of men and women currently serving in the armed forces into the R.S.L., which was purely a body for veterans at that time. Public opinion, he told them, was not on their side. Nor were a lot of ex-servicemen.

'Anyone who has been through war is against it, and these days many people are so against it that they won't serve.'

The speech didn't go down well with the diehards, but others, particularly the younger veterans, saw the sense in what Roden said. Within five years men and women currently serving were admitted.

The second occasion got him into a great deal of hot water. The date was 8 August 1972, and Roden was speaking to the New South Wales branch of the R.S.L. at its 56th State congress. Vietnam had been going on for some years, and public opposition to Australians participating in this war was not limited to the radical fringe. The longer the war dragged on, the more people turned against it. National Service, which was the Federal Government's euphemism for conscription, had been going on for many years, but after 1965 some of the 8,000 Australian troops sent to Vietnam were conscripts, which only increased opposition to conscription. This became compounded when, in an effort to minimise opposition, a lottery element was introduced. All those eligible for national service were put into one group, from which numbers were drawn at random to fill the year's quota. 'Draft dodgers' were at risk of imprisonment.

In August 1971, Prime Minister William McMahon announced that Australian forces would be withdrawn from Vietnam, but some Australian participation was still going on when Roden made his controversial speech to the New South Wales R.S.L. in August 1972, and conscription was still being practised through the lottery system. With an election coming up, Labor was already campaigning vigorously on an anti-conscription platform.

Roden's speech concentrated upon the nature of defence.

'In my view the obvious thing which needs to be kept under continuous consideration is the likely extent and category of defence needs. In Australia there are obvious geographic problems with a very long coastline to be defended by a small population. There are obvious economic problems because money spent on defence must necessarily have its effect on the economy and will reduce money available for other purposes such as housing, roads, communications, factories and general development ... We must also consider defence in the somewhat unpredictable field of foreign affairs—unpredictable simply because it is impossible to see far into the future and to prophesy accurately the political and economic development in each country of the world. It is not only these developments in neighbouring areas which will affect us, but unexpected and initially quite insignificant happenings in any part of the world ... We have formulated a defence system depending upon a well trained and equipped permanent force backed by a citizen military force and national service on a selective basis.

'Taking this in the given order there is no doubt, I should imagine, that a great majority of people would support a proposition of a well trained and equipped nucleus in the Navy, Army and Air Force. It may well be that the Navy and Air Force with their highly technical and costly capital equipment have sound arguments for almost total dependence on career servicemen ... The Army ... will, I think, continue in the future to favour development of weapon systems rather than sheer dependence on manpower.

'The Services, taken in the context of the national economy, are unproductive, but this is also true of a great number of us, including myself, to whom I might add in the economic sense politicians, public servants and public figures. Defence policy must therefore, in my view, be considered very carefully in conjunction with needs in other fields ... The building of roads and national communication networks have a defence aspect and must be considered in these terms also ...

'However, defence has a tendency to be a demanding servant and, surrounded by emotions, tends to grow in complexity and size. *It has to be limited to needs*, and there has to be an element of calculated risk in deciding the appropriate size of the defence force in any country ... The aim should be a viable and effective defence force consistent with our needs, and compatible with our economy and national development in other fields. It could well err on the side of smallness, provided it was efficient and capable of quick expansion, and backed by manufacturing and civil potential.

'... There are areas of defence which have caused considerable public feeling both for and against ... The affluent society and the current outlook among young men has left the Citizen Military Force short of its establishment. I am convinced it is not necessarily money nor conditions which attract men to the Citizen Military Force, but a feeling of motivation. When the need for defence is obvious the recruitment in the Citizen Military Force and the regular Army tends to increase and be sufficient for the purpose ... The type of recruit willing and ready to involve himself ... is the only type of recruit of any use. The unwilling one is not only a hindrance to himself but also to the unit.

'A lack of recruitment for the regular Army and the Citizen Military Force has led to the introduction of a selective system of national service, and on the merits or demerits of this, I know feelings run very high. In the ultimate, the decision must rest with those who have the facts before them and who are in a position to assess defence requirements. However, I must admit personally to doubts about the need for national service and certainly I am doubtful about its efficacy. The ballot system with its introduction of lottery effects on the career of a young man is something to which logical objections can be raised. Many people would say that either national service should be universal or it should be abolished, and I have no doubt the Services would claim that national service is necessary for the maintenance of the strength of the armed forces, but if this national service were universal it would result in the overwhelming swamping of the system . . .

'There is no doubt in my mind that Australia must have an adequate defence system, although it will be obvious that I am inclined to believe that this could be handled with less manpower, with an efficient and small regular armed force—Navy, Army and Air Force—backed in the case of the Army by a voluntary and well-motivated Citizen Military Force . . . This is too important a subject to be a matter of so-called youth revolt or, at the best, division of opinions within the community. It is one which must be continuously looked at and evaluated; one in which members of the community such as yourselves should have a deep interest because ultimately and essentially it is our country's future and our freedom about which we are talking.'

This long extract will give the reader a good idea of how Roden spoke: no Ciceronian rhetoric, no, but crisp, replete with muscle yet devoid of the slightest fat, strong yet tactful—and extremely thought-provoking. Its content is as relevant today as it was at the time he spoke. Balanced, rational and unsparing, even of himself.

Perhaps here is the place to mention two other of Roden's experiences during those bitter years when the Australian people were so divided about participation in Vietnam.

The first occurred on 21 April 1966. Roden was to take the salute on the steps of the Sydney Town Hall to honour a detachment of

New South Wales troops leaving for Vietnam. The police received a tip that someone was going to assassinate the Governor by shooting him from the roof of a building opposite and overlooking the Town Hall (a most imposing and superbly situated edifice in russet sandstone). The anonymous caller notified the police the evening before, so Roden was informed and advised that it might be better if he didn't attend.

'Of course I'll be there! This doesn't deter me in the slightest from doing my job at the parade. It causes me no personal concern at all.'

There were police everywhere, including on top of every building in the vicinity, but Roden took the salute and nothing happened. The tip had come through the Drug Squad; whether or not it was a hoax has never been established.

The second incident was uglier, and occurred on Thursday, 1 May 1969. Again, Roden had been warned that there would be trouble. At 2.30 p.m. he was due as Honorary Colonel of the Sydney University Regiment to inspect it on the lawn outside the Great Hall before being welcomed as the University's Visitor, an honorary and symbolic title.

Trouble or no, he was determined to go ahead. After his old regiment arrived to parade, a big gathering of students staged a 'sit down' on the lawns. When Roden appeared he ignored them, walked through them towards the double line of citizen soldiers; he was clad in striped trousers, black jacket and black hat, as a civilian. One student threw himself in front of Roden, who staggered and would have fallen had his aide-de-camp and the regiment's commanding officer not grabbed him and steadied him.

'He kicked!' shrieked one female demonstrator, others echoing.

'A man with one leg can't kick anyone, even his dog,' says Roden, smiling.

Still ignoring the host of screaming protesters, he proceeded to inspect the guard amid a rain of rotten tomatoes, then walked on to the Great Hall, where the Chancellor, Sir Charles McDonald, was waiting anxiously.

Sir Charles wanted to take action over the incident, but Roden persuaded him to leave matters lie.

To a *Sydney Morning Herald* reporter afterwards, he said, 'Overseas they know how to riot more effectively and vigorously. This is the only difference between our students and rioters I have seen in Egypt, Ceylon and Pakistan.'

'Did you resent being pelted with tomatoes?'

'It is one of those things that seem to be happening in universities. It wasn't personal, and there were more students determined to stop it than there were to start it.'

He went on to say that students ought to be able to express their views, but that it was dangerous when they employed violence. 'This minority talks about democracy, but its actions are the least democratic.'

The outcome of the incident was that Roden emerged the hero of the hour. Most of the student demonstrators had no idea that their target had only one leg; few probably understood that he had won a Victoria Cross. The moral of the story is surely that it pays to choose your adversary wisely. Other public figures may not have emerged so impressively, but to someone who had lain for twenty-six hours with his leg shot to pieces, a few antagonistic students didn't really amount to much.

'I found out afterwards that many of them came from broken homes or were otherwise disadvantaged,' he says.

The duties of the Governor and the First Lady were very heavy— sometimes unnecessarily so, Roden felt. The number of documents

"Our finest hour! A mere thousand or two of us against this one-legged VC winner!"

Paul Rigby, 1969

We dips our lid to Roden Cutler, VC

SIR RODEN CUTLER

IN all the hullabaloo over the ninny-pated student demonstration against the Sydney University Regiment on Thursday, one salient feature failed to get its fair share of attention.

The remarkable dignity and diplomacy of the Governor, Sir Roden Cutler.

His courage in facing the demonstrators was not all that remarkable, perhaps. After all, he once won the Victoria Cross in the face of greater danger than a pack of undergraduate louts.

What WAS remarkable was the fact that he didn't lose his cool, even after getting splattered by rotten tomatoes.

And afterwards, when he might have justifiably sounded off, he was the essence of moderation.

Like most Australians we tend to cast a jaundiced eye on bigwigs, but we can't fault Sir Roden's performance.

Instead, we dips our lids to him.

And it takes a big man to make us say that.

he had to sign was daunting, to say the least. The Governor's study contained a huge dining table which was always completely covered with papers to which he had to affix his signature. Sir Kenneth Street used to entertain himself by timing how many of these documents he could sign in five minutes, but Roden thought it would be better if the job were rendered less likely to cause writer's cramp. Among the papers, for instance, were appointments of juniors to the State public service if the junior already had a relative in the State public service; scout commissions and the transfer of oyster leases had to have his approval. So did certain prisoners being recommended for parole. Never anything he couldn't approve (yet in theory he could, of course), though he used to take private bets with himself over the prisoners, and discovered that almost all those he thought would wind up back on fresh criminal charges did indeed commit further offences.

'Les,' he said to the Chief Justice, Sir Leslie Herron, a friend from university days, 'couldn't I rubber-stamp these reams of routine papers?'

After due consideration, Sir Leslie delivered the legal opinion that, provided the stamp was kept under lock and key and that Roden actually did the stamping himself, it was permissible. From then on, Roden saved his fountain pen for the documents which had genuine significance. After that it wasn't difficult to break Sir Kenneth Street's five-minute record.

He was, besides, the official patron of at least a hundred organisations, many of them charitable. One such was the St. John Ambulance Brigade, in which Helen also took a great interest. As a result, he was made a Knight of the Order of St. John of Jerusalem, and Helen first a Companion of the Order, then a Dame of the Order—which delighted her.

As part of his effort to make the people of New South Wales

conscious that Government House belonged to them, he made sure that every school in the State sent two children per year to G.H. as his guests. Country children had to have billets arranged, and many of them needed fare assistance. Everything possible was done to make the visit a highlight for the children, who came in groups throughout the year. When they arrived at G.H. they were met by Roden's private secretary, who gave them a little talk on how G.H. was run, then they formed a crocodile and walked into the ballroom, where Roden and Helen received them. The girls would try to curtsy and the boys would bob. ('You have to keep a straight face, you know, even when they call you "Your Majesty".') After the greeting they were shepherded outside onto the colonnade and given a sumptuous refreshment—scones with jam and cream, little sandwiches, plenty of fruit squash—and then Roden would personally lead them on a tour of G.H. and its grounds, telling them its history and its importance to the State. The function concluded back in the ballroom, where the children were allowed to ask questions. The family's private rooms were never shown to visitors; Roden considered it dangerous for outsiders to know whereabouts the family slept. Curious. He must have had a presentiment.

There were many, many receptions for sporting clubs of all kinds, for farmers, charitable organisations, the Law Society and other professional bodies—you name it, it was invited to G.H. Roden's A.D.C. perused the visitors' book which was kept in the police box at the gate, and added a card to his card file if a name appeared in it for the first time.

'We would always try to have every name to something at Government House,' says Roden.

One of the little victories which pleased Roden most concerned the Trades Hall, which was headquarters for the various trade unions. Unionists, particularly union executives, were not at all whoop about creaking, antediluvian institutions like governors, but Roden had met one union leader because he was a member of the New South Wales upper house of parliament.

'Look,' said Roden to him, 'I've made it my policy to call on different groups and organisations, including factory operations— if making rubber tyres is important in New South Wales, then I want to know all about making rubber tyres. I say the same thing about trade unions. So why haven't I been asked to the Trades Hall?'

The Legislative Councillor looked dubious, demurred.

'Oh, come on! You're a liberal-minded man, so what's wrong with my visiting the Trades Hall?'

The invitation to call upon the union executives at the Trades Hall duly came through. Everyone was very stiff, extremely uneasy and uncomfortable. Offered afternoon tea, Roden accepted, to find that 'afternoon tea' consisted of huge glasses of beer accompanied by tomatoes, raw onions, nuts and other edibles which went well with huge glasses of beer.

At the time there was a union fracas in Newcastle, where union members had taken exception to certain publicans and were banning huge glasses of beer.

'I see you're not like Newcastle when it comes to the size of the glass,' said Roden, lifting his beer and toasting the union executives. 'You couldn't have chosen a better repast.'

That broke the ice. The meeting went very well, with Roden asking innumerable questions and everyone anxious to reply. Some of the men he already knew through trade missions when serving abroad. As with everything, he was genuinely interested and not at all biased. The importance of Trades Hall could not be over-estimated; fascinated, Roden learned a lot.

To reciprocate, he gave a reception at G.H. for the Trades Hall people. The party went swimmingly save that he noticed two very serious men standing isolated by the fireplace, neither mingling nor partaking of the refreshments. Over he went.

'Won't you have a drink?' he asked.

'We shouldn't be here, Governor,' said one.

'Why on earth not? You had invitations, didn't you?'

'Yes, but we're communists.'

'I don't give a darn about that! The Governor is for everyone, including communists. I meant to invite you, and now that you're here, I'd very much like to see you enjoy yourselves.'

Roden truly did believe that he was there without fear or favour for every New South Welshman and Welshwoman.

'How did you get the unions on side?' asked Richard Casey, now Governor-General.

'It's not a question of getting them "on side". It's simply that I treat their members like ordinary human beings—with real respect. You could do the same.'

But Casey never did. All too often institutions and the people comprising them become ivory towers. Even unions.

For Helen, the years in Government House were absolutely filled to overflowing. She rose at 7 a.m. and was dressed in time to supervise the departure of the three younger boys for school; David was attending the University of New South Wales. Anthony, Richard and Mark went to Shore, a private boys' school on the far side of the Harbour Bridge. The family gathered for a quick breakfast of cereal, toast and fruit, then Helen made sure that the three boys were dressed properly, had done their homework, had their books, had whatever sporting equipment needed on any one day, and had money for the bus fare home as well as lunch. Then she drove them to school herself; this was her time to talk to them and make sure that all was well in their world, discover if they had any problems or things on their minds, listen to their stories. So often were her evenings devoted to public duties that she never made the mistake of thinking there would be other time to keep her finger on the family pulse. It was crucial that they know they were loved and wanted, given that their parents were so busy and sometimes unavailable. The headmaster of Bilton Grange had told the Cutlers that he thought Richard and Mark were good because they could look forward with complete confidence to really pleasant holidays with their parents, who brought them back into the family fold at every opportunity. Love to the Cutlers was not merely an effusive display of hugs and kisses, but also something parents had to prove with interest in the children's doings, in a stable environment and in the cultivation of a sense of self-respect.

When she returned from the trip across the bridge to Shore, Helen immediately met with the butler and the chef, then followed this by a meeting with the housekeeper. She would also see the gardener about flowers for the house, and when the season required it she would inspect the garden beds and make plans; she consulted the staff of the Royal Botanic Gardens (next door to G.H.) about plans, which they loved. Roses were her favourite flowers.

That done, she went to her secretary's office and dealt with mail, invitations, enquiries of all kinds. She concentrated on women's and children's organisations and affairs, feeling that she could ease this burden off Roden's shoulders a little. She was President of the Girl Guides, sat in the Chair of the New South Wales Red Cross, was patron of St. Vincent's and other hospital ladies' auxiliaries, was Honorary Colonel of the Women's Royal Australian Army Corps, and, together with Roden, was a vice-president of the St. John

Ambulance Brigade. Requests that she be official patron of this or that just streamed in, as they did to Roden. She had various uniforms and regalia, as well as many badges and honours. On numerous occasions she worked late into the night, for she wrote all her speeches herself, and—not as fortunate as extemporaneous Roden—toiled over them. Only after every last thing was finished did she go to bed.

Roden had duties of a similar kind. He was Chief Scout of the State, and, in line with his policy that G.H. should be as hospitable as possible, he instituted the practice of bringing the parents of Boy Scouts or Girl Guides inside the G.H. grounds, where they could sit on chairs and listen as the various awards and certificates were presented; unfortunately such occasions were too large to seat the parents inside the ballroom. Helen presided over the Guides.

There were at least two sit-down meals of an official kind per week, and several receptions; in the course of one month, over two hundred meals would be catered for, excluding nibbles for receptions. Every formal dinner was across-the-board; when Cardinal Gilroy retired, for example, the Governor's dinner in his honour saw prelates of assorted creeds at the table—'plus a couple of nuns'. When the Royal Easter Show was on in Sydney, the Show Committee was always invited to a sit-down meal.

Requests would come asking to use G.H. as a venue for some charity drive—the Red Cross, senior citizens, hospital auxiliaries and the like. The answer from Roden was usually affirmative; though the petitioning organisation had to pay for the food and drink, Roden and Helen assisted where they could. If it were a very large function, they obtained marquees from the Army free of charge. The members of the organisation's executive committee were always asked inside afterwards for a drink at the Governor's expense. The one thing Roden wouldn't do was to allow these charity drives to set up the table where people paid their entrance fee on G.H. soil; it had to be outside the gates.

Of official visitors who stayed at G.H. there were many over the years. A good proportion of royalty, various heads of state.

The first member of the Royal House of Windsor to stay at G.H. during Roden's fifteen years as Governor was Prince Charles, who happened to be almost exactly the same age as the second of the Cutler sons, Anthony. Charles had been sent to Timbertop, an ancillary of the famous Geelong Grammar School. On his way to and from he would stay at G.H., where he and Anthony used to raid the refrigerator, make toast and generally behave like the more docile and sweet-natured kind of adolescent male. Charles (who was never to be addressed as Your Royal Highness) leaned a lot on Helen for advice and maternal comfort. Roden and Helen were both very fond of him; his manners were exquisite and his disposition a little shy, though he was a good conversationalist with a broad vocabulary. He was interesting as well as interested.

Almost four years were to go by before the Queen made her first pilgrimage to Australia after Roden became Governor; she arrived in 1970, the two hundredth anniversary of Captain Cook's discovery of Australia's east coast. She was, Roden and Helen found, a very easy guest who did her homework in every minute detail, knew exactly where she had to be at what time, and what she would be called upon to do. Like Charles, she had a natural acting streak, and did very funny impersonations of well-known people. The royal yacht, *Britannia*, was called upon to sail the few miles down the coast from Sydney Harbour to Botany Bay (where

Cook had landed); Roden and Helen made the journey with the Queen and Prince Philip. One does not sit in the presence of royalty unless bidden, but the little voyage was a choppy one, so the large steam yacht rolled. The Queen, watching the suburbs and beaches of southern Sydney slide by, noticed that Roden was having difficulty keeping his balance, and told him to sit down. She was always a thoughtful and noticing person, quick to dispel tension or avert embarrassment.

When a waiter dropped a tray with a loud clang behind her husband's chair, she blinked and said, 'Philip, did you do that?'

On another occasion while she and the Prince were staying at G.H., Roden and Helen gave a dinner to which Madame Marcos was invited; as there wasn't room to accommodate her at G.H. as well, the wife of the President of the Philippines was ensconced at the Boulevard Hotel. And she was late for dinner—so late that the moment for walking into the dining room had to be postponed. Roden, who abhors bad manners, was visibly annoyed. Finally Madame Marcos arrived. Before Roden could move, the Queen spoke.

'Philip, there's Madame Marcos. Do go over and say hello to her,' she said, clearly afraid that if Roden got there first, he mightn't be quite himself.

On this first visit, Her Majesty created Roden a Knight Commander of the Royal Victorian Order, and gave him a pair of cufflinks which say ER II—a rare honour, he is informed. Roden genuinely loves her as a person.

In 1973, when the Queen opened the Sydney Opera House, Roden asked her if she would consider bringing Prince Charles and Princess Anne with her on her next visit; he thought it would be good for the people of Australia to see the parents and two of the children together. In 1974 she obliged, and Roden held one of the few balls given at G.H. (the ballroom was beautiful, but unfortunately G.H. didn't have enough women's toilets for this kind of function). What he hadn't counted on was son David's dancing all night with Princess Anne—it made the papers and speculation was rife. But, as all four parents knew, there was absolutely nothing in it. David and Princess Anne liked each other enough to be friends—and liked the way they danced together.

There were other royal visitors. Prince Philip came on his own several times. When Helen was in London on one occasion Princess Margaret asked her why *she* was never invited to visit Australia. Gough Whitlam was Prime Minister; Roden had known him and been friends with him since university days (they were both born in 1916), so he contacted him and Sir John Bunting, the Australian High Commissioner in London. The result of all these heads put together was an invitation to Princess Margaret as Colonel-in-Chief of the Women's Royal Army Corps to attend the silver anniversary of the Women's Royal Australian Army Corps, of which Helen was the Honorary Colonel. So it was Helen's visit.

Entertaining Princess Margaret was 'fairly hectic'. She loved company but wasn't keen on stuffed shirts, preferred people who were vital and fun-loving. A tiny woman, she liked to dance with Roden, whose tin leg resented such activities. Later she went to the independence celebrations in Vanuatu, where she took ill, was very poorly indeed. Roden received a message asking if he and Helen could put her up at G.H.; he answered, of course, that he would be delighted, but the Governor-General and Lady Kerr were very miffed that *they* hadn't been asked to put her up. However, nothing could be done save what Princess Margaret wanted, so she came to G.H. in Sydney, where Roden and Helen saw to her medical attention and got her back on her feet.

Prince Bernhard of the Netherlands, husband of Queen Juliana, flew in piloting his own plane; Roden and Helen had met him at The Hague, and found entertaining him a great pleasure. As he was plagued by back trouble, he liked a hard bed, with which G.H. provided him; that and plenty of Dom Perignon champagne, and he was delightful company.

Pope Paul VI visited, and as the Premier regarded him as head of the Vatican state, Roden was instructed to receive him formally. His envoy was none other than Bishop (later Cardinal) Marcinkus, to become head of the Vatican bank and wind up amid something of a controversy. As the Bishop's visit was a morning one, Roden had laid on the appropriate refreshments—little sandwiches and cakes, that sort of thing, plus tea or coffee.

His Grace surveyed the spread and sighed audibly. 'Have you got a Scotch and a cigar?' he asked.

The Scotch and cigar were provided, after which the Pope's coming visit was discussed at length. No, His Holiness would prefer to stay with the papal nuncio in Sydney, but yes, he would very much enjoy a State reception in his honour. Roden found Bishop Marcinkus highly likeable, and was very sorry to hear of his later troubles. When he wrote to say so, the Cardinal answered.

The Pope's most peculiar request was to be given a list of *all* the G.H.'s staff, down to and including gardeners and maids. After he arrived at G.H. he asked that they be paraded for his benefit, and gave each of them a papal blessing and silver medal.

'It was interesting to discover how many of my staff were Catholic,' says Roden, who doesn't enquire into such matters.

His State reception presented some problems. Anglican Archbishop Sir Marcus Loane declined to attend because he didn't recognise the Vatican as an autonomous secular state, so for a while it looked as if one of the more prominent New South Wales religions would be unrepresented at the across-the-board gathering.

But after a great deal of scurrying around, the Anglican Bishop Hulme-Moir agreed to come, and all went well.

Of foreign heads of state there were many; Roden remembers two of them very vividly, King Hussein and Queen Alia of Jordan, and the Shah and Shahbanou of Iran.

British educated and absolutely comfortable with the English language, King Hussein proved an enormously likeable and easy guest, but it was Queen Alia with whom Roden fell in love.

'She would kick off her shoes, tuck her feet under her in her chair and talk so interestingly,' he says. 'Oh, I did like her! The most delightful, sensible woman—very able too.'

When she was accidentally killed in a helicopter crash, Roden grieved greatly.

It is customary for heads of state when entertained to tender a reciprocal invitation; King Hussein's was one of those Roden was happy to accept. By the time the Cutlers did manage to visit Jordan, its king had married again; the new wife was Queen Noor, another very likeable person. Roden and Helen were treated royally, put up in Amman's best hotel and given dinners at the palace. They were flown by helicopter down to the rose-red city of Petra, usually entered through a very narrow chasm on the back of a horse or ass. Because of Roden's leg they were conveyed through in a large, jeep-like vehicle which had about a centimetre of clearance on either side. Jordanian hospitality was generous and wholehearted.

The King and Queen of Jordan still send a Christmas card.

The Shah was quite different—very aloof, touchy and on his guard. Though the Shah had none of his own, Roden found a sense of humour essential in his dealings with the Shah; Shahbanou Farah, much younger than her husband, stayed very much in the background. He had to be addressed correctly, as Your Imperial Majesty or Your Supreme Majesty. However, both of them were undemanding guests in domestic terms. On the night before the imperial couple departed, Roden and Helen took them to a youth concert at the Sydney Opera House. When the orchestra played 'God Save the Queen' a considerable number of the concertgoers ostentatiously kept sitting, though when the Iranian national anthem was played everyone got up.

'What is the matter? Why do they sit?' the Shah demanded.

'Oh, it has nothing to do with you, Your Imperial Majesty, it's me they're objecting to,' said Roden with a smile.

On the way to the airport they encountered a group of demonstrators with posters saying GET OUT OF OMAN!

This upset the imperial visitor very much.

'Please don't worry, Your Imperial Majesty,' soothed Roden. 'None of them even knows where Oman is. They're just here to make a show, that's all.'

Which calmed the imperial visitor down; he was perpetually worried about security.

As indeed he still was when Roden and Helen passed through Iran on their way to London in 1978, not many months before the Shah fell. He and the Shahbanou were very hospitable, but clearly the Shah understood that his hold on the Peacock Throne was inexorably loosening.

'If he were able to go out and let the people see him, he'd be much better off,' said Queen Elizabeth II sadly to Roden and Helen. 'But, alas, it isn't in his nature.'

While the Cutlers were in Iran the Shah arranged for them to see Isfahan, Shiraz and ancient Persepolis; in each place the local satrap held a dinner in their honour, replete with caviar.

'Oh, but I was fed up with caviar by the time we left, I can tell you!' says Roden.

When asked for the names of those royal guests he liked the most,

Roden nominated the Queen, the Queen Mother, Prince Charles, Princess Anne, Prince Philip and King Hussein—not necessarily in that order. His opinion of all of them is very high, his emotions very fond.

And then, of course, there was The Dismissal.

Several times during his fifteen years in G.H., Roden was sworn in as Administrator of the Commonwealth of Australia—that is, as acting Governor-General and Commander of the Australian Defence Forces. 'There's not much to do when one is Governor-General,' he says. 'The busy places are Sydney first and Melbourne second. For me, Canberra was a holiday. The Governor-General worked, but he took major things, didn't have the day-to-day grind I had in Sydney.'

Lord Casey was Governor-General when Roden entered office; he was succeeded by Sir Paul Hasluck, whom Roden thought 'a cold fish, but most scrupulous in his attention to duty. He never, for instance, missed an Executive Council meeting—*and* he had input.'

By the time that Hasluck's term was up early in 1974, Canberra had seen major changes. Late in 1972, Australians had elected a Labor federal government for the first time in twenty-three years. The new Prime Minister was Gough Whitlam, Q.C., a controversial figure whom, like his old *inimicus*, Menzies, one either loved or hated. Physically he was very tall and imposing, intellectually he was outstanding, and politically he was the first of Labor's Australian leaders to endeavour to overcome the old saws about socialism, the working class and Labor's traditional image. Certainly he collected a large white-collar vote; after Gough Whitlam, no analyst would be able to divide the electorate up into discrete sociopolitical strata. From Whitlam's time onwards, some of the blue-collar vote would migrate away from Labor, while a lot of the white-collar vote would migrate towards it. The new Labor image was humanitarian. Like John F. Kennedy, Whitlam appealed to the young, the disadvantaged and the disenchanted. His bright-eyed and bushy-tailed government was seen as Australia's new hope.

It was his misfortune to enter into office (19 December 1972) through a House of Representatives election only; the Senate contained 26 Labor senators, 26 Coalition senators, 5 senators of Santamaria's splinter group (the Democratic Labor Party), and 3 full independents. As neither the full independents nor the Santamaria group could be relied upon to vote with Labor on every issue, Whitlam did not control the upper house.

His second misfortune lay in the fact that global economics were about to undergo catastrophic upheavals: OPEC and the petroleum crises of September–December 1973 were to play havoc with the whole world, including Australia.

As if all this were not enough, two shadowy sections of the Australian Constitution combined to bring about Labor's downfall. Section 53 arguably gives the Senate the power to reject or defer money bills sent to it from the House of Representatives, including bills asking for 'supply'—that is, seeking the release of public moneys to fund the machinery of government not contained in specific areas like pensions—public service wages and contractors, for example. Section 64 arguably gives the Governor-General the power to dismiss his ministers if he perceives that they can no longer govern—a power the Queen lacks, either in the U.K. or Australia.

In May 1974, the Leader of the Opposition, Billy Mackie Snedden, used the Senate to force a 'double-dissolution' election by having it refuse to pass six separate bills. The Governor-General at the time was Sir Paul Hasluck, such a meticulous stickler for proper procedure that, though Whitlam had had his differences with him in earlier (political) days, Whitlam asked him to stay on in the job for two more years. Hasluck declined.

The election of May 1974 did not alter anything. Though Labor was returned in the House of Representatives, it failed to carry the Senate, from which the Santamaria splinter group had disappeared. The new upper house contained 29 Labor senators, 29 Coalition senators, and 2 independents. The best Whitlam could say was that for the first time in the Commonwealth of Australia's history, a Labor prime minister had been re-elected.

With Sir Paul Hasluck out of the running, Whitlam had a list of eight likely candidates for the job of Governor-General, among them Sir Roden Cutler, Governor of New South Wales. His own preference, however, inclined towards Ken Myer, a businessman who had supported Whitlam's Labor and was a famous patron of the arts. When Myer refused, Whitlam settled on John Kerr, Q.C. At one time Kerr had been a protégé of Dr. Herbert Vere Evatt; though he had let his Labor membership lapse during the 1950s, he was considered a 'Labor man'. He and Whitlam had known each other for many years, had worked out of adjacent chambers during their days at the New South Wales bar; Kerr's wife, Peggy (who was ailing), was a great friend of Margaret Whitlam's. He was currently serving as Chief Justice and Lieutenant-Governor of New South Wales.

The rather epicene handsomeness of Kerr's face in youth had dwindled, marred by a downturned mouth and extra weight, though he still had a spectacular shock of hair, gone snow-white. He had toyed with the idea of politics, but his passion was the Law; in the Law, he seems to have decided, he could shine more brightly. When Whitlam offered him the governor-generalship, Kerr accepted—on conditions. He wanted a good pension on retirement and a ten-year term in office (twice the usual length). Whitlam agreed.

On her royal visit in February 1974 the Queen created Kerr a Knight Commander of the Order of St. Michael and St. George (the same degree as Roden); Sir John Robert Kerr became Governor-General of Australia on 11 July 1974. Soon afterwards Lady Kerr died. Sir John remarried in April 1975; the curtsy, which Kerr had abolished on entering office, was reinstated under the second Lady Kerr, who liked ceremony.

Kerr set out to enhance the status and role of the Governor-General, and was the first Governor-General to travel abroad as Australia's official Head of State. His choice of Administrator during his absences was Sir Roden Cutler, who was acting Governor-General[†] on six separate occasions—and should have been during that fatal November of 1975, for Kerr had planned to go away.

In March 1975, the Liberal Party spilled Billy Mackie Snedden from its leadership and replaced him with John Malcolm Fraser, a rural landowner from the State of Victoria who had an excellent rapport with the Country Party, the Coalition's other segment; in May its name was changed to the National Country Party.

Like Whitlam, Fraser was immensely tall and towered over his colleagues, though his style of leadership was very different from the more flamboyant, lusty Whitlam's—cool, rational, a trifle austere. Neither man was unattractive, though each appealed to a very different spectrum. Each man had a very tall wife.

[†] Any of the six State governors could act as Administrator. Lord Casey had used Sir Edric Bastyan, Governor of South Australia; Hasluck had used Sir Rohan Delacombe, Governor of Victoria; Kerr used Sir Roden Cutler, Governor of New South Wales; and Kerr's successor, Sir Zelman Cowen, used Sir Stanley Burbury, Governor of Tasmania. Interestingly, in October 1975 Whitlam removed Sir Colin Hannah, Governor of Queensland, from the list of potential Administrators after Hannah publicly criticised the Labor Federal Government—a deed which may have reinforced Kerr's impression that if Whitlam knew a dismissal was in the offing, he would act to remove Kerr from office first.

The main difficulty the second Whitlam Government had was financial; inflation had soared to 14.4 per cent and was predicted to hit 20 per cent by 1980, unemployment was skyrocketing, and a Treasury credit squeeze during the latter half of 1974 and into 1975 had gone too far too fast, with the result that the business community was in severe trouble. Nor was Whitlam himself a fiscal man; his interests lay in social reform, education, the arts and foreign affairs. By nature he was not parsimonious, and that led to much criticism of how, for instance, he travelled—which he did a lot. He didn't supervise his ministers stringently, and some abused this leniency.

Two scandals in 1975 led to his dismissing his Treasurer, Dr. Jim Cairns, and his Minister for Minerals and Energy, Rex Connor, for much the same reason: both men had pursued overseas loans in a way which caused them to mislead the Prime Minister and the Parliament. Polls revealed that Labor's stocks were falling, and Whitlam knew that it would take the three full years of his second mandate from the people to improve Labor's position to the point whereat he could be at all confident of re-election.

The Coalition Opposition therefore set out to force an early election, fully aware that Whitlam would resist to the top of his bent. The new Treasurer, Bill Hayden, gained office a scant two months before his department was to bring down the budget for the coming year: it was due in August. Fraser's obvious ploy was to block the budget in the upper house, but in that lay the seeds of disaster; too many of his own senators were of the opinion that the Government should be let eke out its full three-year term.

Unfortunately for the Coalition, Hayden's budget when it was presented on 19 August 1975 turned out to be one which was a radical departure for Labor in that it recommended drastic cuts in public spending and reduced the deficit to a mere $2.79 billion. So

Fraser went one further and introduced a Coalition alternative containing some measures of little appeal to Coalition voters. It did, however, pick up and run with some of Labor's ideas on tax reform which Labor had not fully espoused, concentrated even more upon curbing public spending and less on Hayden's heavy increases in indirect taxes; it postulated that income and company tax should be tied to the Consumer Price Index as well as wages.

But where to next? To reject Supply in the upper house would send the bill back to the lower house; Fraser decided instead to defer the passage of Supply, a measure that would keep Supply in the upper house for however long he could steel some of his senators to hew to his line. His hold on the Senate had been increased when two Labor senators died in office. The practice was that the premier of the State from which the senator came appointed a new (the term was 'casual') senator from the same party as the old one, but first Tom Lewis, Coalition Premier of New South Wales, chose to appoint an independent, and then Joh Bjelke-Petersen, the ultra-conservative Premier of Queensland, followed suit. Neither of the new senators, though independent, was likely to support Labor.

It was more subtle than that, however. The ex-Solicitor-General, Robert Ellicott, had drawn Fraser's attention to Section 64 of the Constitution, which could be interpreted as endowing the Governor-General with the power to terminate his Prime Minister's commission should the Governor-General decide that his Prime Minister was unable to govern. And if, on being denied Supply by the Senate, the Prime Minister refused to ask his Governor-General to dissolve both houses of parliament, that would constitute more than sufficient grounds to dismiss him, after which the Governor-General could have both houses of parliament dissolved and hold new elections. What better grounds for dismissal could there be than a government denied access to money, and therefore unable to pay its employees, contractors and other obligations?

The tussle that commenced when the Senate deferred passage of the Government's Supply bill on 16 October 1975 was enormously complex and involved the accuracy or inaccuracy of three men's readings of each other's character: Gough Whitlam, the Prime Minister determined not to ask for a new election but to tough it out until Fraser's more reluctant senators crumbled; Malcolm Fraser, the Leader of the Opposition, determined to hold up Supply until the Governor-General acted; and Sir John Kerr, the Governor-General with an illustrious legal background and a high opinion of his active constitutional position. On the surface of it, Whitlam knew Kerr a great deal better than Fraser did, but beneath the surface, Fraser had formed the opinion that Kerr would not let his chance to enter the history books go by.

The whole nation watched, among its members Roden Cutler, who also knew Sir John Robert Kerr very well. As Lieutenant-Governor and Chief Justice of New South Wales, Kerr had often imbibed too freely at G.H. dinners, with the result that either friends had to drive him home or he had to be half-carried to a car. At that time he drank continuously, and no evidence has been tendered to say that he changed his habits after moving to Canberra. The problem is that dependence upon alcohol has never been regarded as a reason *not* to appoint (or elect) persons to some of the highest positions in the land. The fact is usually not publicised, nor, apparently, considered detrimental to proper cerebral functioning. The author would say only that it surely indicates a basic weakness if the sufferer has not managed to overcome it, and that it certainly does inpede proper cerebral functioning.

Though at these G.H. affairs Kerr always wanted to talk at length about politics, Roden considered him without political sense.

After the crisis in the Senate blew up, Kerr invited Roden and Helen to dinner at the Governor-General's Sydney residence; upon the ladies' withdrawing, Kerr told Roden that though his trip overseas had already been planned and booked, in view of what was occurring in Canberra, he had decided to stay in Australia.

'As you like,' said Roden. 'However, I am prepared to take the responsibility if you'd rather go away.'

'I don't know what is going to happen!' Kerr cried.

'Well, several things could,' said Roden. 'You could let the Parliament solve the mess itself. Or you could tell the Prime Minister that he ought to ask for a double-dissolution, otherwise you'd act to dismiss him. In that event, I suppose as a last resort Gough might move to dismiss you first.'

Kerr jumped, waved his hands in the air. 'Yes! Yes, he would!' he yelped.

Roden was not the first to tell Kerr this, nor was he the last. His consistent advice to Kerr was that, as the Parliament had made the mess, the Parliament ought to be left to solve it. What went through Kerr's mind during those weeks leading up to 11 November no one will really know, despite Kerr's later book. One thing is sure, however; he could never have expected popular reaction to the dismissal to take the form it did, or last so long. Public odium would certainly have deterred him had he dreamed of it. He wanted to be a hero, not a villain.

Roden was in Melbourne to see Think Big win the Cup for the second time in succession on the first Tuesday in November, the 4th. Kerr was also there, staying with Sir Henry Winneke, the Governor of Victoria. One of the suggested solutions to the Supply stalemate was the holding of a half-Senate election, due around the middle of 1976. Whitlam was seriously considering it as one way to break the Opposition, as the polls were showing a distinct swing back to Labor. The three men, Kerr, Winneke and Cutler, discussed the possibility of a half-Senate election. The State governments in New South Wales and Victoria at the time were Coalition, and both governors told Kerr that they thought if Whitlam were to ask for a half-Senate election early, their premiers would instruct them not to issue writs permitting it. Though they agreed that to be forbidden to issue writs would be a flouting of convention, Winneke and Cutler both said that they were bound to accept the advice of their premiers. As was the governor-general to accept the advice of his prime minister. So Kerr knew that the possibility of a half-Senate election was unlikely to involve four of the eight electing entities— the biggest four at that. He had also heard two governors state categorically that, whatever their private views were, they were bound to take the advice of their premiers.

'Had I been acting as governor-general, I would *never* have gone against the advice of my prime minister,' says Roden flatly. 'I still think that Kerr should have let the Parliament sort the mess out itself. It would have.'

Be that as it may, Kerr (terrified that if Whitlam knew the direction of his governor-general's thoughts, he would himself be dismissed from office) resolved to say nothing to anyone. The only outside legal opinion he sought—an opinion Whitlam had instructed him *not* to seek—was Sir Garfield Barwick's. The Chief Justice of Australia was an ex-Coalition attorney-general, so it was perhaps not surprising that Barwick didn't warn Whitlam what was happening. Instead, he confirmed Kerr's own interpretation of Section 64—also Barwick's first cousin Robert Ellicott's interpretation.

Kerr acted on 11 November, Remembrance (or Armistice) Day. While Whitlam was convinced that some of Fraser's senators would give in before the money ran out, Fraser had banked everything on the fact that the eleventh of the eleventh was the last day on which a double-dissolution could result in writs to hold new elections before, in practical terms, February 1976—too far away. Writs issued this day would see an election on 13 December, the last feasible date before Christmas and summer vacation.

Shortly after 1 p.m. on this day, Sir John Kerr dismissed Edward Gough Whitlam, Prime Minister of Australia, and dismissed Whitlam's ministers. He then installed John Malcolm Fraser as the 'caretaker Prime Minister'. The Labor Government still had at least three weeks before the money ran out, and had made what it was sure were legal arrangements to issue vouchers so that its debtors could borrow against them at the nation's banks until the Senate gave in. However, there were ominous signs that many of the banks would not oblige.

As soon as the news of Gough Whitlam's dismissal was known, the public outcry was gargantuan. Huge mobs of people congregated in a passion of fury and grief, ran riot through shopping malls, stoned Coalition premises and forced Sir John Kerr to remain, a virtual prisoner, inside the official residence he had been absolutely determined to hang onto.

In Sydney, Roden's chauffeur was reluctant to take the old grey tank of a Rolls out unless he had Sir Roden in it because he was sure people would think the car belonged to Kerr. With Roden inside it, State flag flying, no one made the mistake of thinking the tall figure was Sir John Kerr.

'Good on you, Governor!' someone would shout when the Rolls stopped in traffic. 'You wouldn't have done it!'

Kerr was very anxious to tell Roden his side of the story, but

Roden refused to listen. When Gough Whitlam tried to recount his side of the story, Roden refused to listen. Fraser was never to volunteer his version.

Appearances can be deceptive. Those huge mobs of people had given the impression that the entire country was outraged, but in actuality they were but a minute percentage of Australia's thirteen millions. At the federal elections on 13 December 1975, the Coalition under Malcolm Fraser went into government with the biggest majority in the nation's history—and held the Senate very comfortably. Nor, when the next election came around, did Labor get in. Whitlam retired from parliament in favour of an academic career and handed over the Labor leadership to Bill Hayden.

Kerr hung on as Governor-General until 1977, worn down by the rotten eggs, squashy tomatoes and vilification which accompanied his progress whenever he poked his nose out of his burrow. With the degree of his knighthoods raised from Knight Commander to Knight Grand Cross, he resigned to take up a position as Ambassador to UNESCO, but after three weeks of hue and cry, he laid that down too. The rest of his life was spent living in exile in Surrey, England.

After a State funeral at St. Andrew's Anglican Cathedral one day in Sydney a long time later, the cars were arriving to pick up the dignitaries when Gough Whitlam, noticing Roden, turned and walked over to him.

'I should have appointed you,' he said.

The television cameras recorded the picture of this encounter and Whitlam's comment was lip-read, but it didn't make the news because of the lack of sound.

Malcolm Fraser as prime minister remained the same rather aloof kind of man he had always been.

'He was very difficult to get hold of and talk to, but Helen always had the solution,' says Roden. 'She'd ring Tammy up and ask them to come and have a quiet dinner with us. Tammy would say she'd love to come, and Helen would ask her to let Malcolm know. Then he'd turn up. Even after I was chairman of four boards on which he was a director, it was very hard to get alongside him, though he has never been unpleasant. Just correct and stiff. It's his nature, that's all.'

There were four premiers of New South Wales during Roden's fifteen years as Governor. The first three—Robert Askin, Tom Lewis and Eric Willis—were Coalition, and the last—Neville Wran—was Labor. Of none of them does Roden have anything nasty to say; he kept his office and his person totally apolitical, not very difficult for him.

'I liked Rob, he was a very good premier to get on with,' says Roden of Askin. 'I found him most receptive to anything I had to say, and we had an easy, friendly relationship.'

Tom Lewis he deemed 'a poor premier. He'd been an excellent minister for lands, and Rob had preferred him to Eric Willis for the job because he thought Tom would have a better rapport with the public. But as premier he used to bring up all sorts of ideas, very few of them workable. He was convinced he could handle the responsibilities of premier wonderfully well, but my own view is that he could not. His own party stabbed him in the back—while he was at a meeting the rest of them got together and decided to replace him with Eric Willis.

'I was in Canberra acting as Administrator at the time, and I had invited Tom Lewis and his wife, Yutta, and Warwick and Mary Fairfax to come down and dine with me at "Yarralumla" and stay for the night.

'Tom got the news that he was no longer premier that morning, and rang me in Canberra to say that he didn't think he ought to come. I told him he'd better, because he had to face people sooner or later. He was on my list and he was expected. It—ah—wasn't really a brilliant dinner, as Tom blamed Warwick Fairfax's *Sydney Morning Herald* for his overthrow. I think otherwise, but at any rate, they arrived. Warwick Fairfax in a cap and jacket driving the Rolls. Yutta, Tom's wife, I think did nothing but cry all night. I finally went to bed.'

Eric Willis's nickname was 'Stainless Steel'.

'Eric was a very co-operative premier. He saw me regularly each week and we discussed things and what was happening. He wanted to have an early election. I said that I would not approve it because he had the numbers in the House and he had six months to run before he had to go to the polls. With three months to run, he came back and asked me if he could have the election now. I said yes, but if he wanted my opinion, I thought he'd lose. He thought he would not. But he lost, and in came Neville Wran.'

And what of Neville Wran?

'Very pleasant, friendly and co-operative. He was a very good politician, very clever. On several occasions I suggested that he might like me to resign so he could appoint someone from the Labor Party, but he kept me on. Helen and I were extremely popular, so he saw no reason to change things.'

When he entered office as Governor of New South Wales, Roden was forty-nine years old, and Helen forty-two. Though G.H. was far more a home than any of the diplomatic residences abroad had been, they were both very aware that sooner or later they would have to find somewhere else to live.

In the meantime, they decided that they needed a retreat, somewhere fairly remote wherein they could live without servants or strangers in the house—have cookouts—hike—fish—canoe— spend time alone with the boys, growing into young men. So in 1968 Roden acquired the lease on a beautiful property bordering Lake Eucumbene in the Snowy Mountains, and built a four-bedroomed house upon it. Whenever they could, they headed down there; Roden loved to fish for trout, Helen loved to walk, the boys loved it all.

By 1976, entering upon his third term as governor not long before Neville Wran, Q.C., entered upon his first term as premier, Roden decided that they really ought to find a house in Sydney. He asked a friend in real estate, Max Raine, to produce some suitable places for them to inspect, and used his third son, Richard (who had gone into real estate on the commercial side and dealt with the sale of industrial and business premises), as his outside opinion. They had furniture in storage, having commissioned it at the time when they had lived those two years in Canberra. The first place they looked at was the one they ended up buying; situated in Bellevue Hill at the end of a long driveway past other houses, it offered them real privacy. Because of his leg Roden liked to exercise by swimming, and the house possessed a pool right outside the living room. It also had a room at the end of the pool with a bathroom attached that would make a study for Roden. Its only true disadvantage was the number of stairs everywhere, but in 1976 the leg was manageable. So they bought the property on April Fool's Day.

While he remained at G.H., Roden rented the house to the French director of Credit Lyonnaise in Australia, who turned out to be a faultless tenant. Perhaps they bought then because they were not sure whether Roden would continue to be governor after Labor came in, as Roden knew it would. If so, he hasn't said. And, of course, Premier Neville Wran did keep him on.

Being governor had its funny side. One mayor asked Roden to convey his council's loyal greetings to Queen Victoria.

'I will most certainly convey the council's loyal greetings to Her Majesty,' said Roden solemnly.

Another mayor called him 'Your Majesty', as did a lot of the visiting schoolchildren.

On one occasion a newspaper referred to the gubernatorial couple as 'Lord and Lady Cutler'.

But the best—the one Roden was most embarrassed by—was an elderly sergeant of police down Wagga Wagga way. 'A grand old chap, heavily built, the absolute salt of the earth. Every time I met him he gave me a massive curtsy, and I must have met him four or five times.'

None of the boys wanted to follow in Roden's footsteps, which doesn't disturb him in the least. Neither he nor Helen tried to channel them in directions they didn't want to go.

David, the most cautious of the four, always wanted to run his own company; after the University of New South Wales he did his Master's degree at the Harvard Business School, which led to a bit of a contretemps over his passport. A high commissioner or ambassador can issue passports; Roden had always done this for his boys. But the Governor of New South Wales is not so empowered. While he was in the U.S.A. David's passport expired; he applied to the Australian Consul-General in New York for a new one. To discover that, as he had been born in New Zealand, the

Consul-General didn't think him entitled to an Australian passport. It took Roden and quite a few people in Canberra to sort the problem out, but eventually David got his Australian passport.

Anthony went through exactly the same thing when he applied in Australia for a new passport, but Roden told the recalcitrant officials to consult David's papers in Canberra; they did, and decided that Anthony could have an Australian passport. He topped the State in Mathematics when he sat for his exams at the end of high school, and did Science at university. While he sat beside the trout stream down at Eucumbene waiting for a nibble on his line, he would amuse himself by doing mathematical conundrums.

Richard, as mentioned, went into commercial real estate, and Mark, the one whose younger age had meant he remained with his parents, turned out to be another 'brainbox'. He went into computers.

By the end of 1981 all four sons were married, and at the time of the writing of this book, mid-1998, the marriages of Roden's and Helen's boys were still thriving. No divorces, no separations.

David is now fifty-one. He married Vanessa, the only daughter of Sir Rupert and Lady Clarke, and has three boys and a girl. Anthony is now fifty. He married Rhonda, an American girl (also a computer whiz), and has two boys. Richard is forty-six; he and his wife, Jenny, have two boys and a girl. Mark is forty-two; he and his wife, Michelle, have two girls.

Roden is the last person in the world to wish his experiences as a soldier on any of his sons, and still gives thanks that, such has been the direction the world has taken, his boys have been spared a war. However, there is some evidence that his own kind of courage is also present in his offspring.

In 1970, Richard was sitting for his Higher School Certificate and studying hard. His mother and father had gone away by train on an official country tour; the only one at home, he had gone to bed to continue his reading.

A young man about twenty years of age, dressed in what one would today call SWAT regalia, broke into Government House through a servants' entrance and wandered around. When he appeared in Richard's doorway, Richard genuinely thought himself the victim of a joke.

'Where's the Governor?' the stranger demanded.

It was then that Richard saw he was carrying a .22 rifle.

'The Governor's away—why do you want him?'

'I was going to take him hostage—but you'll do.'

'I don't have any money,' said Richard.

'The Government will give the money. I want ten thousand.'

When Richard picked up the phone beside his bed the intruder became agitated, but Richard calmed him down by explaining that if he wanted money from the Government, then the telephone was the only way to get it. He rang the police box at the G.H. gate and told the man on duty that he was being held hostage and please could he have ten thousand dollars? One of the two policemen thought it was a hoax, but the other one took it seriously and radioed for a patrol car. Unfortunately they turned the G.H. police alarm on; the racket panicked the intruder, who started waving the rifle around. Richard launched himself off the bed and tackled the fellow, laid him flat on the floor. The two wrestled for a moment, then Richard managed to grab the rifle; it had one round in the chamber and seventeen in the magazine. By the time the police burst in, Richard had unloaded the rifle and was sitting on the intruder, who was hauled away.

Roden and Helen learned of it from the police, who boarded the train in Goulburn and told them not to worry, it was over.

Richard was awarded a Brave Conduct medal.

•

Sooner or later the old ones have to go. Aunt Dais had been the first; Mr. Morris followed in 1971. His financial circumstances had deteriorated and the house at Bronte Beach became too big to look after, so the Morrises moved to a small apartment at Double Bay. Always a little on the frail side, he became steadily more transparent, found it difficult to get about. When Roden and Helen came to see him before they left on a trip to England, they were very saddened; he had made such a brave effort to dress himself in a suit, but had forgotten to attach the celluloid collar to his shirt, and his shave hadn't been very successful. However, they had no kind of presentiment that his time had come, so the Cutlers left on their journey. He slipped away peacefully some days later; Helen and Roden were already on their way home and arrived before he was buried.

Always inclined to be withdrawn, Mrs. Morris didn't fare well after her husband died; he had done the looking after. Though Helen would never admit that her mother suffered from dementia, she wandered a great deal, would walk into a shop and demand to be taken to the Governor. The death in 1979 of Joan, the eldest daughter, didn't help. Clare Morris herself died in 1981.

As for Ruby, she seemed unquenchable. She lived alone at 'Kyeema', relished every visit Roden, Helen and the grandchildren paid her, took pleasure in her other sons and grandchildren, saw a lot of Doone, kept active and interested in everything, including frequent invitations to G.H. Though she had had but two trips abroad—to New Zealand and to Ceylon when Roden was the High Commissioner in each place—she very much enjoyed holidays down at Lake Eucumbene, and also spent time on Geoff's property outside Gloucester, inland from the central coast of New South Wales.

In April 1974, Geoff asked Ruby to Gloucester for a visit, and took her for a ride around the property in a vehicle which broke down. He went off to get the tractor, but it refused to work either. So Ruby had to hike a considerable distance back to the house; Geoff noticed that the walk distressed her too much. A surgeon himself, he sent Ruby to see a physician in Sydney, who diagnosed cancer in both lungs and secondary deposits elsewhere; she had three months to live. A prognosis that was correct almost to the day. Ruby died in July, just three months short of her ninetieth birthday.

She had never smoked a cigarette in her life, nor allowed anyone to smoke in her house; even Arthur had gone outside to enjoy a cigarette, or else had one in his little 'den'.

It had been a long life very well lived, with perhaps more than its share of grief, worry and trouble, but its rewards were very great too. Her later years were very comfortable and she had survived to see all of her children do splendidly well. She died as gracefully as she had lived. At Manly there is a plaque in her honour; she was one of its most memorable citizens.

No one wanted to live in 'Kyeema'. It was sold.

Helen received a formidable honour while Roden was still Governor. The federal Honours List was published on Australia Day, 26 January. Not long before Australia Day 1980, Helen's secretary said that the Governor-General had telephoned to speak to her, but didn't want her to ring back—he would try again later. Helen was very perturbed.

'It must be something very serious—I do hope nothing is wrong,' she said anxiously.

'It's probably about an honour, dear.'

She looked taken aback. 'Oh, no! Definitely not!'

When Sir Zelman Cowen phoned again, Helen's secretary switched the call through to Roden, explaining that the Governor-General had spoken to Helen already, but would like a word with him too.

'Is there a problem?' Roden asked Sir Zelman.

'No, not at all! I've told your wife that the Queen would be pleased to give her the Companion of the Order of Australia, but I don't think I've really convinced her, and I don't think she understands the seniority of the order. Would you talk to her?'

A rather puzzled face appeared around Roden's study door.

'I've just spoken to the Governor-General,' said Roden.

'Yes, so have I,' said Helen, edging inside. 'This is quite silly, isn't it? He kept saying that it's very senior.'

'Darling, you're senior to me! If you leave the Victoria Cross out of it, every honour I've got is subordinate to your A.C.'

When she still refused to believe him, Roden got a book and showed her. 'She went away looking a bit like a stunned mullet—but then, she never did rate her efforts very highly.'

Towards the end of 1980, Roden asked Neville and Jill Wran to a quiet lunch at G.H.

'Premier, it's time I went,' he said. 'I'm sixty-four, and next January I will have been Governor for fifteen years. That's quite long enough.'

Wran frowned. 'You make it difficult for me,' he said.

'I don't want to do that, but I do think it's time that the people of New South Wales saw a new face in Government House.'

'Well . . .' said Wran, still frowning.

'Look, Premier, I don't want to make it hard for you, but it is time. If there's anything I can do for New South Wales, I would be happy to do it, and I don't mean something I'd be paid for. Just anything for New South Wales.'

Roden then asked that he be allowed to make the announcement of his retirement himself, when he opened the new session of the New South Wales Parliament. An occasion on which, as was the custom, he delivered a speech prepared by the Premier's Department. It was, not unnaturally, critical of Malcolm Fraser's Federal Government, with which Wran, a Labor premier, did not see eye to eye. To Roden's great surprise, Fraser castigated him for giving this 'disgraceful' speech.

'He ought to have understood that, as the servant of my government, I say what my government wants me to say.'

Typically, after Roden did step down as Governor, he and Helen went abroad for six months in order to make life easier for the new incumbent of G.H., Sir James Rowland.

When he returned to Sydney, Premier Neville Wran offered him the chairmanship of the revamped State Bank of New South Wales (formerly called the Rural Bank). Roden objected because of his age, but Wran had the Parliament extend the retirement age for chairman of the State Bank to seventy; Roden accepted gladly.

RETIREMENT

The people of New South Wales mourned Roden's departure from Government House, and the newspaper editorials were glowing. Certainly the author cannot think of any other Governor of New South Wales in this century or the latter half of the last century as well remembered and as greatly loved as Roden Cutler. Nor of any governor during those same 150 years with as splendid a wife and helpmate as Helen.

He doubted that he held the record for length of service as a governor, and rightly so. His nomination was Sir Dallas Brooks of Victoria, but in actual fact Sir Dallas didn't serve for quite as long as Roden. The record-holder, however, is Sir James Mitchell, who governed Western Australia from 1933 to 1951. The title of Most Notorious would probably have to go to Sir Philip Game, the governor of New South Wales who dismissed Jack Lang in 1932.

It was very nice to move into their own home at last, have less duties and more time for themselves. Not that either Roden or Helen had given up their interest in the Scouts, the Guides, Legacy, the R.S.L., St. John Ambulance, the Red Cross ...

The author asked Roden how Helen had coped with the fact that, save for those two years in Canberra, until 1981 she had always had cooks, maids, even butlers.

'She never blinked an eyelid. Aside from someone to do the heavy cleaning, she ran our own home herself—acted a bit like my secretary as well as her own, kept house, did the cooking. She was a good cook, though after so many years of banquets and chefs, we both preferred plain roast dinners to pheasant-under-glass. If we had a large group in to dinner or some kind of party, she'd use a caterer.'

Their chief pleasure was to travel, and they did a lot of it; in London in April of 1981, the Queen acknowledged Roden's contribution to New South Wales by creating him a Knight of the Order of Australia, which is the senior among his three knighthoods.

There was time to go to cricket matches, Rugby matches, and to see more of great friends like Dr. Adrian Johnson and Judge Jack Nagle.

Not that anybody as active and vigorous as Roden Cutler ever really retires. His appointment as Chairman of the State Bank (the Managing Director was Nicholas Whitlam, Gough and Margaret Whitlam's son) led to directorships in other companies, and he was finally able to make use of that degree in Economics. Over the years he has sat in the chair or served on the boards of companies and foundations like the Permanent Trustee Co. Ltd., the Milton Foundation, Rothmans Holdings Ltd., Ansett Express Ltd., the First Australian Fund, Occidental Life Insurance, the Rothmans Foundation, and more. According to men like Brian Sherman and Sir John Carrick, having Roden on your board means no malfunctions at the top. His interest in these commercial or directorial activities is so keen and personal that he still flies off to foreign places for board meetings of companies not headquartered in Australia.

In the northern autumn of 1990, Roden and Helen were in the U.K. again, this time to attend a meeting of the Victoria and George Cross Association and be among those received by the Queen afterwards at Buckingham Palace. By this time their association with Her Majesty had extended over a period of thirty-five years, so it was never strange to set eyes on the face under the hat or tiara— save that it is only when gazing at someone else's ageing face that one realises with a shock that one is no longer young oneself.

Because Roden was almost as ardent a Rugby Union fan as he was a cricket fan, he and Helen attended an important Rugby match at Twickenham the day before they were to fly home to Sydney. The football committee had arranged for the Cutlers to sit in its box, which was a hundred-metre walk from the nearest gate. When their car reached the gate, the driver explained that Sir Roden was disabled—could he please drive right in and drop his passengers at the back of the stand? The policeman on duty gave permission.

After the match was over the Cutlers found their car and driver waiting in the same spot behind the stand, and climbed in. The crowd was immense, the drive back to the gate a slow one.

At the gate they were pulled up by a senior policeman. The man who had given the driver permission to go in had reported this fact to his superior, who was waiting for them—and not in a good mood. At first he concentrated his abuse on the driver, who explained that Sir Roden Cutler was disabled.

The senior policeman walked to stare in through Helen's window, from which vantage spot he could see the length of Roden's form clearly.

'Disabled, eh? He doesn't look disabled to me!' he snapped.

Helen rolled her window down and he stuck his head inside the car. It was obvious that he was suffering from some kind of upper respiratory ailment—eyes and nose running—but that didn't stop his breathing heavily in Helen's face and spluttering on her as he kept up his tirade about rank having too many privileges. Roden chose to ignore him; after it became plain that the car's occupants were not going to gratify him by arguing, the senior policeman let them go.

The Cutlers arrived in Sydney about eleven in the evening. The next morning Helen was up and prowling in her garden, which she had planted with roses. But during the day she began to feel a little off-colour, and passed a restless night. Most unusual for her, she rang the doctor herself; he came at once. Her own theory was that she must have eaten something tainted, but the doctor demurred. He told her to take things quietly; if she did not feel any better on his treatment, she was to phone him at once.

Roden accompanied the doctor out. 'What is it?' he asked.

The doctor gave a list of two or three things, then added, 'There's a slight chance it's meningitis.'

This appalled Roden, who said to Helen that he would cancel his afternoon board meeting. Helen wouldn't hear of it. When he came home he thought she was sleeping, and didn't disturb her. But when he couldn't rouse her in the morning he rang the doctor, who took one look at Helen and summoned an ambulance. She was rushed into intensive care at St. Vincent's Hospital, where a lumbar puncture revealed clear fluid under no increase in pressure. Then the pathology indicated a meningococcal meningitis. Helen died at ten o'clock that night, 9 November, of massive systemic failure due to meningococcal septicaemia. She was sixty-seven years old.

It happened so *quickly*! The sons were devastated, but Roden—

For forty-four years she had been wife, friend, lover, constant companion, mother of his children, object of his respect and esteem. There had never been anyone else, and it wasn't supposed to happen this way. He had been so sure that he would go first—husbands always did, didn't they? Illness and Helen? They just didn't go together. One moment among the roses, the next moment the beloved eyes closed for the last time. It should have been him!

But he soldiered on, though Helen's death was the worst of all his ordeals. A devout and practising Anglican all her life, she was buried from St. Andrew's Cathedral amid a host of mourners.

His only bitterness about Helen's death still rankles: he blames the senior policeman at the Twickenham Rugby match. The St. Vincent's doctors said that the incubation period put her acquiring the infection—a rare one—on that day, given that one doesn't get from London to Sydney in less than one full day.

Of his loneliness and grief in the months and years which followed he has not spoken. Nor has the author asked. It is not the proper function of a biographer to probe into the kind of deep feelings which are absolutely private, and best unrecalled. She is just sorry that Roden will have to read this.

He did soldier on. He gave up neither his much treasured charities nor his companies. A man of such eminent good sense understands that nothing cures grief, but that work keeps mind and spirit going. Those with true courage never retreat permanently from living. And Time's droplets slowly, slowly coat the naked wound until it is bearably crusted over—not forgotten nor any less acute, yet incorporated into a fresh dimension of experience that enhances, cannot diminish.

People were wonderful, especially his sons, his brothers, Doone; Helen's younger sister, Mim, was a tower of strength, as were his friends.

•

The invitations kept coming in; the only difference was that now they said, 'Sir Roden Cutler and Friend'. Sometimes he asked Doone to accompany him, sometimes he asked Mim.

Two years after Helen's death Mim, a psychiatrist, told him that he ought to marry again. The advice wasn't something he wanted to think about, nor did he, but it was not long after Mim had spoken to him that he met one of Helen's old friends at St. Mark's Church of England, Darling Point; he hadn't seen her since Helen's funeral.

Her name was Joan Goodwin. They had met in New York while he was Consul-General. Her father, the Reverend Clive Goodwin, and his wife were very good friends of Helen's parents, whom they knew from Canon Goodwin's days as Rector of St. Mark's. When Mrs. Morris learned that Joan was working in New York, she told the Goodwins that she would make sure Helen contacted Joan. All these elderly heads probably thought that it would cheer Joan up to meet some other Australians; she was just emerging from a short but very damaging marriage.

Helen called Joan, and asked her to come and have lunch at the apartment on Fifth Avenue.

Until that point in the earlyish 1960s, Joan Goodwin had had a peculiar and painful life. Being an Anglican minister's child was not easy in a day and age when the Church of England still tended to think of its ministers as privately funded by their families or by some wealthy local pillar of the Establishment. The Rev. Goodwin was never in one place for more than two or three years, and did not have the connections to ensure that he was given a good parish during the early years of his service. Or perhaps he chose this.

Joan was born in Huskisson in southern New South Wales, not far from Nowra, where her father was the curate. From there he went to Hobart in Tasmania; from Hobart he went to Rockdale, a Sydney suburb; after that he was in St. Marys, a turbulent hamlet west of Sydney; and then he went to the steel town of Port Kembla. A second girl and then a boy came along, which meant three Goodwin children to worry about.

Mrs. Goodwin was frantically busy, as were the wives of all ministers as truly good and dedicated as was Clive Goodwin. She helped care for the church premises, kept her own house, acted as her husband's secretary, entered the parish accounts, had her own good works to do, and answered the rectory doorbell twenty-four hours a day. Her financial circumstances were no better in those days than her unworldly husband's, but somehow Mrs. Goodwin managed to scrape up the money to send Joan, aged three-and-a-half, to boarding school. That sounds like *Jane Eyre* or some other mid-Victorian novel, but one of the Goodwins' very real troubles was that so many of their parishes were, for want of a stronger word, 'rough'. At least in a good Church of England boarding school the tiny girl was safe and protected.

Until she turned five, Joan boarded at the Meriden school in Sydney; St. Catherine's, the school of Mrs. Goodwin's choice, refused to take a child under five. Joan remembers that she slept in a cubicle off the Meriden headmistress's own bedroom. Then at five it was St. Catherine's at Waverley, where she remained until she turned sixteen. Sometimes (depending upon the parish) she went home for holidays, sometimes she went to an aunt or an uncle. Among the girls at St. Catherine's was Joan Sutherland.

It certainly wasn't easy to go home for the holidays during the Second World War; the Rev. Goodwin was the chaplain at the Seamen's Mission in George Street North—not exactly the right district or premises to harbour a young girl for five minutes, let alone five weeks in summer.

But all those years of uncomplaining and hardworking service were rewarded in 1950, when the Rev. Goodwin went as Rector to St. Mark's, the church at which Roden and Helen had been married in 1946. A very good address and a very good 'living'. Apart from his expected duties he began the task of helping the aged in the community; this was to earn him an M.B.E. (Member of the Order of the British Empire) in 1968. When he died in retirement in 1981 he was a Canon of St. Andrew's Cathedral, Archdeacon of Sydney, and entitled the Venerable Goodwin.

At sixteen Joan had had enough of school and left, went to work in an assortment of jobs. An uncle died when she was twenty and bequeathed her sufficient of an inheritance to enable her to do what all girls wanted to do then: have a couple of years in England. After the couple of years she returned to Sydney, only to develop itchy feet again; she went to the U.S.A.

There she married—disastrously. It lasted but a short time. Scarred and wary, she came to New York and secured a job with the Australian airline Qantas as a ground hostess.

And went to lunch at the Cutlers' apartment on Fifth Avenue. Helen had been very warm on the phone, but the Joan who arrived was apprehensive, not at all sure that the wife of such an eminent man should have bothered inviting her.

Roden intimidated her at first glance—so tall, so splendid. But it wasn't long before she realised that he had a wonderful sense of humour, and she departed after that very pleasant lunch thinking wistfully that he was just the man for her. However, that could not be. He was a happily married man and she liked his wife enormously—so much so that she knew she had made a real friend. Helen and Joan had a lot in common, though they were very different too. Which is the right combination for friendship.

She was appointed the V.I.P. hostess by Qantas, and found her *métier*. This was work she enjoyed thoroughly and was good at. It meant that she had to be on hand to meet the incoming Qantas V.I.P.s as well as shoo the outgoing V.I.P.s onto the plane before it departed several hours later. Occasionally Roden, as Consul-General, also had to be on hand to meet some V.I.P., or shoo a V.I.P. onto the plane home. The Qantas flight came in at 6 a.m., which meant that Joan and sometimes Roden would be there in the sleet, the snow, the rain or the humidity to make sure that the Honourable So-and-so or Sir So-and-so had no trouble with the immigration authorities, his luggage, the lounge refreshments or the company. Owning equally keen senses of humour, Joan and Roden made the best of these dawn patrols.

But it was Helen she saw more than Roden.

After two years in New York, she went home to be with her parents again; in 1964 Canon Goodwin was transferred from St. Mark's to St. Philip's on Church Hill, not really so very far from the old Seamen's Mission, but in a better area. She spent three months helping her father clean out the church and the rectory, then went back to work with Qantas, this time on the ground staff at Sydney airport; soon she was back in her old slot as the V.I.P. hostess, and that she remained for the next eighteen years. When Qantas offered her an early retirement she accepted, though she was not at leisure for long. Sir Peter Abeles asked her to become room manager at Ansett Airlines, a job she filled for the next seven years.

Off and on she saw Helen and Roden when they travelled; she attended functions at G.H., was a part of Helen's circle in Bellevue Hill after Roden retired.

She had never found a man who measured up to him, though she cast no lures in his direction. He was married to Helen and she admired them both. It was as simple as that. Though she was at Helen's funeral, she made no attempt to contact Roden afterwards. Life was pleasant enough, and her widowed mother was beginning to fail, to need more attention.

So when, after that chance meeting at St. Mark's more than two years after Helen's death, Roden telephoned her and asked her if she would accompany him to a function as his friend, she accepted without suspecting that he would pursue the acquaintance.

The author asked her if she and Roden went out together for long before they decided to marry.

'No,' said Joan. 'You know Roden—he made up his mind, and that was that. I was the one who hesitated.'

Not because she didn't love him enough; she had admired him for thirty years. No, she hesitated because, though she knew Roden and Helen well, she had met their sons very rarely, and she knew that a second wife for their father would come as a shock to them. They had adored their mother and, while they sorrowed for their father, they probably had him tucked away in their minds as a widower for the rest of his life. Or so Joan reasoned. She agreed to marry Roden only if his sons and their wives approved.

The news did come as a shock, but they were generous.

Roden and Joan were married at the end of April 1993.

The author never knew Helen, save through the medium of this book, listening to Roden talk about her so much, so warmly, so lovingly, so loyally—the full gamut of a rich enduring marriage from its joys through its spats to its griefs. Yet his relationship with

Joan is not a light convenience, a second-best kind of thing. It is as if, with the going down of one sun, he has turned his face to a different part of the sky and found another source of warmth. He and Joan are happy together, like being together. They still share that same sense of humour, and strike sparks off each other. Nice sparks.

'Roden says that if Helen knows, she'll be very pleased,' Joan told the author.

At the time of writing he is eighty-two, and the leg is a terrible burden. He has had several bad falls, but he resists the idea of a wheelchair strenuously.

'After one shocking fall recently he got up after dinner and delivered a speech,' says Joan. 'I don't understand where he gets the strength from—he's amazing.'

The Bellevue Hill house with all those steps has become too much; the Cutlers are about to move into something on one level. They still entertain, and Roden still flies off to foreign climes to enjoy the cricket with his friend Paul Getty (who has his own cricket pitch), attend the Victoria and George Cross Association meetings, sit on his overseas boards. He hasn't quit yet. He never will.

In conclusioN

There are those who will read this book and end by refusing to believe that men like Roden Cutler do walk the face of this earth. They will decide that I, the biographer, have conflated and exaggerated. But it is all as distinct as it is true: the heroism, the almost limitless willpower, the degree of intelligence and commonsense, the ability to control primal instincts, the uncanny knowledge of people and events, the warmth, the humour, the fidelity, and—most astonishing of all—the humility. I do not think that he has ever of his own choice let anyone down. Not country, not government of the day, not wife, not children, not even his own humanity. When he saw the look on his wife's face at the moment he mentioned the post in New York, he took a job he did not want. When his ambitions and his interests prompted him to stay in the sphere he loved most—diplomacy in Asia—he thought of his sons and returned home to be a governor so that the family could be together. There is neither misanthropy nor misogyny in his nature, yet he has standards. When those standards are not measured up to, one meets not enmity, but disappointment.

After living with him so long, after pursuing the path of his life so exhaustively, I find myself unable to put my finger on any why or what or how. We live in a world which desperately wants to know why, what, how? We fund research programs into human motivation, we publish thousands of books about it, we expend magnetic tape and film by the megamile in our quest for why and what and how.

Yet here I am without any answer for Roden Cutler. Religion has been an influence in his life, but never in a way suggesting that God—in Whom he does believe—has been a crutch or even much of a comfort. The energy and the stamina are phenomenal, the humility a paradox. But what fascinates me by far the most is the *balance* inside this man. The mind which never stops thinking and analysing, the emotions which are so strong yet never blur perception or perspective. He stands poised at the exact centre of what mind and spirit should be, coming down on neither side. Whatever has to be done, he will do—provided that it is just, moral, ethical and necessary. Not in a furore, not for base reasons, not coldly, not intemperately. And with all of it, such an essential simplicity. Others may fret, stew, go round and round in circles. He never does.

Maybe the only answer lies in the myth of Sir Galahad: that heroism endures as long as the soul remains untainted. In which case, there is no likelihood that Roden Cutler will ever be less than a hero. His soul remains untainted.

AUTHOR'S AFTERWORD

Just a brief thank you to all the people who helped, in particular Christopher Jobson, late of Australian Defence Headquarters, now of the Australian War Museum, and the Historical Documents Unit at the Australian Department of Foreign Affairs; both have been wonderful. I am indebted to the history of the 2/5th Field Regiment, *Guns and Gunners* (published by Angus & Robertson in 1950), beautifully written by Brigadier John W. O'Brien, D.S.O. The maps in it done by Sgt. K.C. Baird were of immense assistance to me in preparing my own maps of Merdjayoun and Damour.

Thank you to Peggy, Pinky and the rest of the folks at the Norfolk Island R.S.L., through whose offices I first met Sir Roden Cutler quite a few years ago. Thank you to Sir Roden's family and friends, and a special thank you to Joan, Lady Cutler.

Thank you to my loyal and unflagging team 'Out Yenna': Pam Crisp, Kaye Pendleton, Ria Howell, Fran Johnston, Lyn McCowan, Joe Nobbs, Mike and Clinton Sharkey, Dallas Crisp, Phil Billman, and—of course—Poindexter the cat. Thank you to Jan and to Brother John. Thank you heaps to Selwa Anthony, who did the Australian agenting for this book free of charge. Thank you to Melinda with love. Thank you to Ian Sinnott, who has been such a good friend and support.

Finally, thank you ILYBHGMz to my husband, who went without a game of Scrabble for weeks.